Critical, Constructive Assessment of CEFR-informed Language Teaching in Japan and Beyond

To Morg Lee,

What I am now owes you tremendously.

With the deepest gratitude & love,
Noriko

Also in this series:

Criterial Features in L2 English
John A Hawkins and Luna Filipović

Language Functions Revisited
Anthony Green

Immigrant Pupils Learn English
Bronagh Ćatibušić and David Little

The CEFR in Practice
Brian North

English Profile in Practice
Edited by Julia Harrison and Fiona Barker

Critical, Constructive Assessment of CEFR-informed Language Teaching in Japan and Beyond

Edited by

Fergus O'Dwyer
University College Dublin and University of Münster

Morten Hunke
Aoyama Gakuin University

Alexander Imig
Chukyo University

Noriko Nagai
Ibaraki University

Naoyuki Naganuma
Tokai University

Maria Gabriela Schmidt
Tsukuba University

CAMBRIDGE
UNIVERSITY PRESS

University Printing House, Cambridge CB2 8BS, United Kingdom

One Liberty Plaza, 20th Floor, New York, NY 10006, USA

477 Williamstown Road, Port Melbourne, VIC 3207, Australia

4843/24, 2nd Floor, Ansari Road, Daryaganj, Delhi – 110002, India

79 Anson Road, #06–04/06, Singapore 079906

Cambridge University Press is part of the University of Cambridge.

It furthers the University's mission by disseminating knowledge in the pursuit of education, learning and research at the highest international levels of excellence.

www.cambridge.org
Information on this title: www.cambridge.org/9781316638231

© Cambridge University Press 2017

This publication is in copyright. Subject to statutory exception and to the provisions of relevant collective licensing agreements, no reproduction of any part may take place without the written permission of Cambridge University Press.

First published 2017

20 19 18 17 16 15 14 13 12 11 10 9 8 7 6 5 4 3 2 1

A catalogue record for this publication is available from the British Library

Library of Congress Cataloguing in Publication data
Names: O'Dwyer, Fergus, editor. | Hunke, Morten, editor. | Imig, Alexander, editor. | Nagai, Noriko, editor. | Naganuma, Naoyuki, editor. | Schmidt, Mariela Gabriela, editor.
Title: Critical, constructive assessment of CEFR-informed : language teaching in Japan and beyond edited by Fergus O'Dwyer, Morten Hunke, Alexander Imig, Noriko Nagai, Naoyuki Naganuma, Mariela Gabriela Schmidt.
Description: Cambridge University Press : University Printing House, [2016] | Series: English Profile Studies, 6 | Includes bibliographical references and index.
Identifiers: LCCN 2016036662 | ISBN 9781316638231 (alk. paper)
Subjects: LCSH: Common European Framework of Reference for Languages (Project)--Japan. | Language and languages--Ability testing--Japan. | Language and languages--Study and Teaching--Japan. | Language teachers--Training of--Japan. | Language policy--Japan. | Second language acquistion--Japan.
Classification: LCC P118.75 .C83 2016 | DDC 418.0071/052--dc23 LC record available at https://lccn.loc.gov/2016036662

ISBN 978-1-316-63823-1

Cambridge University Press has no responsibility for the persistence or accuracy of URLs for external or third-party internet websites referred to in this publication, and does not guarantee that any content on such websites is, or will remain, accurate or appropriate. Information regarding prices, travel timetables, and other factual information given in this work is correct at the time of first printing but Cambridge University Press does not guarantee the accuracy of such information thereafter.

This volume is dedicated to Kevin Cleary: we have fond memories of his general encouragement and 'Can Do' attitude.

Contents

Acknowledgements	x
Series Editors' note	xi
Notes on contributors	xii

Section 1   1
The context

1. Introduction: Towards critical, constructive assessment of CEFR-informed language teaching in Japan and beyond   3
   Fergus O'Dwyer, Morten Hunke, Alexander Imig, Noriko Nagai, Naoyuki Naganuma and Maria Gabriela Schmidt

2. The past, present and future of the CEFR in Japan   18
   Maria Gabriela Schmidt, Judith Runnels and Noriko Nagai

3. The perception of the CEFR in secondary-level English language teaching in Japan   49
   Tomoko Takada

Section 2   65
Materials design

4. Marugoto: Japanese Language and Culture – the series of coursebooks based on the JF Standard for Japanese Language Education   67
   Noriko Yokoyama

5. Applying the CEFR to English for Academic Purposes textbooks   77
   Naoyuki Naganuma, Noriko Nagai and Fergus O'Dwyer

Section 3   95
Curriculum reform

6. Applying the CEFR to renew a General English curriculum: Successes, remaining issues and lessons from Vietnam   97
   Pham Thi Hong Nhung

7	A 'Can Do' framework-based curriculum in a university-level English language learning programme: Course goals, activities and assessment *Etsuko Shimo, Carlos Ramirez and Kaori Nitta*	118
8	Implementing the CEFR as a benchmark for 'action-oriented' syllabus design *Mark de Boer*	155
9	Using the CEFR-J and the CEFR as frameworks for renewal of an English language curriculum at a Japanese university: An action research study	175
9A	Aligning a Japanese university's English language curriculum and lesson plans to the CEFR-J *Jack Bower, Judith Runnels, Arthur Rutson-Griffiths, Rebecca Schmidt, Gary Cook, Lyndon Lusk Lehde and Azusa Kodate*	176
9B	Developing ELP-informed self-access centre learning materials to support a curriculum aligned to the CEFR *Azusa Kodate*	226
9C	The key questions in Bunkyo *Jack Bower, Arthur Rutson-Griffiths, Gary Cook, Rebecca Schmidt, Lyndon Lusk Lehde, Azusa Kodate and Judith Runnels*	247

Section 4 267
Portfolio approaches

10	A CEFR-informed e-portfolio in blended learning at a German university *Astrid Buschmann-Göbels and Bärbel Kühn*	269
11	Using the CEFR-based European Language Portfolio in a non-CEFR English course *Paul Wicking*	285
12	Developing a portfolio for English as a tool for global communication *Yukie Saito*	292
13	Using the 'Can Do' descriptor list as a checklist for short-term Chinese study in China *Qu Ming*	303

Section 5 313
Conclusion

14 Bringing critical and constructive assessments of CEFR-informed
   language teaching forward 315
   *Fergus O'Dwyer, Morten Hunke, Alexander Imig, Noriko Nagai,
   Naoyuki Naganuma and Maria Gabriela Schmidt*

Author index 325
Subject index 327

Acknowledgements

The editors of the volume would like to thank all the contributors for working with us for the two years or so it took to complete the volume. This involved putting practices down on paper, tweaking these ideas, and giving feedback on other contributions. We do appreciate your patience and hard work.

The Series Editors, Fiona Barker and Nick Saville, provided support and encouragement throughout the process. The Publications Assistant, John Savage, was great to work with: thank you for being very helpful while getting the volume toward publication. We would also like to thank the reviewer Brian North for contributing many ideas which improved the content of the chapters, and the volume in general. On a more general note, we would also like to extend our gratitude to those who have developed the CEFR and ELP, and to those who continue to develop its ability to facilitate language learning. We hope the action research approach taken in the volume will be deemed valuable, and in some small way, hope the publication helps bring language education efforts forward.

This volume was edited by members of the Framework and Language Portfolio Special Interest Group (FLP SIG), which is established within the Japan Association of Language Teaching (JALT). Many people within JALT have provided help, support and encouragement over the years. This volume was supported by a KAKENHI Grant-in-Aid for Scientific Research (26370624) from the Japan Society for the Promotion of Science. This grant allowed us to hold events and workshops in Chukyo University, Osaka University, and Tokai University. Thanks to all who contributed their ideas and energy at these events. Gregory Birch and Jerry Miller, among several others, helped organise these events. Many thanks to Ryan Richardson who proofread earlier versions of the chapters during the submission process. We would also like to thank our reviewer from outside the box, Julia Wirtz, for her thorough check of all chapters.

Finally, Cambridge English Language Assessment and Cambridge University Press are grateful to the following publishers for their permission to use copyrighted material: the Japan Foundation for the use of Figure 2 on page 70 and Figure 3 on page 72; the Council of Europe for the use of Figure 5 on page 88; and Taylor & Francis for the use of Figure 1 on page 294.

Series Editors' note

This is the sixth volume in the English Profile (EP) Studies series and it complements the first five volumes by reporting in detail on the implementation of the Common European Framework of Reference for Languages (CEFR, Council of Europe 2001) in a variety of educational contexts, taking a broad view across Asian and European contexts. With its critical evaluation of the challenges and successes of implementing the CEFR in various language learning contexts, including state secondary and tertiary education, it provides further exemplification through detailed case studies of the approach described in volume 4 in this series, *The CEFR in Practice* (North 2014), which focuses on challenging misconceptions about this framework. The team of six editors have collated and contributed to an insightful collection of papers which cover five main aspects of how the CEFR is shaping pedagogical practices and curricula in Japan and beyond.

Since its publication in 2001, the CEFR has increased its influence beyond Europe, notably in Japan, as shown by the extensive research and support from policy makers which resulted in the publication of the CEFR-Japan (CEFR-J) (Tono 2013; see also Chapter 9A of this volume). This strong regional support for a CEFR-informed approach to language learning is evidenced by this volume, which showcases the adoption and adaptation of the CEFR in Japanese and other educational contexts; materials design using CEFR principles; curriculum reform; the use of portfolios in language teaching; and the future of CEFR-informed language pedagogy. The whole volume is learning oriented, mirroring the action-oriented nature of the CEFR.

The main aim of EP is to produce reference level descriptors for English based on a triangulation of pure and applied linguistic and educational research, involving empirical investigation using learner and native user data, expertise from educators worldwide and an exploration of the relationship between linguistic theory and real-life evidence (see earlier volumes in this series). Taking a wider perspective, the EP Studies series publishes work that explores all aspects of the CEFR and how this framework relates to the fields of English language learning, teaching and assessment. This sixth volume reports in detail on how the CEFR is being used in various educational contexts and its impact on the teaching, learning and assessment of English and other languages, therefore filling a gap in the EP Studies series and extending its reach to anyone interested in the broader implications of the CEFR for language education in Japan, Vietnam and Germany.

Alongside the other books in the EP Studies series, this volume presents timely studies that report on interesting and challenging applications of the CEFR which add to the existing literature and seek to encourage the adaptation and use of the CEFR in more educational contexts worldwide. To aid this undertaking, this volume presents a clear checklist of questions about CEFR implementation and provides contextualised answers for each situation described, which aims to engender an understanding of what choices led to the effective learning practices and outcomes reported for each study. A major intention of this volume is to enable replication of the positive aspects of CEFR-informed practice described here by other teachers, policy makers and researchers, who will also benefit from understanding the challenges faced by the authors in developing or applying CEFR-informed language learning practices.

Since its launch in 2006 at the International Association for Teachers of English as a Foreign Language (IATEFL) conference in Harrogate, UK, EP has been concerned with international collaboration between English language researchers, teachers and policy makers, with active members of the EP Network providing data from language learners, carrying out research projects or hosting events in many countries. This volume supports the aims of EP and additionally presents significant implications for all language education professionals, whether teachers, assessment experts or policy makers, in a variety of contexts. We believe that this volume will be of interest to anyone interested in language learning in general and in the application of the CEFR to any language learning environment.

Fiona Barker
Nick Saville
July 2017

References

Council of Europe (2001) *Common European Framework of Reference for Languages: Learning, Teaching, Assessment*, Cambridge: Cambridge University Press.

North, B (2014) *The CEFR in Practice*, English Profile Studies volume 4, Cambridge: UCLES/Cambridge University Press.

Tono, Y (2013) *CAN-DO list sakusei katsuyou: Eigo toutatsu shihyou CEFR-J guidebook [CEFR-J Guidebook: Resources for Establishing and Utilizing 'Can-Do' Lists for English Language Teaching]*, Tokyo: Taishukan.

Notes on contributors

Jack Bower is the Director of the Bunkyo English Communication Center at Hiroshima Bunkyo Women's University. His research interests include aligning curricula and language tests to the CEFR, and vocabulary learning through Computer Assisted Language Learning (CALL). He is currently a PhD candidate at Macquarie University, Australia.

Astrid Buschmann-Göbels is the Project Coordinator of the tutorial programme at the Foreign Languages Centre of the University of Bremen. Hence, she is responsible for the training and supervision of the student tutors as well as for the overall concept of the tutorial programme. Her research interests lie in developing concepts and learning spaces for fostering autonomous language learning and setting the stage for out-of-classroom learning.

Gary Cook is currently a Curriculum Coordinator at Hiroshima Bunkyo Women's University. He is interested in language testing, particularly vocabulary, and materials development.

Mark de Boer is a Lecturer at Akita International University in Northern Japan. He is a PhD candidate at the University of Birmingham. His research interests are in peer-to-peer dynamic assessment and the ecology of online learning.

Morten Hunke (MA English, German as a Foreign Language, Linguistics) worked as an Associate Professor for globalization at Aichi Prefectural University from 2013 to 2016. Before, he was a Teaching Fellow at the University of Leeds from 2006 to 2010. He has taught English, German and Swedish at university level in four different countries, and is currently teaching English at a number of universities in the Greater Tokyo area. His research interests include the use of the CEFR and the European Language Portfolio (ELP), learner autonomy, prosody and speech performance, improving study abroad mobility, and Computer Assisted Language Learning (CALL).

Alexander Imig is an Associate Professor at Chukyo University (Nagoya, Japan), and has been teaching German as a foreign language since 1991, with previous positions in Berlin and Prague. He was a Lecturer at Aichi Prefectural University from 2001 to 2007 and has been teaching in his current position since April 2008. His fields of study include rhetoric and curriculum development, especially in multilingual contexts.

Azusa Kodate is currently an Associate Professor at the Institute for the Advancement of Teaching and Learning at Kokugakuin University in Tokyo. She was the Self Access Learning Center (SALC) Coordinator at Hiroshima Bunkyo Women's University from 2012 to 2015, and led a wide range of projects including CEFR-based self-access centre materials development as part of curriculum renewal. She has also been an external consultant for faculty development in the field of self-access learning in both private and public universities in Japan. Her research interests are in learner autonomy and materials development.

Bärbel Kühn was the Director of the language centre of the four public universities of the federal state of Bremen (Germany) until November 2015, with previous positions at the Goethe-Institut in Frankfurt, München and Helsinki. She is the present Chair of the Council of Languages of Bremen, and has been responsible for the implementation of the European Language Portfolio (ELP) in the e-portfolio system Elektronisches Europäisches Portfolio der Sprachen (EPOS). She is also co-coordinator of the EPOS Collaboration and coordinator of the Training and Consultancy Activity of the European Centre of Modern Languages (ECML) of the Council of Europe. Her special interests are first, second and foreign languages, learning autonomy and the principles of the CEFR and the ELP.

Lyndon Lusk Lehde is a Lecturer at Hiroshima Bunkyo Women's University, where he teaches Pop Culture, Tourism English and International Communication Strategies. His interests include cross-cultural pragmatics, as well as the use of film analysis and video production in the classroom.

Qu Ming is an Associate Professor of Muroran Institute of Technology, Japan. Her interests include language testing, CEFR-based language teaching, and Chinese culture research.

Noriko Nagai received her PhD in Linguistics from the University of Michigan and is currently a Professor of English and Linguistics at the College of Humanities, Ibaraki University in Japan. Her research interests lie in cross-linguistic influence, explicit instruction of English grammar based on comparative analyses of English and Japanese, CEFR-informed criterial lexical and grammatical features, and the implementation of the CEFR to English education in the Japanese higher education context.

Naoyuki Naganuma PhD is an Associate Professor of the International Education Center at Tokai University. He got his doctor's degree in 2006 from Tokyo University of Foreign Studies. His research interests are mainly on language learning motivation and language testing, especially 'Can Do' oriented assessment to promote learning and motivation. He was a member of a Ministry of Education, Culture, Sports, Science and Technology – Japan

(MEXT) committee relating to setting learning attainment targets in the form of 'Can Do' lists in foreign language education.

Kaori Nitta is a Professor of English at the Faculty of Applied Sociology, Kindai University in Osaka. She received her MA in Linguistics from California State University at Long Beach in 1980, and has been teaching as a full-time teacher at Kindai University since 1993. She is interested in English for Specific Purposes (ESP), and effective teaching methods to raise students' awareness for social issues, as well as their motivation and English productive skills.

Pham Thi Hong Nhung is an Assistant Professor of Applied Linguistics at Hue University of Foreign Languages, Vietnam. She has been training English language teachers for 20 years. Her research interests include intercultural communication and foreign language teaching.

Fergus O'Dwyer taught at Osaka University between 2010 and 2016. He was principal investigator of the Japan Society of the Promotion of Science (JSPS)-funded 'Critical, constructive assessments of CEFR-based language teaching' project, which formed the basis of this edited volume. His interests include action research, the use of the CEFR and the European Language Portfolio (ELP), Dublin and Irish English, and sociolinguistics. He is currently a lecturer in Linguistics at the University of Münster, Germany, and a PhD candidate at University College Dublin, Ireland.

Carlos Ramirez is an Associate Professor in the Faculty of International Studies at Kindai University, Osaka, Japan. He has taught EFL in Japan for the past 20 years. His research interests are oral communication development and language testing theory and practice.

Judith Runnels has taught English in China, Korea, Japan, England and Australia. She holds an MA in English Linguistics and is currently a PhD candidate at the Centre for Research in English Language Learning and Assessment (CRELLA), University of Bedfordshire, UK. Her research interests lie in evaluation and the usage of the CEFR.

Arthur Rutson-Griffiths is Assistant Director of the Bunkyo English Communication Centre at Hiroshima Bunkyo Women's University. His professional interests include the CEFR in Japan, task-based language teaching, extensive reading and techniques to foster student motivation.

Yukie Saito teaches at Waseda University as a part-time lecturer. Her interests include the application of the CEFR and the European Language Portfolio (ELP), teachers' cognition, and pragmatics. She is a PhD candidate at Temple University, Philadelphia.

Maria Gabriela Schmidt is currently an Associate Professor for German Studies and Linguistics at Tsukuba University (Japan), and has 30 years' teaching experience in Germany, South Korea and Japan at university level. She holds an MA degree in Philosophy and a PhD degree in Comparative Linguistics, both from the University of Mainz (Germany). Her research interests include first/second/third language acquisition, applied linguistics, phonetics/phonology and listening, teaching methods, learner autonomy, intercultural communication and the CEFR.

Rebecca Schmidt is currently a Lecturer at the Bunkyo English Communication Center at Hiroshima Bunkyo Women's University. Prior to that she taught for 10 years in Japanese public schools, where she also helped establish a curriculum for an elementary school's English language programme. She has a Master's in Applied Linguistics from Macquarie University and a BA in Public Policy with a focus on Education from Vanderbilt University. Her research interests involve collaborative learning, classroom group dynamics and ludic uses of language in teaching practice.

Etsuko Shimo, Associate Professor in the Faculty of Applied Sociology, Kindai University, teaches English and other related courses in their undergraduate programmes. Her research interests include learner autonomy, collaborative learning activities, student and teacher beliefs, and language education policy.

Tomoko Takada is a Professor at Meikai University in Chiba, Japan. She received her PhD in TESOL from New York University, and now teaches English language pedagogy in the teacher training programme. She was a member of a project that developed CEFR-J, a modified version of the CEFR to the Japanese educational context. She is interested in using the CEFR-J in secondary school syllabus design and material development.

Paul Wicking is an Associate Professor at Meijo University Faculty of Foreign Studies. He is currently researching the ways in which assessment is conceived and practised in Confucian heritage cultures, with a particular focus on learning-oriented assessment.

Noriko Yokoyama is a Professor for Japanese language education at Showa Women's University. She worked for the Japan Foundation for 27 years until March 2016 as a Japanese language specialist contributing to its teacher training programmes as well as learning materials development. Her research interests are second language acquisition (SLA) in general, and particularly the role of listening in second language acquisition.

Section 1
The context

1 Introduction: Towards critical, constructive assessment of CEFR-informed language teaching in Japan and beyond

Fergus O'Dwyer, Morten Hunke, Alexander Imig, Noriko Nagai, Naoyuki Naganuma and Maria Gabriela Schmidt

1 Introduction

This edited volume deals with some of the factors and salient issues to be considered when using the Common European Framework of Reference for Languages (CEFR, Council of Europe 2001). It is often suggested the CEFR has been misused, both within and outside Europe. Many focus on the 'Can Do' descriptors[1] and CEFR scales used to create attainment levels and for validation purposes. This ignores the original purposes of the CEFR, which include promoting plurilingualism and action-based learning for the purpose of developing autonomous, interculturally competent citizens (Parmenter 2014:203). The CEFR needs to be contextualised in a suitable way, based on current conditions and salient issues in specific contexts. The CEFR can become a shared point of reference to compare contextual choices (Coste 2007:42) in language-related areas such as policy, pedagogy, textbook development, assessment, etc. By outlining issues relating to these choices, this volume contributes to the ongoing debate on use of the CEFR. The adverse effects of language testing (e.g. teaching to the test) may be reversed should a more learner-centred pedagogy produce more effective and autonomous language learners.

The most widely recognised aspect of the CEFR is probably the 6-level proficiency scales and their 'Can Do' descriptors. Depending on the usage of the 'Can Do' scheme, the result may be positive or negative. Positive results generally occur when implementation focuses on the original aims of the CEFR as mentioned above. This volume, and the research project[2] which made it

---

1 'Can Do' descriptors are also often referred to as 'Can Do' statements: all chapters in this volume use the former term.
2 This work is supported by a KAKENHI Grant-in-Aid for Scientific Research (26370624) from the Japan Society for the Promotion of Science, and coordinated by members of the

possible, attempts to create critical and constructive assessments of current practices, so that such a pedagogy can be advanced in Japan and elsewhere. Assessment in this case refers to assessing how the CEFR is currently used in language education. The volume is designed to critically but constructively assess and interpret which aspects of the CEFR are being implemented in an effective way in specific contexts. We also try to highlight elements that can be improved in the future. One aim of this publication is to suggest further ways in which the principles and practices encouraged by the CEFR can permeate the foundations of language education. This generally touches upon issues such as the processes involved in the use of the CEFR, and accounting for factors, or contextual choices, which contributed to institutions using the CEFR in a certain way. The purpose of this process is to allow for others to be able to make informed decisions about practices that may be relevant to their contexts. This includes those who currently use the CEFR in some form, and would like to evaluate their own practices.

So as to set the scene, the next section of this chapter briefly introduces issues relating to using the CEFR in language education. We then explain the rationale and purpose of the edited volume, and outline a set of key questions that are at the centre of the publication. It is hoped the key questions will provide a basis for generating ideas about current practice that can be adapted and implemented by others.

2 Setting the scene for critical assessments of the CEFR

A central benefit of applying the CEFR in language education is that it provides a way of aligning individual achievement to global standards. Byram and Parmenter (2012) note that this is often how policy-makers, keen to be seen to be achieving high standards, engage with the CEFR. The CEFR can serve as a 'common language' that can be shared by language educators internationally. It also provides clear goals and measurable achievement by reference to the levels. As a result, those involved in language education, who are 'shopping around' globally for answers to their problems, often turn to the principles of the CEFR as a solution. This is especially relevant in cases beyond Europe, such as Argentina (Porto 2012, Porto and Barboni 2012) and Japan (Sugitani and Tomita 2012). Use of the CEFR in Japan includes the score interpretation of high-stake proficiency tests, attempts to create Japanese proficiency standards for foreign languages, and the use of 'Can Do' descriptors to improve foreign language education as well as to promote autonomous learning (Nagai and O'Dwyer 2012).

Japan Association of Language Teaching (JALT) Framework and Language Portfolio Special Interest Group (FLP SIG).

Chapter 2 of this volume provides an overview of past, present and future application of the CEFR in Japan in more detail. While CEFR-related research has a certain amount of prominence in academic circles in Japan, and some enthusiastic educators have developed CEFR-informed initiatives in their classrooms, the influence of the CEFR on language learning curricula has yet to go beyond surface level (e.g. using 'Can Do' descriptors as proficiency aims). As noted, the volume suggests how the principles of the CEFR can influence language education in Japan and beyond (Chapter 6 also relates to developments in Vietnam, with some reference to the home of the CEFR – Europe – in Chapter 10).

The Council of Europe (2008:9) recommends that the appropriate use of the CEFR adheres to the principle that the CEFR is descriptive, and should not be applied in a prescriptive way. One criticism of the CEFR is that the framework lacks validity and reliability in empirical and statistical terms. Coste (2007:42) advises to be wary of unhelpful 'attention to psychometric technicity', as well as a tendency to adopt the CEFR levels too readily, ignoring the detailed CEFR scales of illustrative descriptors, and limiting possibilities of contextualisation. This is particularly relevant to applying the CEFR to classroom language education, where effective contextualisation of 'Can Do' descriptors is key. The Council of Europe also stresses that the CEFR:

- is not exhaustive
- can be a common language for stakeholders to evaluate existing practices, and to situate their efforts in relation to others
- can contribute to the promotion of basic educational values such as autonomy and lifelong learning
- encourages further elaboration and development (2008:9).

For more about the principles such as learner autonomy that underline the CEFR and the related European Language Portfolio (ELP), see Council of Europe (2001), Little (2010, 2012), North (2014), section 2 of Chapter 10, section 1 of Chapter 7, and section 2 of sub-chapter 9B of this volume. We try to elaborate on possible contextual choices to consider when using the CEFR as a shared point of reference (Coste 2007:42; North 2014:8–44). While these learning situations are mostly from the country of Japan, the salient language learning issues will apply in many other contexts.

2.1 The rationale and purpose of this volume

The fundamental rationale of this volume is that, up until now, there has been little in the way of critical and constructive assessment of CEFR-informed pedagogical practices in Japan or beyond. Since the three case studies in the

Morrow (Ed) (2004) volume, research on implementation of the CEFR has very much focused on the macro level (e.g. Broek and Van den Ende 2013, Figueras 2012, Martyniuk and Noijons 2007, Piccardo, Germain-Rutherford and Clement (Eds) 2011, Takala 2013). Policy issues have been dominant; the edited volume of Byram and Parmenter (Eds) (2012), for example, predominantly presents a policy-maker perspective. The complexity of language policies can be shown in a 3-level model, which we exemplify in the case of Japan. The macro or national level includes the role of testing and examinations, and the creation of the CEFR-J as a national reference project. The CEFR-J, a modified version of the CEFR, is aimed at Japanese learners of English (Tono 2013, Tono and Negishi 2012 see also section 2 of Chapter 2 of this volume). Some 120 'Can Do' descriptors correspond to five skills (listening, reading, spoken interaction, spoken production, and writing), and 12 proficiency levels from Pre A1 to C2. Analysis suggested the need for finer-grained divisions for the A and B levels, according to typical learner profiles. The meso or institutional level features the role of universities and teacher organisations for shaping language policies. The micro level deals with syllabuses, teaching on a lesson level and individual learning.

As this volume focuses on the implementation of the CEFR in language education institutions, it is important to be aware that the CEFR and its 'Can Do' descriptors must be adapted and changed to suit the specific context they serve. We aim to progress pedagogical implementation of the principles and practices related to the CEFR by showing exemplars. This work is complementary to North (2014), which provides examples of the implementation of the CEFR, with a focus on misconceptions of the CEFR and how these could be addressed. We carry on the work of North, providing in-depth case studies. For a comprehensive description of processes it is necessary to unfold the complexity of language policy and then reduce it by concentrating mainly on the institutional levels (universities, language centres and, to some extent, teacher networks).

There is certainly scope for investigation of the role of institutions such as teacher associations in the globalising of educational and cultural policy. Teacher associations seem to be important networks all over the world. Byram and Parmenter (2012) give the example of the role of the American Association of Teachers of German in promoting the CEFR in the United States. Another example, which is interesting in terms of its border-crossing role, is the influence of the Association of Japanese Teachers in Europe on debates on the CEFR within Japan. This edited volume, co-ordinated by a teacher organisation (the Japan Association for Language Teaching Framework and Language Portfolio Special Interest Group, abbreviated to JALT FLP SIG), is a further example of the role of these networks. The results of this collection can help focus the role of universities, teacher organisations and individuals in shaping and implementing language policies, and

Introduction

the importance, on the institutional level, of the amalgam of top-down and bottom-up implementation of the CEFR.

Research (e.g. Martyniuk and Noijons 2007) shows that the CEFR has been successfully applied to a wide variety of curricula leading to course improvement in Europe, positively impacting language education. It should be noted that there are still unresolved issues. For example, Buschmann-Göbels and Kühn report in section 2 of Chapter 10 that there is still a large focus on testing in Europe, which may not always be helpful. In countries and regions outside Europe, implementation of the CEFR has not been without difficulty. Specifically, to adapt the CEFR to the entire language programme, teachers and other stakeholders must share its basic philosophy and ideas, which can be realised through top-down and bottom-up implementation facilitated by strong leadership. However, how this is realised in actual practice is extremely context dependent, and plans readily deployed in certain contexts may face unique obstacles in another. Institutions face obstacles unique to their circumstances, and how successfully they can navigate these obstacles partly depends on the availability of a rich amount of information around CEFR programme implementation and innovation. This volume seeks to add to the information available through the presentation of carefully implemented studies which demonstrate the range of initiatives possible, from relatively small-scale classroom implementations to larger institutional innovations, and also from a wide variety of institutional contexts, including several types of universities.

This publication contains contributions on how the principles and practices of the CEFR are being successfully applied. What hasn't worked is also introduced, for example see sub-chapter 9A. While many feel that a CEFR-informed, learner-centred pedagogy can produce more effective and autonomous learners of language, it is difficult to bring about change. This is particularly true in areas such as textbooks, curricula, and teaching practices. We aim to critically but constructively assess and discuss the implementation of the principles and practices suggested by the CEFR in these three interrelated areas. In order to give the entire volume a sound theoretical basis, particularly with regard to transfer of elements of one education system to another, a central focus is needed. This is addressed by examining key questions, which outline the processes involved in the use of the CEFR, and the factors which can contribute to institutions using the CEFR in a certain way. The key questions are outlined below.

2.1.1 Key questions regarding curricula

- **What type of implementation has been adopted? What specific practices have been implemented? What practices have been seen to be effective?**
  The aim here is to generate ideas of current practice that can be adapted and implemented by others.

- **How are all stakeholders involved? Can the people engaging in CEFR-informed teaching and learning develop a sense of ownership? How?**
  The 'Can Do' descriptors of the CEFR are unwieldy if not contextualised effectively. The focus of this question is that teachers and learners should engage with the 'Can Do' descriptors (and the general principles of the CEFR and ELP), contextualising the 'Can Do' descriptors for individual classes and learners. In this way, they may develop a sense of ownership of the practices.

- **Has the CEFR promoted a system for in-house evaluation of curricula and learning targets? Do curricula and courses include transparent and concrete learning objectives, with accepted 'Can Do' descriptors at the centre? How?**
  This question is in response to the prevalent focus on testing (e.g. teaching to the test) and language knowledge over language use in language curricula in Japan. By focusing curricula on the competencies put forward by the CEFR, classroom learning may be focused and improved.

- **Is it possible to compare the results of instruction in different classes?**
  This is particularly relevant for tertiary level, where in many cases individual teachers work alone, with little co-ordination between classes. There is little relationship between what learners undertake in a first year class and second year class, for example. There is also the issue of a lack of links between what is learned at high school and university. Scaffolded, CEFR-informed curricula could be one solution.

2.1.2 Classroom instruction

While the latter two questions in section 2.1.1 most definitely apply to the classroom, key questions specific to this area include:

- **Do 'Can Do' checklists serve as the key reference point for processes of reflective learning in which self-assessment plays a central role? How?**
  This is based on the viewpoint of Little (2010:171): that initiatives in the university context are most likely to succeed if 'Can Do' checklists serve as 'the key reference point for processes of reflective learning in which self-assessment plays a central role'. Reflection and self-assessment are important practices in which learner autonomy can be developed. Learning to learn is an important concept. Learners can become self-directed by finding out how to get to their desired learning 'destination'. It is thought that the effectiveness of reflection and self-assessment can be improved if they are combined with the learning progress mapped out in the CEFR self-assessment grid and illustrative scales. Learners often encounter this learning map via 'Can Do' checklists, which 'explode' a global scale of the

CEFR. An example of reflective learning could include learners, aiming to write to the B2 level, defining the elements that contribute to the quality mentioned in a 'Can Do' descriptor 'expanding and supporting points of view at length' (Council of Europe 2001:61). If 'Can Do' checklists are used as reference points in assessment and reflection, then the learners are guided towards an appropriate learning 'destination'.

- **What are the interpretations of teachers, students and other stakeholders, of the philosophy and ideas of the CEFR?**
  Some initiatives have been pushed from the 'top-down', with little effort to engage teachers and others from the 'bottom-up'. It is important that those pushing initiatives consider those involved with language learning at other levels in the institution in question. This is directly related to the penultimate question below.

- **Are the CEFR-informed materials (textbooks, teaching content etc.) action-oriented, and easily applicable by both teachers and students? How?**
  Putting a CEFR stamp on the back of a book, or a 'Can Do' descriptor at the top of a chapter opening page may not be the most effective way to implement a CEFR-informed programme. Appropriate learning outcomes should be at the centre of learning efforts.

- **Can all involved readily see the benefits of the CEFR-informed approach for their own teaching/learning?**

- **Is autonomous learning beyond the specified materials (e.g. textbooks) supported and encouraged? If so, how?**
  Autonomous learning, discussed above, is central to the lifelong view of learning that the CEFR and ELP movement promotes.

The textbook-related element of this volume (Chapters 4 and 5) analyses texts in relation to two elements: the correlation of the learning materials with the descriptive scales of the CEFR, and implementation in terms of a connected pedagogy (O'Dwyer, Imig and Nagai 2014) aligned to the principles and practices of the CEFR (e.g. action-oriented, reflective learning). The action research perspective of the contributions will suggest improvements that future textbooks can incorporate. In terms of CEFR-informed language education, there is little action research. Contributors to Chapter 3 to 13 were encouraged to pursue a dynamic action-reflection cycle (McNiff and Whitehead 2009:20): observe what is going on; think about how they can improve it; act; gather data to show the transformational nature of the actions; test and modify existing thinking and practices; communicate the significance of what they are doing, and try new ways of acting. For other interpretations of action research see section 3 of Chapter 6, and sub-section 3.3 of sub-chapter 9A.

2.2 The outcome of this volume: An assessment grid for learning programmes

The key questions make up a grid (Table 1) which can be used to assess what language learning institutions are doing in terms of learning outcomes. The main focus of this volume is aligning curricula to the CEFR. This includes contextualising 'Can Do' descriptors for specific purposes, while also incorporating some important principles that underlie the CEFR including learner autonomy. The principal purpose is to assess how institutions have achieved these aims (curricula alignment, contextualisation, incorporating principles of the CEFR), and to outline the important issues (or contextual choices) that are involved. North (2014) outlines some important steps for aligning a curriculum to the CEFR, and developing descriptors for communicative language activities. In terms of successful projects that have developed descriptors for communicative language activities, important components involve conducting a needs analysis to identify target situations and tasks, and find suitable 'Can Do' descriptors for these. The next step could be formulating 'Can Do' descriptors that briefly and positively describe tasks in a concrete manner. In validation teachers, learners, or both sort 'Can Do' descriptors, and give comments (North 2014:145). Aligning a curriculum to the CEFR revolves around providing a clear idea of practical course aims. Steps, after needs analysis and presenting objectives, include: specifying

Table 1 Assessment grid for learning programmes

Language learner can receive tuition informed by the following * = reasonably well, ** = well, *** = very well	*	**	***
Teachers, students and other stakeholders accept the philosophy and ideas of the CEFR (e.g. learner-centred, forward-looking assessment)			
In-house evaluation of curricula and learning targets, informed by the CEFR			
It is possible to compare the results of instruction in different classes			
People engaging in CEFR-informed teaching and learning develop a sense of ownership			
All stakeholders are involved			
All can readily apply, and see the benefits of the CEFR-informed approach for their own teaching/learning			
'Can Do' checklists serve as the key reference point for processes of reflective teaching/learning in which self-assessment plays a central role			
Autonomous learning beyond the specified materials (e.g. textbooks) is supported and encouraged			

objectives for different levels, sequencing objectives into short units of work, analysing the specific needs and interest of learners to decide final schedules and plans, presenting objectives and plans to learners, and involving learners in monitoring their achievement. These steps form the background of the assessment of the practices outlined in the chapter. Several frameworks are possible for analysing models of learning programme evaluation (e.g. Shufflebeam 2000).

What we aim to do through this grid is not to suggest ways to evaluate programmes, but to outline effective learning practices and learning outcomes, with an understanding of the contextual choices that underline these practices. The case studies in this volume are of innovative individuals who have successfully implemented their own CEFR-informed practices. Future endeavours can implement elements of these exemplars so that CEFR-informed practices underlie language learning efforts in Japan and beyond in the future. We use the grid, and accompanying interpretations, to outline how the practices in certain situations follow the steps to align a curriculum to the CEFR (North 2014:145) mentioned in the previous paragraph, and to present the strengths and weaknesses found in the practices. This is done to outline to the reader the aspects they can replicate. We hope that if some negative aspects associated with specific situations are highlighted, some suggestions can be found to show how to turn the situation towards a better learning environment. The grid is learning oriented, with the outcomes placed in terms of what language learners will receive as a result of receiving tuition at a certain institution. The case studies presented in the book will be assessed in terms of this grid. The positive points of each case study are presented together, which will form an exemplar for those who wish to use CEFR-informed practices in their own context. This is the main focus of Chapter 14.

An important consideration is that many factors will be context dependent, and it is not reasonable to expect any one use of the CEFR to fit all situations. It is important to consider that use of a framework such as the CEFR depends on varying needs, aims, rationales and outcomes. Those who intend to use elements of the CEFR must take these issues into consideration. The case studies present some of the factors that affect certain types of use.

3 Organisation of this volume

In the next chapter, 'The past, present and future of the CEFR in Japan', Maria Gabriela Schmidt, Judith Runnels and Noriko Nagai overview the use of the CEFR in Japan, and outline the role the framework has played in language education. Some thoughts are also offered regarding future implementation. It is noted that there is still a lot of work to be done before the CEFR is fully embedded in the system. The development of the CEFR-J (Tono 2013,

Tono and Negishi 2012) creates a better environment for implementation in classrooms. Initiatives implemented by the Ministry of Education, Culture, Sports, Science and Technology – Japan (MEXT) further facilitate the use of the CEFR-informed practices by mandating learning attainment targets in the form of 'Can Do' lists for junior and senior high schools.

In Chapter 3, 'The perception of the CEFR in secondary-level English language teaching in Japan', Tomoko Takada reports on a teacher training project for a group of high school English teachers who developed and used such lists. Not all teachers are ready for this, and teacher training is an important consideration. Another challenge they faced is that students need a great deal of specific help and guidance for reflection. The introduction of CEFR-informed practices has had positive effects (e.g. increased promotion of a 'Can Do' approach and activities that may foster autonomous learning), but there are many remaining issues including the amount of 'buy-in' and sense of ownership from stakeholders. All parties may not be able to readily see the benefits of the CEFR-informed approach for teaching and learning. It must be remembered that the proponents of more teacher-centred and knowledge-based teaching must face a 'paradigm shift' in accepting the underlying principles of the CEFR and the ELP (Majima 2010:61). The challenges for the education system as a whole can be seen in these details.

Chapters 4 and 5 present critical, constructive assessment of CEFR-informed language teaching textbooks. Noriko Yokoyama in Chapter 4, 'Marugoto: Japanese Language and Culture – the series of coursebooks based on the JF Standard for Japanese Language Education', describes the characteristics of a series of coursebooks that illustrate the use of the Japan Foundation Standard (which is directly based on the CEFR 'Can Do' descriptors) in classroom practice. Each level consists of two volumes and offers the following two different types of learning: (a) implicit learning through listening and speaking for communicative language activities, and (b) explicit learning of grammar, vocabulary and characters for communicative language competences. Chapter 5, 'Applying the CEFR to English for Academic Purposes textbooks' by Naoyuki Naganuma, Noriko Nagai and Fergus O'Dwyer, overviews a research project that developed English language integrated skills textbooks that suitably adapt and apply the CEFR for the higher education context in Japan. These textbooks also developed supplemental learning materials, such as a language portfolio, to support learner and teacher autonomy, and to support the classroom implementation of the text.

In regard to using the CEFR for Japanese as a foreign language in various countries, the following question could be a supplementary issue raised by this volume: how can the common European yardstick, the CEFR levels as defined in 'Can Do' formulations, be applied to languages such as Japanese, and what kind of interpretations of the philosophy and ideas of the CEFR do active or aspiring Japanese language instructors actually have in a European language teaching context?

Chapters 6 to 9 address elements of the implementation of the CEFR in curricula. These chapters can be framed in terms of contextual choices, and the process of familiarisation of teachers and other stakeholders with the CEFR (North 2014). Chapter 6, 'Applying the CEFR to renew a General English curriculum: Successes, remaining issues and lessons from Vietnam', by Pham Thi Hong Nhung, describes the low level of CEFR familiarity in Vietnam, and the need for explicit familiarisation of teachers with the main concepts of the framework. The ambitious government-mandated top-down policy is being imposed upon educators with little consultation. For the policy to be accepted and efficiently implemented, there needs to be involvement from the bottom-up (i.e. teachers, learners and other stakeholders). This contribution from Vietnam outlines how training workshops and other collaborative initiatives can aid the acceptance and effective use of the CEFR.

Etsuko Shimo, Carlos Ramirez and Kaori Nitta (Chapter 7, 'A 'Can Do' framework-based curriculum in a university-level English language learning programme: Course goals, activities and assessment') then explain a context-specific 'Can Do' framework based on the CEFR, with the purpose of providing specific goals and simple assessment tools for both students and teachers, implemented in a university-level language curriculum. The contextual choices are based on a low to medium level of familiarity: implicit familiarisation with CEFR concepts is needed and achieved by some faculty development and to a greater extent by teacher involvement in curriculum implementation. A policy has been set in place but only a low level of teacher involvement is possible. A group of full-time faculty staff are driving the change by guiding a large group of part-time teachers.

In Japan, we see a distinct movement to use the CEFR as a tool to provide coherence and transparency. In Chapter 8, 'Implementing the CEFR as a benchmark for 'action-oriented' syllabus design', Mark de Boer relates the implementation of curricula and classroom instruction based on the general measures of CEFR for a faculty-wide English education. The initiatives are designed to help develop 'communicative language competences, provide context, support language activities and language processes, text, domain, strategies, and tasks' (Council of Europe 2001:9–10). In this case the contextual choices are based on a low level of CEFR familiarity; with implicit familiarisation with the concepts of the CEFR the most viable option. This is achieved by teacher involvement in curriculum implementation. There is no policy set in place: individuals are driving the change.

Conversely, Chapter 9 ('Using the CEFR-J and the CEFR as frameworks for renewal of an English language curriculum at a Japanese university: An action research study', comprising three sub-chapters written by Jack Bower, Judith Runnels, Arthur Rutson-Griffiths, Rebecca Schmidt, Gary Cook,

Assessment of CEFR-informed Language Teaching in Japan and Beyond

Lyndon Lusk Lehde and Azusa Kodate) presents a case where contextual choices are based on a relatively high level of CEFR familiarity. A prolonged and focused familiarisation process involved workshops, expert involvement, action research cycles and a tight group working towards a common goal. The institutional policy is supported both from top-down and bottom-up, with a high level of involvement from a small group of full-time faculty members who are leading the change for their own classes. Acceptance of the CEFR in that institution is widespread, from all stakeholders. The case involves the alignment of curricula to the CEFR-J, curriculum mapping, and the development of related self-access materials. Procedures involved in the alignment project included:

- teacher education and training workshops
- rewriting the General English (GE) curriculum goals based on CEFR-J descriptors
- writing detailed 'Can Do' descriptors for all lesson handouts to serve as a reference for teachers
- receiving expert feedback on the lesson 'Can Do' descriptors
- mapping the existing curriculum against the CEFR-J grid
- writing simplified 'Can Do' descriptors for students and placing them in checklists at the beginning and end of lesson handouts
- recreating learning activities in the Self Access Learning Center (SALC) based on the CEFR-J.

A second stage of curriculum renewal is also described. This offers hints for the application of action research in CEFR-informed practices. It should be noted that the practices adopted in this chapter are extensive, and require a large amount of space to sufficiently explain and present the case to the reader. The editors feel this is justified, as this is a fine example of using the CEFR for the design and continual improvement of language education curricula. These initiatives positively influence multiple aspects of learning and teaching at the institution.

Chapters 10 to 13 present implementation of the CEFR in classrooms through portfolio approaches, with a focus on the pedagogical function of promoting learner reflection and self-assessment. Chapter 10, 'A CEFR-informed e-portfolio in blended learning at a German university', by Astrid Buschmann-Göbels and Bärbel Kühn from Bremen University in Germany, provides an example of how language learning initiatives have been implemented in Europe, the home of the framework. The contextual choices in Bremen are based on a high level of familiarity with the CEFR, and its underlying principles. Linguistic pluralism is a reality and a specific need in this context. Chapter 11, 'Using the CEFR-informed European Language Portfolio in a non-CEFR English course' by Paul Wicking, discusses how the author integrated an ELP into an English programme that is not based on CEFR descriptors. In the next chapter (Chapter 12), 'Developing a portfolio for English as a tool for global communication', Yukie Saito exemplifies how 'Can Do' descriptors are used to draft a portfolio for students to learn English as tool for global communication, and reflect the cyclical phases of self-regulated learning. Similarly, in Chapter 13, 'Using the 'Can Do' descriptor list as a checklist for short-term Chinese study in China', Qu Ming outlines how 'Can Do' checklists serve as the key reference point for processes of self-assessment and reflective learning based around study abroad trips to China. These four contributions outline the efforts of enthusiastic educators, who are bringing the principles of learner involvement in reflective learning to the classroom, something that has not been fully applied or appreciated inside and outside Europe.

Chapter 10 discusses both the use of the CEFR in curricula, and how CEFR-informed e-portfolios are implemented in blended learning supported by tutoring. As is demonstrated in Chapter 7 in particular, dealing with large numbers of part-time teachers places very particular obstacles for implementations of CEFR-informed curricula and classroom instruction. Novel and creative approaches like using tutors, learning advisors, or even training student facilitators may provide workable and viable solutions for institutions struggling with such issues. The inclusion of e-portfolios is another very important element of the future implementation of the CEFR in Japan and elsewhere. We understand individuals have started negotiations to bring the EPOS portfolio used in Bremen to Japan. However, there are no examples or exemplars for practitioners to reference. These are some of the reasons for including Chapter 10 in the volume. Furthermore, the contribution by Buschmann-Göbels and Kühn begins the 'Portfolio approaches' section as the learning approaches discussed in Chapters 11 to 13 could benefit greatly from the integrated technology and tutoring processes. Section 2 of Chapter 10 briefly outlines the development and history of the CEFR and ELP in Europe: these are important for teachers and others to understand before undertaking their own initiatives. The final chapter, 'Bringing critical and constructive assessments of CEFR-informed language teaching forward' by Fergus O'Dwyer, Morten Hunke, Alexander Imig, Noriko Nagai, Naoyuki Naganuma and Maria Gabriela Schmidt, concludes the volume by assessing the case studies in terms of the grid (Table 1). Final remarks outline the important ideas for users of the CEFR to consider when undertaking pedagogic enterprises.

Acknowledgements

The authors would like to thank Theron Muller and Judith Runnels for the thoughtful feedback they gave on earlier drafts of this chapter.

References

Broek, S and Van den Ende, I (2013) *The Implementation of the Common European Framework for Languages in European Education Systems*, Brussels: Policy Department B: Structural and Cohesion Policies, European Parliament, available online: www.eur oparl.europa.eu/RegData/etudes/etudes/join/2013/495871/IPOL-CULT_ET(2013)495871_EN.pdf

Byram, M and Parmenter, L (Eds) (2012) *The Common European Framework of Reference: The Globalisation of Language Education Policy*, Bristol: Multilingual Matters.

Byram, M and Parmenter, L (2012) Introduction, in Byram, M and Parmenter, L (Eds) *The Common European Framework of Reference: The Globalisation of Language Education Policy*, Bristol: Multilingual Matters, 1–12.

Coste, D (2007) *Contextualising Uses of the Common European Framework of Reference for Languages*, Strasbourg: Council of Europe.

Council of Europe (2001) *Common European Framework of Reference for Languages: Learning, Teaching, Assessment*, Cambridge: Cambridge University Press.

Council of Europe (2008) *Recommendations CM/Rec(2008)7 of the Committee of Ministers to Member States on the Use of the Council of Europe's Common European Framework of Reference for Languages (CEFR) and the Promotion of Multilingualism*, Strasbourg: Council of Europe.

Figueras, N (2012) The impact of the CEFR, *English Language Teaching Journal* 66 (4), 477–485.

Little, D (2010) The European Language Portfolio and self-assessment: Using 'I can' checklists to plan, monitor and evaluate language learning, in Schmidt, M G, Naganuma, N, O'Dwyer, F, Imig, A and Sakai, K (Eds) *Can Do Statements in Language Education in Japan and Beyond – Application of the CEFR*, Tokyo: Asahi Press, 157–166.

Little, D (2012) The European Language Portfolio: History, key concerns, future prospects, in Kühn, B and Pérez Cavana, M L (Eds) *Perspectives from the European Language Portfolio: Learner Autonomy and Self-assessment*, London: Routledge, 7–21.

Majima, J (2010) Impact of can do statements/CEFR on language education in Japan: On its applicability, in Schmidt, M G, Naganuma, N, O'Dwyer, F, Imig, A and Sakai, K (Eds) *Can Do Statements in Language Education in Japan and Beyond – Applications of the CEFR*, Tokyo: Asahi Press, 49–65.

Martyniuk, W and Noijons, J (2007) *Executive Summary of Results of a Survey on the Use of the CEFR at National Level in the Council of Europe Member States*, Strasbourg: Council of Europe.

McNiff, J and Whitehead, J (2009) *Action Research*, California: Sage.

Morrow, K (Ed) (2004) *Insights from the Common European Framework*, Oxford: Oxford University Press.

Nagai, N and O'Dwyer, F (2012) The actual and potential impacts of the CEFR on language education in Japan, *Synergies Europe* 6, 141–152.

North, B (2014) *The CEFR in Practice*, English Profile Studies volume 4, Cambridge: UCLES/Cambridge University Press.

O'Dwyer, F, Imig, A and Nagai, N (2014) Connectedness through a strong form of TBLT, classroom implementation of the CEFR, cyclical learning, and learning-oriented assessment, *Language Learning in Higher Education* 3 (2), 231–253.

Parmenter, L (2014) Globalization in Japan: Education policy and curriculum, in Stromquist, N P and Monkman, K (Eds) *Globalization and Education: Integration and Contestation across Cultures*, Maryland: Rowman and Littlefield, 201–215.

Piccardo, E, Germain-Rutherford, A and Clement, R (Eds) (2011) Adopter ou adapter: le Cadre européen commun de référence est-il seulement européen? *Synergies Europe 6*, available online: gerflint.fr/Base/Europe6/Europe6.htmlhttp://gerflint.fr/Base/Europe6/Europe6.html

Porto, M (2012) Academic perspectives from Argentina, in Byram M and Parmenter, L (Eds) *The Common European Framework of Reference: The Globalisation of Language Education Policy*, Bristol: Multilingual Matters, 129–137.

Porto, M and Barboni, S (2012) Policy perspectives from Argentina, in Byram, M and Parmenter, L (Eds) *The Common European Framework of Reference: The Globalisation of Language Education Policy*, Bristol: Multilingual Matters, 119–128.

Shufflebeam, D L (2000) The CIPP model for evaluation, *Evaluation Models* 89, 279–317.

Sugitani, M and Tomita, Y (2012) Perspectives from Japan, in Byram, M and Parmenter, L (Eds) *The Common European Framework of Reference: The Globalisation of Language Education Policy*, Bristol: Multilingual Matters, 198–211.

Takala, S (2013) The CEFR in use: Some observations of three Nordic countries, in Figueras, N (2013) (Ed) *The Impact of the CEFR in Catalonia*, APAC Monographs No 9, 9–18.

Tono, Y (2013) *CAN-DO list sakusei katsuyou: Eigo toutatsu shihyou CEFR-J guidebook [CEFR-J Guidebook: Resources for Establishing and Utilizing 'Can-Do' Lists for English Language Teaching]*, Tokyo: Taishukan.

Tono, Y and Negishi, M (2012) The CEFR-J: Adapting the CEFR for English language teaching in Japan, *Framework & Language Portfolio (FLP) SIG Newsletter* 8, 5–12, available online: dl.dropboxusercontent.com/u/33808898/FLP%20SIG%20NL%208%20Sep2012%20CEFR-J.pdf

2 The past, present and future of the CEFR in Japan

Maria Gabriela Schmidt
University of Tsukuba
Judith Runnels
University of Bedfordshire
Noriko Nagai
Ibaraki University

1 Introduction

The success of the Common European Framework of Reference for Languages (CEFR, Council of Europe 2001) in Europe has been based on the 'common currency' it has provided governments, applied linguists, educators and other stakeholders who desired a real-life and comprehensive approach to language learning, teaching and assessment (Figueras 2007:478). The CEFR does not yet appear to have had as substantial an effect on language education outside of Europe as within, although that is not to say that it may not eventually do so. In this regard, significant increases in the popularity of the framework within language education in Japan have recently become evident.

This chapter gives an overview of the usage of the CEFR in Japan from 2004 to the present and also interprets the CEFR's role in the past, present and future landscape of foreign language education in Japan. In this first section, after the CEFR's history in Japan is presented, a number of attempts to use the CEFR in language education in Japan are outlined. Particular focus is given to the development of the Japanese adaptation of the CEFR, known as the CEFR-Japan (CEFR-J). The challenges associated with the previous usages of the CEFR and recommendations for overcoming them are discussed.

The subsequent section evaluates the present role of the CEFR in Japan through three studies within various contexts of language education: national, institutional and individual. The first examines research activities on the CEFR in Japan by exploring CEFR-related Japan Society for the Promotion of Science (JSPS) Grant-in-Aid funded projects. Over 136 funded research projects related to the CEFR have been undertaken since 2004, with 31 ongoing at the time of writing. To explore the impact of the CEFR at an institutional level, the second study focuses on the analysis of the foreign language curricula of 50 Japanese national universities, concluding that the CEFR has had an underwhelming influence on foreign language curricula: only a single one of the 50 universities surveyed has adopted the CEFR at more than a surface level. The final study reviews teachers' perceptions of the CEFR's past usage, present impact, and potential future applications. This study also revealed an underwhelming impact of the CEFR overall, but indicated that some stakeholders are clear and strong adopters of the framework. These teachers claim that the CEFR has benefited their language programmes substantially but nonetheless suggest a list of tools and supplementary materials that they think would be required in increasing and improving usage of the CEFR at their institutions. The final sections discuss the CEFR's future in language education in Japan. Particular focus is given to the needs of teachers, who are seen herein to be key stakeholders, at the front line of language education and with the power to determine whether the CEFR has any impact on the teaching, learning and assessment of foreign languages in Japan.

2 Past reception of the CEFR in Japan

Following the Japanese translation of the CEFR by Yoshijima and Ohashi in 2004, the CEFR began paving its way through the foreign language education landscape in Japan, and it has become more visible every year since then. The CEFR's first steps in Japan, albeit relatively hidden ones, were in fact taken by a group of teachers of Japanese as a foreign language (JFL) in Europe related to the Association of Japanese Language Teachers in Europe (AJE). In the early 2000s, they built a joint research group focused on the CEFR with Japanese teachers in Japan and in Europe (Majima 2010, Sugitani and Tomita 2012). This was accompanied by a number of expert groups studying the possibility of usage of the CEFR in foreign language education in Japan. However, these studies were not restricted to the use of the CEFR in English language education; rather they focused much more on other languages like French and German, and especially on JFL (Majima 2015, Sugitani and Tomita 2012).

Up to the time of writing, the CEFR's short history in Japan can be divided into five phases (Table 1), with the early studies at AJE and the expert groups representing the first phase. The first CEFR-related JSPS Grant-in-Aid funded project started during the second phase in 2004. Being the only one of its kind at the time, it opened the door for the CEFR's usage in foreign language education. Co-ordinated by Koike (2008), this was also the start-up project for the CEFR-J (2012), the final version of which was published by Tono and Negishi (2012) several years later in Phase 3. In the second phase, the CEFR remained invisible to most language teachers, although publication of the Japanese translation of the CEFR in 2004 spurred a growing interest which resulted in a slight increase in various related academic activities. These included a number of conferences and supplementary resources to support the usage of the CEFR. To provide an example, a 2006 symposium, supported by the Ministry of Education, Culture, Sports, Science and Technology (MEXT) at Osaka University of Foreign Studies entitled 'A new direction in foreign language education: The potential of the Common European Framework of Reference for Languages' was held (Majima 2007, North 2006). In response, some Japanese universities initiated internal research projects on usage of the CEFR, some of which are documented in Schmidt, Naganuma, O'Dwyer, Imig and Sakai (Eds) (2010).

The third phase commenced in the year 2008, with a more markedly visible increase in CEFR-related activity. This included the publication of different kinds of CEFR projects specific to Japan: 1) the founding of the Japan Association for Language Teaching Framework and Language Portfolio Special Interest Group (JALT FLP SIG) in 2008 (Japan Association for Language Teaching Framework and Language Portfolio Special Interest Group 2015), 2) the Japan Foundation standard for Japanese-Language Education in 2010 (Japan Foundation 2015), resulting in a new approach for Japanese language teaching and an overhaul of the tests for the Japanese-Language Proficiency Test (JLPT), and 3) in 2012, the publication of the specially adapted Japanese version of the CEFR, the so-called CEFR-J (Tono 2013, Tono and Negishi 2012). For a more detailed overview of CEFR-informed applications in Phase 3, see Majima (2010) and Sugitani and Tomita (2012).

The most recent phase began in 2013, with a major development being the announcement by the Japan Broadcasting Corporation (known as NHK in Japan) that the CEFR-J would frame their educational language programming on both television and radio (Japan Broadcasting Corporation 2012). A series of new CEFR-informed textbooks were also developed (see Chapter 5). Concurrently, the research project resulting in this volume, known as CriConCef, aimed to evaluate critically and constructively the ongoing process of implementation of the CEFR in curricula, textbooks and classroom practice. Additionally, the Japanese Eiken Foundation for English released a CEFR-informed paper-based test known as the Test of English for Academic Purposes (TEAP). With four skills to be tested, it challenges the long-standing central examination for entering universities (Test of English for Academic Purposes 2015).

As for the fifth phase, the needs of students, teachers and other stakeholders related to the challenges of learning foreign languages should be addressed. The influence of the CEFR is still growing and will likely continue to expand to a point where it has a more noticeable impact on curricula, textbooks and materials, and classroom practices. Table 1 summarises the CEFR's history in Japan so far.

Table 1 A summary of the history of the CEFR in Japan

Phase 1: Invisible (2001)	Phase 2: Perceptible (2004)	Phase 3: Visible (2008)	Phase 4: Growing (2013)	Phase 5: Expanding (2016)
JFL builds a joint research group, AJE. Expert group studies on applicability of CEFR in Japan.	Translation of CEFR into Japanese. Research projects start to appear. Some conferences are held.	JALT FLP SIG founded (2008). JF standard established (2010). CEFR-J published (2012).	NHK uses CEFR for programming. CEFR-informed textbook published. This edited volume developed. CEFR-informed tests developed e.g. TEAP.	CEFR expands into practice. Stakeholders' needs addressed.

Other scholars seem to agree with the history of the CEFR presented in Table 1. Parmenter and Byram suggested that:

> An increasing number of quite powerful figures in language education policy circles advocating use of the CEFR together with more professional networks ... are gradually raising the profile of the CEFR in Japan ... [Yet] ... the influence of the CEFR in Japanese language education policy is still muted, there is little doubt that the CEFR will be the subject of increasing attention (Parmenter and Byram 2010:16).

Their usage of the expression 'powerful figures' seems to make reference to the invisible first and perceptible second phases of the CEFR's history, where only a small number of those involved in language education were aware of and interested in it. Parmenter and Byram also refer to events in the years 2009 and 2010, just around the time that the awareness of the CEFR and discussions surrounding its usage became more visible, or in their words, the 'subject of increasing attention' (Parmenter and Byram 2010:16). Since then, an increasing number of studies, research projects and activities show the rising interest in the CEFR and the need for its usage.

However, its impact thus far has not been consistently widespread across language education in primary, secondary and tertiary contexts. Sugitani and Tomita (2012) give a detailed introduction of the first few years of the CEFR in Japan, pointing out that:

> There is a significant gap in the influence of the CEFR between school education and university education. In school education, which is very tightly controlled by the central government, reference to the CEFR is scarcely evident, and there is little general interest at present in appropriating the CEFR in national policy for compulsory education ... In university education, on the other hand, there is a great deal more freedom,

and this has facilitated much greater interest and influence (Sugitani and Tomita 2012:198).

In any case, to discuss the CEFR's 'past' as if it has indeed truly passed is questionable: the CEFR in Japan is still a very recent phenomenon, and in terms of implementing the CEFR for language learning in a Japanese learning context in the years ahead, the present situation may provide the key for the future. Since it is expected that, during the forward-looking Phase 5 (Table 1), usage of the CEFR will continue to expand into the practices of language education stakeholders (namely teachers) it is important to first review previous attempts to use the CEFR in Japan, described in the following section.

2.1 Previous attempts to use the CEFR in Japan

Nagai and O'Dwyer (2012) highlighted three major applications of the CEFR in a Japanese foreign language educational context: for score interpretation of high-stake proficiency tests, for the creation of Japanese proficiency standards for foreign languages, and for various pedagogical uses of 'Can Do' descriptors to improve foreign language education and to promote autonomous learning. The influence of the CEFR and its underlying philosophies are detectable in various degrees within these three areas of language education in Japan, each discussed in turn in this section.

In terms of high-stake proficiency test score interpretation, focus on standardised testing in Japan has given rise to long-standing concerns about the distortion of the curriculum, and subsequently, the quality of language learning, to accommodate such high-stake testing. Nagai and O'Dwyer (2012) argue that the focus on standardised testing can bring greater benefit to learners if the mainstream tests are closely aligned to the CEFR. In doing so, this would encourage learners to progress according to the CEFR's illustrative scales, while reducing the distortion of the curriculum (Nagai and O'Dwyer 2012). Thus far, there are very few known attempts to use the CEFR in Japan for the purposes of test design, with the exception of one example described in Chapter 9 and a further from Negishi (2006). It is expected that this is one area which will continue to grow as the CEFR moves into its next phase of development in Japan.

In terms of Nagai and O'Dwyer's (2012) second potential application of the CEFR, an example of the development of Japanese proficiency standards for foreign languages includes the Japan Foundation Standard for Japanese Language Education (Japan Foundation 2015). The Japan Foundation Standard (JFS), released by the Japan Foundation in 2010, like the CEFR, is a framework consisting of six levels, and is described in the form of 'Can Do' descriptors (see also section 2 of Chapter 4). The JFS proposes a portfolio approach and values learners' autonomy of their own learning and assessment. It specifies tasks assigned to each language activity and their conditions of performance. It suggests that the usage of the scaled descriptors is necessary for self-assessment checklists or as goals of a language course. This shows that there is the potential to integrate the CEFR and its related concepts into a Japanese language teaching environment, which is argued to bring the benefit of greater transparency for all stakeholders including learners, teachers and administration. Doing so, however, touches upon one challenge of using the CEFR: the local standards based on the CEFR should match the original CEFR proficiency levels. This issue is also central to the CEFR-J enterprise, which is perhaps the most notable development throughout the CEFR's history in Japan.

A further example of the creation of Japanese proficiency standards for foreign languages is the CEFR-J, a contextualised version of the CEFR for English Language Teaching in Japan (Tono 2013, Tono and Negishi 2012). It provides a finer grained self-assessment grid of the CEFR's A and B levels. A1 level is divided into four sub-levels: Pre A1, A1.1, A1.2 and A1.3. Each of the levels A2 to B2 is broken down to two sub-levels: A2.1, A2.2; B1.1, B1.2; and B2.1, B2.2, respectively. Tono and Negishi (2012) state the purpose of the CEFR-J is to meet the imminent demand for transparent attainment goals for learners of English. They believe that the CEFR-J will encourage action-oriented approaches in English language teaching (ELT) in Japan. Consequently, this will help develop communicative abilities and skills of Japanese learners of English, which have long been acknowledged as insufficient compared with those of learners in other industrialised nations and need to be improved to meet the demands of the current globalised world (Sugitani and Tomita 2012, Tono and Negishi 2012).

Nagai and O'Dwyer's (2012) third potential application of the CEFR in Japan was related to the use of 'Can Do' descriptors for the purposes of improving the transparency and cohesiveness of language education programmes. Some of these initiatives are documented in Schmidt et al (Eds) (2010). Thus far, the CEFR seems to have been most widely applied to the improvement of language education curricula although the implementation of such institution-wide curricula has generally been found to be difficult (Schmidt et al (Eds) 2010). Although one of the most challenging and ambitious adaptations of the CEFR is perhaps the curriculum development of an entire language programme in an institution, a number of reforms of the English curriculum at a tertiary level have been conducted, many of which have been renovated with reference to the CEFR. The first instance of a CEFR-informed curriculum development in Japan on an institution-wide context was in 2005, when Osaka University used the CEFR as the achievement goals in each of their 25 foreign language programmes (Majima 2010, Sugitani and Tomita 2012). A more down-sized but equally successful adaptation of the CEFR to a number of language programmes at a tertiary institution was undertaken at the Muroran Institute of Technology (Krause-Ono 2010). Another example comes from Ibaraki University (Nagai 2010).

These case studies indicate that a CEFR-based language curriculum reform is neither easy nor straightforward and that the amalgam of top-down and bottom-up implementation with a strong leadership is necessary (Schmidt et al (Eds) 2010). While top-down implementation brings the benefits of integrated, effective decision-making and curriculum control, there is the risk of the loss of both teacher and learner autonomy. Conversely, bottom-up implementation of CEFR-based language reforms can likewise bring effective results, but may face administrative or other institutional hurdles if top-down stakeholders are not supportive of the project. As discussed in Schmidt et al (Eds) (2010), when the implementation was forced top-down without much adaptation of the CEFR to a particular Japanese educational context, the good intention of the language curriculum reform may be in vain. Keio University's attempt may be such a case (Horiguchi, Harada, Imoto and Atobe 2010). If educators are encouraged to use the principles and practices encouraged by the CEFR, there should be suitable training for stakeholders at all levels along with a bottom-up movement to appropriately contextualise the CEFR for the specific context.

Despite these examples, increasing usage of the CEFR in Japan has not occurred without critique. Sakai (2014) pointed out that Japanese language teaching tries to avoid the taxonomy of *communicative categories*, which is precisely one of the main rationales behind the CEFR. In other words, in using the CEFR without considering the implications it makes on the act of communication, its pragmatic approach to language learning and teaching is neglected or lost entirely. As Sakai states (2014:73): 'In Japan, however, the use of the CEFR has largely been limited to the "Can Do" statements, and this use has become widespread in the language teaching profession.'

The use of 'Can Do' descriptors as checklists in a course to facilitate learners' self-regulatory learning is indeed widespread in Japan and it has also been rather successfully implemented (Schmidt et al (Eds) 2010). Sato (2010) demonstrated a great success in improving learners' ability to monitor their learning. The main positive impact of the pedagogical use of 'Can Do' descriptors can be said to be the perceived shift from teacher-centred knowledge-driven classes to student-centred communication-oriented instruction (Collett and Sullivan 2010, Sato 2010). Nonetheless:

> ... there are also suggestions that reform of understanding about "teaching and learning foreign languages" is important, in that the development and application of "Can Do" statements is in itself insufficient for the overarching aim of "foreign language education reform", both for educators and students (Sugitani and Tomita 2012:201).

A major criticism therefore, is that key tenets of the CEFR are either ignored or overlooked by the selective attitude with which some stakeholders approach using it. Going into more detail, Sakai notes that:

> Two major problems concerning the contextualization of the CEFR within the Japanese educational system are apparent: one is that the studies ... have a tendency to regard the CEFR merely as a means by which to categorize standards of competence in one language and to see the six levels as a suitable scale for evaluating an individual's proficiency in one foreign language ... there is hardly any indication that the CEFR will be considered as a cross-sectional tool for improving the whole [of] foreign language education in Japan. The other problem is that, although the "Can Do" statements are discussed, other principles of the CEFR are rarely mentioned (Sakai 2014:76).

To elaborate, Sakai (2014) believes that the two main aims of the CEFR are overlooked: firstly, the CEFR aims to aid communication between stakeholders, and secondly encourages stakeholders to continually reflect on their own language education practices (Council of Europe 2001:6). On the side of classroom instruction, these principles are the task-based and pragmatic approach, as well as learner autonomy via tools such as the learner biography. By restricting the CEFR's implementation to its 'Can Do' descriptors, perhaps because they are the CEFR's easiest facet to handle, the CEFR is stripped of many of its underlying concepts and the various potential uses the CEFR suggests are neglected. These may include the planning of language learning programmes, materials and assessment in consideration of the assumptions they make about learners' prior knowledge, how they relate to and build on learners' previous experience with language education, how criteria are set, their ultimate objectives and how the content reflects this. Additionally, the importance of raising a learner's awareness of their present abilities and knowledge, aiding them to self-set learning goals, self-select materials or self-assess are paramount in the CEFR's approach to language learning, teaching and assessment (Council of Europe 2001:6). Sakai concluded by showing his support for the judgement of David Newby (European Centre of Modern Languages, Graz, Austria):

> In implementing the CEFR and when devising support measures, language policy makers and researchers should therefore consider exactly why it might benefit teachers to be informed about the CEFR and which aspects should be highlighted and which principles and sections deserve detailed attention (as cited in Sakai 2014:77).

Although it is evident that strides and positive changes have been made, particularly since the start of Phase 2 (Table 1), the integration of the CEFR in the Japanese language education system may be thus far a rather reduced or tokenistic adaptation, and a better understanding of the present situation is required before the future of the CEFR can be discussed.

3 Evaluating the present situation

To shed light on the present situation of the CEFR in Japan, three studies were conducted. Firstly, a database of publicly funded CEFR-related research projects in universities was searched (section 3.1). Secondly, university curricula from national universities across the country were consulted (section 3.2), and finally a questionnaire on tertiary level language teachers' perceptions of the CEFR was conducted (section 3.3). A general increase in publicly funded research projects was evident from 2004 to 2015, and although many studies and scholars are involved in detailed research projects, traces in the curriculum are yet to be seen. The survey of foreign language curricula at 50 national universities revealed only four which referenced the CEFR and of these four, only one appeared to use the CEFR comprehensively. Public universities seem to show reluctance in using the CEFR and are under pressure to fulfil ministerial guidelines in their curricula. The teacher perceptions study revealed a general desire to use the framework among participants who are aware of the CEFR's advantages but seem to be hindered by the CEFR's complexity, noting that its use is associated with significant challenges.

3.1 Research activities on the CEFR in Japan

The JSPS Grant-in-Aid funded projects are a visible part of the science and education system in Japan. All such projects are publicly accessible on the so-called KAKEN database[1]. Following the completion of funding, the projects must present their findings, which are also published for public access. To evaluate the present situation of research on the CEFR, the KAKEN database was searched on 30 July 2015 and on 10 December 2015 to confirm the numbers for the year 2015. The search terms of 'CEFR' and its Japanese translation ('youroppa gengo kyotsuu sanshou waku' or 'oushuu sanshouwaku') were used to find projects using these terms either in their title or as a relevant keyword of the research project. This produced a list of 136 projects, with the first project dating back to 2004: the initial project of the CEFR-J research group, headed by Koike (2008). When searches were performed using other related keywords (in both Japanese and English) such as the 'English Language Portfolio', 'ELP' or 'Portfolio', '"Can Do" list' or '"Can Do" statement', 'autonomous learning' and so on, more hits for related

---

[1] kaken.nii.ac.jp

The past, present and future of the CEFR in Japan

research projects were found. However, these same terms have a variety of meanings across a number of areas in language education, so searches of this nature may be misleading with regard to the CEFR's usage in Japan. They were therefore excluded from the analysis.

Figure 1 shows the number of funded CEFR-related research projects per year from 2004 until 2015. The 136 projects are either completed or ongoing. At the time of writing, there were 31 ongoing CEFR-related research projects. For a span of 10 years, 136 projects may not seem to be many. However, two things have to be taken into account: firstly, these are only the projects in foreign language teaching related to the CEFR, and secondly, these are the projects which successfully obtained grants. As a general tendency, only one third of all proposals submitted are granted funding. This implies that a larger number of researchers and teachers interested in the CEFR exist, but may not be reflected by the numbers presented here.

Figure 1 CEFR-related JSPS research projects granted per year from 2004 to 2015

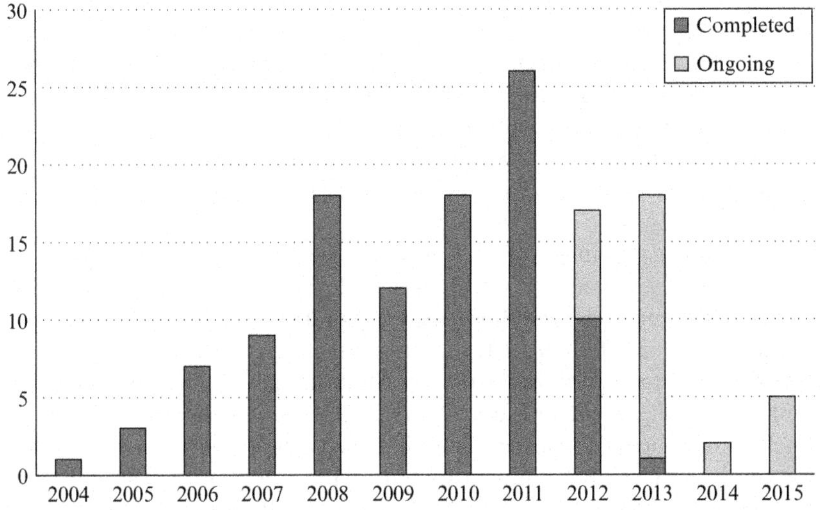

As can be seen in Figure 1, since the first project granted in 2004, there was a steady rise in projects until the year 2008. Between the years 2008 to 2013, there have been between 12 (in 2009) and 26 projects (in 2011). Thus far, these findings fit within the description of the CEFR's history in Table 1. Conversely, during the so-called 'growing' phase (Table 1), the number of projects granted for 2014 and 2015 show a sharp decline. It should be noted however, that many of the projects were conducted in co-operation between several universities: in total 156 universities, colleges, research institutes and high schools were involved. Taking the number of researchers into consideration, two thirds were conducted by research groups with two to 16 members. Only one third of the research projects involved researchers from a single university. Therefore, these simple figures strongly suggest that a large number of universities (both private and public) as well as nearly 600 researchers at university level are directly involved in studying a topic of foreign language education, linguistics, culture or social science related to the CEFR (although researchers involved in multiple projects cannot be accounted for).

Of the 136 projects that mention the CEFR, 58 of these projects explicitly referred to the CEFR in the title and/or listed it as a keyword. Conversely, 78 projects in the KAKEN database were less explicit in their relation to the CEFR: in these cases the CEFR was not referred to in the title, but rather in the description or reports associated with the project. These projects focus more specifically on certain facets of the CEFR, thus showing that the CEFR as a whole is not only being discussed, but various aspects of the CEFR are forming an essential part of the discussion on foreign language education in Japan. It is suspected that the decline in research projects in 2014 may be partly due to the increasing specificity of the research project topics. It is also possible that projects which were embarked on in these years were scheduled to last for several years, such as the one described in Chapter 9. It is thought that when their results become publicly available, this will spur a more significant increase in research related to the CEFR once again.

Regarding the foreign languages being taught, out of the 136 retrieved research projects, the majority of the projects (roughly 90) were related to ELT. Thirty were related to teaching JFL, and other projects focusing on various languages including French, German, Spanish, Russian, Italian, Chinese, Czech, or on multilingual/plurilingual aspects were also found. This suggests that those working in JFL and other foreign languages are aware of the CEFR and its potential applications: the CEFR's usage in Japan is not restricted to English language education. This finding is in alignment with one of the CEFR's tenets that its usage facilitates communication and collaboration between stakeholders of various foreign languages and is not restricted to those within the same foreign language.

Besides the JSPS Grant-in-Aid funding, many universities (public and private) also grant internal research projects for one or two years. Sometimes these projects work towards internal revision of curricula or developing novel teaching materials, but their results may not be publicly accessible or are perhaps only partially visible through specialised conferences, internet searches, or searches through university reports, for instance. Examples of such internal projects include those of Keio University (Horiguchi et al 2010), the Center for Education of Global Communication of the University of Tsukuba that promotes trilingual education and uses CEFR-based tests for the second foreign languages German and French (Hamana 2015), Kanazawa University (section 3.2 of this chapter) and Hiroshima Bunkyo Women's University (Chapter 9).

Although the total number of 136 research projects may seem to be low, it should be noted that as they strictly concern CEFR-related research in foreign language education and do not represent all research on the CEFR, this number should in fact be interpreted as substantial. It is therefore puzzling that this amount of CEFR-related research over the last 10 years has left few visible traces in language education curricula or textbooks in Japan (as discussed in sub-section 3.2 of this chapter). Some traces do exist for example, and include, in senior high school English education the approved textbook *Crown English Communication* (Shimozaki, Imoto, Iwasa, Kuroiwa, Kono, Tsutimoto, Matsubara, Mochizuki, Yui, Watanabe, Deaux, Slater and Kitagawa 2014), and recently, as a result of a KAKEN project, an English for Academic Purposes (EAP) textbook (see Chapter 5) for universities. It seems that there is nonetheless a wide gap between research and practice: on one hand, study and data collection about the usage of the CEFR is ongoing, but the implementation of the CEFR into practice appears to be lacking on the other. This is not a novel issue as Figueras (2007) also noted that in Europe, despite the effort invested into 'discussions, debates, seminars and congresses' on the framework, 'it is still not possible to say that these language policies have been effectively transferred to classrooms or to teaching materials' (Figueras 2007:478).

This returns to Parmenter and Byram's (2010) point that the influence of the CEFR has remained muted, and (as discussed in section 4 of this chapter) that it is up to stakeholders on the front line of language education, namely the teachers, to determine the course of the CEFR's future. Nonetheless, this is not to say that the CEFR has not exerted any change on the teaching, learning and assessment of foreign languages in Japan. The next sections explore its modest impact on tertiary level curricula and teachers.

3.2 The CEFR and university curricula

In order to investigate how the CEFR has been implemented into foreign language education at the tertiary level, general education foreign language programmes of national universities were examined. In this survey, only national universities were investigated because they are directly influenced by MEXT's policies and guidelines through their budgetary subsidiary[2]. Among the 86 national universities in Japan, 50 universities (at least one university

---

2 Japanese national universities are to design their curricula depending on their own diploma policies. However, their running costs are almost entirely subsidised by the Government and hence the MEXT's policies and guidelines for higher education severely affect curricula of national universities.

from each of the 47 prefectures) were selected for inclusion in the study to avoid any regional bias. National colleges or institutions whose education is focused on specific or professional studies, such as medical and engineering colleges, were excluded from the survey.

Data was collected online and any information on curricula and course syllabuses of general education foreign language programmes of the 50 universities were searched. When the online information was not enough to judge how and to what extent the CEFR was implemented, clarification from relevant local stakeholders was sought through email or interviews.

The following two points were investigated for each of the 50 national universities:

1. Whether their programme is proficiency based, and if so, how the students are streamed.
2. Whether their curricula exhibit some application of the CEFR.

If foreign language programmes were proficiency based, it was assumed that they must use some sort of measure to stream students into different levels and to assess their achievements against the target levels. It was thought that the CEFR might be used as a guiding tool to build coherent proficiency-based foreign language programmes, hence the inclusion of the first research question. It was found that 34 universities out of the 50 surveyed use proficiency-based language curricula. Although it was expected that the CEFR would be used, the CEFR was not mentioned as a streaming tool: 11 programmes used the Test of English for International Communication (TOEIC), while three programmes used the Test of English as a Foreign Language (TOEFL), Global Test of English Communication (GTEC) and General Test of English Language Proficiency (G-TELP). The remaining 20 universities did not mention how students are streamed.

The 50 universities' foreign language programme descriptions and course syllabuses were then examined for reference to the CEFR or 'Can Do' lists. Four universities referred to the CEFR and none referred to the CEFR-J. The universities whose language programmes referred to the CEFR included the German programme at the University of Tsukuba, the French programme at Yokohama National University, and the English programmes of Kanazawa University and Mie University (case studies of private and public universities which have adapted the CEFR are found in Chapters 7, 8 and 9).

The Center for Education of Global Communication at the University of Tsukuba indicates that some German classes are related to CEFR levels (Sugitani and Tomita 2012). For instance, 'Oyo kaiwa', or 'Applied Conversation A1', aims at CEFR Level A1/A2, and 'Applied conversation A2' at the CEFR's B1 level. One of the professors currently teaching in the programme states that some of the students are preparing for the CEFR Level

A1 and A2 test of the Goethe-Institut 'Start Deutsch A1/A2'[3]. However, the German programme as a whole was not designed with the CEFR as a foundation. The descriptions of aimed objectives of classes in the German programme varied significantly across instructors. According to one of the instructors of the programme, some instructors who are familiar with the CEFR may use the CEFR descriptors to set the goals of their classes, but others who are unfamiliar with it, naturally do not. In fact, this could also be the case for many of the sampled universities: while their online information pages do not refer explicitly to the CEFR, it remains a possibility that instructors within each of the programmes may in fact do so.

For the French programme at Yokohama National University, the curriculum map, which illustrates the learning outcomes of their General Education programme, suggests that some French language courses relate their objectives to the CEFR levels[4]. For instance, their Basic French course describes its objectives in terms of CEFR levels. 'Furansugo jisshu', or 'Practical French 1' and 'Practical French 2' target CEFR Levels A1 and A2, respectively. However, other French courses do not do so. Instead, the course descriptions simply state that the course is targeted at an intermediate or advanced level of conversation. It should be noted here that the CEFR is drawn from solely for the purpose of communicating the approximate difficulty level of the course, and that it is not referred to in any other capacity. All in all, the French programme as a whole is not based on the CEFR.

According to the English language syllabuses at Mie University, two courses of the General Education English programme refer to the CEFR[5], indicating that a prerequisite to register is that students should be above a B1 level. However, according to an interview with the co-ordinator of the programme, the remaining classes of the English programme neither refer to nor are based on the CEFR at all.

Among the 50 national universities surveyed in this study, Kanazawa University is the only university which applies the CEFR to an institution-wide English language programme. The English programme at Kanazawa University is entirely based on the CEFR (Sugitani and Tomita 2012). In January 2010, Oyabu and her colleagues (2012) conducted a survey to assess students' proficiency levels using 'Can Do' descriptors and on the basis of the results of the survey they determined the learning outcomes of each course in the English programme. They adapted the CEFR descriptors to fit their contexts and used them to evaluate students' proficiency levels in four language skill areas: communication (including spoken interaction and production), writing production, listening, and reading. Based on the results of the survey they set the target levels for three types of English courses: English I,

---

3 www.flang.tsukuba.ac.jp/page/page000032.html
4 www.ynu.ac.jp/education/plan/pdf/map_kyoyo_09.pdf
5 syllabus.mie-u.ac.jp/?action=display&id=16489

II and III. Their target levels roughly correspond with Levels B1, B2 and C1, respectively. In addition to the English I courses, Kanazawa University offers three other English courses which target students whose proficiency levels are below the designated targets of English I courses. The course is a preparatory course for English I which is aimed at A2 to B1 levels.

Overall, the survey of the CEFR's influence on national universities in Japan revealed much less influence on language programmes than expected. It is possible though that the CEFR may in fact be adapted on a smaller scale. For instance, Osaka University does not have a CEFR-based institution-wide foreign language programme. However, the School of Foreign Studies in the university adapts the CEFR for the curricula of the languages they offer[6]. It is also possible that some universities have adopted the CEFR, but do not use any of the relevant terms, such as the CEFR, 'Can Do' descriptors and 'Can Do' list, in their programme descriptions and online information, meaning that the CEFR usage in the initial net search would go undetected. The General Education English programme at Ibaraki University, for example, states the learning outcomes of their programmes using 'Can Do' descriptors based on the CEFR. However, the programme description does not refer to the terms such as the CEFR, 'Can Do' descriptors and 'Can Do' list at all, since it is in the midst of making a shift towards a TOEIC-based programme.

Kanazawa University appears to be one of only a few universities which seem to follow the philosophy of the CEFR and adopt the CEFR's descriptors within their language education programmes, although even then its usage is limited to the English language programmes. At Kanazawa University, descriptors are used to set transparent learning objectives in order to make all the English classroom instructions cohesive and coherent in working towards achieving the lesson's goals. However, Kanazawa University's well-designed CEFR-based curriculum had to be greatly reduced due to anxious and hasty demands from administration for more visible results like higher test scores on the TOEIC.

In fact, other national universities are facing similar situations; in the academic year commencing in 2016, national universities will start the third term of a 6-year plan whereby they have to present their new curriculum plans for the new term to MEXT. Because MEXT is demanding more visible goals for English education, the majority of universities state their learning outcome using TOEIC or TOEFL scores. This does not appear to contribute to a more cohesive, transparent, or communication-centred approach to language teaching and learning. Indeed, developing new and more profound ways of teaching foreign languages in Japan certainly presents a challenge, especially considering that key stakeholders, namely language teachers, have been found

---

6   The present School of Foreign Studies (SFS) at Osaka University was the former Osaka University of Foreign Studies (OUFS). Both were merged in 2007. The curriculum for foreign languages remained separated for each school.

to struggle when it comes to the CEFR. Some of their issues are discussed in the following section.

3.3 Japanese university language teachers' perceptions of the CEFR

The final study to explore the present situation of the CEFR in Japan was a questionnaire investigating the current perceptions of the CEFR held by tertiary level language teachers in Japanese universities. Any of their previous applications of the framework and any future plans for its usage were also investigated. This entailed examining teachers' familiarity with the CEFR, the areas of language education in which it has been used, its estimated impact, problems arising through its previous usages, and intended future usage. Particular focus was given to the issues that CEFR users have previously faced and the suggestions they made to resolve them.

The participants in this study were 36 English language teachers from tertiary institutions in Japan. Out of Japan's seven regions, responses from all except Hokkaido were obtained. In general, although 36 responses represent a very small sample size, it was considered sufficient for a general overview, especially since previous surveys of stakeholders' perceptions of the CEFR and its usage reported similar sample sizes (Council of Europe 2005, Martyniuk and Noijons 2007). The majority of participants were JALT FLP SIG members from both private (55.2%) and public (44.8%) institutions, all of which offered English as a Foreign Language (EFL) courses. Over 65% of the universities also offered foreign language courses in Chinese, Korean, French, German, Spanish, and Japanese. Russian and other languages were also available at some of the universities (Arabic, Portuguese, Italian, Okinawan, Indonesian, and Catalan).

The questions employed in the teacher survey were as follows:

1. To what extent are you familiar with the CEFR?
2. Among language education staff at your institution how widely known is the CEFR?
3. How much impact overall has the CEFR had on your language education at your institution?
4. At your institution, to what extent has the CEFR been used within a number of areas in language education?
5. What plans (if any) are there to make further use of the CEFR at your institution?
6. What struggles (if any) has your institution encountered with using the CEFR? What do you think are the reasons for these struggles?
7. What kind of 'CEFR support' tools do you think would be useful for you to have access to?

For questions 1 and 2, participants used a 5-point scale with the categories of none, a little, somewhat, considerably and strongly familiar to indicate their own and institutional staff's familiarity with the framework. For question 3 and 4, respondents used no, little, some, considerable and strong impact and usage respectively to indicate the impact and usage of the framework in various areas of language education at their institutions. Mean scores for the teachers' perceptions of their own familiarity with the framework, staff at their institution's awareness of the CEFR and overall impact are shown in Figure 2. Participants' mean ratings of their own familiarity with the CEFR were close to the 'considerably familiar' option on the response scale, while they estimated that the familiarity with the CEFR of staff at their institution was in between the 'a little' and 'somewhat familiar' options. Respondents rated the overall impact of the CEFR on language education at their institution as being between 'little' and 'some impact'. Respondents also indicated how much the CEFR had been used within a number of areas in language education at their institution, the mean ratings of which are shown in Figure 3.

Figure 2 Mean scores for respondents' familiarity with the CEFR, the familiarity with the CEFR among staff at respondents' institutions and perceived impact of the CEFR

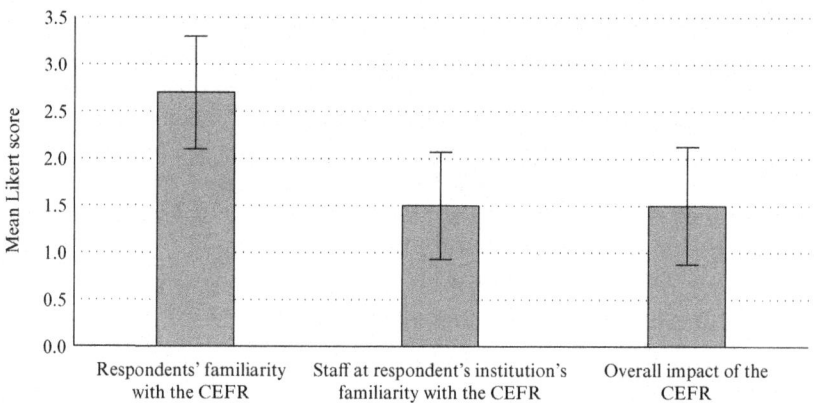

For half of the 14 surveyed areas of language education, a mean response closest to no usage whatsoever was selected (in Figure 3, this is shown as a mean closest to 1.0, or all areas below teaching methods). Minimal usage of the CEFR was found within the remaining seven areas (teaching methods and above in Figure 3), which means that none of the areas surveyed have experienced considerable application of the CEFR. However, for nearly each area of language education, it is evident that the standard deviation is often nearly the same size as the score itself, meaning that there was a substantial range in responses. Indeed, it should be noted that 74% of respondents only

Figure 3 Mean ratings for the usage of the CEFR in various areas of language education at the respondents' institutions*

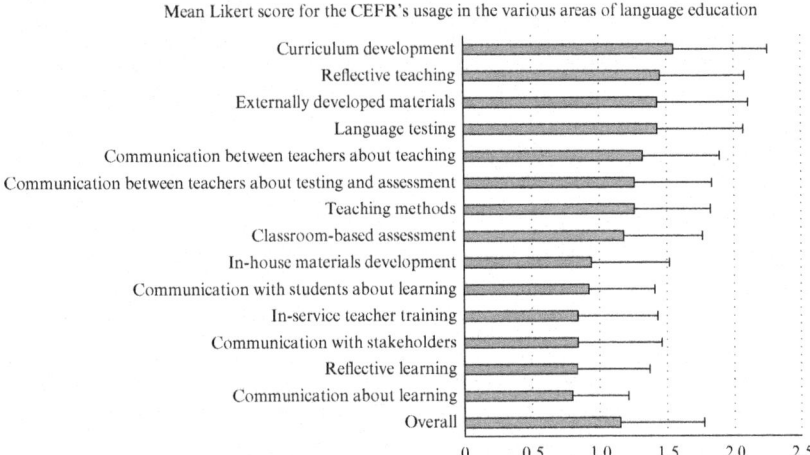

* The error bars show the standard deviation, which represents the variation in the data, or the spread of respondents' ratings

selected options on the low end of the scale, indicating very little usage of the CEFR at their institution. If the responses from that 74% are ignored, every area listed in Figure 3 (except for communication between teachers and students about testing) was rated as being significantly affected by the CEFR. This finding implies a dichotomy between institutions which appear to be either strong adopters of the CEFR or non-adopters (Rogers 2010).

When such a division is made, respondents at the 12 adopter institutions in the current survey indicated that the CEFR had been used in eight out of the 14 total areas of language education investigated, with a mean usage overall of 3.3 as opposed to a mean usage of 1.6 at the non-adopting institutions. The CEFR has been used most in curriculum development. Other areas of strong CEFR usage include reflective teaching, communication between teachers about teaching, the usage of externally developed materials, classroom-based assessment, and reflective learning.

Despite the dichotomy in the types of CEFR users (strong and non-adopters), respondents from both of these groups nonetheless pointed out challenges and struggles that they have faced in implementing the CEFR. The results derived from respondents' feedback on this question suggest the most substantial struggles in using the CEFR have stemmed from three areas: a) a lack of supporting resources; b) a lack of teacher training; and c) a lack of understanding of the framework among institutional staff.

A lack of understanding of the framework led to resistance to its implementation at an administrative and an individual teacher level. One respondent even accused their colleagues of complete disinterest, despite the availability of local 'experts' and resources and the departmental requirement that they work more closely with the framework. Conversely, successful curriculum reforms have occurred at institutions with a CEFR-advocating director or a small number of teaching staff who have avidly adopted the framework.

A general lack of understanding of the framework is also attributed to a high turnover of staff. The issue of staffing is reiterated in two comments related to the role of part-time staff in the usage of the CEFR, which leads into the second area where struggles have occurred: in teacher training. It was suggested that there was no support for the training of part-time teachers and that they were largely left out when it came to any relevant professional development. Indeed, even full-time staff struggled with learning sufficiently about the framework. Finally, in addition to the difficulty of informing, supporting or training teachers, respondents indicated that a lack of access to or existence of resources has prevented the CEFR's usage from progressing at their institutions.

To address these issues, participants provided a wishlist of resources, which reflected the challenges respondents have faced. In fact, many of the requested resources can be divided according to the same three categories of struggles: those that relate to increasing understanding of the framework, those that would address a lack of supplementary resources describing previous usages of the CEFR, and those that would support the training of teachers or other stakeholders on the CEFR's local usage and implementation. Regarding the suggested resources, respondents suggested that brochures, handouts and other training materials which summarise the framework and explain what it does would be beneficial. Practical guides on how to train teachers were also suggested: one respondent lamented that there is only theoretical literature available thus far, but that 'how to implement the CEFR' guides are required. Other suggestions for potentially useful supplementary resources included guides about CEFR-informed classroom instructions, case studies of previous usages and examples of CEFR-informed materials. A user-friendly website which could be accessed by both teachers and learners, and provided performance samples for each level and descriptor were also suggested. Other participants reiterated the request for illustrative examples of learner output and typical listening and reading texts at various levels, which could be used for goal setting, and be modified according to the local learning context. Three respondents wished for tests of various kinds: to certify CEFR level, to use as placement tests, and to compare to the results of other tests.

Responses about future uses of the CEFR related mostly to curriculum development (42% of the comments) and testing and assessment (25%). 'Can Do' descriptors were referred to three times (20%), and increasing training related to the CEFR was mentioned once. Altogether, these findings are akin to those of Martyniuk and Noijons who noted that their respondents stressed:

> ... the need for general clarification (such as comments on theoretical concepts, examples and good illustrations, sets of tasks for use in specific contexts, a bilingual terminology glossary for each country), as well as the need to familiarise more teachers with the document by organising national and international events, exchanging good practice, etc. [Respondents also exhibit] a strong need for the creation of materials in many areas where the CEFR has been found to be useful [and] a guide on how to develop a CEFR-based curriculum or a training kit for the development of CEFR-based tests. In addition, CEFR-based tests and benchmarks to illustrate what performances at CEFR-levels entail should be produced. Similarly, banks of test items for language skills at specific levels are required (Martyniuk and Noijons 2007:6–8).

This quotation is of great interest because it shows that the needs of stakeholders in language education around the globe are similar, whether they work in Egypt, the Council of Europe's member states, Mexico or Japan. In fact, it appears that the needs of teachers in various contexts within Japan are also similar: the respondents of this survey came from both private and public universities, all over the nation and varied in their institution's foreign language offerings.

Overall, as in the previous two studies of this section, the CEFR's influence on language education appears to be consistently unremarkable. The CEFR does not yet play an important role in many areas of language education, with the exception of a limited number of strong adopters of the framework who use it widely. However, even teachers from non-adopting institutions did state that they would make use of the CEFR in the future, and suggested a number of resources they believed would be beneficial. These suggestions make serious implications on the future of the CEFR at Japanese universities and provide evidence for the potential and importance of collaboration between stakeholders in language education.

4 The future of the CEFR in Japan

Given the understanding of the current situation of the CEFR in language education in Japan, there are two main areas of development which seem likely in the future. The first is an increase in local implementation projects of the CEFR at various institutions, which would build on the foundations set in Phase 2 and 3 of the CEFR's history (Table 1). It is expected that the growth in Phase 4 will largely consist of publicly available examples of case studies, such as those in this volume, and eventually lead to changes in the classroom practices of tertiary level language teachers especially. This section discusses the reasons for why an increase in interest in the CEFR is expected. It proposes an evidence-based model for top-down CEFR implementation derived from the findings of the three studies. The suggested CEFR-implementation resources are used to contextualise this model so that it can also be applied from the bottom-up. The second area of development is likely to be situated in secondary and primary institutions, where curriculum decisions are not left to individual institutions, but must reflect MEXT policies. It is also thought that the CEFR-J will play a substantial role in mediating these policies in the future due to its applicability beyond tertiary level language education contexts. Indeed, the CEFR-J is perhaps the resource with the greatest potential to impact language education in Japan, and it is also discussed in the following section and in section 4.4.

4.1 Diffusion and adoption of the CEFR in Japan

In all three studies described in section 3, at a national, institutional and individual context, the CEFR was found to have a very modest impact on foreign language education in Japan, a result different from that of the studies from the Council of Europe (2005) and Martyniuk and Noijons (2007). In Martyniuk and Noijons' (2007) survey on the impact of the CEFR on language education at a national level in the Council of Europe's member states, the CEFR was found to have impacted a number of official documents at national policy levels. The general conclusion was that 'the CEFR seems to have a major impact on language education. It is used often as the exclusive neutral reference – in all educational sectors. Its value as a reference tool to co-ordinate the objectives of education at all levels is widely appreciated' (Martyniuk and Noijons 2007:7).

When the Council of Europe (2005) survey enquired about the familiarity, usage and usefulness of the CEFR in an institutional level in Europe, Egypt and Mexico, they found that the CEFR was widely known, used mostly by teachers, teacher trainers, test and material writers, for teacher training, language testing, curriculum development, materials development, and communication with stakeholders (Council of Europe 2005:3). Valax (2011) also conducted a survey on the impact of the CEFR in France, the UK, Taiwan, Hong Kong, New Zealand and Australia. His findings were markedly different from those from Europe but similar to those of the present three studies. A third of participants indicated that they had never heard of the framework and over two thirds could not rate the framework's impact and usefulness in a variety of areas, due to lack of knowledge. Valax concluded that for respondents outside of the Council of Europe's member states 'there is little interest in, or enthusiasm for the CEFR among those frontline professionals who will ultimately determine whether it has any real impact on the teaching and learning of languages' (Valax 2011:i–ii).

The Council of Europe (2005) and Martyniuk and Noijons (2007) studies both occurred within seven years after the CEFR's publication, but the CEFR had still not strongly impacted language education outside of Europe three years after that (Valax 2011). Indeed, time is likely a major explanatory factor for the results of the three studies reported herein, as the CEFR is comparatively a relatively newly discovered innovation for language teachers in Japan. For Japan, the CEFR is suggested to be in a growth phase (Table 1) where it has been referred to and used in a number of contexts around the country, and has been researched for further use but has not yet had any significant influence on teaching materials or teaching practices in classrooms, even though it has been fully adopted at the national level for TV and radio educational programming, and referred to in MEXT policies (see section 4.4). Scholarly interest in the CEFR appears to have peaked in 2011 (Figure 1), with the CEFR-J being published in 2012, which means that very little time has passed since. If the phases suggested in Table 1 follow through, then it will likely be at least another few years until Phase 5 is reached, where the CEFR becomes well established in the practices of language education stakeholders at either the national, institutional or individual level, as it seems to have done in many locations in Europe.

In fact, Rogers (2010) has found that time is one of the major elements related to the adoption and spread of innovations (the others being the innovation itself, the communication channels through which information about the innovation is spread, and the social system). His theory of diffusion of innovations explains why, how and at what rate innovations spread throughout social systems consisting of various types of adopters. If Europe is considered to be the first group (on a global scale) to adopt the innovation of the CEFR, according to Rogers (2010) they would be classified as Early Adopters (and represent 13.5% of a population). The next group is known as Early Majority Adopters (and consists of 34% of a population). Assuming that adoption of the CEFR will increase globally over time, the results presented here suggest that Japan as a whole may fall within the world's Early Majority Adopters of the CEFR.

Within Japan however, the situation is vastly different, as it cannot be argued that adoption of the CEFR has reached an early majority. In fact, the results of all three studies suggest that those using the CEFR at the moment are likely classifiable as innovators (the 2.5% of the population who are first to adopt the innovation). At the adopter institutions, the CEFR's impact was strong, but also perhaps, only partial (restricted to certain areas of language education), and among a select or small number of staff. This was also suggested by the findings of the survey of national curricula and also through the review of previous usage of the CEFR (section 2.1). In general, feedback from previous literature on the CEFR (section 2) as well as the three studies reported in this chapter, indicates that innovators have found implementing the CEFR complex, time consuming and difficult. To address this, the following section presents the development of a model to be applied in local CEFR implementation projects, both from the top-down and the bottom-up.

4.2 From the top-down: A CEFR implementation model

In the teacher survey, respondents identified three areas of challenges to their efforts to use the CEFR: a lack of understanding of the framework by relevant stakeholders, a lack of supporting resources, and a lack of training for relevant stakeholders (such as teachers) about the intended CEFR implementation project within their institutions. These three areas appear to be related to each other in a type of vicious circle where an issue with one leads to an even greater lack in another, hindering progress on any implementing of CEFR-informed practices. For instance, a lack of supporting or supplementary resources for users may result in a lack of understanding of the framework, meaning that effective training on the local implementation project may not occur, or it may only occur at a tokenistic or surface level. Alternatively, a lack of understanding of the framework in the first place leads to disinterest in learning more, which precedes a general lack of published supporting resources. A lack of resources may then lead to a lack of training, resulting in a lack of understanding. The result is unsuccessful completion or even incompletion of the CEFR implementation project (sub-chapter 9A of this volume provides an example of unsuccessful implementation of the CEFR). Nearly any order of these three areas seems possible, thus suggesting that addressing all three may be imperative in successful implementation of the CEFR at an institutional level. To summarise, feedback from the study's participants suggests that understanding of the framework among all stakeholders, accessibility of supporting resources, and adequate training for those directly involved in the implementation project are the three areas which need to be addressed in order to ensure successful local implementation of the CEFR. Figure 4 shows these relationships incorporated into the CEFR implementation model proposed by the authors for application in any context with a variety of stakeholders involved in using the CEFR.

Figure 4 The CEFR implementation model: Facets requiring management for successful implementation of the CEFR

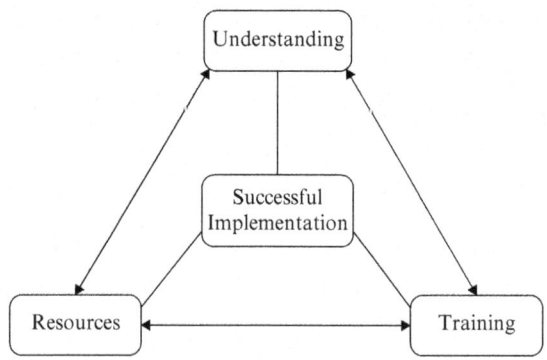

The past, present and future of the CEFR in Japan

Understanding refers to the process of ensuring a common understanding of the framework among stakeholders. *Resources* consist of examples of successful CEFR implementation or previously determined practical usages of the framework that can be drawn from to aid understanding, or planning of the current implementation project. *Training* involves ensuring that stakeholders have a mutual understanding of the intended implementation project, and feel that they are sufficiently knowledgeable to carry it out. Materials relevant to the first two modules are likely context independent, and can be applied anywhere. Conversely, those within the *Training* module are relevant to and dependent on the demands of the local CEFR implementation context. In ensuring that an amalgam of both top-down and bottom-up implementation is achieved, it is hoped that this model will aid leaders in the top-down management of CEFR implementation projects. Conversely, the following section discusses the needs from those on the ground: the teachers.

4.3 From the bottom-up: Teachers' needs

In addition to the model presented in section 4.2, a major implication of the teachers' comments from the third study is the clear need for a publicly accessible resource bank of materials that can be drawn from for any CEFR implementation project. Teachers suggested specific materials which they believed would be valuable and useful, and could contribute to overcoming the hurdles they had previously faced in their CEFR usage. These materials were then classified within each of the three areas of the CEFR implementation model from Figure 4, producing a hypothetical toolkit which contextualises each of the three facets requiring management for successful implementation of the CEFR. Figure 5 illustrates this proposed CEFR implementation toolkit for application in any context with a variety of stakeholders involved in using the CEFR.

Looking at Figure 5, the sparsity of the training module may be noted: this is because the materials used within this stage of the CEFR implementation project will likely differ according to the needs of each local context. For instance, goals and plans for courses throughout four years of university study have been included in the training module, rather than in resources as it is unlikely that all institutions would be able to use the same plans: goals and plans for each year would depend entirely on the learners at that institution and therefore require local contextualisation (Chapters 9, 11, 12 and 13 of this volume describe the processes and the types of materials that were used within local implementations, tailored to suit each individual context).

Given the respondents' intended future usages of the CEFR reported in section 3.3, a CEFR implementation toolkit as a general resource would certainly be useful for many tertiary institutions of Japan. The toolkit would complement resources currently available, for example the European Centre for Modern Languages' 'Training teachers to use the European Language

Figure 5 The CEFR implementation toolkit: A teacher-derived wishlist of resources to support implementing the CEFR

Understanding
- User-friendly brochures
- A 'CEFR for Dummies' handout
- CEFR-J handbook translated into English

Resources
- Classroom instruction
- Case studies
- CEFR-informed materials
- Illustrative examples of Japanese learner output (speaking and writing)
- Examples of typical listening and reading texts at each CEFR level
- CEFR level placement tests or tests to certify CEFR level
- A CEFR website in Japanese and English for both teachers and students
- Dossier
- A list of other institutions in Japan employing it
- Previous examples of teacher training

Training
- Concrete, achievable goals and plans from 1 to 4 years

Portfolio project'[7], North's (2014) book *The CEFR in Practice*, the Oxford Online Placement Test (Pollit 2009, Purpura 2010), the Cambridge English series of exams (2015) or the free tool DIALANG (Alderson and Huhta 2005, DIALANG 2015). In any case, this CEFR implementation toolkit currently does not exist, and producing it would require significant work and collaboration between stakeholders.

4.4 The CEFR-J

The model presented in Figure 4 is most likely best applied to tertiary contexts and it is expected that substantial CEFR growth will occur in universities. Going beyond a tertiary context however, it is the CEFR-J that is also very likely to have a future impact on language education in Japan, in both secondary and primary institutions. Indeed, the CEFR-J might be best received by teachers in primary education, where English language activities were obligatorily included in the curriculum in 2011, and in 2018, will become a compulsory subject for all schools (Ministry of Education, Culture, Sports, Science and Technology 2011). Teachers in primary

---
7   elp-tt2.ecml.at/ELPTT3/tabid/2330/language/en-GB/Default.aspx

schools, who are not professionals in teaching English, are unlikely to possess knowledge about how English should be taught and may feel that they do not have sufficient English knowledge themselves to teach it. Yet, they have to design classes which develop students' attitudes and desires to use English in the future. The sub-divisions of the CEFR-J were developed with these kinds of issues in mind, and are well designed to help teachers choose suitable activities. Furthermore, the sub-divisions help novice learners, who command limited communicative competence or do not yet even know the alphabet, become aware of their own step-by-step progress and develop self-efficacy.

For secondary schools, MEXT (2011) proposed that each school in secondary education should create transparent learning outcomes of English education, with junior and senior high schools establishing learning attainment targets in the form of 'Can Do' lists. As noted in Chapter 3, this is challenging for teachers who may not be familiar with 'Can Do' lists or the CEFR, and training initiatives are therefore required. MEXT has stated that teachers are free to develop their own descriptors, without any stipulation for how to do so. In other words, what constitutes useable, transparent and coherent 'Can Do' descriptors is not specified. Many CEFR adopters (including the editors and authors of this volume) feel that leaving teachers to develop their own descriptors without an overarching framework is a mistake and believe that CEFR-J or CEFR descriptors are sufficiently well developed to fulfil MEXT's demands. Teachers are of course due a certain amount of autonomy in contextualising their own 'Can Do' descriptors and lists, but there appears to be little detriment in having outcomes linked to the internationally recognised benchmarks inherent in the CEFR and CEFR-J.

While it seems certain that setting concrete attainable goals will be an initial step towards reforms in English education in Japan, to further facilitate reforms of English education in Japan and to gain desired results, the philosophy of the CEFR should also be well understood. 'Can Do' descriptors and lists do not simply represent achievement goals, but also act as guiding tools for designing curricula and courses, planning daily classroom instructions, and determining tasks and activities to be performed in classrooms. Unless teachers understand why 'Can Do' descriptors as they are in the CEFR are developed and how they can be used, the real reform of English education will not be achieved. Once again, the need for sufficient training is iterated.

In terms of the CEFR-J's use in higher education however, simply increasing the training of teachers to better understand the CEFR-J and the rationale behind the usage of 'Can Do' descriptors may nonetheless not lead to reaching MEXT's goals. In the CEFR-J, there are five sub-levels within A1 and A2 alone, and it is difficult for both learners and instructors to distinguish proficiency between these sub-levels. In fact, Runnels (2013) examined if university students could identify the difficulty of each of the A1.1, A1.2, A1.3, A2.1 and A2.2 descriptors. While a distinction between the CEFR's original A1 and A2 levels was found, there were statistically significant differences in ratings among the adjacent levels in the sub-divisions of A1 and A2 of the CEFR-J. The 'Can Do' lists of the CEFR-J may not be useful for the assessment of learners at the tertiary level, and this may be the basis for future versions of the framework.

How the CEFR-J is hoped to contribute to reforms in English education remains to be seen. The real renovation nonetheless may only be done when all stakeholders who are involved in language education (including policymakers, administrators, teachers and so forth) realise the profound philosophy behind the content of 'Can Do' descriptors and their usage. Once again, for this to occur, there is an urgent need to demonstrate how to use the CEFR and CEFR-J as a guiding tool or as a basis for reflective practice in considering what language learners need to learn and how. As discussed throughout section 4, this also requires exemplars and resources. On this issue, Tono (2015) noted there is hope in the form of CEFR-J corpus-based reference level descriptors, alignment of lessons in secondary school English textbooks to CEFR-J descriptors, annotations of the NHK English database using the CEFR functional categories and CEFR-J descriptors, and the use of CEFR-J in language education at the Tokyo University of Foreign Studies, among other institutions.

5 Conclusions

In this chapter, the history of the CEFR in Japan was classified into four phases, with a newly emerging fifth phase commencing around the time of writing of this volume. Reviews of previous work on the CEFR's usage in Japan suggested a continually increasing awareness of and familiarity with the framework across a variety of educational contexts in Japan. To interpret the present situation of the CEFR in Japan, three studies were conducted. They revealed a moderate amount of research on the CEFR over the past 15 years. They also demonstrated that the CEFR has had a modest impact on the curricula of foreign language education at national universities, and that there is a range of CEFR adoption among teachers and institutions around the country. This feedback led to the development of a descriptive model of the various factors which appear to require management in applying the CEFR to local language education contexts (the CEFR implementation model) in future applications of the framework. The need for a resource bank of materials for Japanese university language teachers to draw from when engaging in their own implementations of the CEFR, whether on an individual or an institutional level (the CEFR implementation toolkit), was also highlighted as a requirement if development of the CEFR is to continue in Japanese language education. Finally, the potential of the CEFR-J in primary, secondary and tertiary contexts was discussed. While the contents of this volume present case studies of innovative individuals or institutions that have successfully implemented their own CEFR-informed projects, it is clear that they are simply setting the foundation for what is to come, as awareness and usage of the CEFR continues to increase to the point where it makes a substantial impact on the practices of language education professionals in Japan. Ultimately, there is little doubt that 'the adaptation of the CEFR will be a major step ahead toward more drastic reforms in English education [in Japan]' (Tono and Negishi 2012:6).

References

Alderson, J C and Huhta, A (2005) The development of a suite of computer-based diagnostic tests based on the Common European Framework, *Language Testing* 22, 301–320.

Cambridge English (2015) *Cambridge English exams*, available online: www.cambridgeenglish.org/exams/

Collett, P and Sullivan, K (2010) Considering the use of Can Do statements to develop learners' self-regulative and metacognitive strategies, in Schmidt, M G, Naganuma, N, O'Dwyer, F, Imig, A and Sakai, K (Eds) *Can Do Statements in Language Education in Japan and Beyond – Applications of the CEFR* (2nd edition), Tokyo: Asahi Press, 167–183.

Council of Europe (2001) *Common European Framework of Reference for Languages: Learning, Teaching, Assessment*, Cambridge: Cambridge University Press.

Council of Europe (2005) *Survey on the use of the Common European Framework of Reference for Languages (CEFR): Synthesis of Results*, Strasbourg: Council of Europe, available online: www.coe.int/t/dg4/linguistic/Source/Surveyresults.pdf

DIALANG (2015) *Information about DIALANG*, available online: www.lancaster.ac.uk/researchenterprise/dialang/about

Figueras, N (2007) The impact of the CEFR, *English Language Teaching Journal* 66 (4), 477–485.

Hamana, E (2015) Project report: Grant project for undergraduate education enhancement (Academic year 2014), *Studies in Foreign language education (Foreign Language Center, Tsukuba University)* 37, 127–129.

Horiguchi, S, Harada, Y, Imoto, Y and Atobe, S (2010) The implementation of a Japanese version of the 'European Language Portfolio – Junior version' in Keio: Implications from the perspective of organizational anthropology, in Schmidt, M G, Naganuma, N, O'Dwyer, F, Imig, A and Sakai, K (Eds) *Can Do Statements in Language Education in Japan and Beyond – Applications of the CEFR* (2nd edition), Tokyo: Asahi Press, 138–154.

Japan Association for Language Teaching Framework and Language Portfolio Special Interest Group (2015) *Home of FLP SIG*, available online: sites.google.com/site/flpsig/home

Japan Broadcasting Corporation (2012) *The new standard CEFR for introducing the NHK English course for the 2012 fiscal year?*, available online: b.hatena. ne.jp/entry/eigoryoku.nhk-book.co.jp/cefr.html

Japan Foundation (2015) *JF Standard for Japanese Language Education*, available online: jfstandard.jp/summary/ja/render.do

Koike, I (2008) *Pioneering basic research using second language acquisition research to ensure coherent, linked English education from elementary school through junior high school to university*, Grants-in-Aid for Scientific Research 2004–2007: Scientific Research A, Report on research results.

Krause-Ono, M (2010) Using German Can Do statements as model for other languages like Russian and Chinese: A special project, in Schmidt, M G, Naganuma, N, O'Dwyer, F, Imig, A and Sakai, K (Eds) *Can Do Statements in Language Education in Japan and Beyond – Applications of the CEFR*, Tokyo: Asahi Press, 111–125.

Majima, J (2007) *Osaka University of Foreign Studies Committee for Educational Improvement Report on Japan–Europe International Symposium 2006: A New Direction in Foreign Language Education: The Potential of The Common European Framework of Reference for Languages*, Osaka: Osaka University.

Majima, J (2010) Impact of Can Do statements/CEFR on language education in Japan: On its applicability, in Schmidt, M G, Naganuma, N, O'Dwyer, F, Imig, A and Sakai, K (Eds) *Can Do Statements in Language Education in Japan and Beyond – Applications of the CEFR* (2nd edition), Tokyo: Asahi Press, 49–65.

Majima, J (2015) *Homepage of Junko Majima on CEFR*, available online: majimajunko.sakura.ne.jp/bukosite/cefr/pg35.html

Martyniuk, W and Noijons, J (2007) *Executive Summary of Results of a Survey on the Use of the CEFR at National Level in the Council of Europe Member States*, Strasbourg: Council of Europe.

Ministry of Education, Culture, Sports, Science and Technology (2011) *Kokusai kyotsugo to shite no eigoryoku kojo no tame no itsutsu no teigen* [*Five Proposals and Specific Measures for Developing Proficiency in English for International Communication*], available online: www.mext.go.jp/component/b_menu/shingi/toushin/__icsFiles/afieldfile/2011/07/13/1308401_1.pdf

Nagai, N (2010) Designing English curricula and courses in Japanese higher education, in Schmidt, M G, Naganuma, N, O'Dwyer, F, Imig, A and Sakai, K (Eds) *Can Do Statements in Language Education in Japan and Beyond – Applications of the CEFR* (2nd edition), Tokyo: Asahi Press, 86–104.

Nagai, N, and O'Dwyer, F (2012) The actual and potential impacts of the CEFR on language education in Japan, *Synergies Europe* 6, 141–152.

Negishi, M (2006) How much do we have in common with the Common European Framework of Reference? The applicability of the CEFR to an IRT-based English proficiency test in Japan, in Yoshitomi, A, Umino, T and Negishi, M (Eds) *Readings in Second Language Pedagogy and Second Language Acquisition: In Japanese Context*, Philadelphia: John Benjamins Publishing Company, 83–100.

North, B (2006) *The Common European Framework of Reference: Development, theoretical and practical issues*, paper presented at the symposium 'A New Direction in Foreign Language Education: The Potential of the Common European Framework of Reference for Languages', Osaka University of Foreign Studies, Osaka, Japan, March 2006.

North, B (2014) *The CEFR in Practice*, English Profile Studies volume 4, Cambridge: UCLES/Cambridge University Press.

Oyabu, K (2012) Student survey on English language competence based on CEFR Can-Do descriptors, *Forum of Language Instructors (Kanazawa University)* 6, 63–77.

Parmenter, L and Byram, M (2010) An overview of the international influences of the CEFR, in Schmidt, M G, Naganuma, N, O'Dwyer, F, Imig, A and Sakai, K (Eds) *Can Do Statements in Language Education in Japan and Beyond – Applications of the CEFR* (2nd edition), Tokyo: Asahi Press, 9–17.

Pollit, A (2009) *The Oxford Online Placement Test: The meaning of OOPT scores*, available online: www.oxfordenglishtesting.com/uploadedFiles/Buy_tests/oopt_meaning.pdf

Purpura, J E (2010) *The Oxford Online Placement Test: What does it measure and how?*, available online: www.oxfordenglishtesting.com/defaultmr.aspx?id=3048

Rogers, E M (2010) *Diffusion of Innovations*, New York: Simon and Schuster.

Runnels, J (2013) Preliminary validation of the A1 and A2 sub-levels of the CEFR-J, *Shiken Research Bulletin* 17 (1), 3–10, available online: teval.jalt.org/sites/teval.jalt.org/files/SRB-17-1-Runnels_0.pdf

Sakai, S (2014) Towards implementing the principles of the Common European Framework of Reference for Languages within the Japanese educational system, in Merkelbach, C (Ed) *The CEFR in an East Asian Context*, Taipei: National University Press, 71–99.

Sato, Y (2010) Using Can Do statements to promote reflective learning, in Schmidt, M G, Naganuma, N, O'Dwyer, F, Imig, A and Sakai, K (Eds) *Can Do Statements in Language Education in Japan and Beyond – Applications of the CEFR* (2nd edition), Tokyo: Asahi Press, 184–199.

Schmidt, M G, Naganuma, N, O'Dwyer, F, Imig, A and Sakai, K (Eds) (2010) *Can Do Statements in Language Education in Japan and Beyond – Applications of the CEFR* (2nd edition), Tokyo: Asahi Press.

Shimozaki, M, Imoto, Y, Iwasa, Y, Kuroiwa, Y, Kono, T, Tsutimoto, C, Matsubara, K, Mochizuki, N, Yui, R, Watanabe, Y, Deaux, G, Slater, A and Kitagawa, T (2014) *Crown English Communication*, Tokyo: Sanseido.

Sugitani, M and Tomita, Y (2012) Perspectives from Japan, in Byram, M and Parmenter, L (Eds) *The Common European Framework of Reference: The Globalisation of Language Education Policy*, Bristol: Multilingual Matters, 198–211.

Test of English for Academic Purposes (2015) *Test of English for Academic Purposes*, available online: www.eiken.or.jp/teap/

Tono, Y (2013) *CAN-DO list sakusei katsuyou: Eigo toutatsu shihyou CEFR-J guidebook [CEFR-J Guidebook: Resources for Establishing and Utilizing 'Can-Do' Lists for English Language Teaching]*, Tokyo: Taishukan.

Tono, Y (2015) *From CAN-DO to classroom: How to pedagogically contextualize the CEFR-J*, plenary presented at second conference on 'Critical, constructive assessment of CEFR-based language teaching in Japan and beyond', Tokai University, Tokyo, 6 June 2015.

Tono, Y and Negishi, M (2012) The CEFR-J: Adapting the CEFR for English language teaching in Japan, *Framework & Language Portfolio (FLP) SIG Newsletter* 8, 5–12, available online: dl.dropboxusercontent.com/u/33808898/FLP%20SIG%20NL%208%20Sep2012%20CEFR-J.pdf

Valax, P (2011) *The Common European Framework of Reference for Languages: A critical analysis of its impact on a sample of teachers and curricula within and beyond Europe*, unpublished PhD thesis, University of Waikato, available online: researchcommons.waikato.ac.nz/handle/10289/5546

Yoshijima, S and Ohashi, R (2004) *Gaikokugokyouiku (2): gaikokugo no gakushuu, kyouju, hyouka no tame no yooroppa kyoutsuu sansyou waku*, Tokyo: Asahi Syuppansha.

3 The perception of the CEFR in secondary-level English language teaching in Japan

Tomoko Takada
Meikai University

1 Introduction

The Common European Framework of Reference for Languages (CEFR, Council of Europe 2001) has been contextualised in Japan's educational policies in a unique way. The present paper describes how it has become visible in the secondary-level English language education policy in Japan since the Ministry of Education, Culture, Sports, Science and Technology (MEXT) first mentioned 'Can Do' lists in *Five Proposals and Specific Measures for Developing Proficiency in English for International Communication* released in 2011. First, it examines three documents issued by MEXT to explore how the CEFR, not as a whole but with modification, has fit into the existing educational system in Japan. It then reports how the 'Can Do' initiatives proposed by MEXT have been accepted by secondary school English teachers, based on two studies conducted by Eiken Foundation of Japan (2013) and Wada (2015). It is followed by an example of the implementation of a 'Can Do' list, a small-scale pilot study conducted at a prefectural high school that was designated as a hub school of the MEXT's 'Can Do' initiatives. The paper concludes with some reflections, and future challenges to be addressed.

2 Background to MEXT's suggestion for establishing 'Can Do' lists

2.1 Reference to the CEFR in the MEXT Five Proposals

The first official document that reflects some influence of the CEFR is the *Five Proposals and Specific Measures for Developing Proficiency in English for International Communication* (the 'Five Proposals' for short) (Ministry of Education, Culture, Sports, Science and Technology 2011a), which was compiled by the Commission on the Development of Foreign Language Proficiency, a panel commissioned by MEXT. It aims at improvement of the command of English of secondary school students so that they can function effectively in the international community. Proposal 1 recommends that each junior and senior high school establish and publicise learning attainment targets in the form of 'Can Do' lists, monitor attainment, and make results public. Considering that 'Can Do' lists are an essential part of the CEFR, if not equivalent to the CEFR, we could safely say that the Five Proposals is the first document in which Japan's English language teaching (ELT) policy referred to the concept of the CEFR. The rest of the proposals, Proposal 2 through to Proposal 5, refer to the following: 2) stimulating students' motivation for English learning, 3) effective utilisation of assistant language teachers, information-communication technology, and other means, 4) reinforcement of English skills and instruction abilities of English teachers, and 5) modification of university entrance examinations towards global society (Ministry of Education, Culture, Sports, Science and Technology 2011a).

The Five Proposals, as its introduction states, stemmed from the perception that the current ELT practice in Japan is inadequate when improvement of English ability is important as globalisation advances at a rapid pace (Ministry of Education, Culture, Sports, Science and Technology 2011a). According to the Commentary on The Course of Study for Lower Secondary Schools (Ministry of Education, Culture, Sports, Science and Technology 2008) and the Commentary on The Course of Study for Upper Secondary Schools (Ministry of Education, Culture, Sports, Science and Technology 2009), which are national standards for each school to design curricula, the overall objective of foreign language teaching is to develop students' communicative abilities. However, Proposal 1 describes that, whereas many schools conduct classes in compliance with the Courses of Study (Ministry of Education, Culture, Sports, Science and Technology 2008, 2009), some schools are reported to focus on grammar-translation learning or on preparation for high school or university entrance examinations.

The reality that Japan's ELT at the secondary level has fallen short of expectations has been a persistent problem, although MEXT has reiterated the objective of ELT in many ways. For instance, the Courses of Study require that teachers give sufficient consideration to actual language-use situations and functions of language in order to comprehensively cultivate communication abilities. To support this principle, the Courses of Study give examples of language-use situations and functions of language such as explaining, reporting, offering, requesting, and inviting. They also require that teachers provide students with more opportunities to use English for communication. The MEXT's assumption that language is acquired through language use activities is consistent with the CEFR's approach that language learners and users act in social contexts.

Another impetus to the inclusion of 'Can Do' lists in the Five Proposals may have been the publication of the CEFR-J, a modified version of the CEFR geared to Japanese learners of English. It is a 'Can Do' list with a total of 120 descriptors for five skills and 12 proficiency levels from Pre A1 to C2 (Negishi, Takada and Tono 2013, Tono 2013). The CEFR-J was developed to respond to the need for a common language framework mainly for school use. Koike (2008), the mastermind of the CEFR-J, claims that a comprehensive system that integrates primary, secondary, and tertiary levels of Japan's ELT is needed to reform the traditional teaching practice, which fails to prepare learners to meet the demands of the globalised community. He notes that Asian countries like China, Korea, and Taiwan, which have reformed their ELT systems, have surpassed Japan in developing learners' English proficiency. Thus, the 'Can Do' initiatives that followed the release of the Five Proposals in 2011 were launched in a situation where policy-makers, researchers, teachers, and other stakeholders were looking for a solution to a long-overdue problem with ELT in Japan.

2.2 Reference to the CEFR in two of MEXT's documents following the Five Proposals

After the Five Proposals (Ministry of Education, Culture, Sports, Science and Technology 2011a) requested that each junior and senior high school establish and publicise learning attainment targets in the form of 'Can Do' lists, monitor attainment, and make the results public, MEXT published the *Handbook for Setting Learning Attainment Targets in Foreign Languages in Each Junior and Senior High School in the Form of 'Can Do' Lists* (2013b, the 'Handbook' for short). Eight months after its publication, the *Action Plans to Reform ELT to Meet the Needs of the Globalised Community* was released (Ministry of Education, Culture, Sports, Science and Technology 2013a, the 'Action Plans' for short). Both of these documents directly refer to the CEFR. The Handbook cites the global scale and the self-assessment grid of the CEFR in the appendix, whereas the Action Plan explicitly shows CEFR proficiency levels as attainment targets for English abilities required of students.

The reference to the CEFR is rather limited in the Action Plans. It uses the CEFR's six-level scale of language proficiency as a tool for summative assessment with corresponding TOEFL iBT scores and Eiken grades. According to the Action Plans, in a new ELT system that will be fully inaugurated in 2020 under the upcoming revised Courses of Study, students, upon graduation from senior high school, should reach from B1 to B2 level. Upon graduation from junior high school, they should reach from A1 to A2 level. These attainment targets are higher than those under the current system, in which senior high school students are to reach A2 to B1 at the point of graduation, whereas junior high school students are expected to reach A1. The upgrade of the targets is made possible, theoretically, by enhancing the foreign language education offered at primary schools.

In contrast, the Handbook, a 46-page document mainly addressed to secondary school teachers, principals, and prefectural supervisors, has more emphasis on pedagogical aspects of the CEFR. It was published in concert with one of the specific measures to implement Proposal 1, which reads as follows (Ministry of Education, Culture, Sports, Science and Technology 2011a:5):

> Junior and senior high schools shall establish and publicise learning attainment targets in the form of 'Can Do' lists, and *monitor* attainment. The Government and education boards shall provide schools with reference information and other support as necessary for establishment and *utilisation* of learning attainment targets (Italics added).

The Handbook further states that establishing a 'Can Do' list, which is a list of behavioural objectives, will make the implementation of the contents of the Courses of Study easier, enabling teachers to refine and improve their teaching techniques and assessment methods.

The Handbook, in other words, serves as a guide to implement the contents of the Courses of Study. Starting with the purposes of each school establishing a 'Can Do' list, the Handbook provides practical information regarding how to establish one, and how to utilise it for teaching and assessment. It also illustrates how 'Can Do' lists should be reflected on annual teaching plans and lesson plans. According to the Handbook, 'Can Do' descriptors are to be converted into goals of each unit of MEXT-authorised textbooks. The achievements of the unit goals, then, are assessed by appropriate methods including performance tests, and the test results are to be used to improve teaching and learning.

2.3 'Can Do' lists of MEXT and 'Can Do' lists of the CEFR

The Five Proposals, the Handbook, and the Action Plans spell 'CAN-DO' lists in upper-case letters (for the purpose of clarity, this paper generally uses 'Can Do', unless directly citing text from other documents; however, in this sub-section only I use 'CAN-DO' for comparison purposes). MEXT is careful about making a clear distinction between upper-case 'CAN-DO' lists in these official documents and lower-case 'Can Do' lists in the CEFR. On one hand, MEXT 'CAN-DO' lists are in line with some of the educational philosophy from the CEFR 'Can Do' lists: lifelong learning, learner autonomy, and the action-oriented approach. On the other hand, one differs from the other in terms of how they are utilised in teaching and assessment. This section first describes how these two are similar, followed by how they are different.

The concepts of lifelong learning and learner autonomy are explicitly described in the purposes for developing the 'CAN-DO' lists. According to the Handbook, the purposes are three-fold:

(a) To clarify abilities students need to acquire in order to express themselves in foreign languages and to understand foreign languages, and to utilise the 'CAN-DO' lists to improve current practice of teaching and assessment.

(b) To help students to develop communication abilities in foreign languages, with equal emphasis on four skills, so that they will be able to appropriately convey their ideas taking into consideration their interlocutor's social background, as well as to foster ability of thinking, making decisions, and expressing themselves.

(c) To foster students' positive attitude towards learning, which is necessary to be autonomous learners, by sharing learning attainment targets with students from the perspective of lifelong learning (Ministry of Education, Culture, Sports, Science and Technology 2013b:5, translated by the author).

Purposes (b) and (c) echo Article 30 of School Education Act (Kaisetsu kyoiku roppo henshu iinkai 2016:180), which specifies that 'a basis of *lifelong learning* should be established by helping students acquire basic knowledge and skills, develop abilities to use them to solve problems, as well as abilities to think, make decisions, and express themselves, and foster *positive attitude toward learning*' (italics added).

Whereas (b) and (c) remind us of lifelong learning, one of the CEFR's principles, (a) seems to reflect the action-oriented approach, which is another educational concept of the CEFR. Figure 1 shows MEXT's suggestion that 'Can Do' descriptors should be written in two areas: ability to express themselves in foreign languages (i.e. speaking and writing skills) and ability to understand foreign languages (i.e. listening and reading skills). This suggestion was probably prompted by the suspicion that at some schools most language activities fall in the farthest right category shown in Figure 1, that is, knowledge and understanding of language and culture. This implies that most of the class time is spent on teaching grammar. This is why teachers are requested to write 'Can Do' descriptors in listening, reading, speaking and writing. If a descriptor says, for example, 'I can exchange simple opinions about familiar topics', teachers have to engage their students in the exchange of opinions. When they exchange their opinions with their classmates and teachers, they behave as language users. They function as a 'social agent', in CEFR terms, taking part in the authentic communication in the classroom.

Figure 1 How 'Can Do' lists are related with criterion-referenced evaluation (Ministry of Education, Culture, Sports, Science and Technology 2013b:36; translated by the author)

	Learning attainment targets in the form of 'Can Do' lists		
Interest, willingness, and a positive attitude towards communication	Ability to express themselves in foreign languages	Ability to understand foreign languages	Knowledge and understanding of language and culture
Basic elements of criterion-referenced evaluation			

As we have seen, upper-case 'CAN-DO' lists share some basic principles with lower-case 'Can Do' lists. However, the former differ from the latter in other aspects. First, the target users of 'CAN-DO' lists are limited, whereas the CEFR 'Can Do' lists are for a wide range of users. The CEFR is for language specialists, including policy-makers, curriculum designers, testing institutions, material writers, as well as for teachers and learners. In contrast, the upper-case 'CAN-DO' lists of MEXT are specifically for English teachers for secondary schools and their students in Japan. They are expected to serve as a tool to improve and refine the secondary-level ELT based on the Courses of Study.

Second, 'CAN-DO' lists are to be custom tailored by each secondary school whereas the CEFR 'Can Do' lists are context neutral. The former is the description of outcomes of English language learning envisioned by teachers at each school with specific groups of students in mind. The Handbook requests that all the English teachers at each school participate in the 'Can Do' initiative, think about the bigger picture of their students as language users at the time of graduation, and set up a 'Can Do' list for each grade based on the Courses of Study.

Third, 'CAN-DO' lists serve as learning attainment targets that must be reached by all the students, at least theoretically. This is because the overall purpose of 'CAN-DO' lists is the thorough implementation of the Courses of Study, which are ordinances of MEXT (Ministry of Education, Culture, Sports, Science and Technology 2013b). This shows a striking contrast with the CEFR 'Can Do' lists, which are meant as illustrations of CEFR proficiency levels (Jones 2012). Descriptors in MEXT 'CAN-DO' lists do not have to be aligned to the common scale.

2.4 Secondary school English teachers' perceptions of the 'Can Do' initiatives

'Can Do' lists[1] were thus introduced in the context of educational policies in Japan, followed by 'Can Do' initiatives, which entail the establishment and implementation of 'Can Do' lists. The entire process has faced challenges at each step as the Eiken Foundation of Japan (Eiken for short) (2013) and Wada (2015) show. As is the case with any educational reform plan, there is always a time-lag between the announcement of a package of measures and its implementation. The 'Can Do' initiatives are no exception.

Proposal 1, which requests that each junior and senior high school establish and publicise learning attainment targets in the form of 'Can Do' lists, monitor attainment, and make results public, has received a slow response

---

[1] The capitalisation of 'CAN-DO' is abandoned hereafter and 'Can Do' is used as in other chapters of this volume.

from secondary school teachers, according to a questionnaire survey conducted by Eiken in 2013, two years after the Five Proposals was released. Eiken sent a questionnaire to a total of 5,000 randomly selected secondary schools nationwide, receiving responses from 915 schools. Its purpose was to capture the progress of the 'Can Do' initiatives and to clarify what support is needed for teachers. The results revealed that 58% of the teachers at responding schools do not understand the relationship between 'Can Do' lists and the Courses of Study whereas 42% of teachers understand the relationship to some extent. The number of schools that had already set up 'Can Do' lists was 10%. Schools in the process of making the required changes amounted to 11% while 43% were planning to do so, and 35% had no plans (Eiken Foundation of Japan 2013).

Even the schools that had established their own 'Can Do' lists have not necessarily derived full pedagogical benefits from them. Out of 197 schools that had, or had almost, established 'Can Do' lists, 36% had not started using them. It suggests that effective use of 'Can Do' lists is another challenge that awaits teachers who have made them. Out of the 58% that have been using them, the majority of those schools admitted that they are struggling to figure out how to use them.

The Eiken survey results show that the sources of difficulty in the implementation of 'Can Do' lists vary: time constraint (48%), difficulty of assessment using 'Can Do' lists (35%), wide disparity in students' English proficiency (33%), and wide disparity in teachers' perception (33%). A fundamental problem, though, seems to be that 21% said that the purposes of 'Can Do' lists are not clear, as some respondents from junior high schools described in their answers to an open-ended question:

> We make annual plans for teaching and assessment, setting learning objectives of each unit of textbooks in four areas, which include ability to express themselves in English and ability to understand English. We do not understand why we need to set objectives in the form of 'Can Do' lists in addition to the existing objectives.
>
> Learning objectives of each unit of textbooks that we set can serve as a 'Can Do' list. There is no need to write a list since we already have learning objectives.

These reactions suggest that learning objectives of each unit, which are short-term targets, have been mixed up with 'Can Do' descriptors, which are long-term targets. This is not surprising since secondary school teachers, particularly junior high school teachers, are used to the current evaluation system, in which learning objectives for each unit are set in the four areas as is shown in Figure 1 and serve as criteria for evaluating students' achievements. Their achievements are shown on a 3-point scale for each of the four areas for each unit, which are counted towards a final grade of a semester (Ministry of Education, Culture, Sports, Science and Technology 2011b, 2012).

Wada (2015), in an attempt to examine how 'Can Do' lists are accepted and to sort out related problems, interviewed high school English teachers and supervisors in eight prefectures, and junior high school English teachers and supervisors in six prefectures. He also collected approximately 100 'Can Do' lists written by junior and senior high school teachers. He found that, whereas the majority of teachers who were interviewed were in the process of establishing 'Can Do' lists, the 'Can Do' lists he collected showed a wide variety. For example, one high school 'Can Do' list was a mixture of the Eiken 'Can Do' list, the CEFR-J, and the grade system established by the school itself. Another showed evaluation criteria together with descriptors. Processes of establishing 'Can Do' lists varied too. Whereas most schools wrote 'Can Do' lists on their own, one local board of education wrote one and the junior high schools in the district followed suit. He attributes this variety to each 'Can Do' author's perception of the Handbook, which requests that each school establish learning attainment targets *'based on the reality of the students of each school'* (Ministry of Education, Culture, Sports, Science and Technology 2013b, italics added) as well as on the Courses of Study. His interpretation is that teachers acted on their own judgement instead of following step by step the procedure provided by the Handbook. Their judgement, he claims, needs to be carefully assessed.

Wada's list of problems related to the 'Can Do' initiatives is long and daunting. He raises the following questions:

- For what part of the Courses of Study do 'Can Do' lists facilitate teaching and how?
- 'Can Do' lists are supposed to improve current teaching practice and assessment methods. If there is a need for improvement, exactly what is to be improved? How is it to be improved?
- 'Can Do' lists are supposed to foster learner autonomy. How is it to be fostered?
- In designing tasks based on descriptors, how should the task difficulty be set?
- How often should performance tests be administered to assess communication abilities validly?
- How should we set the standard to judge whether or not students have reached a given learning attainment level? (Wada 2015:3–5; translated by the author.)

These problems suggest that the 'Can Do' initiatives do not make up a project that is to be successfully completed after a certain period of time but are a project we have to live with. Even so, each one is such a controversial issue that it is difficult to decide which one to start with. Under these circumstances, there are some pilot studies in which high school teachers attempted to carry out MEXT's 'Can Do' initiatives. One of them, which adopted the portfolio-oriented approach, will be described in the following section.

3 Adoption of a 'Can Do' list to fit to a high school context

3.1 A portfolio-oriented approach as a means to realise MEXT's 'Can Do' initiatives

The portfolio-oriented approach was inspired by the European Language Portfolio (ELP), which Little (2009) dubs as a companion piece of the CEFR. The ELP consists of three components: language passport, language biography, and dossier. It reports the owner's communicative language proficiency, records their personal history of language learning and intercultural experiences, and keeps an archive of their works such as speech scripts and essays (Lenz 2004). In addition to its reporting function, the ELP has the pedagogical function of helping its holders reflect on their learning using a 'Can Do' list (Kohonen 2000, Lenz 2004). A portfolio-oriented approach adopts the concepts that underlie the ELP, particularly focusing on the development of learner autonomy through reflective learning and self-assessment (Kohonen 2006). This approach makes the language learning process more visible, helping students gradually take increasing charge of their learning with guidance provided by the teacher (Kohonen 2001, Little, Hodel, Kohonen, Meijer and Perclova 2007). It was piloted in Finland from 1998 to 2001 as part of a European ELP development project sponsored by the Council of Europe (Kohonen 2006, 2009).

This approach was adopted in the implementation of a 'Can Do' initiative in a prefectural high school in Chiba in two phases: one each for the school years 2013 and 2014 (Takada 2014, 2015a, 2015b, Takada, Tomura, Habakari and Kimura 2013, 2014, 2015). This pilot study adopted three principles proposed by Little et al (2007). They are (a) learner involvement, (b) appropriate target language use, and (c) learner reflection. These principles, integrated with the site-based syllabus and MEXT-authorised textbooks, were put into practice as follows:

(a) Learner involvement: The teachers establish learning attainment targets in the form of a 'Can Do' list (i.e. long-term objectives) and share them with the students and their parents at the beginning of a school year. The involvement of stakeholders was ensured this way. Next, they set objectives of each unit of the textbooks (i.e. short-term objectives) in relation to the 'Can Do' list. The unit objectives appear on the top of a worksheet, which is prepared by a group of teachers in charge of each grade, to make students have a clear idea of what they are going to learn. The same objectives are also printed at the end of the worksheet to help them reflect on their learning.

(b) Appropriate target language use: Tasks are generated from the objectives of each unit, which correspond to particular 'Can Do' descriptors. Opportunities for the students to use English interactively are secured. For example, the task of writing a brief introduction or explanation about familiar topics starts with brainstorming in pairs. Also, students exchange their written products and comment on each other's writing. Thus, social interactive aspects of learning are emphasised.

(c) Learner reflection: The students reflect on their own learning process and learning products as they refer to the objectives of a particular unit that are shown at the end of the worksheet.

The first phase of the implementation of the portfolio-oriented approach faced a major challenge in terms of how to help and guide students with reflection. Reflection itself is not an unfamiliar concept in educational practice in Japan. In fact, it is common in primary and secondary schools to set aside a few minutes at the end of each class for learners to reflect on what they learned and what they thought during the class. The problem is that they tend to reflect on an affective level rather than on a cognitive level. Their typical descriptions are 'I enjoyed the class', 'The activity was fun' and 'I want to do it again'.

In an attempt to go beyond this level, criteria for self-assessment were developed to promote reflection in the second phase. For research purposes, it focused on one descriptor for writing, 'I can write a brief explanation or introduction about myself, my family, my school, my community, and other topics of my interest'. This descriptor was broken down into more concrete terms. Descriptors, which are mostly general statements, allow a variety of interpretations. For instance, 'a brief explanation' may be just one paragraph or three paragraphs. 'Topics of my interest' also vary. The teachers at the research site and this researcher discussed what consists of 'a brief explanation' and 'introduction about topics of one's interest' written by their 10th graders. We came up with the following three criteria:

(a) The explanation or introduction has a topic sentence.

(b) The topic sentence is followed by supporting sentences.

(c) The topic sentence and supporting sentences are consistent.

These criteria served as a guide for reflection on *language products*. It was also agreed that a topic sentence consists of a topic and an assertion (Williams 1969).

To help students reflect on their *learning process*, three open-ended questions were prepared as follows:

(a) What exactly did you do to organise a reader-friendly paragraph?
(b) What was difficult in writing the paragraph? Was there anything you wanted to express but could not write?
(c) Write anything that came to your mind while writing.

These open-ended questions, together with the assessment criteria, were printed on worksheets to be used for self-assessment.

The students worked on four writing tasks derived from the given descriptor during an 8-month period, and their learning outcomes and development of learner autonomy were examined through quantitative and qualitative data analyses. The results show that the students performed better in the fourth writing than in the first writing in each of the three criteria. The quantity of writing also increased, which suggests their fluency improved. Their awareness for language products and the learning process was also enhanced. There were descriptions that reflected their awareness of the organisation of a paragraph and their ability to read their own writing from the readers' perspective. There are some cases, though, where their reflection was not necessarily to the point. For example, some students described that they wrote enough supporting sentences to make their points clear, but their writing showed that all the supporting sentences were not necessarily relevant to the topic. In other words, they thought their writing was semantically consistent when in reality it required improvement. More guidance is needed to help them enhance their task awareness by, for instance, holding a conference on a one-on-one basis. This small-scale pilot study is limited in its implications, but it at least suggests that the portfolio-oriented approach can be an option to realise the objectives of the 'Can Do' initiatives in Japan. More such case studies are expected to be conducted in the future.

3.2 Discussion

In terms of the possible influence of the 'Can Do' initiatives described above, there are positive signs reflected by addressing three of the key questions of this edited volume: 'Can Do' descriptors as the key reference point for processes of reflective learning, applicability of lesson materials to the action-oriented approach, and the benefits of the action-oriented approach for teaching.

First, the present implementation indicates that the use of 'Can Do' descriptors, which are officially called the learning attainment targets in the form of 'Can Do' lists in Japan's educational system, can promote reflective learning in a high school. In order for 'Can Do' descriptors to serve as the key reference point, however, they need to be easier to access for students. Since 'Can Do' descriptors are written in general terms by nature, more specific learning objectives and assessment criteria aligned with them should be prepared. Setting specific learning objectives for each unit of a textbook based on a 'Can Do' list and showing them to students before they start learning a particular unit will provide them with clearer descriptions of objectives and motivate them to use English for communicative purposes. The same learning objectives shown at the end of the unit will help students evaluate their own performance. Self-assessment, however, tends to be impressionistic if they are not provided with appropriate guidance. Therefore, assessment criteria aligned with the learning objectives are called for so that students can reflect on their own language products from the perspective of a 'Can Do' list. In sum, a 'Can Do' list cannot be utilised effectively as it is; it must come with more transparent and concrete learning objectives and assessment criteria, both of which are closely related to a 'Can Do' list.

Second, through the implementation of a 'Can Do' list, applicability of lesson materials to the action-oriented approach was examined by the teachers involved. This is a crucial issue in Japan's school system, where the use of MEXT-authorised textbooks is a requirement in primary and secondary education. MEXT-authorised English textbooks reflect the philosophy of the action-oriented approach to some extent since the Courses of Study stipulate that the overall objective of foreign language teaching is to develop students' communication abilities in listening, speaking, reading and writing. However, some communicative activities included in the textbooks do not fit with target student proficiency levels. There is also a problem that they just provide topics for discussion and presentations without showing step-by-step procedures to complete the task, leaving novice teachers at a loss about how to guide students. The 'Can Do' initiatives can provide teachers with opportunities to examine their textbooks from the perspective of their applicability to the action-oriented approach. At the research site, the teachers decided to discard some communicative activities in the textbook that are above their students' level of English proficiency and generated one for each unit based on their 'Can Do' list. They then discussed the instruction procedure and created worksheets that show every step towards the completion of the task.

Third, the teachers involved reaped benefits from the action-oriented approach, which was revealed through interviews with them after the two-year implementation. First and foremost, the students had more opportunities to act as language users in class than before. Language learning requires years of painstaking efforts. In order to achieve learning attainment targets in the form of a 'Can Do' list, which are long-term targets, teachers set a number of short-term targets and prepared tasks to achieve them. What is more, these tasks were not independent but were related to each other, which served as stepping stones towards the final goal.

Also, the philosophy and ideas of the action-oriented approach were shared with the group of teachers who participated in the 'Can Do' initiative at the research site. The teachers' background varied in terms of teaching experience and the view of language teaching and learning, and so did their perception of the action-oriented approach. A 'Can Do' list connected those who have understood the philosophy and ideas of this approach and those who are halfway through their understanding. When they observed each other's classes and had feedback sessions afterwards, they discussed their teaching practice from the perspective of the 'Can Do' descriptor that was relevant to a particular lesson, making the discussion more focused and productive. Creating lesson worksheets as a team was another opportunity for all the teachers to confirm that their overall objective of teaching English is to develop students' communication abilities, and that it is achieved by having them use the target language. Thus, a 'Can Do' list can function as 'a common language' for teachers who strive for an effective form of communicative language teaching.

4 Future challenges

As was described previously, the perception of the CEFR in Japan's educational system is unique. For this reason, we face some challenges. One is that the concept and ideas of the CEFR contextualised in Japan's educational setting have not been fully understood. Since the CEFR and 'Can Do' lists were mentioned in MEXT's official documents, they have often been highlighted in journals, educational magazines, conferences, and in-service seminars for secondary school English teachers. The pitfall of this movement, however, is that the understanding of the educational philosophy of the CEFR, along with the notion of 'Can Do' lists, has remained on a superficial level. There is a general tendency to become insensitive to the definitions of educational buzzwords and use them with vague knowledge about them. This can mislead secondary school teachers. For example, the use of the CEFR's six proficiency levels as learning attainment targets in official documents could be misunderstood. Whereas its message is that the objective is to attain communication abilities, the CEFR's proficiency levels could be perceived as equivalents for scores of standardised tests, since the levels are sometimes shown with corresponding test scores. Careful attention and explanation are needed in the use of the CEFR's six proficiency levels.

A 'Can Do' list is another buzzword. Although it was an unfamiliar term to the majority of secondary school teachers several years ago, it is now often mentioned in English teachers' classrooms. However, as the Eiken Foundation of Japan (2013) and Wada (2015) suggest, there is still confusion among them regarding what 'Can Do' lists are and why they should be developed. Teachers should understand that behind 'Can Do' lists are educational ideas including lifelong learning, learner autonomy and the action-oriented approach, before they start establishing the lists. The Handbook was published in 2013, and prefectural education boards have been holding in-service seminars, but we still seem to have a long way to go.

Another challenge is that departure from traditional knowledge-based, teacher-centred instruction, which is one of the objectives of MEXT's 'Can Do' initiatives, requires change on the part of teachers. There is always some resistance to change. Schärer (2008), in his interim report on the ELP, states that change is rarely perceived as comfortable, and that energy and sustained effort are needed to produce lasting results. We should remember that even in Europe the implementation of the CEFR has been a difficult endeavour. In fact, the impact of the CEFR on pedagogy is less visible than that on testing (Little 2007). Policy-makers and researchers should understand that time and patience are needed to reap pedagogical benefits from the 'Can Do' initiatives, and should help teachers who have been struggling to improve their teaching techniques and assessment methods.

References

Council of Europe (2001) *Common European Framework of Reference for Languages: Learning, Teaching, Assessment*, Cambridge: Cambridge University Press.

Eiken Foundation of Japan (2013) *Gaikokugo kyoiku ni okeru CAN DO list no katachi deno gakushu totatsu mokuhyo settei ni kansuru genjo chosa* [*Current Situation Survey on Setting Learning Attainment Targets in the Form of 'Can Do' Lists in Foreign Language Education*], Tokyo: Eiken Foundation of Japan.

Jones, D (2012) *The CEFR and its impact on learning: The Asset Languages case study*, paper prepared for the International Symposium on the Application of the CEFR for English language teaching in Japan: The potential of the CEFR-J, Tokyo, 2012.

Kaisetsu kyoiku roppo henshu iinkai (2016) Kaisetsu kyoiku roppo [*Commentaries on Six Acts of Education*], Tokyo: Sanseido.

Kohonen, V (2000) Part One: Exploring the educational possibilities of the 'Dossier': Suggestions for developing the pedagogic function of the European Language Portfolio, in Council of Europe *Enhancing the Pedagogical Aspects of the European Language Portfolio (ELP)*, Strasbourg: Council of Europe, 5–31.

Kohonen, V (2001) Developing the European Language Portfolio as a pedagogical instrument for advancing student autonomy, in Karlsson, L, Kjisik, F and Nordlund, J (Eds) *All Together Now: Papers from the Nordic Conference on Autonomous Language Learning*, Helsinki: University of Helsinki Language Center, 20–44.

Kohonen, V (2006) Student autonomy and the European Language Portfolio: Evaluating the Finnish pilot project (1998–2001), in Wolff, L B and Batista, J L V (Eds) *The Canarian Conference on Developing Autonomy in the Classroom: Each Piece of the Puzzle Enriches us All*, CD-ROM Lecture 2, Canarias: Gobierno de Canarias.

Kohonen, V (2009) Autonomy, authenticity and agency in language education: The European Language Portfolio as a pedagogical resource, in Kantelinen, R and Pollari, P (Eds) *Language Education and Lifelong Learning*, Helsinki: Sense Publishers, 9–44.

Koike, I (2008) *Pioneering basic research using second language acquisition research to ensure coherent, linked English education from elementary school through junior high school to university*, Grants-in-Aid for Scientific Research 2004–2007: Scientific Research A, Report on research results.

Lenz, P (2004) The European Language Portfolio, in Morrow, K (Ed) *Insights from the Common European Framework*, Oxford: Oxford University Press, 22–31.

Little, D (2007) The Common European Framework of Reference for Languages: Perspectives on the making of supranational language education policy, *The Modern Language Journal* 91, 645–655.

Little, D (2009) *The European Language Portfolio: Where Pedagogy and Assessment Meet*, Strasbourg: Council of Europe.

Little, D, Hodel, H, Kohonen, V, Meijer, D and Perclova, R (2007) *Preparing Teachers To Use The European Language Portfolio*, Strasbourg: Council of Europe.

Ministry of Education, Culture, Sports, Science and Technology (2008) *Chugakko gakushu shido yoryo kaisetsu* [*Commentary on The Course of Study for Lower Secondary Schools*], Tokyo: Kairyudo.

Ministry of Education, Culture, Sports, Science and Technology (2009) *Kotogakko gakushu shido yoryo kaisetsu* [*Commentary on the Course of Study for Upper Secondary Schools*], Tokyo: Kairyudo.

Ministry of Education, Culture, Sports, Science and Technology (2011a) *Kokusai kyotsugo to shite no eigoryoku kojo no tame no itsutsu no teigen* [*Five Proposals and Specific Measures for Developing Proficiency in English for International Communication*], available online: www.mext.go.jp/component/english/__icsFiles/afieldfile/2012/07/09/1319707_1.pdf

Ministry of Education, Culture, Sports, Science and Technology (2011b) *Hyoka kijun no sakusei, hyoka hoho nado no kufu kaizen no tame no sanko shiryo (chugakko gaikokugo)* [*A Guide to Setting Criteria and Improving Evaluation Methods for Foreign Language in Lower Secondary Schools*],Tokyo: Kyoiku Shuppan.

Ministry of Education, Culture, Sports, Science and Technology (2012) *Hyoka kijun no sakusei, hyoka hoho nado no kufu kaizen no tame no sanko shiryo (koto gakko gaikokugo)* [*A Guide to Setting Criteria and Improving Evaluation Methods for Foreign Language in Upper Secondary Schools*], Tokyo: Kyoiku Shuppan.

Ministry of Education, Culture, Sports, Science and Technology (2013a) *Global ka ni taio shita eigo kyoiku kaikaku jisshi keikaku* [*Action Plans to Reform ELT to Meet the Needs of the Globalised Community*], Tokyo: Kyoiku Shuppan.

Ministry of Education, Culture, Sports, Science and Technology (2013b) *Kaku chu koto gakko no gaikokugo kyoiku ni okeru CAN DO list no katachi deno gakushu totatsu mokuhyo settei no tame no tebiki* [*Handbook for Setting Learning Attainment Targets in Foreign Languages in Each Junior and Senior High School in the Form of 'Can Do' Lists*], Tokyo: Kyoiku Shuppan.

Negishi, M, Takada, T and Tono, Y (2013) A progress report on the development of the CEFR-J, in Galaczi, E D and Weir, C J (Eds) *Exploring Language Frameworks: Proceedings of the ALTE Kraków Conference, July 2011*, Studies in Language Testing volume 36, Cambridge: UCLES/Cambridge University Press, 135–163.

Schärer, R (2008) *European Language Portfolio: Interim Report 2007*, Strasbourg: Council of Europe.
Takada, T (2014) *Jiritsu teki gakushusha wo ikusei suru 'Can Do' list no sakusei to katsuyo ni muketa torikumi* [*A pilot study on the establishment and implementation of a 'Can Do' list to foster learner autonomy*], paper prepared for the 40th annual convention of Japan Society of English Language Education, Tokushima, 2014.
Takada, T (2015a) Chiba project hokoku [A report on Chiba project], in Takada, T (Ed) *Portfolio teki approach ni yoru mirai shiko gata eigo shido model no kochiku* [*Development of a Future-oriented English Teaching Model Based on the Portfolio-oriented Approach*], report on Chiba project sponsored by the Japan Society for the Promotion of Science (No. 23320117), 37–74.
Takada, T (2015b) *Gakushu totatsu mokuhyo wo katsuyo shita writing shido: Naisei kijutu ni miru jiritsu ishiki no henyo* [*Sharing a learning attainment target with students in teaching writing: Development of learner autonomy through reflection*], paper prepared for the 41st annual convention of the Japan Society of English Language Education, Kumamoto, 2015.
Takada, T, Tomura, R, Habakari, S and Kimura, K (2013) *Koko ni okeru 'Can Do' check list sakusei, kaitei, katsuyo no kokoromi* [*A pilot study on the establishment, revision, and implementation of a 'Can Do' checklist*], paper prepared for the 37th annual convention of the Kanto-koshin-etsu Association of Teachers of English, Matsumoto, 2013.
Takada, T, Tomura, R, Habakari, S and Kimura, K (2014) *Gakushu totatsu mokuhyo ni itaru michi: 'Can Do' list no igi wo kangaeru* [*How to achieve learning attainment goals: Why we need a 'Can Do' list*], paper prepared for the 38th annual convention of the Kanto-koshin-etsu Association of Teachers of English, Urayasu, 2014.
Takada, T, Tomura, R, Habakari, S and Kimura, K (2015) *Noryoku kijutubun wo gutaika suru jugyo jissen no katei to kadai* [*Designing lessons based on 'Can Do' descriptors and related issues*], paper prepared for the 39th annual convention of the Kanto-koshin-etsu Association of Teachers of English, Uenohara, August 2015.
Tono, Y (2012) *CEFR-J: Sono haikei to kaihatsu no keii* [*CEFR-J: How it was conceived and developed*], paper prepared for the International Symposium on the 'Application of the CEFR for English language teaching in Japan: The potential of the CEFR-J', Tokyo, 2012.
Tono, Y (2013) *CAN-DO list sakusei katsuyou: Eigo toutatsu shihyou CEFR-J guidebook* [*CEFR-J Guidebook: Resources for Establishing and Utilizing 'Can-Do' Lists for English Language Teaching*], Tokyo: Taishukan.
Wada, M (2015) *Gakushu totatsu mokuhyo to shite no 'Can Do' list sakusei ni tsuite: Genjo to kadai wo saguru* [*Establishing 'Can Do' lists as learning attainment targets: Exploring current situations and related issues*], paper prepared for a monthly lecture of the Kanto-koshin-etsu Association of Teachers of English, Tokyo, 2015.
Williams, S H (1969) *The Logic of the English Paragraph*, Tokyo: Kenkyusha.

Section 2
Materials design

4 Marugoto: Japanese Language and Culture – the series of coursebooks based on the JF Standard for Japanese Language Education

Noriko Yokoyama
Showa Women's University

1 Introduction

The Japan Foundation (hereafter, JF) is a non-profit public organisation funded by the Japanese government engaged in international cultural exchange. Supporting Japanese language education overseas is one of the three major fields JF focuses its activities on, together with arts and cultural exchange, and finally Japanese studies and intellectual exchange. Developing teaching materials is among the activities JF is engaged in to promote Japanese language education overseas. Other activities include training teachers and conducting the Japanese Language Proficiency Test. This paper introduces a series of coursebooks entitled *Marugoto: Japanese Language and Culture* (The Japan Foundation 2013a, 2013b) which JF has been developing based on 'JF Standard for Japanese Language Education' (hereafter, JFS). JFS is a framework for Japanese language learning based on the Common European Framework of Reference for Languages (CEFR, Council of Europe 2001) and does not by itself prescribe any teaching methodology. On the other hand, the coursebook is an actual plan of teaching and should provide users with ways to apply the framework. While the CEFR-informed, action-oriented coursebooks challenge the traditional style of form-focused Japanese language teaching, I argue that the coursebooks are easily applicable by both teachers and students. 'Can Do' descriptors are at the centre of reflective learning in which self-assessment plays a central role, while other principles of the CEFR, like intercultural understanding, are also emphasised in the coursebook series. The following sections explain in detail how the characteristics of JFS are realised in *Marugoto*.

2 The characteristics of JFS

JFS, released in 2010, has the following characteristics:
1. The six levels of proficiency are in common with the CEFR.
2. The six levels are described in the form of 'Can Do' descriptors. The JF has so far developed 532 original 'Can Do' descriptors and has uploaded them together with 493 CEFR 'Can Do' descriptors in the database called the *Minna no "Can-do" Website*, where users can log in, search for 'Can Do' descriptors by category and level, and save selected and/or edited 'Can Do' descriptors in an individual user's own folder. (jfstandard.jp/cando/top/ja/render.do)
3. JFS focuses on competence in intercultural understanding.
4. JFS proposes a portfolio and values learners' self-management of their own learning and assessment.

The levels of the *Marugoto* series are set along the levels of JFS as follows: Starter (A1), Elementary 1 (A2), Elementary 2 (A2) and Pre-Intermediate (A2/B1). These levels have already been published for sale, while Intermediate 1 (B1) has been issued as trial version that is also scheduled to be for sale.

3 Learning objectives as 'Can Do' descriptors

The second characteristic of JFS is that the levels are described in 'Can Do' descriptors. In other words, proficiency is defined in terms of actual performance rather than in terms of language knowledge. In order to realise the principle of this 'performance-based instruction' the challenge *Marugoto* has made is to clearly divide performance practice and conventional learning of language forms. Each of the first three levels consists of two volumes, *Katsudo* (communicative language activities), and *Rikai* (communicative language competences), which offer two different types of learning.

The model of Japanese language proficiency adopted in the *Marugoto* series is illustrated by a JFS tree, which is shown in Figure 1. The upper part (the branches) are called communicative language activities, and include receptive, productive and interactive activities. The lower part (the roots) of the tree are called communicative language competences, and include linguistic, socio-linguistic and pragmatic competences. *Katsudo* offers learning of communicative language activities aiming for 'implicit learning' (Ellis 2008:449–454) through listening and speaking, and basically excludes the learning of grammar. On the other hand, *Rikai* offers learning of communicative language competences aiming for 'explicit learning' (Ellis 2008:449–454) of grammar, vocabulary and written characters. Traditional Japanese language teaching has, for a long time, been based on the PPP model (Presentation–Practice–Production, which focuses on language forms), and

Marugoto: Japanese Language and Culture

Figure 1 The two types of learning in the Marugoto coursebook series

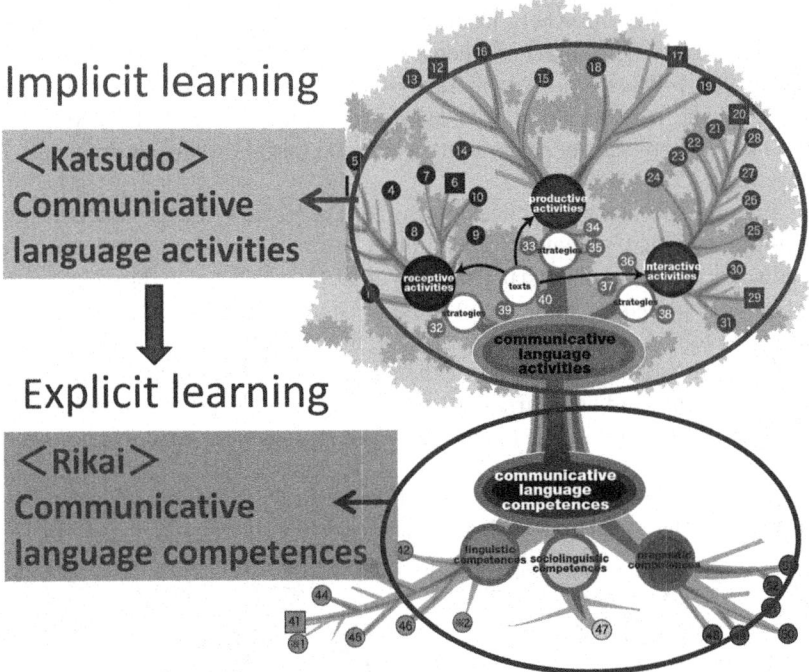

Marugoto challenges this tradition by recommending learners start with implicit learning using *Katsudo*, followed by *Rikai*, which aims to reinforce what they have learned in *Katsudo* through explicit learning. This recommendation is based on Second Language Acquisition research (Ellis 2006, 2008) that suggests insistence on grammatical accuracy from the start may impede the development of communicative ability (Ellis 2006:91). The precedence of implicit learning through task-based activities without explanation about language forms is a challenging trial in the context of the traditional style of form-focused Japanese language teaching. The respective contents of *Katsudo* and *Rikai* are explained below with a sample lesson from the Starter volume.

3.1 Katsudo (activities) contents

In *Katsudo*, the objectives of each lesson are described on the first page in the form of 'Can Do' descriptors. For example, the 'Can Do' descriptors for lesson 6 are the following four: 1) 'Say what your favorite dish is', 2) 'Talk with a friend about where to go for lunch', 3) 'Read a menu', and 4) 'Order food and drinks at a hamburger shop'. Those 'Can Do' descriptors are written in short, simple phrases in the textbook for learners to easily understand. They

Assessment of CEFR-informed Language Teaching in Japan and Beyond

are then rephrased with elaborate descriptions so that the level of performance would conform to CEFR level, and are included in the database called *Minna no "Can-do" Website* where teachers/learners of *Marugoto* can share their learning objectives and achievements with those outside the institution who do not know *Marugoto*. An example of the rephrased version of the 'Can Do' descriptors is as follows: 'Can ask a friend questions about what food he/she likes and answer questions about what food one likes, while having a meal together' (A1 level).

Figure 2 shows the first page of lesson 6. The learning starts with listening without explicit explanation. The implicit learning is expected to happen in deductive ways as explained in the following. Learners listen to the sound such as *Karee o tabemasu* (to eat curry) and *Sushi o tabemasu* (to eat sushi) and are expected to make form-meaning mapping in their mind with the help of pictures. After listening several times, the teacher may pronounce names of the food randomly and ask learners to point out the food that was pronounced, in order to confirm that the form-meaning mappings were satisfactory.

Figure 2 The first page of lesson 6 under the theme of Tabemono (food), from Katsudo © The Japan Foundation

After learning basic words and phrases needed in this lesson, learners listen to some short dialogues. The dialogue shows the situation, for example, where someone is talking with a friend about where to go for lunch. Explicit explanations about sentence patterns like 'Doko de tabemasuka?' ('Where shall we eat?') or 'Ano mise de tabemashoo' ('Let's eat at that restaurant') are not given. However, looking at the picture marked with ★ in Figure 2, learners are assumed to understand the overall meaning. When learners listen to several dialogues of the similar pattern, they gradually better understand the meaning, as well as get familiar with the basic patterns like those shown previously.

The significant point about the process in learning the dialogue is that learners are not required to understand everything, but to infer the meaning from the context, to be tolerant of ambiguity, and eventually notice the language forms repeated in the dialogues. Inferencing and tolerance of ambiguity are among the important strategies that researchers (Brown 2000, O'Malley and Chamot 1990) point out that learners need to acquire in the course of learning another language.

After being exposed to enough input, learners finally have an opportunity to produce original output in the form of interaction between classmates. In role-playing with a partner in the activities of Figure 2, they ask their partner and/or answer questions about what kind of restaurant they are going out to for lunch. If their communication breaks down or they face any problems in the course of role-playing, they are advised to go back to the input and listen to the dialogue again. Swain (1995) claims in her output hypothesis that 'in producing the target language (vocally or subvocally) learners may notice a gap between what they want to say and what they can say, leading them to recognize what they do not know, or know only partially' (Swain 1995:125–126). The trial of role-playing makes them aware of what they need to find out about the language form used in the dialogue, which gives the prime opportunity to return to listening to the model dialogue again. Hence, this process of going back and forth between output and input is important for inner learning to happen.

3.2 Rikai (understanding) contents

Rikai offers explicit learning about language forms which language teachers have traditionally been familiar with. The objectives of each lesson in *Rikai* are given in the form of grammatical patterns such as 'Sukina ryoori wa karee desu' ('My favorite dish is curry') and so on. One special characteristic of *Rikai* is that the answers to the exercises are offered in audio format. The principle that *Marugoto* values spoken language is extended to the thought that explicit learning of language forms should be done with spoken language that involves accents and phonetic change.

4 Intercultural understanding

The third characteristic of *Marugoto* is an emphasis on intercultural understanding. Each topic includes a 'Life and Culture' page like that shown in Figure 3. The left page is from the topic of food and shows various fast food restaurants with questions like 'What kinds of restaurant do you have in your country? Are they inexpensive? Delicious? Fast?' and so on. The aim of this page is not to reach a single answer or conclusion, but to notice differences and similarities among cultures. The learners are exposed to a number of different topics such as family, shopping, Japanese seasonal events and so on, and encouraged to discuss differences and similarities with their own cultures. It is also expected that they reflect their own culture through such discussions and notice variety among individuals even among the same culture.

Figure 3 'Life and Culture' page © The Japan Foundation

5 Portfolio approach

The last characteristic of *Marugoto* is the proposal of a European Language Portfolio (ELP)-type approach. Learners are expected to create learning achievements like recorded speech samples and essays, or records of linguistic and cultural experiences such as learning plans and reflections, which may include photos, tickets and bills of receipt. They also create assessment tables like a self-assessment checklist. The final page of the coursebook includes the self-assessment checklist where the learning objectives of all the lessons are listed. Every time they finish a lesson, they evaluate their own learning by colouring the stars and writing comments. For example, in lesson 6, learners review their own performance with the 'Can Do' 'Talk about your favorite foods', and colour one, two or fully three stars and comment on what learning activities they liked, what they found difficult or whatever impressed them. This process encourages learners to reflect on what they have learned and to realise what more they would like to learn. If teachers/learners look in the *Minna no "Can-do" Website*, they would see what other 'Can Do' descriptors in the same level with the same topic are available for further learning. The *Minna no "Can-do" Website* includes English language versions of 'Can Do' descriptors in addition to Japanese versions so that the 'Can Do' descriptors could be shared with learners and stakeholders.

6 Feedback from the users

Although JF has not yet formally planned research based on data collection, feedback from the teachers who used *Marugoto* is quite positive, as exemplified by these comments:

- learners enjoy learning
- learners have better listening comprehension
- learners have better pronunciation
- learners are not scared any more to speak out.

Feedback has also included some comments expressing concern about the treatment of grammar:

- it's difficult to teach dialogue without teaching grammar
- learners ask for grammar explanations; is it all right to start with *Rikai* first?

Such feedback suggests that some teachers were sceptical about the method of having performance practice precede grammar practice. However, some reported episodes from teachers indicate that such scepticism has been replaced with a more positive attitude towards the method after observing their learners' successful performance and positive response. Concurrently, however, JF should continue to observe what happens in problematic teaching situations and add necessary descriptions to teaching manuals.

7 Conclusion: The key questions and Marugoto

To conclude this chapter, I discuss how the *Marugoto* coursebook series reflects the principles of JFS/CEFR, how these practices relate to the key questions of this edited volume, and present general steps for compiling textbooks aligned with the CEFR-based standards.

Through the experience of introducing CEFR-informed textbooks, there are several important points to consider for both Japanese language education, and language education in general. An important element of the *Marugoto* series, as explained in section 3 of this chapter, is the foregrounding of 'Can Do' descriptors at the centre of the learning enterprise, with self-assessment and reflection clearly encouraged. Other key issues are also discussed here.

7.1 Are the CEFR-based materials (textbooks, teaching content etc.) action-oriented, and easily applicable by both teachers and students? How?

The JF provides Japanese language courses in 31 cities around the globe. Most of the courses are taught using the *Marugoto* series, with approximately 16,000 learners in fiscal year 2013. According to the reports collected from those courses (The Japan Foundation Japanese Language Institute 2015), the majority of teachers and students accept the action-oriented learning of *Marugoto* very positively. For example, an Indonesian teacher of Japanese reports that the use of *Marugoto* has replaced the traditional grammar-oriented teaching with a learner-centred way of learning and has caused active mutual learning among students through group work. On the other hand, teachers in Ukraine report on the difficulty in getting used to the *Marugoto* way of teaching, and compiled grammar notes and a teacher's manual for the learners and teachers who are still familiar with grammar-oriented instruction.

7.2 Can all readily see the benefits of the CEFR-based approach for their own teaching/learning?

As mentioned previously, the majority of teachers have been familiar with grammar-oriented instruction by way of the PPP model and have to a greater or lesser extent confronted difficulties in getting used to learner-centred, performance-preceded instruction in introducing *Marugoto*. However, most of those teachers have overcome such difficulties as the following comment from a teacher in Kazakhstan mentions:

> The *Marugoto* way of teaching that excludes grammar explanation in *Katsudo* differs greatly from the way we have been familiar with. In the

Marugoto: Japanese Language and Culture

first place, we could not understand why we should not teach grammar from the first part of the lesson. It was also shocking to us since we felt as if we were deprived of our professional technique. However we were gradually getting to understand that our professionalism can be found in waiting for learners to notice. What they notice by themselves is kept in their memory more effectively than what they are explicitly taught (The Japan Foundation Japanese Language Institute 2015:81).

7.3 Is autonomous learning beyond the specified materials (e.g., textbooks) supported and encouraged? If so, how?

According to the collected reports, the portfolio approach has been mostly effective in promoting autonomous learning beyond the classroom. The JF Japanese language course in Australia devised the practice called 'Japanese in action' which is a form of homework given in the form of questions such as: 'What Japanese is there around you? Where did you find it? What is it? Please include any photo examples in your portfolio.' The target could be focused with specific learning such as reading food menus or using a Japanese way of addressing family members and friends, or could be broadened into culture learning such as observing the gestures Japanese people make when exchanging business cards. Some learners find portfolio assessment a burden, but practice reports say that sharing of the experiences and products included in the successful portfolio can encourage other learners who used to be less motivated.

7.4 General steps for compiling textbooks aligned with CEFR-based standards

To conclude I am outlining some steps for others who may engage in similar textbook-related activities.

- Make a list of 'Can Do' descriptors of the appropriate level, situated in the real world that the target users are most likely to encounter and would need to achieve. The best selected 'Can Do' descriptors should be both the objectives of the lessons of the textbook as well as the index of assessment.
- Extract essential language forms from the above-mentioned 'Can Do' descriptors. The selection of language forms should follow the selection of 'Can Do' descriptors, NOT vice versa.
- Include learning of strategies in the textbook for learners to cope with the real-world 'Can Do' descriptors: both comprehension strategies such as inferencing and production strategies such as questioning and substitution are necessary.

- Make each lesson flow from abundant input to moderate output. The fact that the language level of comprehension is higher than that of production should be kept in mind when creating listening scripts and conversational dialogue.

References

Brown, H D (2000) *Principles of Language Learning and Teaching* (4th edition), White Plains: Longman.

Council of Europe (2001) *Common European Framework of Reference for Languages: Learning, Teaching, Assessment*, Cambridge: Cambridge University Press.

Ellis, R (2006) Current issues in the teaching of grammar: An SLA perspective, *TESOL Quarterly* 40 (1), 83–107.

Ellis, R (2008) *The Study of Second Language Acquisition* (2nd edition), Oxford: Oxford University Press.

O'Malley, J M and Chamot, A U (1990) *Learning Strategies in Second Language Acquisition*, Cambridge: Cambridge University Press.

Swain, M (1995) Three functions of output in second language learning, in Cook, G and Seidlhofer, B (Eds) *Principle and Practice in Applied Linguistics*, Cambridge: Cambridge University Press, 125–144.

The Japan Foundation (2013a) *Marugoto: Japanese Language and Culture Starter (A1) Katsudo*, Tokyo: Sansyusha.

The Japan Foundation (2013b) *Marugoto: Japanese Language and Culture Starter (A1) Rikai*, Tokyo: Sansyusha.

The Japan Foundation Japanese Language Institute (2015) *'JF Nihongo kyooiku sutandaado' junkyo koosu jireisyuu 2014: JF kooza ni okeru jissen* [*Collection of Teaching Practices in Japanese Language Courses Based on the JF Standard for Japanese Language Education 2014*], Saitama: The Japan Foundation Japanese Language Institute, available online: www.jpf.go.jp/j/project/japanese/education/jf/case/2014/index.html

5 Applying the CEFR to English for Academic Purposes textbooks

Naoyuki Naganuma
Tokai University

Noriko Nagai
Ibaraki University

Fergus O'Dwyer
University College Dublin and University of Münster

1 Introduction

This chapter explains a research project which developed an English language integrated skills textbook – *Connections to Thinking in English: The CEFR-informed Textbook Series A2+/B1 to B1+*, or 'Connections' for short – (Naganuma, Nagai and O'Dwyer 2015) that suitably adapted and applied the Common European Framework of Reference for Languages (CEFR, Council of Europe 2001) for the higher education context in Japan. The textbook focused on English for Academic Purposes (EAP), rather than focusing on the everyday conversation approach that is typical of many lower-level textbooks on the market. These materials incorporated a Content and Language Integrated Learning (CLIL) approach that fosters global personnel skills such as cognition and collaboration, two of the key concepts other than content and language, suitable for university graduates entering the workforce. Themed units require discussion, presentation and academic writing tasks relating to controversial issues on topics such as technology and health issues. Furthermore, in order to support learner and teacher autonomy and the classroom implementation of the text, we aimed to develop supplemental learning materials and autonomy-informed resources. The significance of this current project is that it develops a contextualised CEFR-informed integrated skills textbook for Japanese learners of English. The textbook is connected to recent results of research on the CEFR, and develops the principles and practices encouraged by the CEFR and European Language Portfolio (ELP).

In the initial year of the project, in order to assess the need and availability of CEFR-informed resources, we analysed texts to see how they correlated to the CEFR, surveyed teacher needs, and gathered examples of actual classroom practices in Japan. In the following year, we developed the textbook materials, with a piloting of the text to determine effectiveness and to assess the need for revisions in the final year. This textbook encourages learners to acquire a deeper understanding of social issues familiar to university students by providing multiple resources from different perspectives based on tasks that involve all of the major skills. The illustrative scales of the CEFR are contextualised for peer- and self-assessment and used for task design and goal settings. As the tasks are similar across all units, the textbook encourages cyclical learning, or spiral learning in confidence building. Furthermore, several CEFR-informed resources are provided for learners to scaffold their learning appropriately. These resources also provide helpful hints for teachers to apply a reflective type of learning based on the CEFR.

In this chapter we first outline the general context on matters such as textbook use in language education in Japan, and the background of the textbook. We then explain the practices that the textbook tasks implement, before situating the results of the research project in terms of the key questions of this volume. The conclusion outlines implications for future development of CEFR-informed textbooks in Japan and beyond.

2 Textbooks in Japan and the CEFR

There are often a large number of students in language learning classes in universities in Japan (many institutions typically have 30 to 40 learners in a class), and some teachers have a lot of classes to teach. Textbooks are an indispensable tool for the reduction of teachers' workloads. Some of the reasons why learners favour the use of textbooks include that they provide a structure, and, importantly for the Japan context which we feel has a heavy focus on testing, they facilitate test preparation. CEFR-informed textbooks are still not common, and we observed that use of the CEFR often involves merely placing 'Can Do' descriptors at the beginning of units, without any real engagement with the tools of the CEFR such as the illustrative scales, and related principles such as contextualised learning aimed to assess and reflect in terms of progression on these scales.

In recent years, it has become apparent that clear goals and assessments, in the form of 'Can Do' lists and related curricula, are required to connect junior high school, senior high school, and university-level education in Japan. The need for syllabuses and learning materials based on concrete action-oriented language achievement goals and performance assessment inspired by the CEFR for all levels of education has been a prescient topic since the Ministry of Education, Culture, Sports, Science and Technology (MEXT) published the *Five Proposals and Specific Measures for Developing Proficiency in English for International Communication* (Ministry of Education, Culture, Sports, Science and Technology 2011) and promoted the learner achievement goals in the form of 'Can Do' lists in secondary education (see section 2 of Chapter 3 in this volume).

There is a great need for the dissemination of specific CEFR-informed ideas and resources for educators to bring into the classroom. With the contextualisation of the CEFR for the Japanese context (CEFR-J, see Tono 2013, Tono and Negishi 2012, and section 2.1 of Chapter 2), and accompanying resources, there are encouraging signs of the use of language achievement levels in the form of 'Can Do' lists that are contextualised to the Japanese context, along with continuing development of exemplar practices in relation to the use of 'Can Do' lists. However, such practice stops at arranging and creating 'Can Do' lists for the materials in question. While know-how has accumulated regarding the use of 'Can Do' lists etc., we cannot say that existing textbooks and materials reflect this know-how. The majority of textbooks only show their levels in relation to the CEFR and do not take responsibility for the establishment of learning goals and related pedagogical practices. Materials from international publishers are also informed by the CEFR, but generally just display a 'Can Do' list. There is a need to develop know-how to implement these tools in the classroom. Furthermore we suggest that the practices and principles that encourage teacher and learner autonomy, which is one of the principles in the CEFR and can be found in the form of the ELP, need to be more prominent in learning materials. These were some of the ideas that guided the textbook project. We now outline the basic structure of the textbook.

2.1 Aim and structure of the book

Connections (Naganuma et al 2015) has five chapters (Technology, Health, Economics, Environment, and Learning) and students will learn related themes on a particular social issue across three units in each chapter, which allows them to acquire a deeper understanding of the issue from multiple perspectives. This textbook targets Level B1 learners (A2+ with scaffolding) with the goal to help them achieve B1+.

In Unit 1 of each chapter, learners read a main academic text analytically with a graphic chart (with learners scaffolding through the use of a parallel text in the level below: A2+) and explain the ideas in the text through oral reproduction as a basis for spontaneous speaking. Contextualised 'Delivery' and 'Organization' scales – based on the 'Spoken Fluency' scale (Council of Europe 2001:129) and that for 'Addressing Audiences' (Council of Europe 2001:60) – are provided for peer- and self-assessment. For homework, learners draw a graphic chart to summarise a short passage related to the main text. Groups of three choose different texts so that they have different information to provide opportunity for information-gap activities and independently draw a chart as a homework assignment.

In the beginning of Unit 2 of each chapter, groups conduct a summary presentation based on the graphic chart prepared at home. The 'Delivery' and 'Organization' scales are again used for peer- and self-assessments. Learners then listen to a main academic talk analytically by creating questions for confirmation (literal and inferential) and opinions, and a summary of the talk as a basis for spontaneous writing (short to extended summary). Further scaffolding, such as a parallel audio track in the level below (A2+) is provided in the appendix at the end of each chapter. For homework, based on the given prompt related to the contents learned in Unit 1 and 2, learners write an essay after organising the ideas and opinions from different perspectives summarised in a table. They can also look at the supplementary texts for further information when writing their essay. 'Descriptive' and 'Argumentative' scales based on the CEFR (Council of Europe 2001:59) are provided for self-assessments. Model essays with annotations in writing level-appropriate to A2+, B1 and B1+ are provided to show the process of writing development. Learners can analyse criterial features that distinguish writings at each level and take notes on the expressions and discourse flow (e.g. use of discourse markers) from the models they can use in their own essay.

In Unit 3 of each chapter, with an integrated understanding of the contents they have learned through Unit 1 and 2, learners organise information and exchange ideas based on their essays, and finally give a presentation using a graphic chart created collaboratively in a group. The 'Delivery' and 'Organization' scales are again contextualised and used for peer- and self-assessments. Learners are encouraged to give comments to each other and write a reflection note for further learning. For homework, learners revise and develop the essay written previously, based on the discussions in the group in class. The 'Descriptive' and 'Argumentative' scales are again used for self-assessments. Learners can use model essays in A2+, B1 and B1+ as their reference.

In the next section we discuss the use of the resources provided in the book. We first start with the design process of the textbook, and the implications for individuals who would like to develop CEFR-informed materials.

3 The processes of designing a CEFR-Informed textbook

With the purpose of developing a contextualised text for the Japanese higher education classroom, we analysed recent CEFR-informed textbooks from international publishers, for example *English Unlimited* (Cambridge University Press), *New Cutting Edge* (Pearson Longman), *New Headway* (Oxford University Press) and *Straightforward* (Macmillan). There was an emphasis on performance-based language learning tasks, and comparing these with the proficiency descriptors of the CEFR. We also looked at the preparation of instructional materials supplementary to textbooks, and other additional resources, along with language portfolios that can be used to foster an environment that encourages learner and teacher autonomy. We anticipated that the text will be suitable for English language classes at the university level, so we correlated this with the current *A Guide to Setting Criteria and Improving Evaluation Methods for Foreign Language in Upper Secondary Schools* (Ministry of Education, Culture, Sports, Science and Technology 2012) implemented in 2013. Keeping these study guidelines in mind, we saw that there was a need for a 4-skills integrated textbook written in English. In light of current learner achievement levels and social needs in Japan, the text aimed for a progression from Level B1 to B1+. However as a remedial measure, we developed resources that facilitate learning progression from A2+ to B1. While the learning content aimed at A2 and B1 is typically less academic and more related to everyday topics, this EAP textbook provides level-appropriate academic content on familiar social issues for tertiary level education.

By using the Common European Framework of Reference for Languages: level estimation grid for teachers (CEF-ESTIM) Grid (European Centre for Modern Languages 2011) which helps us identify level-specific tasks and texts, and by analysing the CEFR learner proficiency descriptors and illustrated scales for texts and tasks, we established relevant basic content and tasks for the textbook. We specified the wordlists and grammar items relevant for the textbook by analysing the language level descriptions and wordlists from the CEFR T-series (van Ek and Trim 1991a, 1991b, 2001), the British Council Core Inventory (North, Ortega and Sheehan 2010), the English Vocabulary and Grammar Profiles (see Hawkins and Filipović 2012), and the CEFR-J wordlist (based on an analysis of major English textbooks in Asian regions, see Tono 2013). By analysing exemplar practices in classrooms using teaching materials used in CEFR-informed curricula, we suggested possible measures that should be incorporated into the textbook. We also examined challenges when implementing the CEFR in Japanese university classes. A needs survey of English language educators in universities in Japan investigated the possibility of the acceptance of CEFR-informed texts and other matters, including the scope of current classroom practices. The general results of the survey were that many teachers were interested in implementing the CEFR in their classroom, but they were not happy about current provisions in popular textbooks in Japan. Another common viewpoint was that teachers did not feel comfortable with, or have the relevant experience for, guiding learners through the illustrative scales of the CEFR, and reflective practices encouraged by the CEFR and ELP. Our principal interpretation of the survey results was that there is a need for a textbook that provides guidance to both teachers and learners in these aspects.

In order to supplement classroom learning, we developed learner resources that meet the needs of learner self-study, and ELP-type practices to promote learner autonomy through setting learning targets and assessing progress. This is a very important element of the textbook, and we will now detail how action-oriented, suitably scaffolded materials include reflective learning, with 'Can Do' descriptors at the centre of the above learning procedures (e.g. goal setting and reflection).

Resources for scaffolding at the end of each unit include chunk-based reading, adjusted for three levels (A2+, B1, and B2). Vocabulary appropriate for Level B2 and higher is highlighted in bold, and paraphrased or given meanings in the glossary (see Figure 1). Both reading and listening texts are chunked with slashes (double slashes at the end of sentence) in sense groups and also formatted to be used in timed reading. Listening scripts and parallel main reading and listening texts in the lower level (A2+) are also provided. See Figure 2 for an example, which shows adjusted content of the text in Figure 1 at a level appropriate for A2+. Sentence structures in B1 and beyond are modified with A2 grammar, showing the major changes in grey highlight at both levels (see A, B and C in Figure 1 and 2) and the rewriting processes step by step. Other scaffolding tasks include a graphic organiser task (learners present a graphic organiser based on a text like Figure 1), and an extended summary task (again based on text like Figure 1). Audio files are recorded in natural and chunked slower voices in reading and listening. Most of the files are found in the CD except parallel (A2) chunked tracks, which are available online[1].

Each chapter ends with self-assessment checklists. Learners can use these checklists to review what they have learned, and have become able to do, in each task in the form of 'Can Do' descriptors. The self-assessment checklists provided in this textbook are modified from the CEFR illustrative scales. Learners can assess their progress and set goals for the next chapter. They can reflect on learning by both thinking about what they 'Can Do' (confidently with ease or under normal circumstances) and setting goals (primary or secondary goal) by double or single checking the boxes. Learners are recommended to leave a reflective comment for critical review of their learning. These checklists are central to the reflective-type learning suggested in Figure 3. The grey highlights show key action in the activities.

The lexical and grammatical items listed in grammar-processing scaffolding are selected based on the publication *Criterial Features in L2 English* by Hawkins and Filipović (2012). They analysed the Cambridge Learner Corpus and propose lexical and grammatical criterial features from A2 through to C2. Because this corpus data is based on written production data, it may not be appropriate for receptive activities such as reading and listening. However, they are used as one of the guiding materials to adjust the level of reading texts as well as the listening manuscripts in the textbook.

---

1   text.asahipress.com/free/English

Figure 1 Chunk-based reading text example

Chapter 1 Unit 1 Task 2: Chunk-based reading text (B1)

Various **concerns** / with social networking / are **voiced vigorously** these days. // Students spend more time / reading "tweets" and Facebook "**statuses**" / than doing their homework. // A) They seem to care more about / what their friends' friends are doing / than to update themselves on the latest **current events** / or jogging for 30 minutes. // Social networking seems to make / people's minds **numb**. // Is this good for us? // Is this a **destruction** / of our creative and private lives? // Not quite. // In fact there are as many good points as bad points / to social networking. // First of all, / social networking **promotes** communication / among friends as well as family. // Not all family members / live together. // The child who studies abroad / can talk with his/her parents with Skype / as if they were living together. // Grandparents and grandchildren communicate easily / even if they live far apart. // Not all people are good / at communicating in person. // People who are shy and have difficulty / in talking face to face / may feel more at ease and more comfortable /when communicating through the internet. // Social networking helps us communicate more / and **reinforce** our relationships. // Social networking also **unites** people / with common interests and opinions. // They can **collaborate** / and **enrich** their personal lives. // Some people may form a group / to talk about works by famous architects / and plan a short trip to visit buildings / designed by them. // Social networking makes it easy / to communicate as well. // Social networking makes it possible / for people in different countries and regions / to exchange their ideas, values and cultures. // People can share their experiences / and **deepen** their understanding of different cultures. //
B) Without social networking / society today would seem to have difficulty in functioning. //
Most workplaces heavily depend on social networking. // C) Workers are expected / to be **competent** with computer **literacy** / and to use various networking sites / to gain **relevant** and necessary information. // Social networking makes our life / simpler and more satisfying. /Despite the **defects** of social networking, / social media will not stop growing, / and will continue to have a great impact on our lives. //

Glossary – Words beyond B1 or equivalent level

*concern: fear *voice (v): say *vigorously : actively *status: current news (which Facebook users post on their account for others to see) *current: present *numb: unable to work well *destruction: to destroy something *promote: support, help *reinforce: increase *unite: put together *collaborate: work together *enrich: improve *deepen: develop *function: work *competent: clever *literacy: knowledge *relevant: useful *defect: bad point

The lexical and grammatical items listed in the step-by-step guidelines of grammar processing for scaffolding from A2 to B1 in the textbook are classified into six categories: sentence length, verb argument structure, sentence structure, adverbial clause, noun modification and others. According to Hawkins and Filipović (2012) the average length of utterance at the B1 level is 10.8 words. Note that sentences in reading texts can be longer than utterances at B1, but this norm is used as one of the guiding principles to evaluate sentences in reading texts concerning whether or not they are appropriate for target learners. Some lexical and grammatical features which are not listed in

Figure 2 Parallel main reading text, which adjusts the content of the text in Figure 1 at a level appropriate for A2+

> Chapter 1 Unit 1 Task 2: Parallel reading text (A2+)
>
> Today people worry about Social Networking very much. Students spend more time reading "tweets" and Facebook "statuses" than doing their homework. A) They care more about their friends' daily activities than their own. Social networking makes people's minds numb.
>
> Is this good for us? Is this a destruction of our creative and private lives? Not quite. Social Networking has many good points, too. First of all, social networking helps communication among friends and family members. Not all family members live together. The child who studies abroad can talk with his or her parents with Skype every day. Grandparents and grandchildren communicate easily even if they live far apart. Not all people are good at communicating in person. Some people are shy and afraid of talking face to face. They may find it easier to communicate through the internet. Social networking helps our communication and strengthens our relationships.
>
> Social networking also links people with common interests and opinions. We can work together and improve our personal lives. Some people may form a group to talk about works by famous architects. They may plan a short trip to visit buildings designed by the architects. Social networking also makes it easy to communicate. People in different countries can exchange their ideas and cultures easily through social networking sites. People can share their experiences and understand different cultures more deeply.
>
> B) Today society does not work well without social networking. Most workplaces heavily depend on social networking. C) Workers need to have good computer skills because they have to get important information from various social networking sites. Our lives are becoming simpler and more satisfying thanks to social networking. Despite the bad points, social media will grow and continue to affect our lives.

Hawkins and Filipović (2012) are also included. They have similar grammatical patterns and functions to those listed as B1. For instance, adverbial subordinate clauses with '-ing' that precede the clause to which they are attached is NOT listed as a B1 criterial feature although a very similar construction, adverbial subordinate clauses with '-ing' that follow the clause to which they are attached, is listed as a B1 criterial feature. Consequently, both constructions are listed as B1. Constructions such as passive clauses and most types of the relative clauses are not listed as criterial features by Hawkins and Filipović (2012) but they are listed simply because our target learners may not be able to process them with ease.

Most of the sentences treated in the grammar-processing scaffolding include more than one grammatical feature. Each grammatical feature in a sentence is listed in the order that appears when reading from left to right. Or a local grammatical feature precedes a global grammatical feature which covers the entire sentence, for instance a word order change. Some examples of the lexical and grammatical features listed in the scaffolding are presented in Figure 4 (the changes are shown in italics at both levels).

Applying the CEFR to English for Academic Purposes textbooks

Figure 3 Task-based self-assessment checklist

Unit 1	What is good about Social Networking?	
can-do		goal
☐☐	B1: Can take notes as a list of key points following a straightforward conversation about the problems of social networking, if speech is clear. [U1T1: Listening to Conversation] Ⓛ	☐☐
☐☐	B1: Can guess the meaning of occasional unknown words from the context and deduce sentence meaning, if the topic discussed is familiar. [U1T1: Guessing Words in Context] Ⓡ	☐☐
☐☐	B2: Can understand articles concerned with social networking in which the writers adopt particular stances or viewpoints. [U1T2: Reading Article] Ⓡ	☐☐
☐☐	B1: Can draw graphic organizer to illustrate the line of the argument in the issue presented and the main conclusion of the article, if arguments and the conclusion are clearly signaled in the text. [U1T3/U1HW: Graphic Organizer Reading] Ⓡ	☐☐
☐☐	B1: Can give a prepared straightforward presentation on social networking, which states some concerns and positive aspects of social networking. [U1T4: Graphic Organizer Reproduction] Ⓢ	☐☐

Reflective comments:

85

Figure 4 Grammar-processing scaffolding

Grammar Processing for Scaffolding	
A. Subject-to-subject raising + Relative clause + Sentence length	
B1	A2
Step 1 They *seem to care* more about what their friends' friends are doing than to update themselves on the latest current events or jogging for 30 minutes.	**Step 1** They *care* more about their friends' daily activities than *their own*.
Step 2 They seem to care more about *what their friends' friends are doing* than to update themselves on the latest current events or jogging for 30 minutes.	**Step 2** They care more about *their friends' daily activities* than their own.
Step 3 They seem to care more about what their friends' friends are doing than *to update themselves on the latest current events or jogging for 30 minutes.*	**Step 3** They *care* more about their friends' daily activities than *their own*.
B. Subject-to-subject raising + Word order	
B1	A2
Step 1 Without social networking society today would *seem to have* difficulty in functioning.	**Step 1** Today society *does not work* well without social networking.
Step 2 *Without social networking* society *today* would seem to have difficulty in functioning.	**Step 2** *Today* society does not work well *without social networking.*
C. Subject-to-Object raising + passive	
B1	A2
Step 1 Workers *are expected to be competent* with computer literacy and *to use various networking sites* to gain relevant and necessary information.	**Step 1** Workers *need to have good computer skills* because they *have to get important information from various social networking sites.*
Step 2 Workers are expected to be competent with computer literacy and *to use various networking sites to gain relevant and necessary information.*	**Step 2** Workers need to have good computer skills *because they have to get important information from various social networking sites.*

Using this type of scaffolding, learners can compare a B1 level sentence with its paraphrased sentence at the A2 level. Through such a task learners are expected to become aware of the lexical and grammatical items they should learn at the B1 level. Furthermore, the observation of the sentences for the two different levels may raise learners' awareness of grammatical features suitable for each level and help them to establish their writing from A2 to B1 and higher levels.

As noted above learners produce an essay after Units 2 and 3. They can also look at the supplementary texts when writing an essay. The 'Descriptive' and 'Argumentative' scales in the CEFR (Council of Europe 2001) are provided for self-assessment (see Figure 5). The grey highlights show key actions and the underlines show key features.

Model essays (Figure 6) in A2+, B1, and B1+ are given to show the process of writing development. Learners can analyse criterial features that distinguish writings at each level and take notes on the expressions and discourse flow (e.g. discourse markers) they can use in their own essay. Please note that the expressions used in the model essays especially in A2+ may be above the target level as a result of the encouragement of borrowing and applying key ideas and useful expressions from the main and supplementary texts.

We aimed to develop materials that supplement classroom activities and facilitate learners working towards individual goals at their own pace. As such CEFR-informed materials are not so prevalent, these will also be a great resource for teachers, and promote teacher autonomy. The reflective learning approach suggested by the Language Portfolio (LP) of this textbook allows teachers and learners to plan for, reflect on and record progress in learning activities. This approach is in line with the ideas of the European Language Portfolio. The LP is downloadable online[2]. This type of LP was designed to be a tool to implement the CEFR in the classroom and beyond.

The LP is designed to be used alongside the tasks of the textbook to encourage learners to use 'Can Do' descriptors in self-assessment, goal setting and reflection. In general, the learning practices suggested by the LP promote a cyclical type of learning: learners are encouraged to see progress throughout the course by using their thoughts on reflections after tasks and chapters to inform goals and directions for future learning.

---

[2] text.asahipress.com/free/English

Assessment of CEFR-informed Language Teaching in Japan and Beyond

Figure 5 The 'Descriptive' and 'Argumentative' scales in the CEFR are provided for self-assessment

Description Scale（描写）[WRITING]

B2 Can write clear, detailed descriptions of events and experiences indicating the relationship between ideas in clear connected text. / Can write clear, detailed descriptions on a variety of subjects related to a specific field of interest.
B1 Can write about experiences, describing feelings and reactions in simple connected text. / Can write straightforward, detailed descriptions on a range of familiar subjects.
A2 Can write very short, basic descriptions of events, past activities and personal experiences.

Argument Scale（論述）[WRITING]

B2 Can write an essay that develops an argument systematically with appropriate highlighting of some significant points and relevant supporting detail. / Can evaluate different ideas or solutions to a problem. / Can write an essay which develops an argument, giving some reasons in support of or against a particular point of view and explaining the advantages and disadvantages of various options. / Can synthesize information and arguments from a number of sources.
B1 Can write short, simple essays on topics of interest. / Can summarize texts and give an opinion about accumulated factual information on familiar matters with some confidence. / Can write about familiar topics, comparing and contrasting different opinions.

Adapted figure based on descriptors from page 62 of the Common European Framework of Reference for Languages: Learning, Teaching, Assessment by the Council of Europe. © Council of Europe. Reproduced by permission.

Learners can first use the LP for initial self-assessment. Based on this self-assessment, they can set goals for both the whole textbook/course, and chapter 1. The next part can be used to start cyclical learning. For example, based on initial self-assessment, learners can set goals for chapter 1. After performing chapter 1 tasks, learners can reflect on how well they have achieved their goals for chapter 1. Based on this reflection learners can then self-assess and set goals for chapter 2, using the 'My next language learning target' sheet from the LP. As chapter 1, chapter 2 and the other chapters involve similar tasks and 'Can Do' descriptors, learners can use this learning cycle to gradually improve in language learning. In this way, learners can be encouraged to develop self-efficacy.

The 'My next language learning target' is first used for goal setting at the beginning of a chapter. When the chapter has been finished the learners can use hints in the final section of the sheet ('Review of learning progress on or near my target date') or a separate page to evaluate how well they have carried out the tasks involved in terms of the 'Can Do' descriptors. They should note the things they have done well and the things they could improve upon. Other learners and the teacher may give advice as to how these improvement points can be incorporated into upcoming learning stages. Learners could also be advised to make personal learning goals as a result. By using the LP learners can take action, step by step, in creating, planning, and working towards goals related to the textbook tasks and 'Can Do' descriptors. It is hoped that by working through this learning cycle, learners can get into the habit

Figure 6 Excerpts of model essays

Chapter 1 Unit 3 Homework: Essay writing

Please revise your essay based on your presentation.

For you, and people close to you, what are the most relevant and important positive and negative points of social networking? Please include possible solutions to overcome the demerits of social networking.

Model Essay: A2+ (158 words)

We should use SNS for the good points they offer. The most positive point of Social Networking Sites (SNS) for me is talking with people. I can talk with friends who live far away on Facebook etc. I can also make friends with people who are interested in the same thing. For example, I can join a Haruki Murakami group, and talk about his books. SNS are good because we can meet interesting people, who you cannot meet in normal life.

However, I spend time on SNS, rather than studying or working. It is useful to make a list of important things, and do them first. Then if we have time, we can use SNS. People can say bad things about people. If you would not say it face-to-face, don't write it on SNS. Some people also use SNS too much, and don't meet people. SNS is a good way to relax, but remember to take a break!

Model Essay: B1 (296 words)

We should use SNS for the good points they offer. The most positive points of Social Networking Sites (SNS) for me are connecting with friends and people with common interests. I cannot see my friends everyday but I can talk with them on Facebook and other sites. I can connect to their daily lives, even if they live far away. We can also make connections with people who have common interests. For example, my favorite writer is Haruki Murakami. I can join a group interested in this writer, and talk about his books. I don't have this opportunity in my work or home, so SNS gives me new opportunities.

For me and people around me SNS is time-wasting and creates poor communication. Using SNS can also waste time, and we don't manage to do some important things in our lives. Sometimes I choose to spend time on SNS, rather than thinking about more important things like study and work. A good thing to do is to make a list of important things, and do them first. Then if we have time, we can use SNS. If you have time games can be fun. But be careful not to waste too much time!

People can also forget normal communication rules, and say bad things about people online. This leads to people killing themselves in some cases. We have to be careful what we say on SNS. A good rule is to think 'would I say this face-to-face?'. If the answer is no, then maybe you shouldn't write such things on SNS. Some people use SNS too often, and meet people face to face less. SNS is a good way to relax, but remember to take a break! We should turn off our phones, and talk with people around us.

of reflecting upon their learning, and thinking about and working towards achieving the steps for their next goal.

The steps in the learning cycle are briefly described in Figure 7, in terms of the procedures learners may undertake.

The learners can use the dossier to keep a sample of their learning from the textbook and elsewhere. This can be used as proof of learning and learning progress. The learners can be encouraged to continue to use the LP after the textbook by providing a link to the LP for Japanese University[3].

4 Discussion

This project set out to design a textbook with activities which include transparent and concrete learning objectives informed by accepted 'Can Do' descriptors, using reflective learning in which self-assessment plays a central role. The result of the project, the textbook, was aimed to be a first step to achieving this goal. This is an iterative process, and we feel that the textbook can provide useful hints for others who wish to create similar learning materials.

One of the key questions for classroom instruction (are the CEFR-based materials – textbooks, teaching content etc. – action-oriented, and easily applicable by both teachers and students? How?) is an important issue. One teacher commented:

> As there is plenty of scaffolding for both the teacher and learner, we feel it is easily applicable for the teacher. The textbook provides various listening and reading supplements to initiate and stimulate classroom activities step by step. For instance, learners first read short articles which describe either positive or negative aspects of an issue and then commit themselves in considering the issue deeply from both sides. Next they present their own ideas and opinions in a group and discuss them. Finally they write up an essay about the issue. Tasks assigned to learners in each step help them engage in these productive activities.

Many educators do not have the resources to create CEFR-informed learning resources outlined in the previous section. These resources also provide helpful hints for teachers to apply a reflective type of learning based on the CEFR. This is something that teachers will typically struggle with if faced with doing this alone. Furthermore, there are not many textbooks that present such detailed, CEFR-informed language resources. This in turn facilitates the teaching of lessons that are suitably scaffolded for learners. This also relates to the key question: Do 'Can Do' checklists serve as the key reference point for processes of reflective learning in which self-assessment plays a central role? How? The materials are clearly mapped to relevant 'Can Do' descriptors and illustrative scales of the CEFR, with relevant resources and reflective learning activities that promote cyclical learning, with peer- and self-assessment practices throughout. As a result, it becomes more possible that all can readily see the benefits of the CEFR-based approach for their own teaching/learning. Once learners become accustomed to working in a

---

3   sites.google.com/site/flpsig/flp-sig-home/language-portfolio-for-japanese-university

Applying the CEFR to English for Academic Purposes textbooks

Figure 7 A learning cycle, as applied to the textbook

Step 1: Self-assessment (beginning text repeated from section 3)

The following self-assessment and goal-setting checklists can be used for self-assessment as well as for setting the goals for the whole course and each chapter. For example, based on initial self-assessment, learners can set goals for chapter 1. After performing chapter 1 tasks, learners can reflect on how well they have achieved their goals for chapter 1. Based on this reflection learners can then self-assess and set goals for chapter 2. As chapter 1, chapter 2 and the other chapters involve similar tasks and 'Can Do' descriptors learners can use this learning cycle to gradually improve in language learning. The self-assessment and goal-setting checklists are general in nature, the 'Can Do' lists for each chapter are related to the content of the chapter in question.

Learners can check their self-assessment according to their criteria (*, ** or ***). They can also set this as a goal (e.g. ** to ***), and record progress.

Decide what evaluative criteria you want to use, and enter dates to set goals, and record progress.

Language biography

The language biography enables the owner to set intermediate learning goals, review progress, and record significant language learning and intercultural experiences.

Unlike the language passport, which you should update once or twice a year, the language biography is designed to accompany your language learning from day to day, unit by unit. You will probably need to use the "My next language learning target" sheet more than once so it is suggested to keep the originals in a safe place and make copies as necessary.

Step 2: Setting for goals for the each chapter

You can now set goals for chapter 1, based on your self-assessment.

Step 3: Reflecting on your progress, and thinking about future learning

After performing chapter 1 tasks, reflect on how well they have achieved their goals for chapter 1. Please try to see gradual improvement in learning. Use the following questions:

Step 2: Setting for goals for the each chapter

Based on your reflection for chapter 1, self-assess and set goals for chapter 2. You can repeat steps 2–4 for each chapter (and other learning you do elsewhere!).

Step 3: Reflecting on your progress, and thinking about future learning

Step 4 Record work: Dossier

---

reflective, forward-looking manner, they may begin to become more autonomous learners.

A wider issue is presented in this key question: can the people engaging in CEFR-based teaching and learning develop a sense of ownership? How? The textbook was created on the premise that the 'Can Do' descriptors of the CEFR are unwieldy if not contextualised effectively. The teachers and learners are encouraged to engage with the 'Can Do' descriptors (and the general principles of the CEFR and ELP), by contextualising the 'Can Do' descriptors for individual classes and learners. In this way, they may develop a sense of ownership of the practices. The second element of the former key question (Is it possible to compare the results of instruction in different classes?) is also relevant at the tertiary level, where in many cases individual teachers work alone, with little co-ordination between classes. There is little relationship between what learners undertake in a first year class and second year class, for example. There is also the issue of lack of links between what is learned at high school and university. Scaffolded, CEFR-informed curricula could be one solution, and this textbook provides a logical step from high school to university, and more critical thinking in the tertiary level.

5 Conclusion

The six levels of the CEFR, and the 'Can Do' descriptors, are now familiar to many in language education in Japan and beyond. It is important to realise that the levels and 'Can Do' descriptors are descriptive, and should not be applied in a prescriptive way. They provide the means by which to estimate ability, thus providing a starting point and direction for future learning. This textbook was a first step in trying to foreground this idea in general language education circles. It is key for learners to effectively contextualise the scales of the CEFR through learning: to elaborate and develop the CEFR levels and 'Can Do' descriptors in ways that are suitable for them. One purpose of this textbook is to encourage learners to see how 'Can Do' descriptors can be used in self-assessment, goal setting and reflection of level-appropriate learning goals. The tasks and assessment tools were created so learning can be appropriately scaffolded, with goals suitable for the current level of the student (even in a class of several different levels of proficiency).

The focus is to use the CEFR for action-oriented learning. There are several language-centric resources in and around this textbook, but the purpose of these materials is to create level-appropriate learning materials informed by the CEFR levels and scales. The important step is to encourage learners to use the scales of the CEFR in action-oriented learning. For example learners can be asked to judge, and provide reasons, in e.g. writing if the main points 'are explained in detail, with precision' (Council of Europe 2001:78). Once aware of what is expected, the learners can take action, step by step. By creating, planning, and working towards the goals of writing 'with precision', learners have to work out for themselves how the action of writing precisely is performed, and then work towards efficiently writing in this way, step by step. Focusing on language features is one part of this action, but focus on language alone will not be sufficient. The learning outcome of writing with precision will only be successfully achieved by carefully focusing on the development of ideas through language. Here one important goal of the CEFR is realised: the beginning of learner autonomy and lifelong learning. The learners see the logical steps to aim for next, and work towards achieving these steps.

We hope that this textbook – in a small, humble way – can help learners navigate the lofty goals the CEFR has set for language learners and educators. Furthermore, the processes followed in creating the textbook – needs analysis, gathering examples of classroom practices, contextualising the illustrative scales of the CEFR and incorporating them into a reflective learning cycle that is based around chapters that incorporate tasks on similar skills for different topics – can be further developed by writers in other CEFR-informed materials.

Acknowledgements

This work was supported by a Kakenhi Grant-in-Aid for Scientific Research (24520611) from the Japan Society for the Promotion of Science, and co-ordinated by members of the Japan Association for Language Teaching (JALT) Framework and Language Portfolio Special Interest Group (FLP SIG).

References

Council of Europe (2001) *Common European Framework of Reference for Languages: Learning, Teaching, Assessment*, Cambridge: Cambridge University Press.

European Centre for Modern Languages (2011) *CEF-ESTIM Grid*, Graz: European Centre for Modern Languages, available online: www.ecml.at/tabid/277/PublicationID/74/Default.asp

Hawkins, J A and Filipović, L (2012) *Criterial Features in L2 English: Specifying the Reference Levels of the Common European Framework*, English Profile Studies volume 1, Cambridge: UCLES/Cambridge University Press.

Ministry of Education, Culture, Sports, Science and Technology (2011) *Kokusai kyotsugo to shite no eigoryoku kojo no tame no itsutsu no teigen [Five Proposals and Specific Measures for Developing Proficiency in English for International Communication]*, available online: www.mext.go.jp/component/b_menu/shingi/toushin/__icsFiles/afieldfile/2011/07/13/1308401_1.pdf

Ministry of Education, Culture, Sports, Science and Technology (2012) *Hyoka kijun no sakusei, hyoka hoho nado no kufu kaizen no tame no sanko shiryo (koto gakko gaikokugo) [A Guide to Setting Criteria and Improving Evaluation Methods for Foreign Language in Upper Secondary Schools]*, Tokyo: Kyoiku Shuppan.

Naganuma, N, Nagai, N and O'Dwyer, F (2015) *Connections to Thinking in English: The CEFR-informed Textbook Series A2+/B1 to B1+*, Tokyo: Asahi Press.

North, B, Ortega, A and Sheehan, S (2010) *British Council – EAQUALS Core Inventory for General English*, available online: www.teachingenglish.org.uk/sites/teacheng/files/Z243%20E&E%20EQUALS%20BROCHURErevised6.pdf

Tono, Y (2013) *CAN-DO risto sakusei katsuyou Eigo toutatsu shihyou CEFR-J gaidobukku* [*The CEFR-J Handbook, A Resource Book for using CAN-DO descriptors for English Language Teaching*], Tokyo: Taishukan.

Tono, Y and Negishi, M (2012) The CEFR-J: Adapting the CEFR for English language teaching in Japan, *Framework & Language Portfolio (FLP) SIG Newsletter* 8, 5–12, available online: dl.dropboxusercontent.com/u/33808898/FLP%20SIG%20NL%208%20Sep2012%20CEFR-J.pdf

van Ek, J A and Trim, J L M (1991a) *Threshold 1990*, Cambridge: Cambridge University Press.

van Ek, J A and Trim, J L M (1991b) *Waystage 1990*, Cambridge: Cambridge University Press.

van Ek, J A and Trim, J L M (2001) *Vantage*, Cambridge: Cambridge University Press.

Section 3
Curriculum reform

6 Applying the CEFR to renew a General English curriculum: Successes, remaining issues and lessons from Vietnam

Pham Thi Hong Nhung
Hue University of Foreign Languages

1 Introduction

Together with the implementation of the National Foreign Language Project for the period 2008–2020 (the 2020 Project for short), the Vietnamese government adopted the Common European Framework of Reference for Languages (CEFR, Council of Europe 2001) as the standard for language education reform policy 'to upgrade its workforce to an international competition level' (Ministry of Education and Training 2008:3). The decision of the Ministry of Education and Training (MOET) echoes the beliefs of many governments in the Asia-Pacific region (e.g. Japan, Malaysia, Korea, Taiwan, Thailand and China) in the value of adopting global language policies to enhance the quality of teaching and learning languages in their countries (Hu and McKay 2012, Nguyen and Hamid 2015). The adoption of the CEFR in the current Vietnamese educational context, which still constantly faces limited human capital and resources, has created a number of challenges in different areas, varying from language teacher professionalism, through curriculum and materials development to assessment. This chapter describes and reflects on the practices of a university in Vietnam teaching both foreign languages and international studies while in the process of applying the CEFR in a context where it has to both struggle with top-down language education policy and utilise the benefits of CEFR adoption for the sake of its own students and teachers. The reflection on and lessons learned from initial successes and remaining issues from this implementation both at institutional and classroom level may be useful to future practices of contextualising the CEFR within the institution as well as in other contexts in which a similar, under-researched application of the CEFR is imposed top-down.

2 Context

With the implementation of the national socio-economic reform policy in 1986 and the impact of globalisation on various social, economic, educational and cultural aspects of life, English has become the preferred foreign language at all educational levels in Vietnam (Le 2002, Nguyen 2011, Pham 2013, Wright 2002). However, for decades since the introduction of English into the educational curriculum in Vietnam, it has been widely recognised that a majority of English students still cannot communicate well in English after spending years learning it at school and even at university, although they may have accumulated a good knowledge of grammar and vocabulary (Ministry of Education and Training 2013b). In an effort to improve the quality of teaching and learning foreign languages, primarily English in the state-run educational system, the Vietnamese government launched a project named 'Teaching and learning foreign language in the state-run educational system for the 2008–2020 period' in 2008, which is now often referred to as the 2020 Project.

In terms of funding and scope, the 2020 Project has been considered the biggest project on foreign language education initiated by MOET. Central to the operation of the 2020 Project is the adoption of the CEFR (Council of Europe 2001) to set professional standards for both language teachers and for foreign language learning outcomes at all educational levels from primary to tertiary. By introducing a global policy such as the CEFR into a local context, the decision by MOET reflects the desire to use the CEFR as a 'quick fix' (Steiner-Khamsi 2004:58) to the currently low quality of English language teaching and learning within the state-run educational system. Language teachers in tertiary, secondary and primary schools are asked to achieve C2, C1 and B2 levels respectively. University graduates majoring in fields other than a foreign language are expected to achieve B1 level, and those whose major study is in languages are expected to achieve C1 level.

However, no activities or actions to apply the CEFR standards were implemented until the end of 2011 when the initial funding for the 2020 Project was made available. There has still been little official account or explanation from MOET on the adoption of the CEFR in the current reform policy of language education. Indeed information about previous research on applying the CEFR or its use in a pilot in the Vietnamese context remains very sparse (Pham 2012).

In 2010 MOET launched a pilot English language curriculum for primary school education for third to fifth graders (Ministry of Education and Training 2010), which it claimed will get primary school graduates to achieve CEFR Level A1. In 2013 MOET issued a number of documents to universities providing training to language teachers and courses in foreign languages to reinforce their active roles in innovating curricula, materials, teaching methodology and assessment practices in order to help university graduates to achieve the required standards outlined above (B1 for those who are not majoring in languages, B2 for those majoring in a foreign language, and C1 for language teachers) (Ministry of Education and Training 2013a). However, not until 24 January 2014 did MOET officially launch a national framework of reference called *Khung năng lực ngoại ngữ sáu bậc dành cho Việt Nam*, translated as *Six-level Framework for Foreign Language Proficiency in Vietnam* (Ministry of Education and Training 2014), which is in fact a translation of the original CEFR with limited modifications and adaptations.

Hue University College of Foreign Languages (HUFL) in Central Vietnam is one component of Hue University, which now has eight schools and colleges. HUFL has roughly 4,300 full-time students and 1,100 part-time students enrolled in degree-granting foreign language programmes. Nearly half of this student body is being trained to become teachers of a foreign language. Although HUFL has university degree programmes in English, Russian, French, Korean, Japanese and Chinese, more than half of the students are undertaking majors in English. The university has 308 full-time staff members, of whom roughly 50 teach English to students majoring in English. As a component of Hue University, HUFL also teaches English to roughly 17,000 students majoring in subjects other than foreign languages from other schools and colleges within Hue University. These students are enrolled full time in Hue University Medical School, College of Agriculture and Forestry, College of Economics, Law School, College of Sciences, Teacher Training College, Arts School and Tourism School.

Selected at the implementation of the 2020 Project to be one of the five foreign language institutes of excellence (Ministry of Education and Training 2011) authorised by MOET to take part in various re-training and assessment activities for in-service language teachers, HUFL is under pressure to innovate and renew, first and foremost, its curriculum, language teaching materials, and assessment practice to 'fit' into, and in with, the adopted CEFR policy standards. This includes renewing the English language curriculum not just for students majoring in English but also for a large number of non-English majors who are full-time students of other schools and colleges within Hue University. Under the implementation of the 2020 Project, these students are required by the new MOET policy to achieve CEFR Level B1 – the 'Threshold' level where language users are believed to be independent users of the language and have the ability to perform fundamental functions in the language – as a minimum English language proficiency, equivalent to level 3 in the *Six-level Framework for Foreign Language Proficiency in Vietnam*. In fact, in 2012, Hue University together with all its constituent schools and colleges issued an official document which clearly states that from 2017, all of its students not majoring in English must achieve at least B1 before their university graduation degree can be conferred. Given an average of four years at university (medical students take longer, usually from five to six years), this policy will apply to all non-English major students who entered Hue University from 2013.

Until 2015 Vietnamese high school graduates were required to take an entrance examination to secure a place at university. Those who chose not to major in English were not required to take an English test to enter; instead they undertook exams in subjects directly associated with the university programme they wanted to pursue. As a consequence, many have not focused on English studies in high school, and after enrolment in a university degree programme, non-English majors vary greatly in terms of their English language proficiency levels.

Over the last 10 years the academic profile of non-English major students at HUFL has shown that some students enrolled in some colleges often have a higher level of English proficiency and better English learning motivation than those enrolled in other colleges. Typical of the groups more able in English are students of Hue Medical School, of the College of Economics, of some programmes of Teacher Training College and of the School of Law, while students at Hue College of Sciences and Arts School often show much lower proficiency levels.

MOET maintains that each university degree programme in Vietnam must provide at least 140 credits. With each credit being equivalent to 15 teacher-led hours, the total number of contact hours is 2,100 for the whole programme. Seven of these 140 credits are given to foreign language learning, in most cases to English. However, these seven credits are distributed only over the first three semesters of university degree programmes, with the ratio of 2–2–3 with two credits (30 contact hours) in the first semester, two credits in the second semester and the last three credits (45 contact hours) in the third semester of an eight-semester university degree programme, spread, on average, over four years. After these 105 General English instruction hours, students may enter a 30-hour English for Specific Purposes (ESP) course, which is optional, depending on their programme and major.

It is estimated to take 400 contact hours of instruction to obtain the CEFR B1 level (North 2014:98). However, non-English major students in Vietnam, in general, and at Hue University, in particular, have only 105 contact hours to achieve B1 level between the time they enter university to the time they are expected to graduate.

Since 2011, HUFL has initiated activities to renew its curricula to meet MOET requirements for standard-based programmes. Among these curricula is the General English language curriculum for non-English major students, which has been amended to help students achieve the CEFR B1 level.

In a context in which the CEFR stands as a point of reference (Trim (Ed) 2001), its descriptors are neither language nor context specific (Hawkins and Filipović 2012, Little 2007). However, little research on the use of the CEFR

Applying the CEFR to renew a General English curriculum

in the Vietnamese context is available (Pham 2012, 2013, 2015), and the necessary budget and human resources required for effective application of the CEFR remain limited (Nguyen and Hamid 2015). The application of the CEFR to the new General English curriculum requiring non-English majors to achieve B1 has therefore produced tremendous challenges. The following section describes the procedure undertaken to implement this curriculum innovation.

3 Details of practices

In preparation for curriculum innovation, a 1-week workshop on the CEFR was organised for English language teachers of HUFL in September 2011 to help them understand the framework more clearly. Two international experts, sponsored by the 2020 Project, introduced the CEFR, its content, the context in which it was created and the reasons for its creation. Both the values and some of the documented limitations of the CEFR were also addressed in this intensive workshop. As reflected in the workshop evaluation sheets, the participants appreciated the information provided to them and had a clearer idea of the CEFR, its potential values as well as its limitations, helping them realise that the CEFR 'Can Do' descriptors can become useful suggestions for their curriculum. As shared by one HUFL teacher who participated in the workshop:

> Before this [the workshop] I did not know what the CEFR was. I felt like I was the king being naked yet thinking I was wearing something beautiful [the CEFR] because MOET said it was beautiful and valuable. Now I think I understand the CEFR has values and potential uses, especially in defining learning outcomes for my students.

However, because the CEFR is not language specific, there was concern that the CEFR 'Can Do' descriptors may not be directly relevant to English proficiency and English language acquisition may not take place in the order set out in the descriptors, nor in the 'Can Do' descriptors of the six CEFR levels. After the workshop, HUFL English language teachers were asked to elaborate on how they thought the CEFR could be useful to the English language curriculum for non-English majors. The doubt that remained was about the possibility of having non-English majors achieve B1 level within 105 contact hours.

In March 2012, HUFL organised two consecutive workshops on language teaching and English language materials development delivered by two experts from the UK. In these two workshops, the participants learned about English language curriculum design and the theory of designing a curriculum with clearly defined, measurable learning outcomes. Lectures were also given on criteria for evaluating and selecting engaging materials for language teaching. The teachers were then asked to make a comprehensive analysis of the then current curriculum and to work on modifying that curriculum using the backwards approach, linking the learning outcomes with the CEFR A1, A2 and B1 levels respectively. At this stage more teachers recognised the use of the CEFR because, as indicated in the reflections of a large number of the participants in their post-workshop report and evaluation sheets, they thought it was significant to have something to hold on to, to refer to and to assess whether their students can do particular things in English at a specific time after a duration of instruction.

However, as part of the development of the overall curriculum and then of individual unit descriptions, teachers found it difficult to describe different levels of language performance when they were asked to describe how they could measure those learning outcomes. A typical comment was that:

> The CEFR focuses too much on what language users can do, not on how well they can do it. I see "well", "clearly" again and again in the CEFR but it is not clear how well at B1 level is well and how well at B2 level is well. So when I describe the learning outcomes and how I measure them in my unit descriptions, it is not clear. I have to work on further detailed descriptions to help my students understand.

In addition, the teachers found it challenging to assign the CEFR A1–B1 scales appropriately to each semester, given that the entrance level of English proficiency of non-English majors varies greatly between students and that they have three blocks of instruction: 30 contact hours in each of semesters 1 and 2, and 45 contact hours in the third semester. The final decision was that after the first semester the students were expected to attain A1, after the second semester A2, and after the third semester B1. This was considered unrealistic in many cases as the study hours (105) are actually roughly a fourth of the recommended hours (400) (North 2014:98).

When the first draft of the renewed curriculum was ready, it was sent out to MOET specialists (who are not necessarily specialists in applying the CEFR): lecturers of five major universities of Vietnam, who have also taken part in the 2020 Project for external review and returned useful comments and questions, some of which are still challenging to HUFL teaching staff members. Among these are the comments that as the CEFR is not English specific there is little research to show that English language acquisition takes place in the order described across the proficiency levels in the CEFR. Others asked on what grounds the curriculum developers and writers of proficiency units or course descriptions use those descriptors to describe the learning outcomes equivalent to specific levels of proficiency. After the first draft was revised, it was approved in February 2013. Also a 'fast track' proficiency test was implemented to classify students into their appropriate levels of ability. Students attaining a B1 result are not asked to undertake the General English course but go straight to ESP courses if their programme contains any ESP courses. Students obtaining A1, A2 and below are placed in class at their level. Students can also choose to take all English courses across their first three semesters regardless of their fast track test results. The use of fast track proficiency tests is thought to be useful and to provide a solution to the prior variation in student proficiency within each class.

However, due to budget limitations and the very large number of students, it was decided that speaking would not be included in the test. Furthermore, blended learning with online resources was emphasised as a solution to help non-English major students increase the time available for self-study to make up the gap between the actual contact hours (105) of English instruction and the recommended number of hours (350–400) needed to achieve Level B1. The question remaining is that even if non-English major students successfully achieve Level B1 after the first three semesters, how would they be able to maintain this level of proficiency when they have very little or even no contact with English for two and a half more years? If they cannot maintain this level of proficiency by the time they graduate and enter the job market, then what is the significance of having them achieve this level of B1? It has been considered that if the students attain B1 level proficiency, the certificate should be valid for two years, and that the students should be given options to take the test again before the last semester of their programme. The option of providing further English courses has also been discussed.

When the curriculum was approved, HUFL teaching staff members started to identify materials which could be used as an English proficiency textbook series covering the A1–B1 levels. The focus was on the degree of alignment with the curriculum, i.e. with the CEFR A1–B1 levels, the cost-effectiveness of copyright authorisation and the online support for students from teachers that accompanies each series. One observation was that many English proficiency book series, including those which have been around for decades, now claim to be aligned with the CEFR and have been quickly re-labelled as suitable for levels from A1 to C1. *New Total English* by Pearson (Clare, Wilson and Cosgrove 2011), *Solutions* by Oxford University Press (Falla and Davies 2013), and *English Elements* by Hueber Verlag (Roth and Schmid-Burleson 2002) were shortlisted. Among these the *Solutions* series was the first choice, followed by *New Total English* and *English Elements* series. Due to budget constraints, HUFL decided to use the German-authored *English Elements*, the least expensive series, which also came with online support.

In 2013, HUFL started to use the new curriculum and the *English Elements* series for first year non-English major students entering the different schools and colleges of Hue University. These students will graduate in 2017 and be the first cohort expected to attain B1 level as a prerequisite to having their university graduation degree conferred.

Once in use, the textbook series received positive feedback from HUFL teachers and students. The most common compliment was paid to its online resources support. However, soon after the introduction of the new textbook series, HUFL also received complaints about the strong German orientation, cultural bias in the textbook series and the heavy instruction content to be covered in only 30 teacher-led hours. In a meeting at the end of the first semester of using this textbook one teacher said that although the new curriculum gave her a better sense of orientation for teaching, she and her colleagues felt like they had to 'run' (jump) from unit to unit and from section to section to cover the contents of the textbook and they did not feel like they were really *teaching* English. To respond to this complaint, HUFL encouraged its teaching staff to implement an action-reflection cycle (Burns 2010, Kemmis and McTaggart (Eds) 1988, McNiff and Whitehead 2006, 2010) to further explore the issues and how to improve their practice.

Kemmis and McTaggart (Eds) (1988) first introduced the action–reflection cycle in action research. This cycle involves four main stages: planning, action, observation and reflection, which can be summarised as follows:

- *Planning* involves identifying a problem or issue, developing a plan of action so as to bring about improvements in a specific area of the research context, considering what kind of investigation is possible within the realities and constraints of the situation and what potential improvements are possible.
- *Action* involves considering the plan carefully and implementing some deliberate interventions into the teaching situation that the teacher puts into action over an agreed period of time.
- *Observation* involves systematically observing the effects of the action and documenting the context, actions and opinions of those involved. This phase is to collect data and information relevant to the issue under investigation.
- *Reflection* involves reflecting on and evaluating the effects of the action or intervention in order to make sense of what has happened and to understand the issue under investigation more clearly.

This action–reflection cycle can be repeated to improve the situation even more.

In various meetings, teachers teaching English to non-English major students were asked to observe, identify and reflect on the problems they face while implementing the new curriculum and using a new textbook series.

- *Planning* involves the teachers asking themselves what problems they have with the textbook and with the curriculum alignment with the

CEFR, what they are happy and unhappy with in using the new curriculum and textbook series, and what they plan to do to solve the problems and improve their teaching.
- *Action* is where the teachers are encouraged to take action to implement some modifications in their teaching, to spend more time on skills and sections in the textbooks which they think are more important to students rather than paying equal attention and time to every part and activity provided in the textbook.
- In *observation*, the teachers are asked to observe the effect of their actions, the responses of their students to their teaching, to collect more systematic data and information about their intervention and modified teaching.
- Teachers then are provided with an opportunity to *reflect* on their own modifications, changes and experience.

An Australian TESOL expert was also involved in this process at a later time. She was asked to observe on an ongoing basis 25 General English classes of HUFL, make contact with non-English major students and teachers, and collect information about the issues the teachers raised during the period of her classroom observations.

In December 2014, after more than two semesters since the introduction of the renewed curriculum and the textbook series, a 6-day workshop was organised to help teachers reflect on the new curriculum and evaluate the use of the new textbook series, focusing on the extent to which it may or may not facilitate the process of achieving B1 level. Common reflections were that the new curriculum helped teachers see more clearly the learning outcomes their students need to achieve as well as what they need to develop for their students for each semester. The 'Can Do' descriptors remind them of the need to develop communicative competences for their students, not just grammar or vocabulary.

However, these 'Can Do' descriptors were not found to be consistently representative of everything a language learner can do at a specific level. For the textbook, the consensus was that it was a complete package with good online resources and a focus on encouraging learner learning autonomy, but that too many of the exercises involved activities far beyond students', and even teachers', experience and that they have a European, particularly a German, orientation; there was too much material to cover in one teaching hour; students typically tend to have 2 hours per week of block classes for learning English for 15 weeks each semester, and the teachers were not sure whether students really made use of the online resources, which remains an unsolved problem. The textbook series, like many other textbooks, tries to develop all four basic language skills (speaking, listening, reading and writing) equally, but, due to long hours of grammar and vocabulary instruction in high schools, a lot of Hue University students' speaking and listening are much weaker and need more help than reading or writing.

This observation was shared by the Australian expert. She said in her report that the book series presumes that student levels across reading, writing, speaking and listening skills are about the same but this is not the case in Hue University and in Vietnam more generally. She then emphasised the need to look for new and different materials to help develop some skill areas that are showing continued weakness.

Also during this 6-day workshop, the teachers analysed the textbook and compared the textbook series with the 'Can Do' descriptors from CEFR A1–B1 to see whether the tasks and the textbook content are well aligned. They worked together to achieve agreement on what parts of the textbook are 'must-teach' sections, and which parts can or should be replaced with better tasks or materials to help learners better realise things that they 'Can Do' with the language. They also came up with a list of actions that should be taken to help students use the CEFR, to better orient their learning. This includes an orientation session or introductory course for non-English major students to help them understand clearly why they are studying English, what knowing a language really means, what learning outcomes are expected of them for each semester and by the end of their programme, what these learning outcomes are and how they are indicated, and what the students could do to better self-regulate their learning to achieve all of these outcomes. The need to provide better resources for learner autonomy and to develop a detailed checklist which can serve as a key reference point for language learning self-assessment was also emphasised. HUFL teachers have been encouraged to adapt and use the European Language Portfolio (ELP) to support their students' self-assessment. However, the use of the ELP has still remained optional, depending on individual choices, and has been applied only to classes of students majoring in English.

In March 2015, following the results of the workshop, the CEFR-based *Life* series by National Geographic Learning (by Hughes, Stephenson and Dummett 2013) was introduced as supplementary material for teachers and non-English major students, in a format adapted to suit the Vietnamese market. Teachers have a choice to either continue with the *English Elements* series while focusing on the 'must-teach' contents identified in the workshop plus using the *Life* series as supplementary materials, or choose to use the *Life* series in place of *English Elements*. At the same time HUFL staff were asked to compile and design materials to complement the main textbooks, especially to focus on developing more listening and speaking skills for non-English major students.

4 Discussion

Four years after the introduction of the CEFR into curriculum renewal at HUFL, the university has accumulated a number of positive outcomes and gained valuable experiences. On the other hand, the university has also identified issues it has to work with during the process of applying the CEFR to renew its curricula.

4.1 What are teachers' and students' interpretations of the use of the CEFR in English language teaching?

HUFL teachers have attained relatively sound interpretations of the philosophy and idea of the CEFR. Similar to the Vietnamese institution investigated by Nguyen and Hamid (2015:65), where MOET's adoption of the CEFR as a global language policy is observed to bring good outcomes by triggering 'wide alerts' and raising 'critical awareness' among teachers and learners, HUFL has witnessed its staff's rise in positive self-awareness and teacher professionalism as well as in implementing standard-based learning outcomes. This self-awareness is well captured in a young teacher's report after the workshop on the CEFR in 2011:

> The use of the CEFR to set standards for English language teachers and student learning outcomes creates a lot of pressure. For decades now once one becomes teachers here [in state-run organisations], they are teachers forever. Nothing can change that and it does not matter whether they remain qualified or not over years of teaching. This is not fair for many young people who have a degree in language teaching and are good at English but cannot find job vacancies to fill. But now the proficiency test they take will say their level of proficiency level and be indicative of their professionalism and teacher identity. That helps distinguish a qualified teacher from other teachers because when you teach a foreign language you must be proficient in that language . . . on the other hand, this policy [of adopting the CEFR to set standards for teacher professionalism] also triggers alerts that as language teachers we need to continuously improve our English proficiency and pedagogy to remain qualified and secure our job. The CEFR-based standards set as learning outcomes will also let students know what their level of proficiency is in comparison with other students, so that they can choose to take action to improve it.

The reflection above echoes teachers' beliefs in the need to utilise a comprehensive language framework to set standards for both English language teachers and students' learning outcomes. In this case the framework happens to be the CEFR. The use of a 'fast-track' proficiency test to classify new students according to their level of proficiency also creates better conditions for teaching and learning. It helps ease the problems associated with having students of too many different levels of proficiency in one class.

HUFL students have also become more aware of teachers' levels of proficiency when they consider with which teacher they should enrol on a course. This consideration for the teachers' level of proficiency is shown in various HUFL learning advisers' reports, which indicate that to many students of the university, one of the most important influential factors in their decision to enrol with a particular teacher is their level of proficiency. Given that often about 75–82 teachers teach the same General English course per semester at HUFL, the most popular question, especially of those who are in their first semester, is how they can know that a teacher has C1 or C2 level, so that they can make the right 'pick'.

HUFL annual conferences during the 2012–2015 period with its graduate employers, including heads of various provincial departments of education and training and principals of primary schools and secondary schools, show that the employers of a large majority of HUFL graduates have become very concerned about whether their future employees will achieve the required level of proficiency as referenced by the CEFR so that they will not have to invest further for their HUFL-graduate employees.

Despite a common good interpretation and appreciation of the value of the CEFR, there still remains a sense of doubt and distrust in the top-down policy among a number of HUFL staff and students. They show distrust in the feasibility of such a policy working effectively given a context where language classes are very often crowded and suffer from a lack of facilities and resources to support foreign language learning. The test result of 235 non-English major students, who are in their second year and have completed the first three semesters in their programme (with 105 teacher-led hours of English lessons) and chose to take the first gatekeeping proficiency test in July 2015, shows that 116 out of 235 (49.4%) achieved B1 level and 119 (51.6%) failed to do so, obtaining A2 or A1 level. With the release of this test result, many teachers and students express their doubt about the achievability of Level B1 by non-English major students. This concern was expressed in the reports of bi-monthly meetings between the dean and deputy deans of the English department and General English department with the school administrators even before the test was implemented and the test result was released.

4.2 How does the CEFR promote a system for in-house evaluation of curricula and learning outcomes?

Working on the CEFR-aligned curriculum has also helped the teachers appreciate the value of identifying measurable 'Can Do' descriptors as indicators of their student learning outcomes, allowing the curricula to have concrete and transparent objectives. One young teacher wrote in her reflection on the workshop in March 2015:

> The CEFR was confusing to me. Like many other teachers I felt we were blind people trying to make sense of it as an intellectual elephant. Only when we were asked to refer to it to renew the [general English language for non-major students] curriculum did it become clearer why such a framework is needed. The CEFR 'Can Do' descriptors specify to me what my students should be able to do at the end of a semester and at the end of a course. Before [the use of the CEFR] I was just able to say my students can speak or write in English, but now I can be more specific about their ability . . . Students can also self-assess their language ability to know where they are among the scales and levels [of proficiency]. The 'Can Do' descriptors provide more practical evidence about their progress because there is a difference between a general, conventional description of learning outcomes like 'You can write informal texts' and a specified account such as 'You can write a letter to your friend or a postcard' . . . When English teachers refer to the CEFR to renew the general English curriculum, we will gain valuable experiences which can be shared with [teachers] of other [language] departments when they renew their curriculum.

Many other teachers have stated that learning outcomes become concrete objectives through the description of 'Can Do' descriptors, and that such descriptors make the curriculum as well as the quality of learning and teaching more transparent.

4.3 How do teachers and students recognise the benefits of the CEFR-based approach for their own teaching and learning?

Teachers' discussion and annual reports also show that the adoption of the CEFR helps them and their students have a better sense of orientation towards teaching and learning English. They are more aware of what they need to achieve across lessons and how that is relevant to the overall learning outcome at the end. This sense of orientation towards the standard-based learning outcomes is also indicated in their more-frequently-asked-than-ever question of whether students would be able to achieve the defined learning outcomes with that textbook series (*English Elements*) in just 105 contact hours of instruction. As the learning outcomes now become measurable and more transparent, teachers are more strongly oriented towards methods and resources which can help their students achieve those outcomes.

A teacher said in the workshop in December 2014 that now whenever she looked for materials or made decisions about which part and tasks in the textbook she should spend more time on, she often referred to the learning outcomes. She has learned to become more strategic and selective in her choices of teaching materials and methods. While recognising the value of 'Can Do' descriptors in guiding their teaching, after the workshop on the CEFR in 2011, HUFL teachers also remember the shortcomings of this framework. One teacher wrote:

> I keep telling myself that there can be many indications of the same [proficiency] level. What is described in 'Can Do' descriptors may just be the most commonly observed competences and is not everything a language user can do in the language at the specific level. This helps me have a broader picture and not let the CEFR block my way of understanding English language acquisition. That is not let it restrict my choices of English teaching materials and methods to just its 'Can Do' descriptors.

This shows that the CEFR-based learning outcomes do not just guide teachers' act of teaching but that understanding of the shortcomings of this framework also orients them towards a more comprehensive view of teaching, and that they are intuitively realising that the CEFR 'Can Do' descriptors are illustrative only, and an open-ended list.

4.4 How does the adoption of the CEFR lead to better support for autonomous learning?

In a context where the actual contact hours are far below the hours of instruction recommended as necessary to help learners achieve B1 level, more than ever before learner autonomy has become a critical concern for teachers. The number of teachers' proposals for research grants (including learner self-assessment) on non-English major students' autonomy, how they make use of online resources, their perceptions of A1 to B1 levels and the CEFR, their learning strategies, and their evaluation of the new textbook series, have increased dramatically. Indeed they have taken up to two thirds of the total number of proposals submitted by teachers teaching English to non-English major students. This suggests that teachers are much more concerned about their students' responses to different aspects of the new curriculum at the implementation level. These research proposals have one thing in common: they all recognise the significance of learners actively engaging in learning, and investigate ways to support learner autonomy.

Learners' ability to self-assess their learning and their progress is part of learner autonomy and is also emphasised by teachers. As pointed out before, teachers put stress on the need to organise orientation sessions and checklists using the CEFR as the central point of reference for students to evaluate their own learning across lessons and units. In the two years, since the introduction of the new curriculum, HUFL has also tripled the budget spent on resources such as print and online English proficiency materials for students to access by themselves. It is also encouraging that students' library hours were recorded to have doubled in 2014 and tripled in the first six months of 2015. Laboratory access hours have also been doubled. To provide more support to students' learner autonomy, HUFL has actually provided extra training on how to give advice on learning strategies to students for its staff who work as learning advisors.

4.5 How are teachers and students involved and engaged in developing a sense of ownership?

While a large number of teachers are engaged in the implementation of the renewed curriculum and the new textbook, not all teachers feel a sense of ownership of the CEFR-aligned curriculum. The workshops on the CEFR, on curriculum design, on evaluating the renewed curriculum and on the use of the *English Elements* series were all organised while classes were being conducted, and so not all teachers could fully participate in the workshops. As a result, not all teachers really understand the philosophy, values and limitations of the use of the CEFR. These teachers tend to have high expectations of the CEFR as a global, comprehensive framework of reference for languages and often feel disappointed and frustrated by the 'Can Do' descriptors which are by nature neither language nor context specific. This feeling of frustration is multiplied by the impression that the implementation was imposed by a top-down policy, which prevents the development of a sense of ownership of the CEFR-based curriculum. This sense of disengagement is most clearly seen in a reflection at the end of the workshop in March 2015 by a teacher of 25 years of experience:

> We are forced to use the CEFR when it is under-developed. I thought MOET should adopt a more effective comprehensive [framework], not an exotic framework like the CEFR ... Developing the curriculum in alignment with the CEFR requires too much work and causes extra, unnecessary burdens while I already have to deal with heavy teaching loads and big classes.

HUFL does not only have problems with creating a sense of commitment and engagement for all their teaching staff members; it also faces difficulties in communicating the value of the CEFR-aligned curriculum and the use of B1 level proficiency tests for gatekeeping purposes to administration staff and students of other colleges, and also to schools within Hue University, despite the fact that the decision to apply a B1 standard to non-English major students was directed by MOET. In 2014, the first inter-institute conference

Assessment of CEFR-informed Language Teaching in Japan and Beyond

on the teaching and learning of foreign languages was held between the eight colleges and schools of Hue University, and the conference documents indicate four common questions from administrators of the colleges and schools whose students are being taught English by HUFL. These questions are:

1. What is the significance and practicality of using a European framework and standards to apply to the level of proficiency of Vietnamese students when, for decades, without this proficiency, their graduates have competed relatively well in the labour market?
2. What will guarantee that non-English major students will achieve B1 level after 105 hours of instruction and what are HUFL solutions to close the gap of 300 missing hours?
3. If students do not achieve B1 level and cannot have their graduation degree conferred when they have completed their university degree programme, and so miss the opportunity to find a job, who will be responsible for explaining to students and their parents the losses and disadvantages of entering the job market late or even worse never being able to do so?
4. What is the significance of sending their students to HUFL to learn English and get a proficiency certificate issued by HUFL while international English teaching (and testing) organisations such as Cambridge, American Academy (AMA) or the British Council have authorised centres in Hue and claim they can provide Level B1 courses as well as tests?

Some questions, such as 2) and 3), cannot really be answered by HUFL and nor can they be answered immediately as the decision to apply the CEFR to standardise learning outcomes for non-English major students was not made by HUFL. However, together with the other questions, they do raise serious issues that HUFL, as a state-run university, has to work hard to find solutions for.

4.6 How are the CEFR-based materials action-oriented and applicable by both teachers and students?

As mentioned before, the adoption of the CEFR in English education in Vietnam has led to the fact that several English proficiency book series from international publishers which have been available on the Vietnamese market for a considerable period are now automatically labelled as A1–C1, with little modification in terms of content and design. HUFL teachers also have problems identifying which series would be most appropriate to their curriculum and which series requires the least time for evaluation and adaptation so that they can recommend those books for their students as references for self-study.

Testing and assessment materials make up an important issue. Along with the adoption of the CEFR in curriculum design, choice of textbooks, standardisation of student learning outcomes and greater English teacher professionalism, MOET also utilised a domestic test format called Vietnamese standardised test of English proficiency (VSTEP), developed to be used as a gatekeeping test for post-high-school learners including undergraduates and postgraduate students. This test claims to be a proficiency test for the CEFR. The results are said to allow its users to classify test takers into B1–C1 levels. Teachers express concern at the constraint between using the CEFR-aligned curriculum to help their students to develop all-round language competences and the demand from their students to teach to the test. This constraint is expressed most clearly by teachers who teach the second year non-English major students, who are in their third semester of their university programme and enrolled in their last General English course of 45 contact hours. It is not uncommon to hear teachers say that even when they want to focus on the curriculum, the textbook and learning activities, students are not interested and they are motivated only when teachers give them materials and tasks which mimic the VSTEP.

5 Conclusions

When MOET introduced the CEFR as a yardstick to standardise not just learner and learning outcomes but also to assess teacher professionalism, quite a few HUFL permanent teaching staff members were judged as not being qualified. Fifteen teachers failed to achieve Level C1 in the proficiency test they were asked to take in 2012. These teachers were sent to an on-campus proficiency course and granted an online English learning account but still failed to provide evidence that they had acquired a minimum level of C1 in English. This was understandable because some had been just at B1 level in English before they took the training course. After 400 hours of classes it remained difficult for these long-serving teachers with, for example, a background and experience in teaching the Russian language, to achieve C1 or even B2 level in English. Placing teachers with B1 level to teach English has consequences and HUFL will have to deal with this issue.

Suffering from a shortage of qualified staff and a huge number of non-English major students is not the only problem that HUFL has to face in terms of resources. It also has to work on short-budgeted investments in facilities necessary for developing learner self-access and autonomy. In addition, the staff members of the information technology section of HUFL are not sufficiently trained to be capable of delivering good-quality training workshops for teachers and students to integrate technology in teaching and learning. Those are pressing issues that HUFL has to work with.

The 4-year journey that HUFL has taken to develop a CEFR-aligned curriculum and find textbooks to deal with a top-down approach has seen the university achieve some positive impacts on teaching and learning. It opens up opportunities for HUFL teachers' professional development and for students to develop and regulate their own learning strategies. It suggests that the action–reflection cycle can bring positive practices when teachers are encouraged to question the curriculum, the ability of their students to achieve required learning outcomes, the relevance of the textbook, and take action to understand why they do what they do and reflect on their teaching as well as the adoption of the CEFR. In March 2015 HUFL allocated funding for an independent research project on the impact of the *English Elements* series as well as of the *Life* series. This 2-year project explores further teachers' and students' perceptions and practices of using these book series and the impact of the choice of these two series on the implementation of the renewed curriculum. Also starting in 2014 and 2015, HUFL is the supervising school for two doctoral projects focusing respectively on the application of the CEFR to curriculum development and on the teachers' and students' responses to the integration of the CEFR in English education at a grassroots level. The journey thus far, though short and full of difficulties and with it being too early to know how it ends, has shown that in dealing with a top-down policy implementation, there are ways for HUFL to make the best of the CEFR for its students and teachers. Successful adopters should not be obliged to agree, but mutual recognition and dialogue are long overdue.

5.1 General steps for contextualising the CEFR

Based on the above analysis of the positive outcomes as well as the remaining issues in relation to implementing the CEFR at HUFL, this chapter now makes suggestions for contextualising the CEFR within the institution as well as in contexts in which a similar situation of the imposition of an under-researched application of the CEFR is found.

- Instead of criticising the top-down approach of applying the CEFR with little research and guidance or imposing the approach at institutional level with little negotiation with its teachers and students, the institution needs to seek ways to communicate the moral purpose of such an implementation, focusing on how the CEFR can make curricula transparent and the learning outcomes concrete and measurable objectives (Pham 2015). A common vision on the use of the CEFR needs to be shared before further activities take place to apply this framework.
- The institution needs to work on an action plan which helps its stakeholders understand both the values and the philosophy of the CEFR as well as the limitations of this reference framework, build capacity and provide guidance throughout the process of using it as a refer-

ence point to renew curricula, textbooks and assessment practice. In other words, the institution should prepare its teachers and students for potential problems they may face when implementing the CEFR in language teaching and learning and help them understand that adopting the CEFR will bring benefits but also difficulties they have to work with along the way.

- Action research on the use of the CEFR at different implementation levels should be cultivated and promoted so that teachers are able to see for themselves the impact of its application, and to make changes and modifications as necessary to improve this, to become more aware of the change processes and to find evidence of the impact of their teaching and assessment in alignment with the CEFR. They should also be provided with a forum to share their data and findings, which then allows them to come up with more collective decisions regarding, for example, which textbooks should be used, what sections of the textbooks should be emphasised, what materials would be more aligned with the CEFR-based learning outcomes and which assessment practices would facilitate learner autonomy.
- The institution needs to cultivate a learning culture where the authorities are open to teachers' and students' feedback and even criticism of the use of the CEFR-aligned curriculum, textbooks and assessment. In the same way, teachers are prepared to learn from students' feedback on their teaching and assessment practice. The authorities of the institution need also to anticipate issues associated with the implementation of the CEFR-aligned curriculum and work with its teachers and students on those issues in a timely and accepting manner. This learning culture will help create better opportunities for mutual understanding and meaningful negotiation between parties involved so that they feel they are all in the same boat making full use of the CEFR for the sake of the students.
- The institution needs also to provide sustainable tools and resources to empower both teachers and students to encourage both teacher autonomy (i.e. professional development) and learner autonomy (i.e. autonomous learning and self-regulated learning). Blended learning can be one of the tools as long as it is well monitored, evaluated and sustained.

The lessons and experiences from applying the CEFR to renew its General English curriculum that HUFL has undertaken for the last 4 years has shown that, despite various problems that the university teachers and students face when implementing a top-down approach in English language education, there are ways to make better use of this framework. There is initial positive evidence showing that if the CEFR is well contextualised, its application can bring about benefits and values to teachers and students *beyond* just a top-down imposition.

References

Burns, A (2010) *Doing Action Research in English Language Teaching: A Guide for Practitioners*, London: Routledge.

Clare, A, Wilson, J J and Cosgrove, A (2011) *New Total English – Intermediate Level*, Harlow: Pearson Education Limited.

Council of Europe (2001) *Common European Framework of Reference for Languages: Learning, Teaching, Assessment*, Cambridge: Cambridge University Press.

Falla, T and Davies, P A (2013) *Solutions (Elementary – Advanced Level)* (Revised edition), Oxford: Oxford University Press.

Hawkins, J A and Filipović, L (2012) *Criterial Features in L2 English: Specifying the Reference Levels of the Common European Framework*, English Profile Studies volume 1, Cambridge: UCLES/Cambridge University Press.

Hu, G and McKay, S L (2012) English language education in East Asia: Some recent developments, *Journal of Multilingual and Multicultural Development* 33 (4), 345–362.

Hughes, J, Stephenson, H and Dummett, P (2013) *Life (Elementary – Intermediate Level)*, Singapore: National Geographic Learning.

Kemmis, S and McTaggart, R (Eds) (1988) *The Action Research Planner* (3rd edition), Geelong: Deakin University Press.

Le, V C (2002) A historical review of English language education in Vietnam, in Choi, Y H and Spolsky, B (Eds) *English Education in Asia: History and Policies*, Seoul: Asia TEFL, 1,013–1,034.

Little, D (2007) The Common European Framework of Reference for Languages: Perspectives on the making of supranational language education policy, *Modern Language Journal* 91, 645–655.

McNiff, J and Whitehead, J (2006) *All You Need to Know about Action Research*, London/Thousand Oaks/New Delhi: Sage Publications.

McNiff, J and Whitehead, J (2010) *You and Your Action Research Project* (3rd edition), London/New York: Routledge.

Ministry of Education and Training (2008) *Decision 1400/QD-TTg by the Prime Minister on the approval of the project: Teaching and learning foreign language in the state-run educational system period 2008–2020*, available online: jpf.org.vn/iwtcore/uploads/2012/08/1-3Decision_1400_QD-TTg-Eng.pdf

Ministry of Education and Training (2010) *Decision No. 3321/QD-BGDDT– Launching Pilot Primary English Language Curriculum*, Hanoi: Ministry of Education and Training.

Ministry of Education and Training (2011) *MOET Recognition of Foreign Language Universities of Excellence Authorized to Undertake Teacher Training and Assessment Activities*, Hanoi: Ministry of Education and Training.

Ministry of Education and Training (2013a) *Dispatch No.7475 Guidance on Learning Outcomes for University Programs*, Hanoi: Ministry of Education and Training

Ministry of Education and Training (2013b) *MOET Annual Report 2013*, available online: moet.gov.vu/docs/annual-reports/MoET%20Annual%20 Report_2013.pdf

Ministry of Education and Training (2014) *Six-level Framework for Foreign Language Proficiency in Vietnam*, Hanoi: Ministry of Education and Training.

Nguyen, T M H (2011) Primary English language education policy in Vietnam: Insights from implementation, *Current Issues in Language Planning* 12 (2), 225–249.

Nguyen, V H and Hamid, M O (2015) Educational policy borrowing in a globalized world, *English Teaching: Practice & Critique* 14 (1), 60–74.

North, B (2014) *The CEFR in Practice*, English Profile Studies volume 4, Cambridge: UCLES/Cambridge University Press.

Pham, T H N (2012) Applying the CEFR to the teaching and learning of English in Vietnam: Advantages and challenges, *Journal of Foreign Language Studies* 30, 90–102.

Pham, T H N (2013) Obstacles to primary school teachers' implementation of methodological innovations to teach English to young learners, *Hue University Journal of Science* 80 (2), 35–46.

Pham, T H N (2015) *Setting the CEFR-based levels of proficiency as learning outcomes and implications for classroom assessment*, paper presented in Proceedings of National Conference on Language Assessment, Hanoi 2015.

Roth, A and Schmid-Burleson, B (2002) *English Elements*, Munich: Hueber Verlag.

Steiner-Khamsi, G (2004) *The Global Politics of Educational Borrowing and Lending*, New York: Teachers College Press.

Trim, J (Ed) (2001) *Common European Framework of Reference for Languages: Learning, Teaching and Assessment User Guide*, Strasbourg: Council of Europe, available online: www.coe.int/lang-CEFR

Wright, S (2002) Language education and foreign relations in Vietnam, in Tollefson, J W (Ed) *Language Policies in Education: Critical Issues*, Mahwah: Lawrence Erlbaum, 225–244.

7 A 'Can Do' framework-based curriculum in a university-level English language learning programme: Course goals, activities and assessment

Etsuko Shimo
Carlos Ramirez
Kaori Nitta
Kindai University

1 Introduction

Large English language programmes face their own particular challenges as methods for maintaining common goals, content, quality and evaluation practices across numerous teachers, classes and students can be a constant struggle. In such cases it is not always possible to fully familiarise teachers, and other stakeholders, with the principles of the Common European Framework of Reference for Languages (CEFR, Council of Europe 2001). This chapter outlines some ways in which such a familiarisation process can be implicitly implemented over time, through curricula renewal. Founded in 2010, the Faculty of Applied Sociology, Kinki University (currently Kindai University), began using a 'Can Do' framework as the basis for their English learning programme. The faculty is the second newest of the 13 faculties of the university (as of 2015). Kinki University itself is one of the largest private universities in Japan with a student body of over 30,000. The Faculty of Applied Sociology offers three major areas of study: Sociology and Mass Media Studies, Psychology, and Environmental Studies. About 500 students are enrolled each year into the first year programme. In this faculty's English learning programme, students are offered many opportunities to develop their productive skills, mainly speaking and writing, so that they can express themselves and their opinions with appropriate grammar and intelligible pronunciation. Needless to say, this emphasis on the development of productive skills has also favourably affected the development of receptive skills: listening and reading.

The 'Can Do' framework-based curriculum was implemented with the philosophy of helping students become autonomous learners, a main part of the philosophy of the European Language Portfolio (ELP), as one of its main goals. The ELP was developed as an educational tool to help implement CEFR ideas in teaching practice; promoting learner autonomy is part of the ELP's pedagogic function (Schneider and Lenz 2001). The ELP aims to 'incite and help learners to reflect on their objectives, ways of learning and success in language learning, plan their learning, learn autonomy' (Schneider and Lenz 2001:3). Many researchers (e.g. Little 1991, Ridley 2003, Wenden 1991) would agree that the ability to reflect and plan can also be considered a part of learner autonomy. While the teaching context is very different from the European context, our curriculum shared the same philosophy of promoting learner autonomy as the ELP and the CEFR in one respect: helping learners to be able to continue learning even after leaving school, i.e. to become effective lifelong learners. Learner autonomy issues in this volume are also found in section 2 of Chapter 1, section 3 of Chapter 8, section 2 of the second phase of research described in Chapter 9 and section 2 of Chapter 10.

In addition, the faculty aims to encourage students' intrinsic motivation even though many of the students may be obliged to learn with extrinsic motivation at the beginning of the course. The ELP pedagogically functions to 'enhance the motivation of the learners, to improve their ability to communicate in different languages, to learn additional languages, and to seek new intercultural experiences' (Schneider and Lenz 2001:3). This view of language pluralism (for a detailed discussion see Council of Europe 2001:4–5), which is supported by the Council of Europe, is not much reflected in our curriculum, where English receives the strongest focus and the variety of language choices is rather limited. The Council of Europe's pluralistic view towards language learning emphasises the importance of individuals building 'a communicative competence to which all knowledge and experience of language contributes and in which languages interrelate and interact' (Council of Europe 2001:4). Due to the limited number of foreign languages offered, our curriculum perhaps does not aim to enrich individual learners' multiple language experiences as far as the Council of Europe's standard.

However, similar to the CEFR, the curriculum has the philosophy of helping students understand how to learn a language while in the process of becoming autonomous learners; such a lifelong applicable skill can be very useful to students particularly when studying other languages (Council of Europe 2001). The curriculum was also developed with an action-oriented approach, the approach adopted in the CEFR (Little 2012). This approach encourages learner-centred classrooms where students can experience hands-on intercultural exchanges even among classmates of the same first language. It facilitates communicative learning. In such student-centred learning environments, students can increase their motivation to learn while using the language and, as a result, can attain enhanced autonomy in their learning (Macaro 1997, M Sato 2006, Y Sato 2010).

Thus, the following goals have been set for our 'Can Do'-based curriculum:

(a) to improve the four basic language skills in order to use English as a communication tool
(b) to develop a positive attitude amongst students towards writing their own opinions, making presentations, and discussing issues with others in English
(c) to improve students' abilities to work on tasks, to make presentations in English, and to interact with people of different cultural backgrounds on their own initiative
(d) to develop autonomy by learning to set methods and goals that are based on self-evaluation activities.

2 Context

2.1 The framework development[1]

The framework is based on an in-house-developed curriculum called the 'Kindai Can Do Framework (KCF)' (Appendix 1). It provides common goals and guidelines both for students learning English and for English teachers designing and preparing class activities and assignments. In other words, the main purposes of the framework are: (a) to provide specific goals and simple assessment tools for students and (b) to provide common curriculum goals and class objectives, and guidelines for class activities both for students and teachers.

The current version was completed by the Department of Language Education at Kinki University in 2008. Prior to 2008, most faculties at the university were using a Test of English for International Communication (TOEIC)-oriented English language learning curriculum. A committee was formed to consider alternatives to this curriculum. The aim of the discussion was to create a curriculum where students could become active 'language users' by building positive attitudes towards language learning and through the development of autonomous learning skills. This was deemed better than students simply remaining as 'language learners', who cannot use the language as seemed to be the case under the existing curriculum (Nitta 2008). In order to make the new curriculum goals clear and specific for all stakeholders, i.e. students and teachers alike, the committee decided to create a common framework for the curriculum. The developers adopted the name KCF for the new curriculum.

In the development of the KCF, the following two points were considered essential.
(a) to create a framework that accommodates our students' levels and backgrounds
(b) to make 'Can Do' descriptors as concrete as possible so that both students and teachers could use them without much difficulty or confusion.

---

1 This section is based on the explanation about the KCF development in Shimo and Nitta (2011), which has been drastically revised for this section.

In addressing point (a), the KCF adopted language areas and levels which were regarded as more familiar and appropriate for our students. Five language areas were specified for the KCF: listening, speaking, reading, writing, and vocabulary and grammar. They were more familiar categories for students as these terms had been widely used in English learning and education fields, in comparison to listening, reading, spoken interaction, spoken production, and writing in the CEFR document (Council of Europe 2001:26–27). For example, the Society for Testing English Proficiency, Inc (STEP) 'Can Do' lists use the four language skills as their categories of 'Can Do's. These four skill-based categories are used as part of TOEIC 'Can Do' lists as well (Chauncey Group International 2000, Society for Testing English Proficiency no date).

Moreover, while the CEFR has six levels from A1 (basic users) to C2 (proficient users), the curriculum committee decided to target the levels of the majority of our students. The English proficiency levels of most students upon university entrance are A1 and A2, especially in relation to oral communication skills. There were few students whose proficiency levels reached C1 or C2 even among fourth year students. Thus, five levels were specified for the KCF: K–4, K–3, K–2, K–1, and K–Global. These levels covered from upper A1 to upper B2 and above in the CEFR (Table 1).

Table 1 KCF and CEFR: levels

KCF levels	CEFR equivalency
K–4	A1+ and A2
K–3	A2+ and B1
K–2	B1
K–1	B1 and B2+
K–Global	B2+ and above

In developing the descriptors, the curriculum committee referred to several 'Can Do' checklists such as the lists developed within TOEIC, the Test in Practical English Proficiency (STEP), and the Kasumi Can-Do Grade. The *TOEIC Can-Do Guide* was published in 2000 based on a study about linking TOEIC scores to self-evaluation abilities (Chauncey Group International 2000). Its purpose is 'to provide organizations with more detailed information linking TOEIC scores to specific tasks that can be performed in English' (Chauncey Group International 2000:3). Similarly, STEP developed their 'Can Do' lists based on questionnaire surveys of over 20,000 test takers (Society for Testing English Proficiency no date) to provide useful indicators about what STEP qualification holders can do at each level.

Concurrently, English teachers at Kasumigaoka Senior High School, a then super English language high school[2], worked on developing 'Can Do' lists for their students called Kasumi Can-Do Grade, in order to effectively facilitate students' autonomous learning (Naganuma and Nagasue 2006). Their 'Can Do' lists were developed based on actual classroom activities and tasks. They also examined the consistency of their checklists with standardised test scores and levels (e.g. TOEIC, Global Test of English (GTEC) C for STUDENTS), as well as with CEFR 'Can Do' descriptors (Nagasue no date).

Similarly to the *Kasumi Can-Do Grade*, Kinki curriculum developers decided that actual classroom activities and tasks should also become key elements in the development of the KCF descriptors. Some descriptors were specially created for the KCF because the tasks indicated by them were considered to play an important role in the curriculum. For example, specific descriptors were created regarding extensive reading and vocabulary power-building activities as they were among core activities in our language programme. The following are among such descriptors:

- I can read a passage in my textbook, and a relatively easy passage in my major field, at the rate of 100 words or more per minute and understand the gist (K–2/reading)
- I can understand Level 2 (1,000 headword level) ER [extensive reading] materials while hardly using a dictionary (K–3/reading)
- I can understand most words on the 1,000-word-level vocabulary list (West 1953) (K–4/vocabulary and grammar).

The CEFR was the most important reference in the KCF development. It provided the foundation for our curriculum, particularly the philosophy of promoting learner autonomy. Most of the KCF descriptors were created based on the CEFR descriptors, but with special attention to point (b): to make descriptors as concrete as possible so that both students and teachers can use them without much difficulty or confusion. Because of this process, the final descriptors adopted in the KCF were different from the specific CEFR descriptors to which the committee referred (Table 2). Additional words or explanation (e.g. 'for half a minute', 'if preparation time is given', and 'while making use of dictionaries') were included in the final descriptors so that such explanations could provide a clear guide for teachers designing class activities. Such explanations could also help students in their self-evaluation activities as students would actually be doing the activities described by the descriptors

---

2 Super English Language High School (SELHi) Project is a Ministry of Education, Culture, Sports, Science and Technology (MEXT) project that aimed to develop effective high school English language learning programmes. The project started in 2002 and continued for eight years. A total of 169 high schools have participated in this project (Ministry of Education, Culture, Sports, Science and Technology 2011).

A 'Can Do' framework-based curriculum

in classes. For example, in one of the core courses in the programme, students are required to do 3 to 4-minute presentation assignments. For the statement 'I can speak for more than three minutes with notes about topics of personal interests, current affairs, and about my major field of study' (K–1/speaking, number 2 in Table 2) students can evaluate without much difficulty whether they can do it after going through the presentation assignments. In addition, the length of students' speaking time such as 'half a minute' (number 1 in Table 2) act as an objective evaluation indicator both for teachers and students; students do pair conversations and interview activities in class and the number of minutes they are required to speak is often specified.

Table 2 Example descriptors from the KCF and the CEFR originals

	KCF descriptors	CEFR descriptors
1	I can speak for half a minute (making a few sentences) about my family, people around me, living conditions, and school life, if preparation time is given according to the difficulty level of the topic. (K–4/speaking)	I can use simple phrases and sentences to describe where I live and people I know. (A1/spoken production)
2	I can speak for more than three minutes with notes about topics of personal interests, current affairs, and about my major field of study. (K–1/speaking)	I can present clear, detailed descriptions on a wide range of subjects related to my field of interest. I can explain a viewpoint on a topical issue giving the advantages and disadvantages of various options. (B2/spoken production)
3	I can understand most of the passages and articles written for English learners at the college and university level, and passages about content in my major field, while making use of dictionaries. (K–2/reading)	I can understand texts that consist mainly of high frequency everyday or job-related language. (B1/understanding reading)
4	I can understand passages about current affairs, and passages about my major field while making use of dictionaries. (K–1/reading)	I can read articles and reports concerned with contemporary problems in which the writers adopt particular attitudes or viewpoints. (B2/understanding reading)
5	I can write a passage of 300 words or more about various topics in fields I am interested in while making use of dictionaries. (K–Global/writing)	I can write clear, detailed text on a wide range of subjects related to my interests. (B2/writing)

Note: CEFR descriptors are from Council of Europe (2001:26–27).

2.2 Institutional size

Large English language programmes face their own particular challenges as methods for maintaining common goals, content, quality and evaluation practices across numerous teachers, classes and students can be a constant struggle. The first and second year English programme consists of approximately 500 students per year. Each year is divided into 18 to 20 classes. There are far fewer students in the upper year third and fourth year part of the programme as most students have already obtained a sufficient number of language credits by then. The minimum number of foreign language credits for graduation stands at 18 credits including other languages such as Chinese, French and Korean. Of those 18 credits, students must obtain at least eight English language credits. Due to the limited number of other foreign language courses, many students on average earn 10 to 12 English language credits.

To serve this large number of students and classes, the faculty has employed five full-time teachers and some 25 to 30 part-time teachers. Both full-time and part-time teachers are a mixture of native and Japanese English teachers. With more than 30 teachers and 1,000 students participating in the programme, administrators have had to devise a number of practices to ensure programme quality and standards as well as a unified, coherent vision.

2.3 Curriculum revision

Our faculty's curriculum was revised in the academic year 2015. Both the previous (2010–14) and the revised (2015–current) curriculum have offered two types of courses: foundation courses (*kikan kamoku*) and advanced courses (*hatten kamoku*). Foundation courses are designed to help students develop their integrated skills in a balanced way – thus, with a special emphasis on the students' weak skills such as speaking and writing. Advanced courses have more specific purposes (e.g. academic skills) or have a special focus on selected skills (e.g. presentation skills, intercultural understanding skills).

In the new curriculum, more emphasis is placed on linguistic pluralism, and students are encouraged to take English and another foreign language class in their first year in the new curriculum. Due to such curriculum policy amendments, the number of English class meetings for first year students was reduced from four times a week in the previous curriculum (used until the end of the 2014 academic year) to three in the revised curriculum. However, the number of English courses available for students has remained the same (24 courses) as in the previous curriculum (Table 3). The main goals of the

Table 3 Class options in the 2015 curriculum

Year	Semester	Class options (* required for all the students)				
3	6th	ES 6		EQ 4	ESS 4	AES 6
	5th	ES 5		EQ 3	ESS 3	AES 5
2	4th	*ES 4*	*OE 4*	EQ 2	ESS 2	AES 4
	3rd	*ES 3*	*OE 3*	EQ 1	ESS 1	AES 3
1	2nd	*ES 2**	*OE 2**			AES 2
	1st	*ES 1**	*OE 1**			AES 1

Notes: 1) ES = English Seminar, OE = Oral English, EQ = Examination Strategies for English Qualifications, ESS = English Special Studies, AES = Academic English Skills; 2) Classes in italics are foundation courses. The rest are advanced courses.

faculty's English learning programme (see section 1) have also remained the same.

3 Details of practice

Both English L1 and Japanese L1 teachers in our programme are aware of the fundamental principles of the task-based, communicative approach of the CEFR (Little 2012). There is now a widespread consensus within the field of applied linguistics that language learning is most effective when using communicative language teaching methodologies that emphasise communicative interaction rather than rote memorisation of linguistic structures and vocabulary (see, for example, Bachman and Palmer 1996, Hymes 2001). The CEFR is the outgrowth of communicative language theory and grounded in the view that the ability to speak involves multiple competences including grammatical knowledge, pragmatic awareness and phonology (Research and Validation Group, University of Cambridge 2009). In addition, a task-based approach to language learning is based on communicative language use (Bachman 1990), which is emphasised in our CEFR-inspired curriculum goals. Our curriculum and syllabus of core courses, as will be seen later in this chapter, recognise the importance of the functional use of language: communication must be purposeful and goal oriented within a specific context.

In order to implement the 'Can Do' framework, various methods and measures have been taken. Among those are (a) the usage of the *My Can-Do Handbook* (CDH) (Kindai University Faculty of Applied Sociology, Department of General Education, English Language Learning Program Management Team 2010–2015) and other textbooks, (b) utilising unified syllabuses and evaluation systems, and (c) sharing class management information. These three points will be explained in this section.

3.1 The usage of the My Can-Do Handbook and other textbooks

3.1.1 The content of the handbook

Full-time faculty teachers created a learning handbook (CDH) in order for both teachers and students to work effectively to achieve the curriculum goals. This handbook is similar to the ELP in that it contains assessment grids and learning record sheets in it (see 'language passport' and 'language biography' in the ELP; see Schneider and Lenz (2001) for details).

The handbook presents the curriculum goals at the beginning of the book. One of the most important tenets of the framework – helping students become autonomous learners – is included among the curriculum goals. In addition, the goals are designed to provide impetus to teachers to incorporate materials and activities that will assist students in achieving the goals.

The pages following the curriculum goals in the CDH include the KCF itself, the *Dekita Checklists*, manuals of learning tools in certain courses, learning record pages (e.g. reading speed graphs), and vocabulary lists (Coxhead 2000, West 1953) ('dekita' means 'I was able to do it' in Japanese). Since its introduction in the 2010 academic year, the CDH has undergone several revisions. More materials such as guidelines for the unified speaking tests and lists of useful expressions have been added, and some of the pages written in Japanese (e.g. the tables of *Dekita Checklists*) have been made bilingual into English–Japanese.

The CDH is distributed to the English teachers of the faculty at or just prior to the beginning of every academic year, as well as to all the first year students in their first English class at university, to familiarise students with the goals of the curriculum. In the first year English classes, students are given an overview of the KCF and its different levels as well as a basic explanation of the *Dekita Checklists*.

Students do reflection, self-evaluation, and goal-setting activities using the checklists three times in each semester: at the beginning, in the middle, and at the end. Each list has about 10 items (Appendix 2). These items are closely linked to the KCF statements, covering all the five levels (from K–4 to K–Global). The items are connected to the activities covered by the first year and second year foundation courses, and thus the same lists are to be used in the first two years at university. Oral English teachers oversee the completion by students of the listening and speaking *Dekita Checklists* while English Seminar teachers do the same for reading, writing, and vocabulary and grammar *Dekita Checklists*.

The CDH also contains a number of explanations and activities that link to KCF, in addition to the checklists. The explanations within the CDH mainly pertain to software that is used both in and outside the classroom such as vocabulary, pronunciation and writing software. The content of the software is all conducive to improving 'Can Do' abilities described in the KCF and in the checklists. Finally, the CDH includes information on and activities for graded readers and vocabulary. At the back of the CDH, there are two vocabulary lists. They are based on West's (1953) General Service List and Coxhead's (2000) Academic Word List. Teachers are encouraged to incorporate vocabulary from these lists in their class activities while students are urged to study them on their own after class. The words on the lists are also covered by a vocabulary software learning tool that students are required to use in their English Seminar 1 and 2 classes. These parts of the CDH all relate to unified evaluation systems, which will be covered in more detail in section 3.2.

3.1.2 Textbooks

In addition to the CDH, teachers are free to use a textbook of their own choosing for the class. Although there is a short list of eight to 10 textbooks for each of the foundation courses, teachers can recommend and use textbooks not on the list if they can justify their selection. Teachers are requested to choose textbooks that adhere to communicative language theory and, more importantly, conform to the content of the unified syllabus. Programme administrators resolved to permit the free selection of the textbook from a larger list in the belief that if teachers are allowed to choose textbooks, the textbooks will better match their own in-class techniques and teaching styles. This in turn should help in the achievement of curriculum goals including, most importantly, student language improvement. Some teacher autonomy and latitude is beneficial and, indeed, essential in the communicative classroom in regard to sequencing, timing and day-to-day activities in order to achieve student progress.

3.2 Unified syllabuses and evaluation systems

To assess student achievement of curriculum goals, students' abilities need to be periodically evaluated. Abilities are assessed objectively by using class tests and evaluations that are based on the abilities described in the KCF. Since the KCF 'Can Do' descriptors outline specific tasks or performance, class evaluations are also task or action based. The tasks or assignments are not only conducted at the end of the term – they are also administered throughout the term to reinforce student competency in the skill. Many of these evaluations have been implemented on a standardised basis meaning that all teachers use the same question types, format and guidelines for evaluating performance. The standard evaluation activities include (a) extensive reading assignments, (b) interview and conversation tests, (c) essay assignments and tests via writing software, and (d) presentation evaluation.

3.2.1 Extensive reading assignment

Levels regarding extensive reading are covered by the KCF. The *Dekita Checklists* also have a related statement, 'I was able to read one graded reader or more in a week from the library or the language institute'[3]. Until the 2014 spring semester, the assignment was to be covered either in English Seminar 1 and 2, or Oral English 1 and 2. Specific instructions include having students turn in a book report or summary of each book read. Students also kept a record of their extensive reading activities in their CDH for the 2010 to 2014

---

3 Language Institute is a language learning centre at the university, where students have access to more than 1,000 graded readers and other language learning materials for English, Chinese, Korean, and other foreign languages. They also offer free extra-curricular language lessons.

versions, giving a rating to the book according to its level of difficulty and the level of personal satisfaction.

Most of the extensive reading assignments have been shifted to the Oral English classes after the introduction of M-Reader software[4]. An experimental use of M-Reader started in the 2014 fall semester, and was fully implemented the following year with unified guidelines. M-Reader allows registered students to take comprehension tests of graded readers and to be informed of the total number of words read.

3.2.2 Interview and conversation tests[5]

The Oral English foundation course revolves around one main common activity. This is the oral testing that takes place twice a term: a mid-term test and a final test. Both of these tests comprise two parts. There is a pair conversation and an interview test with the teacher. All Oral English classes take the test at the same time. The topics for the test are drawn from the standardised syllabus of the course and are solely task based. Examples of these topics include 'talk about going shopping', 'agree and disagree with your partner about different genres of music, books', 'talk about past experiences or future plans' etc. During final exams in each semester, teachers exchange classes and do not test their own students in a system called the Partner Exchange Teacher (PET) system (see section 4.1.3 for a more detailed discussion of PET).

The assessment rubric of the test is mainly based on CEFR/KCF 'Can Do' descriptors. Listed below are two analytical criteria with their corresponding descriptor from the CEFR and KCF. The KCF descriptor is from the pair conversation test (the rubric and descriptors for the interview test are slightly different). The similarities of intent between CEFR and KCF should be noted. Fluency at CEFR Level A2 is defined as:

> Can make him/herself understood in very short utterances, even though pauses, false starts and reformulation are very evident (Council of Europe 2001:29).

The fluency skill in the rubric of the faculty Pair Conversation Test is:

> KCF K–4/Fluency/Pair Conversation Test
> Speech tends to be slow with some hesitations but does not demand unreasonable patience of the listener. Speed of speech is reasonably paced albeit with a number of pauses.

Their definitions of accuracy contrast as follows:

---

4 mreader.org
5 See Ramirez (2011) for details of discussion on the interview and conversation tests.

Uses some simple structures correctly, but still systematically makes basic mistakes (Council of Europe 2001:28).

KCF K–4/Grammar (or Accuracy)/Pair Conversation Test
Can produce basic tenses such as present, present continuous, past and future and, construct sentences with reasonable structure.

3.2.3 Essay assignments and testing

Essay writing is also covered by the KCF statements. At the K–2 level, students are expected to 'write an essay of one to three paragraphs (100 words) about familiar topics while making use of dictionaries'. At the K–1 level, they are expected to 'write an essay of 150 words about a given topic in 30 minutes without using a dictionary' and at the K–Global level to 'write an essay of 200 words about a given topic in 30 minutes without using a dictionary'. '[B]eing aware of the type of essay (e.g. cause and effect, comparison, list, etc.)' (K–2) is also considered important in the essay writing learning process.

In order to help students to do such tasks, four to five paragraph writing assignments are required in English Seminar 1 and 2. Essay writing activities include the mastering of the introduction–body–conclusion structure of essays, use of topic sentences, cohesive paragraph writing activities, and review of useful expressions and connecting words between ideas and paragraphs.

For these kinds of essay writing assignments and tests, an online software writing tool is used. The software evaluates students' writing performance based on whether students have complied with fundamental grammatical rules and basic paragraph formats. The criteria for grading are grounded in the same communicative principles as the CEFR. During the term there are five major writing assignments (including those labelled as tests) and the software awards a grade of 1 to 6 for each of them. The topics are communicative based: for example, 'write about the career you plan to pursue' or 'what happens if there is no technology'. In addition, for self-reflection purposes, students fill in the *Dekita Checklist* for writing at different times during the semester to evaluate their own progress.

The tests take place twice in each semester. In the first semester, descriptive or narrative essay prompts are provided, and in the second semester, cause and effect, persuasive, or argumentative essay prompts are provided. Students' essays are evaluated by software instantly, and teachers also read the essays and give additional evaluations and comments. The use of this software has enabled all teachers involved to focus on helping their students improve their effective essay writing skills, as described in the KCF.

3.2.4 Presentation assignments

Presentation skills are covered by a number of KCF statements. For example, one of the K–1 speaking statements is 'I can speak for more than three minutes with notes about topics of personal interests, current affairs, and about my major field of study'. By the end of the second year in the programme, students are expected to make a presentation of substantive content and length in English. Many opportunities to practise presentations are provided in the foundation courses in the first two years; presentation assignments are part of the required assignments in English Seminars 1, 2, 3, and 4, as well as in Oral English 3 and 4. In the first year, students are expected to give 2–4-minute presentations, and by the end of the second year, they are given 5-minute presentation assignments. At the end of the second year, an event called the English Presentation Contest is held[6]. The event works as an opportunity to present an achievable goal to first year students sitting in the audience. Topics for the presentation depend on the class, with some teachers opting for more latitude in choice while others offer a choice from some pre-selected topics. In the second year, students must focus on topics related to their major or other academic issues.

Presentation preparations in the second year are done in both the Oral English and English Seminar class with a formal rehearsal presentation given in the former class and, one or two weeks later, a final presentation done in the latter class. Students are encouraged to take both Oral English and English Seminar in the same semester to make the most of their English learning opportunities. English Seminar teachers are mainly in charge of preparing students for their presentations. However, Oral English teachers are also informed of the student presentation topics and evaluation criteria, and work together with their colleagues in English Seminar in building student skills for their presentations.

The evaluation rubric which is used in all English Seminar and Oral English classes and the English Presentation Contest is based on KCF principles and fundamental presentation criteria such as content, pronunciation, fluency, loudness, gestures and visual aids. These standard presentation criteria used in the contest are provided to the teachers and can be utilised throughout the programme. In English Seminar 4 (in the second semester of the second year programme), the PET system is used for presentation evaluation. On the final presentation days, students go to a different classroom to make presentations and have their presentations evaluated by a different teacher (and by students in a different class as well). In this way, teachers work collaboratively to help students go through what the presentation-related descriptors describe in the

---

6 Students, especially first and second year students in the foundation courses, are encouraged to attend and can receive participation points towards their final course grades for attending and completing a short assignment about the presentations.

KCF. As for students, they refer to *Dekita Checklists* to evaluate their abilities regarding presentations; one of the statements in speaking is 'I was able to speak for three minutes or longer, using notes and slides, about personal topics, social issues, and topics relating to my major field of studies, if given time to prepare'.

3.2.5 Other

There are other standard activities and assignments that lead to such standardised evaluation as described previously: pronunciation improvement activities using voice recognition software, participation in E^3 (e-cube)[7] activities, and vocabulary enhancement activities using online vocabulary software (which covers words in the lists included in the CDH) are among them. Students' work in these activities is evaluated as part of their course grades, and a unified grading ratio is specified for each activity. These various kinds of activities help to create a learning environment where students can develop their communicative skills in an integrated manner, the principle of which is supported by our 'Can Do' framework.

3.3 Class management information sharing

Collegiality is very important in order for the curriculum to work effectively (M Sato 2006). The act of sharing and exchanging information is key in developing collegiality. Most of the English classes take place during the same periods on the same days. Part-time teachers use one office room and can exchange information about their class management between classes. Full-time teachers occasionally visit the office and exchange ideas about class management, and hear the opinions of part-time teachers. Feedback and opinions about standard assignments and evaluations are especially valuable because such information sharing will help all the teachers focus on the shared teaching goals and thus prompt them to prepare similar activities in their respective classrooms.

Faculty development (FD) meetings for English teachers, which have been held once a semester since the faculty's inception, are also an additional opportunity for teachers to share class management information. The meetings are held at the end of the semester or during the break between semesters, and most teachers attend. In the meetings, one of the main purposes is for teachers to reconfirm the goals of the curriculum. They also have shared ideas for effective teaching techniques and exchange reactions to their class

---

7 E-cube (www.kindai.ac.jp/e-cube) is a fun learning facility in Kinki University where only English can be used. Various activities and events are held throughout the year. Cafeteria food is also available.

activities. The focus has often been on the standard assignments for the foundation courses, but teachers of advanced courses have also benefited from these meetings. They have learned about the specific role of the advanced courses in the whole programme and about the expectations teachers should have of the students' progress prior to the start of these advanced courses. Teachers, as stakeholders in this context, experience 'familiarisation' with the KCF 'Can Do' descriptors (North 2014) as well as with our curriculum goals, activities, and evaluations through these meetings.

Information sharing among all the teachers concerned on a regular basis in the teachers' room, as well as in FD meetings, has been at the core of curriculum management. Such opportunities have helped the curriculum administrators (i.e. full-time teachers) to reflect on the whole programme and to integrate teachers' opinions when revising the content of standard assignments and the methods of evaluation. The latter has all been done while remaining cognisant of the close connection between these assignments and evaluations and the KCF 'Can Do' descriptors.

4 Discussion

4.1 Content of curricula

4.1.1 What type of implementation has been adopted? What specific practices have been implemented? What practices have been seen to be effective?

As explained in the previous section, the eight foundation courses (English Seminar 1, 2, 3, 4 and Oral English 1, 2, 3, 4) in our curriculum were designed based on the KCF. The KCF provided common curriculum goals and guidelines for class activities to the teachers assigned to these courses. The classroom activities and assignments, especially in these foundation courses, have been designed, prepared, or selected based on the criteria described in the KCF. For example, the online-based essay writing assignments, pair conversations, individual interviews, presentations and extensive reading assignments all have connections to the descriptors in the KCF. In addition, *Dekita Checklists* work as a mediator between the KCF and class activities.

Conveniently, and of course purposefully, the checklists allow the students to reflect on the KCF 'Can Do' descriptors. The students are evaluating their abilities in that framework even if they are not actually referring to the 'Can Do' descriptors in the framework itself because the *Dekita Checklists* are linked to the KCF 'Can Do' descriptors. The same is true for the teachers: even if the teachers are not actually referring to the KCF, they are helping their students to improve KCF-linked abilities by conducting the various kinds of assignments and tests that are required to be included or conducted with unified instructions.

The KCF descriptors outline abilities that are required for authentic and realistic communication. In order to help students to acquire such abilities, there have to be various kinds of practical language learning activities. This 'Can Do' framework-based curriculum was successful in the sense that it allowed all the teachers involved to adopt a communication-focused teaching approach.

The variety of class activities is, in fact, one of the most effective practices, and it was made possible in all the classes taught by about 30 different teachers as a direct result of the usage of a 'Can Do'-based curriculum and the implementation of unified evaluations. The curriculum has adopted an action-based approach as can be seen in the framework descriptors. When the framework presents such action-based descriptors, what is expected of the students in the classroom becomes very clear – both to the students and to the teachers. Those expected actions have to be evaluated in the ways that are specifically described in the framework. In our curriculum such evaluations are realised by using *Dekita Checklists* and standardised evaluation criteria for the standard assignments. Both the checklists and the standardised evaluation criteria were developed based on the KCF.

For example, speaking and listening is referenced back to the KCF through the *Dekita Checklists* for speaking and listening. As with reading and writing, students do self-evaluation periodically throughout the term on their progress in these two skills. For example, one of the speaking KCF statements is 'I can understand short and simple questions and instructions if they are given using slow and clear pronunciation' (K–4). This part is exactly what is evaluated in an interview test. Moreover, 'I can mostly understand what is said in clear and short conversations about familiar topics such as stories about the speaker him/herself or about his/her family' (K–3) can be evaluated in students' performance in the conversation test.

Naturally, these actions that cover various areas of English language abilities (i.e. four skills and grammar and vocabulary in the case of the KCF) should be introduced, used, and performed in class. In this way, a 'Can Do'-based curriculum has great potential to bring a variety of activities to a language classroom (Figure 1). This virtuous cycle triggered by 'Can Do' – descriptors will require teachers to move away from a traditional, teacher-centred, grammar-translation way of teaching. This may not be such a big issue for the teachers in our programme who are already familiar with communicative teaching principles. However, the connection between 'Can Do'-based learning goals (or course objectives), class activities, and evaluations has definitely been one of the most effective parts of our practice.

The PET system and standardised evaluations have also been effective

Figure 1 The 'Can Do' framework virtuous cycle and its by-products

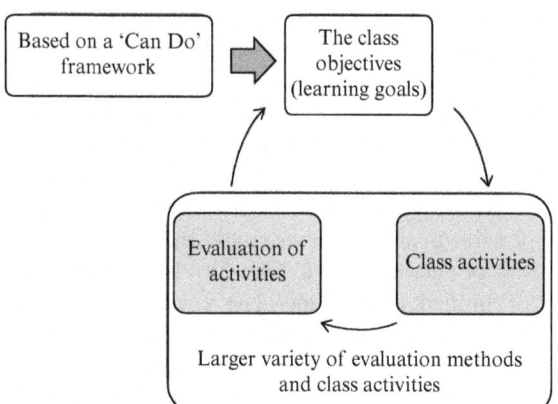

in enhancing evaluation objectivity and driving students and teachers in a single common direction. When students use the KCF descriptors for self-evaluation activities, they may tend to be subjective. This is not a controversial issue since having opportunities for reflection and goal setting is the main purpose of such self-evaluation activities. However, teachers' evaluations should not be subjective. In order to help students improve their skills and to set appropriate goals, students need objective feedback on their progress. The PET system has also ensured that teachers remain faithful to teaching the syllabus and to curriculum goals. All students must be able to perform the same skills on the syllabus regardless of the teacher who is conducting their evaluation. The PET system together with the standard assignments and evaluations has reinforced the awareness of the common objectives among all stakeholders of the English programme.

4.1.2 How are all stakeholders involved? Can the people engaging in CEFR-based teaching and learning develop a sense of ownership?

The CDH and unified evaluation systems are the most important tools for a successful implementation of a 'Can Do' framework-based curriculum which allows all the stakeholders to be involved. However, individual stakeholders seem to hold different levels of sense of ownership.

First, despite its role in implementing the KCF in the foundation courses, the CDH had some issues that need to be addressed. Many of the materials in the earlier versions of the handbook were mainly for two of the four foundation classes, English Seminar 1 and 2. In other words, the handbook was not user friendly for students and teachers in the other foundation courses:

A 'Can Do' framework-based curriculum

English Seminar 3 and 4, and Oral English 1, 2, 3, and 4. A sense of ownership was therefore likely stronger among English Seminar 1 and 2 teachers and less so among teachers of other courses.

In order to improve upon it, the following revisions were integrated into a 2015 version of the CDH:

1. Guidelines and schedule of unified assignments (English) were added.
2. The tables of *Dekita Checklists* were made bilingual and a sample instructional prompt (in English) for a reflection essay assignment was added.
3. The KCF-level graph for students' self-assessment, which previously had space only for the first year, was made for 2-year use.
4. More extensive reading materials (English) were added.
5. Pages of useful websites and useful expressions (English) were added.

The purpose of these additional or revised materials was to make the handbook more user friendly for the first and second year foundation courses.

The teachers provide reflection and goal-setting opportunities using *Dekita Checklists* in the CDH three times in a semester. This means that students need only bring the CDH to the class three times during the semester. However, if that is all that is required of the students, many will simply forget to bring the CDH when they actually need it. Thus, we encourage the CDH to be used in every class. For this purpose, more materials (e.g. useful expressions) have been added. When the students bring the CDH to every class of the foundation courses, their sense of ownership of the CDH is more likely to become stronger. When the *Dekita Checklists* and KCF are referred to regularly, their sense of ownership of the checklists and KCF is also expected to become stronger.

Secondly, the standardised evaluation systems help to strengthen the teachers' sense of ownership. The standard elements of the course syllabus are explained and discussed at regular FD meetings, and on other occasions both formally and casually throughout the semester. The teachers' involvement becomes stronger and deeper especially when the PET system is in effect; teachers have no choice but to share information about their own students' learning progress with other teachers. By conducting information sharing, the teachers' sense of ownership of the KCF-based curriculum is strengthened. More discussion on this point will be provided in the following section.

4.1.3 Has the CEFR promoted a system for in-house evaluation of curricula and learning targets? Do curricula and course include transparent and concrete learning objectives, with accepted 'Can Do' descriptors at the centre? Is it possible to compare the results of instruction in different classes?

The standardised evaluation system is a critical tool for the successful management of the curriculum. The assignments were designed based on the KCF, and the evaluation criteria for these assignments are linked to the KCF descriptors. The criteria are also derived from the standard syllabuses of the foundation courses. In turn, the syllabuses specify shared learning goals, and these goals are directly linked to, and indeed emanate from, the KCF descriptors.

Some of the descriptors are not directly connected to the CEFR, as they were prepared independently from the CEFR descriptors (see section 2.1). However, the CEFR principle that a common basis for assessment should be provided to the teachers and students in different teaching and learning contexts (Council of Europe 2001) is adopted in our curriculum. This principle has promoted a system where we collaboratively reflect upon our course syllabuses, activity guidelines, and task-based evaluations such as essay writing and face-to-face interviews.

The FD meetings, with all the teachers concerned, have become part of such a system. Moreover, countless opportunities are taken, sometimes among only full-time faculty members (the core curriculum development and management members) and sometimes between full-time and part-time teachers in the teachers' common room, to discuss evaluation criteria for specific unified assignments such as presentations and conversation tests. These formal and informal discussions have also led to a constant refining of evaluation criteria for rubrics of different assignments, particularly the criteria in the speaking test's rubric.

PET also plays an effective role in the system. All classes follow the same syllabus and it is incumbent on the teacher to use the task-based topics of the syllabus. The latter is imperative since teachers exchange classes for the final tests and do not test their own students. A 'stray' instructor teaching outside the parameters of the syllabus will put his students at a disadvantage when tested by another teacher. When students' performances are evaluated by different teachers using the same evaluation criteria, every evaluation period turns into an opportunity for teachers to reflect on their own class activities. The teachers are encouraged to reflect on what and how they teach their classes; they examine whether their class activities are helping their students achieve learning targets. These, in turn, are closely linked to the framework descriptors. (For more discussion on PET see section 4.2.3).

4.2 Classroom instruction

4.2.1 Do 'Can Do' checklists serve as the key reference point for processes of reflective teaching/learning in which self-assessment plays a central role? How?

As mentioned, students in the foundation courses are instructed to use the checklists as part of their reflection and goal-setting activity three times in a semester: at the beginning, in the middle, and at the end of the semester. Students in some classes are also asked to write a short explanation about their methods and goals for improving their English. The classroom usage of the checklists in both English Seminar and Oral English courses has been very useful in building awareness among students of the meaning and basic principles of the KCF. It has also given teachers the most direct exposure to and experience with the 'Can Do' descriptors and statements. For students, the time given to fill in the checklists is an opportunity to develop learner autonomy and self-reflection skills. For teachers, it gives them an opportunity to observe how students view their own abilities *vis-à-vis* the checklists and the areas and skills which students wish to improve upon. This information can prove invaluable for teachers in terms of class planning and content prioritisation.

For example, a questionnaire survey conducted among 292 first year students regarding their reactions to the use of *Dekita Checklists* (Shimo 2013) has produced interesting results. The survey focused on the use of speaking and writing *Dekita Checklists* as those two areas of skills were particularly emphasised in our curriculum goals. The survey results indicated that students found it easy to evaluate the ability if they had actually done the task that requires the ability in class. Conversely, they found it difficult to evaluate the ability if they had never used it in a task in class. The results revealed the kinds of activities that teachers did not provide enough of in the students' classes. To put it another way, the use of *Dekita Checklists* not only helps the students evaluate their own abilities but also helps the teachers to decide what kind of activities should be done in their classes. The survey results were shared in an FD meeting, and suggestions for improving their class activities and assignments were discussed at that time. For example, one other finding was that most students thought they could not write specific types of essays such as descriptive and cause and effect essays. Thus, the teachers concluded that clearer instructions about essay types would be beneficial to students.

The time spent on the *Dekita Checklists* is crucial for teachers because they gain further familiarity with the 'Can Do' descriptors and statements. Finally, for both students and teachers, each time the *Dekita Checklists* are used in class, it becomes a reference point for the entire KCF curriculum.

Teachers and students are reminded of the main principles and goals of the programme as well as what remains to be accomplished.

4.2.2 What are the interpretations of teachers, students, and other stakeholders, of the philosophy and ideas of the CEFR?

Even though both teachers and students are exposed to the KCF descriptors (which overlap with CEFR ideas), they both need more familiarity with the application of the descriptors. In-class materials, except for materials included in the CDH, are not explicitly referenced to KCF descriptors and thus this makes it difficult for teachers to become conscious of the framework, let alone the underlying CEFR philosophy.

While cognisant of the different bands and the associated 'Can Do' abilities in KCF/CEFR, many teachers are not explicitly introducing them into classroom activities. This is mainly because teachers have not had sufficient exposure to the descriptors and their levels. They do not know how to explicitly link them to their activities and then to the learning outcomes. In a large English programme such as the programme in this faculty, many of the teachers are hired on a part-time basis. This makes it difficult to have ongoing professional development for teachers. Ware, Robertson and Paydon (2011:12) have underscored the importance of faculty development and have described it as a 'critical step' in the implementation of the CEFR. In their case, five sessions were necessary to train teachers in the new criteria and goals of the programme. According to a study conducted by Barnwell (cited in Fulcher 2003:42), teachers who had undergone training and constant operation of scales and descriptors garnered higher testing reliability co-efficients than those who had not. He deemed this process of learning and understanding the criteria as 'socialisation'. Similarly, if a teacher is not given explicit instruction on the KCF/CEFR principles and 'Can Do' abilities and is not fully aware that the same or similar objectives are embedded within a textbook, learning outcomes can become skewed and disorderly. In our programme, the two faculty development meetings per year are used to instruct teachers on KCF principles. Over time, it is expected that the faculty will experience this socialisation and gain a firmer grasp of the different KCF levels, their descriptors and the 'Can Do' descriptors as they go through North's (2014) familiarisation process.

In regard to testing and evaluations, the rubric has evolved and student assessment has become more precise, which provides valuable feedback to both teachers and students. A 'top-down' process as defined by Ware et al (2011:4) in which 'course goals should be directly linked to assessment "Can Do" statements and in turn to individual assessment rubrics' is slowly taking hold in each reformulation of the rubric. Further refinement of the rubric and descriptors will be necessary through this process. The formality of testing has also provided the programme with added legitimacy in the eyes of the students. It is hoped that this enhanced face validity will result in positive washback: that is, the students will learn by the end of the year that active in-class participation in oral activities will lead to better test grades. There is anecdotal evidence of enhanced legitimacy as animated conversation among students pertaining to test preparations and content can often be heard in hallways and classrooms in the days prior to testing.

Another issue relates to the textbook as the main source of materials for in-class activities for teachers. By allowing teachers to freely select a textbook from a lengthy list, teachers are able to match their teaching style and strengths to the skills and goals of the unified syllabus. However, the drawback is that classes have become textbook driven as opposed to 'Can Do' based. It is fortuitous that most textbooks available on the market have either been given CEFR equivalencies or they have been fully developed based on CEFR descriptors and principles. That said, however, faculty administrators (i.e. full-time English teachers) need to make a more explicit connection between in-class materials and KCF descriptors in order for teachers to use the 'Can Do'-based curriculum as the foundation for language improvement and course goals. Both M Sato (2010) and Collett and Sullivan (2010) have shown the favourable impact of frequent in-class referencing of 'Can Do' descriptors on both reflective learning and language outcomes. In a subsection of a later edited paper, Collett and Sullivan are clear on the importance of this:

> What is essential in helping students to develop the requisite strategies and skills is to explicate expected outcomes of learning, and provide the guidance students need to formulate learning goals along with a clear framework through which they can assess the outcomes of their goal-directed efforts (O'Dwyer, Nagai, Collett, Sullivan and Smith 2011:273).

In their case, they used study progress sheets that incorporated 'Can Do' descriptors. According to their surveys, the results of using the sheets were quite positive: they helped students to identify strengths and weaknesses in the usage of course content and goals, which is a first step towards autonomous learning and reflection (O'Dwyer et al 2011:273). More frequent use of *Dekita Checklists* may be necessary to help the teachers and students focus more on the learning objectives. This would also allow them to make the most of the KCF/CEFR ideas.

Notwithstanding these challenges, both teachers and students have acknowledged the utility of the curriculum. The CEFR is based on communicative theory, which is now the dominant theory in the second language classroom (Little 2012). On the one hand, for teachers this has meant an easy in-class application of the underlying teaching philosophy (i.e. communicative theory). Even though the CEFR principles are not explicit, they are salient in the curriculum through the CDH and *Dekita Checklists* as mentioned earlier. On the other hand, for students, communicative theory can be new to them since in many high school English classes, grammar and language translation teaching methods are still prevalent. They may need time to adapt to the new teaching style and content. However, once students have become immersed in the methodology, they tend to enjoy it as the action-based content provides many opportunities for speaking and physical movement inside the classroom (standing up to communicate with classmates across the room, etc.).

4.2.3 Are the CEFR-based materials (textbooks, teaching content, etc.) action-oriented, and easily applicable by both teachers and students?

Our KCF-based materials are action-oriented and easily applicable by both teachers and students. Required, unified assignments in the programme include vocabulary learning, extensive reading, interview and conversation tasks, essay writing and presentations. Many of these assignments are action-oriented. Students' performances are evaluated based on action-oriented criteria and reflected in their course grades. For example, for presentation assignments the evaluation criteria we use for a total of 30 points are:

- content (appropriate topic, depth of research and discussion, etc.) (10 points)
- expression and grammar (5 points)
- pronunciation, fluency, loudness (5 points)
- eye contact, gestures, and posture (5 points)
- effective use of visual aids (5 points).

All the teachers in different courses (e.g. English Seminar 4 and Oral English 4) use the same criteria in presentation rehearsals and final presentations, for the latter of which the PET system is used. A similar system is used for interviews and conversation tasks (see section 3.2.2).

Moreover, the PET system, which is used in these interview, conversation and presentation assignments, has contributed to a more effective functioning of the 'Can Do' framework-based curriculum. The students need to know the common standards and criteria different teachers will use for their evaluations. The CDH gives both teachers and students such information through *Dekita Checklists* as well as KCF. In addition, the PET system makes the students take their performances more seriously. When PET is in effect during testing periods, students are expected to perform any one of a variety of tasks spontaneously including having a conversation with a partner, taking part in an interview with the teacher on certain topics, or doing a presentation in front of the whole class. This system acts as a tremendous stimulus to students in many different ways. For example, students may feel nervous when doing the tasks but when they complete them, they can be expected to gain confidence in their language abilities. The students will also feel a stronger sense of achievement and their serious engagement with the task will encourage them to reflect more deeply on their learning experience.

While we can see these positive effects among the KCF-based assignments, there are some issues as well. The evaluation criteria for these assignments were developed based on the KCF, but the KCF levels and descriptors themselves will require further refinement and development. It has been recognised that some of the 'Can Do' descriptors of the KCF, even the ones that were based on CEFR equivalents, are ambiguous and difficult to interpret. The emphasis of the descriptors has been on quantity (i.e. how many words can be read/spoken, etc. per minute rather than the actual ability they entail), but more emphasis on quality may be necessary. Also, some of the KCF descriptors are not as aligned to the CEFR as they could be, and thus more overlap between the KCF and the CEFR may be desirable.

4.2.4 Can all readily see the benefits of the CEFR-based approach for their own teaching/learning?

The benefits of a 'Can Do'-based approach are very clear in the faculty's English learning programme. This approach helped to create student-centred classrooms and brought about a variety of activities that cover all five of the language areas specified in the framework. As discussed earlier (section 4.1.1), the connection between learning goals, class activities and evaluation became very effective. When learning goals were specified with 'Can Do' descriptors in the framework and 'Can Do' descriptors in the *Dekita Checklists*, class activities had to be 'Can Do' based or in other words, action based. This in turn meant that evaluations also had to be 'Can Do' based, which is to say once again, action based. The curriculum administrators were expected to prepare unified assignments and evaluation methods for the curriculum to work effectively. For the teachers who were not core members of the curriculum development team, however, the benefits of this 'Can Do'-based approach may have been rather difficult to perceive. Having simply been provided with instructions about these various unified assignments and evaluation methods, it is not their fault if they remained unaware of the benefits of the 'Can Do'-based curriculum. However, teachers could appreciate the positive learning outcomes that resulted from the unified assignments and evaluations even though they may not have associated them directly with the KCF.

For the core members of the curriculum development and management team, the benefits of a 'Can Do'-based curriculum are clear because of the virtuous cycle created by the linkage among class objectives, activities and evaluations. One of the aims that the CEFR has is to provide 'a common basis for the elaboration of language syllabuses, curriculum guidelines, examinations, textbooks, etc. across Europe' (Council of Europe 2001:1) and similarly, the KCF has been functioning as a common basis for the core members of the curriculum development and management team. When they developed course syllabuses including unified assignments and evaluation methods, they based their ideas on the framework.

More exposure, or in North's terms, familiarisation, to the KCF is necessary for the rest of the teachers as well as for the students in order for them to readily connect the positive learning outcomes to the KCF. This would also help in making all actors more aware of the relationship between KCF and its underlying CEFR principles. It should also be pointed out as emphasised above that people can benefit from their surroundings even when they are not aware of the framework within which they work.

4.2.5 Is autonomous learning beyond the specified materials (e.g. textbooks) supported and encouraged? If so, how?

One of the main goals of our programme is to help students to develop autonomy. This is done by having students learn to set methods and goals that are based on self-evaluation activities. Reflection and self-evaluation is encouraged through the use of the CDH and *Dekita Checklists* in the handbook. They have functioned as a tool to promote learner autonomy.

The goal of autonomous learning is crucial to the CEFR. The Council of Europe (2001:6) states the following as the main tenets of self-learning:

- raising the learner's awareness of his or her present state of knowledge
- self-setting of feasible and worthwhile objectives
- selection of materials
- self-assessment.

The goals of the faculty's English programme are consistent with all four of these purposes through the use of the checklists regarding the five language areas (i.e. speaking, listening, reading, writing, and grammar and vocabulary). Since the checklists are filled in three times a semester for each of these skills, students have ample opportunities to review their current state of English knowledge and ability. When completing the checklists, students are asked to think about future goals and methods to achieve these goals. They are also asked to reflect on previous methods and goal statements and to give a sincere account of whether they were able to accomplish them and if not, why not. This is done in some classrooms via a written assignment.

In sum, through the *Dekita Checklists* students have the opportunity to monitor their learning, reflect on their abilities and think about their own learning methods. Moreover, some pages on which students keep their learning activity record (i.e. extensive reading record pages, reading speed record pages, etc.) in the CDH have also helped students better monitor their learning, which is one of the important aspects of learner autonomy. Some of these learning record pages have been revised in the 2015 version of CDH. The remaining learning record pages will keep functioning as a learner autonomy facilitator.

In addition to the handbook, many out-of-class assignments have been set in order to promote autonomous learning. The faculty language programme has included the use of online tools for vocabulary, extensive reading, and essay writing assignments. All of them can or should be used only outside the classroom. The online tools offer students the freedom to choose the time and frequency (the minimum requirement is set) of doing the activities outside the class, which should help to foster their learner autonomy. These assignments entail real-life communicative objectives and emphasise students' learning processes.

For example, M-Reader allows greater freedom for the students in terms of book choice, reading pace and level of difficulty. M-Reader also keeps a record of students' reading activities, while encouraging them to read a certain amount continuously rather than to read a lot at one time and then stop. Through the use of this automated software students will become responsible for searching for their own reading materials and for their own reading time management. These tasks wholly conform to the autonomous learning principles of the CEFR/KCF. When M-Reader became part of the unified assignments, the extensive reading record pages in the CDH were replaced with instructions about M-Reader.

However, many of our students (especially those who do only the minimum amount of work outside the class) may feel that they are simply doing what they are required to do. They may have a similar feeling even when they do reflection and self-evaluation activities, which are in fact supposed to promote learner autonomy. The students should realise that learning and knowledge acquisition are important in themselves so that they can develop a positive attitude towards these activities.

Also, when choices are allowed, students feel that they can make more autonomous decisions. A number of required assignments and activities such as presentations and essay writing may make the students think that they are simply obliged to do those assignments. But when they are allowed to make choices in those unified assignments, they may find the task offers more individual freedom. For example, students can be allowed to select a topic for their presentation assignments and to research appropriate materials at their discretion. In addition, M-Reader has been a part of extensive reading assignments, and this is another area in which students have the opportunity to select their own materials.

Students should feel that they themselves are managing their own learning process through self-generated activities. As discussed above, students are given ample opportunities to self-evaluate and to set goals when using the

Dekita Checklists. Yet, there are few activities that permit them to achieve these goals with their own initiative. Most activities are teacher originated, prompted and guided. This is an area which needs some revision and improvement. That said, the unified assignments do offer much latitude of choice as mentioned above. They also teach the basic techniques for logical thinking, speaking and writing. With these in hand, students can venture to apply these new methods to other challenges. This is the first step towards autonomous learning for the students. The programme administrators however do need to recognise that further development of syllabuses that allow students to generate their own methods and materials for learning will be necessary. One option to be considered is to introduce a portfolio component to the programme. Further programme development will be required to forge ways to help students become true autonomous learners.

5 Conclusion

This chapter was completed with not only the intention of recommending strategies to others who wish to implement a 'Can Do'-based programme but also as a blueprint for these authors to further advance their own programme. It has provided us with ample opportunities not only for reflective teaching but also for reflective curriculum development and management.

We believe our handbook, the CDH, can be utilised as a key to a successful 'Can Do' curriculum. In addition, the standardised evaluation systems play a critical role in the effective management of the curriculum. As for the CDH, by using it as the unifying source of materials for all classes, students and teachers can share their expectations as well as reflect upon their results together. Reflection and goal-setting activities in the CDH help students monitor their learning processes and outcomes more effectively. While the CDH provides guidelines for standard activities such as extensive reading, essay writing, presentations, interview and conversation assignments, the standardised evaluation systems enable all the teachers to actually focus on improving their students for the shared curriculum goals.

Further discussion involving all the teachers will be useful and necessary regarding the future revision of the handbook to make it even more user friendly and thus even more helpful for English language teaching and learning. Moreover, the discussion cannot be done in isolation from the discussion of unified assignments and evaluations. The revision should entail, first and foremost, detailed feedback and suggestions from all of the stakeholders, especially from students and teachers as they are the ones who use the CDH on a regular basis. In this process, it is hoped that all stakeholders will gain a deeper understanding of the CEFR principles underlying the programme. This, in turn, should help us further develop the KCF into a better language learning curriculum.

A 'Can Do' framework-based curriculum

The main recommendations for the implementation of a CEFR-based curriculum in a large institution where maintaining pedagogic consistency across many teachers, classes and students is a challenge are summarised as follows:

- Develop or use existing appropriate 'Can Do' descriptors.
- Create one (or more) main set of guidelines – in our case the CDH – for use by all teachers and students. This text should contain the goals, 'Can Do' descriptors, activities for measuring achievement, explanation of assignments, evaluation criteria and rubrics, etc. This will allow all stakeholders to be in possession of a reference manual on the scope and substance of the language education programme. For the students, possession of such information (e.g. the checklist of 'Can Do' descriptors, the KCF, evaluation criteria, etc.) will make it clear to them the skills they should master. Having the CDH has made it easy for the students to refer to critical information during in-class activities and prior to tests or during self-learning activities outside the classroom.
- Use a common syllabus, assignments, and especially standardised evaluation activities to maintain quality and a single direction of the programme especially among teachers. This can be accomplished through a PET system.
- Encourage autonomous learning by teaching skills that entail real-world communicative objectives and emphasise the learning process. The skills can be basic, but then students should be expected to apply those basic skills to complete their own assignments and projects. For example, we use writing software to improve students' understanding of the basic writing skills and essay formatting. Students' then had to research and write their own essays using the skills and format taught.
- Have students periodically consider their abilities *vis-à-vis* the checklists.

There are still a number of issues and challenges that need to be considered. They are:

1. The 'Can Do' abilities should be better and more often referred to in the classroom by both teachers and students.
2. All teachers need to be fully debriefed and aware of the 'Can Do' descriptors and their value in the language learning process. This should help in avoiding textbook-driven classes as opposed to a principled CEFR-based classroom.
3. If developing your own 'Can Do' descriptors based on the CEFR's statements, they need to be fully grounded in communicative theory (i.e. learning through action-based tasks with authentic, real-world communicative objectives).

4. 'Can Do' descriptors' validity, usefulness, and particularly clarity will need to be demonstrated. They will likely require constant revision and refinement to serve as a context-specific, helpful learning and teaching tool.
5. Teachers will need periodic training on CEFR 'Can Do' descriptors when using them for evaluation purposes.

For our faculty, the CEFR offered us a convenient and theoretically sound structure in which to apply our communicative curriculum that was being used previously. It was easy to adapt the task-based syllabus and mould it together with the clearly defined CEFR 'Can Do' descriptors and precepts. The goals and methods for autonomous learning should be revisited often to ensure students are indeed becoming life-long learners. The CEFR levels, 'Can Do' descriptors and general principles then evolved into the KCF after adapting them to our needs and inserting the modified versions into the curriculum. Finally, the embedding of a standard syllabus, assignment and evaluation system inside the KCF has led to our biggest success: the maintenance of a good quality of English language education among a large teacher and student body.

References

Bachman, L F (1990) *Fundamental Considerations in Language Testing*, Oxford: Oxford University Press.
Bachman, L F and Palmer, D (1996) *Language Testing in Practice*, Oxford: Oxford University Press.
Chauncey Group International (2000) *TOEIC® Can-Do Guide: Linking TOEIC Scores to Activities Performed Using English*, available online: www.ets.org/Media/Research/pdf/TOEIC_CAN_DO.pdf
Collett, P and Sullivan, K (2010) Considering the use of *can do* statements to develop learners' self-regulative and metacognitive strategies, in Schmidt, M S, Naganuma, N, O'Dwyer, F, Imig, A and Sakai, K (Eds) *Can Do Statements in Language Education in Japan and Beyond – Applications of the CEFR* (2nd edition), Tokyo: Asahi Press, 157–166.
Council of Europe (2001) *Common European Framework of Reference for Languages: Learning, Teaching, Assessment*, Cambridge: Cambridge University Press.
Coxhead, A (2000) A New Academic Word List, *TESOL Quarterly* 34 (2), 213–238.
Fulcher, G (2003) *Testing Second Language Speaking*, Harlow: Pearson Longman.
Hymes, D (2001) On communicative competence, in Duranti A (Ed) *Linguistic Anthropology: A Reader*, Malden: Blackwell Publishers, Ltd, 53–73.
Kindai University Faculty of Applied Sociology, Department of General Education, English Language Learning Program Management Team (2010–2015) *My Can-Do Handbook*, Higashiosaka: Kindai University.
Little, D (1991) *Learner Autonomy: Definitions, Issues and Problems*, Dublin: Authentik Language Learning Resources.

Little, D (2012) *The CEFR and Language Teaching/Learning*, paper presented at ACTFL–CEFR Symposium 2012, available online: www.uni-leipzig.de/actflcefr/material/Teaching%20Learning%20CEFR%20Little.pdf

Macaro, E (1997) *Target Language, Collaborative Learning and Autonomy*, Clevedon: Multilingual Matters.

Naganuma, N and Nagasue, A (2006) *SELHi jissen ni motozuku kasumigaoka Can-Do guredo no kaihatsu [Development of Kasumi Can-Do Grade based on the practices at a SELHi]*, presentation given at the 45th National Convention of the Japan Association for College English Teachers, Osaka, 2006.

Nagasue, A (no date) *Eigoka ni okeru Can-Do risuto oyobi "gakushu-hyoka tasuku" kaitatsu-jiritsuteki gakushusha wo mezasu SELHi Post SEL Hi ni okeru 9 nenkan no jissen hokoku [Development of Can-Do lists and "learning-evaluation tasks" at the English Department – A report on nine years of practice for autonomous learners at SELHi and Post SELHi]*, available online: gtec.for-students.jp/cando/cando_pdf/02_example.pdf

Nitta, K (2008) Kinki daigaku ni okersu supikingu raitingu toitsu tesuto donyu no hitsuyosei [The necessity of introducing speaking and writing unified tests at Kinki University], *Kinki University Department of Language Education Bulletin* 8 (2), 235–251.

North, B (2014) *The CEFR in Practice*, English Profile Studies volume 4, Cambridge: UCLES/Cambridge University Press.

O'Dwyer, F, Nagai, N, Collett, P, Sullivan, K and Smith, A (2011) Framework and Language Portfolio SIG Forum: Looking forward, in Stewart, A (Ed) *JALT 2010 Conference Proceedings*, Tokyo: The Japan Association for Language Teaching, 269–280.

Ramirez, C (2011) Some initial considerations of Unified Oral Testing in a Japanese university context, *Kinki University Center for Liberal Arts and Foreign Language Education Journal (Foreign Language Edition)* 2 (1), 307–330.

Research and Validation Group, University of Cambridge (2009) *Examples of Speaking Performance at CEFR Levels A2 to C2*, available online: www.cambridgeenglish.org/images/22649-rv-examples-of-speaking-performance.pdf

Ridley, J (2003) Learners' ability to reflect on language and on their learning, in Little, D, Ridley, J and Ushioda, E (Eds) *Learner Autonomy in the Foreign Language Classroom: Teacher, Learner, Curriculum and Assessment*, Dublin: Authentik, 78–89.

Sato, M (2006) *Gakko no chosen: Manabi no ktodotai wo tsukuru [Challenges by Schools: Creating Communities for Learning]*, Tokyo: Shogakukan.

Sato, M (2010) *Kyoiku no hoho [Education Methodology]*, Tokyo: Sayusha.

Sato, Y (2010) Using Can Do statements to promote reflective learning, in Schmidt, M S, Naganuma, N, O'Dwyer, F, Imig, A and Sakai, K (Eds) *Can Do Statements in Language Education in Japan and Beyond – Applications of the CEFR* (2nd edition), Tokyo: Asahi Press, 167–183.

Schneider, G and Lenz, P (2001) *European Language Portfolio: Guide for Developers*, Strasbourg: Council of Europe.

Shimo, E (2013) *Report from a survey about English learning at Socia (Faculty of Applied Sociology)*, presentation given at the meeting jugyo kaizen kenkyu kai, Faculty of Applied Sociology, Kinki University, March 2013.

Shimo, E and Nitta, K (2011) Developing can-do checklists as a self-evaluation tool for university-level English classes, *Kinki University Center for Liberal Arts and Foreign Language Education Journal* 2 (1),

225–245, available online: kurepo.clib.kindai.ac.jp/modules/xoonips/detail.php?id=AA12508620-20111130-0225

Society for Testing English Proficiency (no date) *Eiken Kyan – Duu Ristuto [The Eiken 'Can Do' List]*, available online: www.eiken.or.jp/eiken/exam/cando/

Ware, J L, Robertson, C and Paydon, S (2011) An implementation of a CEFR-based writing Can Do curriculum, in Stewart, A (Ed) *JALT 2010 Conference Proceedings*, Tokyo: The Japan Association for Language Teaching, 8–19.

Wenden, A L (1991) *Learners' Strategies for Learner Autonomy: Planning and Implementing Learner Training for Language Learners*, New York: Prentice Hall.

West, M (1953) *A General Service List of English Words*, London: Longman, Green and Co.

Appendix 1

A Kindai Can Do Framework (KCF)

Please note that in the framework listed inside the CDH, the statements are provided in a table; however, they will be listed below in this Appendix. The descriptors specified with a CEFR level(s) are from or based on the CEFR 'Can Do' descriptors.

Table 4 Kindai scale, CEFR scale, and TOEIC score

Kindai level	K–4	K–3	K–2	K–1	K–Global
CEFR level	A1/A2	A2/B1	B1	B1/B2	B2
TOEIC	350 <	350 +	450 +	550 +	650 +

1. Listening

K–4

I can understand short and simple questions and instructions if they are given using slow and clear pronunciation. (A1, A2)

I can understand the point of clear and short conversations of familiar topics such as stories about the speaker him/herself or about his/her family.

K–3

I can understand the point of simple spoken messages and announcements if they are spoken using clear pronunciation. (A2)

I can mostly understand what is said in clear and short conversations about familiar topics such as stories about the speaker him/herself or about his/her family. (A2)

K–2

I can understand the points of relatively long conversations, speeches, or announcements, if they are given using clear pronunciation. (B1)

I can understand the point of a 50-word passage utilising clear pronunciation, about personal topics, current affairs, and about introductory content in my major field. (B1)

K–1

I can understand the point of a 100-word passage using clear pronunciation about personal topics and current affairs, about my major field. (B2)

I can understand the point of what is said on TV dramas and in movies if they are easy. (B2)

K–Global
I can understand the content of relatively long conversations, speeches, and announcements. (B2)
I can understand the point of lectures in liberal arts and in my major field. (B2)
I can understand most of the content in TV dramas, movies, and news if they are easy. (B2)

2. Speaking

K–4
I can use expressions frequently used in daily life and use set phrases used for social interactions naturally. (A1)
I can speak for half a minute (making a few sentences) about my family, people around me, living conditions, and school life, if preparation time is given according to the difficulty level of the topic. (A1)

K–3
I can use expressions and respond appropriately to the situation (e.g. making requests, asking for permission, and expressing thanks) with pronunciation clear enough for the listener to understand.
I can speak for one minute about myself or about familiar topics in daily life, if preparation time is given according to the difficulty level of the topic. (B1)

K–2
I can respond quickly in short but proper sentences while understanding the purpose and functions of the other speaker's utterance. (B1)
I can use several kinds of expressions according to the functions and situation (e.g. making requests, suggestions, proposals, apologies, ordering food, etc.), while understanding the level of politeness.
I can speak for more than one minute about topics of my personal interests (e.g. summaries of books and movies and reactions to them, etc.), if preparation time is given according to the difficulty level of the topic. (B1)

K–1
I can respond quickly in proper sentences while understanding the purpose and functions of the speaker's utterance. (B2)
I can continue conversations and discussions by asking questions according to the situation. (B2)
I can speak for more than three minutes with notes about topics of personal interests, current affairs, and about my major field of study. (B2)

I can explain the reasons for my opinion briefly for one minute even if no preparation time is given.

K–Global
I can respond naturally in most situations in daily conversation.
I can explain about various topics for more than five minutes with notes, including discussion in my major field, if preparation time is given according to the difficulty level of the topic. (B2)
I can explain the reasons for my opinion for more than one minute even if no preparation time is given.

3. Reading

Table 5 Level and headwords for extensive reading materials

	K–4	K–3	K–2	K–1	K–Global
Headwords (HW)	HW< 500	HW< 1,000	HW< 1,400	HW< 2,300	HW> 2,300

Please note that (*1) means the level of graded readers.

K–4
I can understand very short, simple English passages (e.g. notes, schedules). (A2)
I can read the passages in my textbook at the rate of 60 words or more per minute and understand the gist.
I can understand Level 1 (*1) extensive reading (ER) materials while hardly using a dictionary.

K–3
I can understand English passages written in the commonly accepted style. (A2)
I can read the passages in my textbook at the rate of 80 words or more per minute and understand the gist.
I can understand Level 2 (*1) ER materials while hardly using a dictionary.

K–2
I can understand most of the passages and articles written for English learners at the college and university level, and passages about content in my major field, while making use of dictionaries. (B1)
I can read a passage in my textbook, and a relatively easy passage in my major field, at the rate of 100 words or more per minute and understand the gist.
I can understand Level 3 (*1) ER materials while hardly using a dictionary.

K–1
I can understand passages about current affairs, and passages about my major field while making use of dictionaries. (B2)
I can read a passage in my textbook, and a relatively easy passage in my major field at the rate of 130 words or more per minute and understand the gist.
I can understand Level 4 (*1) ER materials while hardly using a dictionary.

K–Global
I can understand to some extent essays and articles written for native speakers, academic literature, etc. while making use of dictionaries. (B2)
I can read a passage in my textbook, and a passage in my major field, at the rate of 180 words or more per minute and understand the gist.
I can understand Level 5 (*1) ER materials while hardly using a dictionary.

4. Writing

K–4
I can write short notes, messages, and letters of thanks. (A2)
I can write three to five coherent sentences about topics of personal interests while making use of dictionaries.
I can write information about myself following a format.

K–3
I can write letters of thanks and greetings. (A2)
I can write a paragraph of 50 words about topics of my interests and personal experiences while making use of dictionaries.

K–2
I can write an essay of one to three paragraphs (100 words) about familiar topics while making use of dictionaries. (B1)
I can write while being aware of the type of essay (e.g. cause and effect, comparison, list, etc.).

K–1
I can write a passage of 300 words or more about various topics in fields I am interested in while making use of dictionaries. (B2)
I can write an essay of 150 words about a given topic in 30 minutes without using a dictionary.

K–Global
I can write various types of essays of 500 words or more, while making use of dictionaries. (B2)
I can write an essay of 200 words about a given topic in 30 minutes without using a dictionary.

5. Vocabulary and grammar

Please note that (*2) indicates the word 'level' means the level of word family, and (*3) indicates academic words that come from the Academic Word List (Coxhead 2000).

K–4
I can pay attention to the proper use of grammatical features in activities that require accuracy in grammatical use.
I can use compound and complex sentences properly with 'and', 'but', 'because', 'when', and so on.
I can use the words on the 500-word level (*2) vocabulary list.
I can understand most words on the 1,000-word level vocabulary list.

K–3
I can make use of basic grammatical features in activities that require accuracy in grammatical use.
I can use expressions to connect sentences or paragraphs properly.
I can use the words of the 500-word level (*2) vocabulary list effectively.
I can understand most words on the 1,500-word level vocabulary list.

K–2
I can make proper use of basic grammatical features even in activities the focus of which is on speaking or writing fluency.
I can use sentences and vocabulary for topic sentences and supporting sentences effectively.
I can use most words of the 1,000-word level (*2) vocabulary list effectively.
I can understand most words on the 2,000-word level vocabulary list.

K–1
I can make proper use of various grammatical features even in activities the focus of which is on speaking or writing fluency.
I can correct grammatical mistakes in my own or other students' essays by making use of grammar knowledge.
I can use most words on the 1,500-word level (*2) vocabulary list effectively.
I can understand the words on the 2,000-word level vocabulary list and their derivatives.
I can understand most of the Academic Word List (570 words) (*3).

K–Global
I can make proper use of various grammatical features in using English in various activities.
I can use the words on the 2,000-word level (*2) vocabulary list effectively.
I can use the words on the Academic Word List (570 words) (*3) effectively.
I can understand the words on the 3,000-word level vocabulary list and their derivatives.

Appendix 2

Statements from speaking Dekita Checklists (sample)

1. I was able to use commonly used expressions and set phrases (e.g. greetings and social exchanges) in daily conversations with natural pronunciation. (K–4)
2. I was able to speak for about 30 seconds (a few sentences) using simple words and natural pronunciation, about myself, my family, people around me, living situations, and school life, if I had time to prepare. (K–4)
3. I was able to use expressions and respond appropriately to the function (e.g. request, permission, gratitude, etc.) and situation, with clear, intelligible pronunciation and speed. (K–3)
4. I was able to speak fluently for one minute about myself or familiar everyday topics, if I had time to prepare. (K–3)
5. I was able to speak fluently for one minute about topics of interest to me (summary and reactions to books and movies, etc.) if I had time to prepare. (K–2)
6. I was able to use expressions appropriate to the level of politeness, and return short and appropriate responses without hesitation. (K–2)
7. I was able to ask questions, keep conversations and discussions going, and reply with quick and proper responses according to the situation. (K–1)
8. I was able to express my opinions with reasons for a minute even without time to prepare. (K–1)
9. I was able to speak for three minutes or longer, using notes and slides, about personal topics, social issues, and topics relating to my major field of studies, if given time to prepare. (K–1)
10. I was able to respond naturally in most daily conversations, and was able to express my opinions with reasons for a minute or longer even without time to prepare. (K–Global)
11. I was able to speak for five minutes or longer, using notes and slides, about various topics including topics in my field of studies, if given time to prepare. (K–Global)

8 Implementing the CEFR as a benchmark for 'action-oriented' syllabus design

Mark de Boer
Akita International University

1 Introduction

The purpose of this chapter is to outline how the Common European Framework of Reference for Languages (CEFR) (Council of Europe 2001) is being implemented at Iwate University. In 2010 an Information and Communications Technology (ICT) contents project began at Iwate University (de Boer 2011, de Boer, Onaka and Nakanishi 2012) where the content developed was aimed at providing English education specific to students' areas of study, such as chemistry, biochemistry, education, and humanities. In this way, English is taught using concepts in these areas of study rather than teaching English directly as a subject. This chapter in part outlines an example of a situation where it is not possible or viable to fully familiarise stakeholders with the concepts of the CEFR, so these concepts were integrated into the curriculum content. Through the development of this content came the implementation of skills-based learning designed to provide students with skills that would benefit them once they entered the workforce. On a wider level, I also outline how the CEFR can be used to implement national priorities and policies, in this case developing 'global human resources' in learners. In 2010, the Ministry of Economy, Trade and Industry (METI) released a document which outlined possible reasons for why Japan was falling behind economically and technologically on a global scale. This brought to the forefront the concepts of 'global human resources' and 'globalisation' and this reinforced the need to incorporate a skills-based curriculum into the ICT contents platform. The CEFR criteria, action-oriented approach, and 'Can Do' descriptors were used as the core to develop the ICT contents platform. As will be outlined in this paper, the ICT contents system has been developed as a face for the CEFR and this has been built based on the CEFR guidelines. It is following this concept that this paper will outline what is being done, why and how it is being done, and the effectiveness of this implementation.

2 Context: The underlying reasons for implementation

In order to provide students with the necessary skillset to be more effective in the global market, a change in syllabus design was needed. The term 'globalisation' can be interpreted as a message to begin sending graduates overseas, or to begin to make more of a mark in the global markets with respect to business or culture, or to educate students in more global issues, yet the reasons behind the need for this shift towards globalisation need to be understood before embarking on a complete overhaul of a university system to adapt to this important trend. I have examined the document that was released by METI, which outlines the reasons for the need for 'global human resources' (defined in the next section) and provides evidence for the need for globalisation. This will be discussed next.

2.1 METI mandate and global human resources

In 2010, METI released a document (Ministry of Economy, Trade and Industry 2010), which outlined possible reasons why Japan was falling behind economically and technologically on a global scale. They attributed these reasons to basic cultural issues and the fact that the Japanese are more reluctant to work abroad after they graduate. They state that more education is needed to increase language ability and make students more aware of cultural and working differences, so in their document labelled 'Global Human Resources', the METI outlined three main areas that need to be addressed which would assist in creating university graduates with the knowledge and ability to work overseas. These three areas include communication, cultural knowledge and understanding, and working skills, and are detailed below (Table 1).

METI (2010) stated their definition of what global human resources can do. In this world where globalisation is in progress, global human resources can:

- think independently
- make themselves easily understood by colleagues, business acquaintances, and customers of various backgrounds
- overcome differences in values and characteristics arising from cultural and historical backgrounds
- understand others and consider their standpoints
- further take advantage of their differences to build synergy
- create new values.

Stemming from this definition of global human resources, three abilities have been proposed that identify skillsets that young Japanese people need in order

Implementing the CEFR as a benchmark for 'action-oriented' syllabus design

Table 1 Abilities required for 'Global Human Resources' (Ministry of Economy, Trade and Industry 2010)

Abilities required (METI)	Details		
Communication ability in foreign language	Particularly English, which is widely used in the world		
Ability to understand and take advantage of different cultures	To take actions while being aware of the existence of differences in values and communication methods on the basis of diversified backgrounds and histories (= cultural differences)		
	Not to judge cultural differences as good or bad, but to be interested in and understand differences and take flexible actions		
	To recognise strengths of diverse people with cultural differences and to use such strengths for the creation of new values through a synergetic effect		
Fundamental competences for working persons (This is a concept proposed by METI, for common abilities required for a person to work with various people in the workplace or local society)	Ability to step forward (action)	Identity	
	Ability to try patiently even after failure	Ability to take actual actions	
		Ability to work with others	
	Ability to work in a team (teamwork)	Ability to provide information	
	Ability to co-operate with diversified people in achieving a goal	Flexibility	
		Submission to discipline	
		Ability to listen carefully	
		Ability to understand situations	
		Ability to control stress	
	Ability to think well (thinking)	Ability to find problems	
	Ability to ask questions and think well	Ability to plan	
		Ability to create	

to be competitive in the global market and therefore become 'global human resources'. If we again examine the reasons for why the CEFR was developed, we can identify a number of strikingly similar objectives between the CEFR and METI. 'More effective international communication combined with respect for identity and cultural diversity' (Council of Europe 2001:5), is similar to METI's cultural objectives, and 'better access to information, more intensive personal interaction, improved working relations and a deeper mutual understanding ... reference for learning languages at all levels' (2001:5) is also similar to METI's objectives for language and the workplace. From our perspective, the METI mandate provides some direction to what kind of content and approach is needed to prepare students for their future, so the next step was to examine the CEFR criteria to understand what kind of framework to build within our own university.

2.1.1 The CEFR as a common framework

The CEFR levels and the 'Can Do' lists may be interpreted as a model for assessment, but we have interpreted it as a framework to implement in the curriculum and the 'Can Do' lists are used as a basis for how our curriculum is designed. For the user of the curriculum, either as a teacher or a learner, the CEFR 'Can Do' lists are seamlessly integrated into the syllabus and users are unaware of their existence. The role of the teacher is to work with the learners as they move through the various tasks in the curriculum.

The Council of Europe defined three criteria (comprehensive, transparent, and coherent) for their framework to make it effective so 'that all users should be able to describe their objectives, etc. by reference to it' (Council of Europe 2001:7):

- 'comprehensive' means that there is specified a full range of language knowledge, skills, and use
- 'transparent' means that the criteria are clear and readily comprehensible to all users
- 'coherent' refers to the relationship between needs, objectives, content, creation of material, establishment of learning programmes, teaching and learning methods, and evaluation, testing and assessment (2001:7).

This comprehensive, transparent, and coherent framework needs to be open and flexible so that it can be adapted as necessary to all situations, so it should be multi-purpose, flexible, open, dynamic, user-friendly, and non-dogmatic. These criteria are briefly outlined below (Council of Europe 2001):

- *Multi-purpose*: The framework should be usable for a wide variety of purposes.
- *Flexible*: It should be adaptable for use in different circumstances.
- *Open*: It should be capable of further expansion.
- *Dynamic*: The framework should be in continuous evolution.
- *User-friendly*: The framework should be readily understandable.
- *Non-dogmatic*: The framework should not be attached to any one linguistic theory or practice.

Using this framework as a guide, the ICT content platform was developed. The core of the development was to build courses that taught students subjects using English, rather than teaching English as a subject. Here, the ICT platform outline will be explained followed by a comparison between the ICT and the CEFR framework.

2.2 ICT platform outline

The ICT content platform is created within the learning management system (LMS) Moodle (Dougiamas 2011). The structured courses which teachers use as their main syllabus are divided into the four faculties: agriculture, engineering, education, and humanities and social sciences. There are also self-study courses with content related to all four faculties, designed to assist students' learning vocabulary and understanding of concepts that are related to their field of study. In addition to the self-study courses, there are courses created as parallel courses, which can be used as self-study, but they can also be used in conjunction with a structured course, as the teacher may want the students to learn some additional information or may assign some of these as homework assignments. For example, a teacher may want the students to do presentations in class and the parallel course about giving a good presentation will give them some additional opportunities for developing the skills which will help them achieve gains in that area. Table 2 has a brief outline of the ICT content platform compared with the criteria that the CEFR adopted for itself.

Table 2 Comparing the CEFR criteria with the ICT platform

CEFR criteria	ICT contents platform
Multi-purpose	ICT self-study, parallel courses, regular courses
Flexible	ICT can be used for teaching, for learning, for vocabulary building, for discussion
Open	ICT by adding links, by refining content, adding courses, adding content
Dynamic	ICT input from students, context by students, addition of courses based on learning, linking courses
CEFR user-friendly	ICT visual base, easy to manoeuvre, simple with little scrolling
CEFR non-dogmatic	ICT teachers have free rein of use, no methodological restrictions

The ICT platform core function is to support the learning of subjects through English, rather than learning English as a subject. The content of each of the faculties, with some overlapping areas (organic chemistry may be used by both agriculture and engineering students, world history may be used by education and humanities students), is specific to the needs of those learners and the curriculum content provides them with the study of targeted concepts using English as the medium. The ICT platform was designed to be flexible. The self-study courses are available for learning career-related concepts and vocabulary and for learning specific skills, such as academic writing and presentation skills. Teachers use the content for teaching, for assigning homework and for skill building. The content is not static, it is open and dynamic. Updates to the curriculum are done constantly, and areas are designed based on feedback or requests from teachers or students. The ICT content platform has visual links to all areas and courses of the site specific to the Faculties of education, humanities, engineering, and agriculture.

In addition, there are links to self-study areas of the site, all easily identifiable through icons.

In addition to the fact that the ICT platform has been designed with the CEFR criteria in the forefront and measures have been taken to make sure that all criteria have been met, the 'Can Do' lists are considered benchmarks that the curriculum is developed around. This is one of the key strategies of the ICT contents platform. The content is important, but as will be shown in section 3, the implementation of the content through the activities set up in Moodle is instrumental in linking ICT with the CEFR.

It is important to understand that we maintain the framework as the core based on the CEFR framework, but the implementation of the curriculum is based around the 'Can Do' benchmarks of the CEFR. This is in direct reference to the CEFR's action-oriented approach as is outlined below.

2.3 Action-oriented approach

A comprehensive, transparent, and coherent frame of reference for language learning, teaching and assessment should relate to a very general view of language use and learning. As specified in the CEFR framework, the users of the language encounter different situations where they need to achieve something using language. The action-based approach by the CEFR takes into account '... cognitive, emotional and volitional resources and the full range of abilities specific to and applied by the individual as a social agent' (2001:9). The 'Can Do' illustrative scales reflect these and we will show how this is taken into account in course and resource development. The CEFR introduces their action-oriented approach with the following statement:

> Language use, embracing language learning, comprises the actions performed by persons who as individuals and as social agents develop a range of **competences**, both **general** and in particular **communicative language competences**. They draw on the competences at their disposal in various contexts under various **conditions** and under various **constraints** to engage in **language activities** involving **language processes** to produce and/or receive **texts** in relation to **themes** in specific **domains**, activating those **strategies** which seem most appropriate for carrying out the **tasks** to be accomplished. The monitoring of these actions by the participants leads to the reinforcement or modification of their competences (2001:9, emphases in original).

To create a complete curriculum package as a core for the ICT platform, while providing a curriculum framework that has an action-oriented approach, then the core ideals must be paid attention to (Council of Europe 2001).

Implementing the CEFR as a benchmark for 'action-oriented' syllabus design

- *General competences*: For example, sociocultural and intercultural knowledge as well as language use skills for different situations.
- *Communicative language competences*: Knowledge of the use of grammar, sociolinguistic competences, and pragmatic competences.
- *Context*: Events in which communication takes place.
- *Language activities*: Language is used in reception or production (such as reading course content, or producing a presentation), in interaction (where there are at least two people participating in an oral or written exchange), or mediation (in an instance where communication is not possible directly).
- *Language processes*: The production of speech and writing.
- *Text*: Discourse that supports the completion of a task.
- *Domain*: Where the social agent operates.
- *A strategy*: The actions required to be able to carry out a task, such as using language or organising where there may be no language activity.
- *A task*: Described as a purposeful action that will achieve something in the context of a problem.

Each of these elements is dealt with in various activities of the ICT contents platform. These are compared with the METI and ICT in Table 6 in section 5. For now, I will turn my attention to the ICT content platform and discuss how the framework of the CEFR was closely paid attention to during its inception. I will pay particular attention to the CEFR criteria and the action oriented approach in the discussion.

3 Details of practices

In this section I will outline a section of a course and show how the ICT contents, METI's mandates and the CEFR are brought together. The 'Can Do' benchmarks, as will be explained, are what I use in designing sections of a course. The CEFR is our frame; the ICT content platform is a face for that frame.

3.1 The structure of an activity in a course

The course outlined for the purpose of this chapter is a 15-week university first year General English course for students in the faculties of agriculture and engineering. There are 38 students in this course. The course outline is too extensive to be listed here; one section of the course will serve the purpose of demonstrating the implementation of the CEFR. What will be outlined is the section of the course, and how each section is based on a part of the 'Can Do' list. This will help identify how the courses have been set up and how they aim at providing an attainable goal for the students as they move through the activities.

In this section of the course, the learners are required to create a group 5-minute presentation and an assessment rubric, which they will use to assess their presentations. Below (Table 3) is a visual representation of the section of the course, which outlines the face-to-face discussion, file uploads and the presentation.

Table 3 Course outline for weeks 2 through to 7

Activity	Week 2	Week 3	Week 4	Week 5	Week 6	Week 7
Rubric	Face-to-face		Upload file		Teacher implements rubric	
Workshop		Face-to-face		Face-to-face	Upload file	Presentation

3.1.1 Workshop

Students work in groups of six to create PowerPoint presentations. They work online and face-to-face. In class, students watch video clips related to environmental issues (Lake Chad, Larsen B ice shelf, sea levels rising, Earth breathing, ocean currents, time lapse glaciers, polar ice caps) and choose one of the video topics to do a presentation about. The students use the online Moodle forums to share information about their topics, upload PowerPoint slides, discuss their scripts, and discuss their schedules. Each student is responsible for creating at least one slide for the presentation. Students give a 5-minute presentation, which is peer assessed using the first assessment rubric. The presentation must be done by memory.

Each video has a quiz associated with it and all quizzes need to be completed by each learner. This is to make the students more aware of the topics that the other groups are presenting about since the questions in the quizzes focus on the vocabulary and comprehension for each of the video topics.

3.1.2 Assessment rubric

Learners work in groups to create an assessment rubric using the template provided by the teacher. The rubric has two goals, one from a sociocultural perspective, as McConnell (2006:92) states:

> If students are actively involved in decisions about how to learn and what to learn and why they are learning, and are also actively involved in decisions about the criteria for assessment and the process of judging their own and others' work, then their relationship to their studies will probably be qualitatively different from that of students who are treated as recipients of teaching and who are the objective of others', unilateral, assessment.

Implementing the CEFR as a benchmark for 'action-oriented' syllabus design

The second goal is based on the 'Can Do' lists (see Table 5 in section 4 for the full list). Teachers may have difficulty in getting students to pay attention to peer presentations, and it may be important that students be critical of the content of these presentations. Audiences attending presentations that are linked to their own field of study, as found in many conferences, need to learn how to follow the line of arguments and to critically assess the contents. This rubric exercise addresses the benchmarks that address those.

The template given by the teacher provides an area for category, element and grade based on qualitative measures (Table 4), and the learners fill in the areas based on what they deem to be elements of a presentation. The grade is based on the presentation quality of that category and element. The group leaders from each group collaborate to consolidate all the group rubrics into one final assessment rubric (Table 3). The teacher implements the final assessment rubric into Moodle's workshop activity, which is an activity inside of Moodle which allows students to be involved with peer-assessment. During the presentations, the learners use the workshop activity and assess their peers.

While the process of creating a rubric and then using it as an assessment tool is a tools-and-results activity (Newman and Holzman 1993), the actual contents of the rubric are not based on any CEFR benchmarks. The purpose of the rubric is for the students to create their own benchmarks and in doing so satisfy some of the benchmarks of the 'Can Do' lists by establishing those skills during the activity. Table 5 in section 4 outlines these connections in more depth.

3.1.3 The CEFR's action-oriented approach and the online workshop activity

Comparing the action-oriented approach with the workshop activities, the action-oriented approaches are clearly covered through the components of the workshop as outlined here.

- *General competences*: As much of the work is done within a group and there is a lot of collaboration, existential competence (e.g. a learner's attitude towards new ideas in the group), intercultural skills (when dealing with other students), and learning and study skills are key areas of competence required.
- *Communicative language competences*: Learners need to make themselves understood, especially when explaining concepts that are unknown to others, so competence in grammar structures and discourse competence are required. For learners working in online groups, functional competence is required, especially when dealing with factual information.
- *Context*: Through the use of the forums, learners are communicating, the face-to-face time is also for collaborating using the L2, and the presentations are done in English, which is the final part of the process.

Table 4 Group-created assessment rubric

Category	Element	Grade				
		0	1	2	3	4
Attitude	Eye contact / Movement / Gesture / Voice / Expression / Communication	No eye contact. Not suggesting the state of the other party.	Not much movement. A presenter is a little active.	Standard.	A presenter is very active and presents in a clear voice.	A presenter tries to communicate with the audience. The presentation is very interesting.
Slide	Simple words / Clearly / Simple screen / Use colour	A lot of words. The image is very complicated. Pale colour word.	A lot of pictures.	Statements fairly clear.	The slide is so simple that the audience can understand easily.	Easy to understand. Vivid colour word.
Group	Smoothness / Cohesiveness / Teamwork	Everyone apart. The audience can't feel co-operation of the group.	Some members work hard, the other members don't work.	Moderately together.	All members work hard.	There is a unity. Proceed smoothly.
Picture	Easy to look at / Beautiful / Size / Graph	Small. Confused.	Not clear.	Normal.	Not easy to understand.	Easy to understand. Bright colour. Good animation.
Other	Speak clearly / Time allocation / Spelling / Grammar	Difficult to understand. Many misses.	Not possible to allocate time. Some misspelling, pronunciation and grammar.	Normal.	Speak clearly. Moderate voice. A few missed words.	Possible to allocate time exactly.

Implementing the CEFR as a benchmark for 'action-oriented' syllabus design

- *Language activities*: The learners use the language to provide information to other members of their group, to produce a poster or PowerPoint slides, to negotiate meaning, or to mediate learning where there is misunderstanding.
- *Language processes*: All forum text is done in English; the presentation scripts and slides are also created in English.
- *Text*: In this case, this is similar to Context, where the process is carried out in English, and the language is used to advance the activity forward through asynchronous dialogue in an online forum.
- *Domain*: There are educational domains such as online forums replacing the classroom and face-to-face learning, as well as occupational domains such as offices.
- *A strategy*: The learners need to schedule their work time, they need to organise their information, create slides, provide feedback, improve based on feedback, practise their presentations.
- *A task*: The learners are given this task to do and, as outlined in Table 4 and this section, the task at hand is a purposeful action, with direct targets based on the 'Can Do' list and with respect to the mandates by the METI.

4 The key questions in Iwate

4.1 What type of implementation has been adopted? What specific practices have been implemented? What practices have been seen to be effective?

Table 5 outlines excerpts from the CEFR 'Can Do' illustrative scales (Council of Europe 2001) to illustrate how an activity has been created based on 'Can Do' descriptors. It is not the intention of the teacher to assess the learners with the descriptors; the descriptor determines the activity's purpose within the course. As learners go through the activities, they are being exposed to the 'Can Do' descriptors with the expectation that they will become more proficient with respect to the benchmark each provides. The levels used to make the 'Can Do' list in Table 5 range from A2 to B1, a level comparable to the learners' level for this course. The implementation is done through the content in the ICT content platform and through the activities set up in the courses that deliver the content.

Assessment of CEFR-informed Language Teaching in Japan and Beyond

Table 5 CEFR 'Can Do' English benchmarks linked to workshop presentation activity

Workshop presentation activities	CEFR 'Can Do' descriptors (A2–B1 levels)
Videos and video quizzes	Can understand and extract the essential information from short, recorded passages. Can catch the main points.
	Can identify unfamiliar words from the context.
Workshop activity – preparation	Can give brief comments on the views of others. Can make his/her opinions understood.
	Can understand basic factual information.
	Can develop an argument giving advantages and disadvantages.
	Can read straightforward factual texts.
	Can find and understand relevant information.
	Can develop an argument giving advantages and disadvantages.
	Can follow detailed directions.
	Can discuss plans, routines.
	Can recognise the line of argument.
	Can exchange, check and confirm information.
Workshop activity – presentation	Can give a short presentation, can give a prepared speech on a familiar topic.
	Can define the features of something concrete for which he/she can't remember the word. Can start again using a different tactic when communication breaks down.
	Can work out how to communicate the main point(s) he/she wants to get across, exploiting any resources available.
	Can explain main points in an idea or problem, comprehensibly.
Assessment rubric/ assessment	Can recognise the line of argument.
	Can understand main points of a clear speech.
	Can follow a talk within his or her field.
	Can understand factual information.
	Can understand relevant information.
	Can contribute, account for and sustain opinion.

4.2 How are all stakeholders involved? Can the people engaging in CEFR-based teaching and learning develop a sense of ownership?

The activities within a course have been matched to areas of the 'Can Do' lists and therefore, by implementing the activity within the course, the teachers are in a sense, implementing the CEFR-based curriculum. This can be the equivalent of using a textbook with CEFR 'Can Do' descriptors addressed

Implementing the CEFR as a benchmark for 'action-oriented' syllabus design

within the structure of the activity without the teacher or students being aware of the reasons for the activities or content. In the same way, since in this case it was not viable to fully familiarise stakeholders with the concepts of the CEFR, this is done implicitly by involving teachers and others who implement the curriculum in the target activities concerned.

4.2.1 Administration and developers

The administration and developer roles are important for creating the activities that target the 'Can Do' lists. In order to do this, teachers and learners are consulted on the content that they feel addresses the English needs for learner careers. For example, students are asked about material that they feel would be beneficial to learn in English and those concepts and materials are then researched by both the students and the developer to implement their jointly constructed content into the ICT platform. Teachers are also consulted about what content of their coursework can be implemented in the ICT platform, content they feel would be beneficial to be learned in English. The developer of the ICT platform then takes the content and implements it respecting the CEFR criteria, balancing that with the 'Can Do' descriptors. In other words, while the content is important for the learners, it is the activities that surround the content that address the 'Can Do' descriptors, and the ICT contents platform links the activities with the action-oriented approaches. The ICT content platform remains a face for the CEFR and the content and activities are used to create that face.

4.2.2 Teachers and learners

Teachers, especially part-time teachers, frequently are not aware of the CEFR, so the activities in the ICT platform provide the content that teachers have full access to. Teachers who use the ICT platform, but are unaware of the CEFR, essentially are incorporating the CEFR benchmarks into their courses by incorporating the ICT contents into their syllabus. Through this approach, from the perspective of the university, the teachers are developing a sense of ownership because they have the freedom to design a course with ready-made content, and teach it using their own methodologies, and the learning objectives are transparent and concrete. Examples of these learning objectives are outlined in the section showing the workshop activity. The students on the other hand are unaware of the benchmarks even though they are developing skills outlined in the benchmarks. The feedback these students provide shows that they realise the benefits of this kind of learning despite being unaware, as the course materials and activities help them move towards the goals laid out in the benchmarks.

4.3 Has the CEFR promoted a system for in-house evaluation of curricula and learning targets? Do curricula and courses include transparent and concrete learning objectives, with accepted 'Can Do' descriptors at the centre?

The 'Can Do' descriptors are at the centre of the curriculum, but testing is not done at the classroom level, as the learning targets are implemented through the curriculum and the focus of the curriculum is language skills, not language learning. With any method of evaluation, there are a number of drawbacks either on the teaching side or on the testing side. If the focus is on the testing of grammar, then the teaching will invariably be grammar based. If the teaching is to do with task-based learning, then the evaluation becomes more complicated as pointed out in a number of cases (Butler 2011, Swan 2005, Willis 1996, Willis and Willis 2007). Yet in the instance outlined here, the focus is neither grammar nor language; the focus is on the use of language through the development of skills, such as communication and presentation skills. In Table 5, where the workshop presentation activity is matched with sections of CEFR 'Can Do' descriptors, there is no reference to the absolute accuracy of the language, nor is there any reference to grammar. The 'Can Do' descriptors focus on performance abilities. The ICT contents platform and the various activities surrounding the content provide the student and teacher with concrete goals focused on skills. Research is being done at Iwate University to do with dynamic assessment (de Boer 2013, 2015, O'Dwyer and de Boer 2015), which can be implemented in conjunction with the CEFR 'Can Do' benchmarks.

4.4 Is it possible to compare the results of instruction in different classes?

At this point the implementation is still new and because of the non-dogmatic approach, the results may vary depending on the teacher, class and students. The range of skills of each student may differ from class to class so to pinpoint an exact language level or to compare the results of instruction is difficult. However, one must remember that language is used in these courses as an enabling skill only. As research is being done with respect to dynamic assessment, it may be possible, in the near future, to implement a guideline for teachers to refer to in order to dynamically assess their students as they move through the process of doing each activity in the curriculum.

4.5 Do 'Can Do' checklists serve as the key reference point for processes of reflective learning in which self-assessment plays a central role? How?

In our case, the 'Can Do' lists are not apparent to the learners or the teachers. As has been stated in various parts of this chapter, the CEFR 'Can Do' descriptors are incorporated as content and through the curriculum. Since the focus is on learning the skills to use the language effectively, students encounter similar projects throughout the course. These projects give the students the necessary skills which will be useful in their careers.

4.6 What are the interpretations, of teachers, students and other stakeholders, of the philosophy and ideas of the CEFR?

Teachers and students are not aware of the philosophies and ideas of the CEFR. At this stage, still early in the implementation, more teachers are becoming involved in the development of the curriculum and resources in the ICT contents platform. During consultations with teachers, various 'Can Do' items are discussed, making the teachers more aware of how various content is used to help students develop skills. Without discussing the source of the philosophies (the CEFR), the discussions revolve around skills and how to implement curricula to develop those skills.

4.7 Can all readily see the benefits of the CEFR-based approach for their own teaching/learning? Are the CEFR-based materials (textbooks, teaching content etc.) action-oriented, and easily applicable by both teachers and students?

Those teachers who have used the ICT content platform have seen positive differences in the student reaction to the curriculum, learner motivation, and effectiveness of the lessons. From the student perspective, moving away from learning for the test to a curriculum where they are learning to use the language specific to their careers, encourages a marked interest in the content and increasing confidence in using their voice. From the teacher perspective, seeing the differences in what the students can do with this format of teaching and learning is motivating and they can instantly see the benefits of this type of curriculum.

The language education at Iwate University is not designed to be taught for the test, since the language is learned through using the language and the learners are not taught the structure of the language (deBoer 2013).

Therefore, traditional language testing is difficult to implement, but testing on various concepts in English that are associated with learners' career paths is more conducive to both the mandate proposed by METI and the action-oriented approach shown by the CEFR. Since the 'Can Do' benchmarks are used as the basis for activity development, and the CEFR is a framework for reference, the 'Can Do' lists cannot be used for assessment purposes. The benchmark creates the goal, but there are varying degrees of abilities around that target, so the assessment needs to be on the process associated with the benchmark, not on whether that benchmark has been achieved. Assessment on the process is an entirely different issue not discussed in this paper, but it is under current research. Teachers who are implementing ICT contents into their classes are discovering that assessment of language is superfluous, as each student in the classroom has their own perspective on the language. Over the span of 15 weeks in a course, more emphasis should be on the assessment of skills using language rather than on the structure of the language. As a reviewer of this chapter also noted, future work may relate to integrating 'Can Do' descriptors for aspects of language competence such as pragmatic competences; see section 5.2 of the CEFR (Council of Europe 2001:108).

4.8 Is autonomous learning beyond the specified materials (e.g. textbooks) supported and encouraged? If so, how?

The very nature of the curriculum encourages students to become more autonomous because of the process involved through each activity (de Boer 2015). As shown, students are given only a starting point for their presentation topic and the onus is put on them to work in their groups to research information for their presentation. They have access to the internet, books, and textbooks, and are able to talk to professors on campus. The students determine their own course of action, which is evident each year a new group of students moves through the same project, as the research and outcomes have a different perspective each time. This makes it difficult to provide a test on any given topic as that would stifle student autonomy and force the students to approach their research by the content that would be tested.

5 Conclusion

The implementation of the ICT content platform is still in its infancy; the project was completed in 2013 and not all teachers are using it. The teachers and students who are actively involved with this project can readily see the benefits, and are also involved with further development of curricula, content and course implementation. Initial results of the feedback from teachers and students show that the learning and teaching with respect to the CEFR is beneficial. Positive points include the focus on 'real-life' abilities and not

Implementing the CEFR as a benchmark for 'action-oriented' syllabus design

grammar, the importance of learner co-operation, and the increased sense of learner responsibility. To implement the CEFR into a university curriculum requires careful planning. The ICT content platform puts a face to the CEFR criteria and research on the mandates set by the METI. As the CEFR is a framework, or a set of benchmarks of abilities, our next goal is to be able to regulate those abilities based on the four skills of listening, reading, writing and speaking, so that we might help our students prepare better for going abroad or becoming citizens that can bridge the culture between Japan and other countries.

The main recommendations for the implementation of a CEFR-based curriculum in a large institution, where explicit CEFR familiarisation initiatives may not be viable, are summarised as follows:

- Determine an overall list of abilities and skills for learners for once they graduate. This will help you in determining the structure of your curriculum and syllabus. We have used the report issued by METI identifying the need for 'Human Resource Development' as our guide for identifying the skills students need.
- Examine the illustrative descriptor scales of CEFR 'Communicative language activities and strategies' (Council of Europe 2001) and determine the activities within the syllabus that would help students achieve the relevant descriptors. The activities play the more important role within the syllabus. The focus is placed on the students being able to learn to use the language to hone those skills.
- Place the onus on the student for their learning. The teacher's role in the classroom should be to guide the students through dialogue, not through instruction.
- Provide the students with tools that will help them develop skills. The most effective tools are the ones that are generally used in the workplace, such as Microsoft Office, or the internet.
- Work with students to understand what they feel their needs are for their own learning. The curriculum content can be supplemented with student-developed content.

There are still a number of issues and challenges that need to be considered. They are:

1. Educating teachers on illustrative descriptor scales. Currently, teachers use the platform that has been developed but part-time teachers are less informed as to the underlying reasons for the activities in the curriculum (see section 5 of the first phase of research described in Chapter 9, and section 3.3 of Chapter 7 for teacher training and familiarisation issues).
2. There are still issues with assessment. Research is being done on how to incorporate interactionist dynamic assessment and still be able to

provide a numeric grade at the end of the course. This is one of the key issues that teachers find difficult to incorporate. Testing at the end of a course is still a large part of the university culture, which has prevented this type of curriculum from being accepted university wide.

As a final conclusion, the CEFR (action-oriented approach), METI and the workshop activity from the ICT platform are compared. This has been done to show similarities across all three. To isolate an example, the METI states 'action' in their mandate, which was defined as: identity, ability to take actual actions, and ability to work on others. During the activity, learners are involved in a number of actions that help move the process forward. These actions include planning and carrying out their project but this also is reflective of the action-oriented approach ideals of the CEFR. These are shown in Table 6.

Table 6 Comparison of the CEFR, METI's mandates for global human resources and the ICT contents workshop activity processes

CEFR	METI	Workshop presentation activity
General and communicative language competences	Communication	● Face-to-face communication ● Asynchronous forum dialogue ● Mediated learning
General competences (practical skills, intercultural skills) Communicative language competences (sociolinguistic competences) Language activities (for working in groups or writing emails requiring polite language)	Understand different cultures (working with different kinds of people)	● Working in groups ● Talking with professors ● Emailing companies
General competences (interpersonal relations, attitudes) Communicative language competences (sociolinguistic competences) Strategies (organising, planning) Domains (different areas for communication)	Action	● Their project – their direction ● Scheduling ● Planning ● Work sharing ● Problems arising ● Teamwork issues
Language activities (reception and production, interaction, mediating)	Thinking	● Looking for information ● Planning for uncertainty ● Creating from nothing ● Learning to ask questions ● Learning to get information
General competences (practical skills, intercultural skills) Communicative language competences (sociolinguistic competences) Language activities (for working in groups)	Teamwork	● Flexibility ● Group leader dynamics ● Adapting to different situations ● Listening to group members ● Providing work for the group

The CEFR action-oriented approach for the 'action' component of METI is shown as the completion of a task through the activation of competences, and use of relevant strategies in the context and domain concerned. In order to carry out the various tasks associated with the workshop activity, the learners need to be able to take their current level of experiences, design a strategy to take the activity through to completion, and they can do this either in the face-to-face learning environment, online in the forum, or through their own choice of communication media. The activity warrants the development of their skills as shown in Table 5 and this is linked to the action-oriented approach in Table 6. Understanding different cultures comes from interaction with other students, with the teacher, with professors, and in cases where students interact with companies to gather information.

References

Butler, Y G (2011) The implementation of communicative and task-based language teaching in the Asia-Pacific region, *Annual Review of Applied Linguistics* 31, 36–57.

Council of Europe (2001) *Common European Framework of Reference for Languages: Learning, Teaching, Assessment*, Cambridge: Cambridge University Press.

de Boer, M (2011) ICT contents project at Iwate University, in Stewart, A (Ed) *JALT2010 Conference Proceedings*, Tokyo: The Japan Association for Language Teaching, available online: jalt-publications.org/proceedings/articles/1041-ict-contents-project-iwate-university

de Boer, M (2013) *Dynamic assessment in tool-mediated learning: A theoretical framework*, unpublished PhD thesis module 1, University of Birmingham, 2013.

de Boer, M (2015) *Ecological dynamic assessment syllabus: Assessing the process of learner-centred mediation*, unpublished PhD thesis module 2, University of Birmingham, 2015.

de Boer, M, Onaka, N and Nakanishi, T (2012) English ICT contents program development through collaboration at Iwate University, in Stewart, A and Sonda, N (Eds) *JALT2011 Conference Proceedings*, Tokyo: The Japan Association for Language Teaching, 229–240.

Dougiamas, M (2011) *Moodle Version 2*, available online: docs.moodle.org/dev/Releases#Moodle_2.0

McConnell, D (2006) *E-learning Groups and Communities*, New York: Open University Press.

Ministry of Economy, Trade and Industry (2010) *Release of Report by Global Human Resource Development Committee of the Industry–Academia Partnership for Human Resource Development*, Tokyo: Ministry of Economy, Trade and Industry.

Newman, F and Holzman, L (1993) *Lev Vygotsky: Revolutionary Scientist*, New York: Routledge.

O'Dwyer, F and de Boer, M (2015) Approaches to assessment in CLIL classrooms: Two case studies, *Language Learning in Higher Education* 5 (2), 1–25.

Swan, M (2005) Legislation by hypothesis: The case of task-based instruction, *Applied Linguistics* 26 (3), 376–401.
Willis, J (1996) *A Framework for Task-based Learning*, Malaysia: Addison Wesley Longman.
Willis, J and Willis, D (2007) *Doing Task-based Teaching*, Oxford: Oxford University Press.

9 Using the CEFR-J and the CEFR as frameworks for renewal of an English language curriculum at a Japanese university: An action research study

This chapter, made up of three related sub-chapters, is a reflective analysis of two cycles of renewal of an English language curriculum at a small private Japanese women's university. The first renewal cycle from 2012 to 2013 aimed to align an existing English as a foreign language curriculum to the Common European Framework of Reference-Japan (CEFR-J, Tono 2013, Tono and Negishi 2012), and the second cycle, which will be completed in early 2017, aims to create a new curriculum based on the Common European Framework of Reference for Languages (CEFR, Council of Europe 2001). The two cycles of curriculum renewal are analysed using an action research approach (McNiff and Whitehead 2010).

The first sub-chapter (9A) gives background information about an English language education centre at the university where this action research took place. It explains the reasons for curriculum renewal, and for initially using the CEFR-J as the framework for renewal. Then, the two curriculum renewal cycles are explained in detail. Each component of the renewal process is analysed and reflected upon from an action research perspective. Lessons learned from the renewal process are presented, and recommendations are made for others who may engage in similar attempts to either revise or create a curriculum based on the CEFR or the CEFR-J.

Sub-chapter 9B explains and evaluates the development and renewal of Self Access Center (SAC) activities designed to both support the CEFR(-J)-based curriculum content, and to foster autonomous learning in students. It gives detailed descriptions of CEFR-J-based and CEFR-based SAC activity design, which should serve as valuable examples to other SAC practitioners looking to engage in similar projects. The challenges faced, and the lessons learned from creating these activities aligned to a classroom language curriculum, are also illustrated.

Sub-chapter 9C is a reflective analysis of the entire curriculum renewal process described in 9A and 9B. It addresses each of the key questions of this edited volume and concludes with a summary of the insights we have gained, and our recommendations for other practitioners.

9A Aligning a Japanese university's English language curriculum and lesson plans to the CEFR-J

Jack Bower (Hiroshima Bunkyo Women's University), Judith Runnels (University of Bedfordshire), Arthur Rutson-Griffiths (Hiroshima Bunkyo Women's University), Rebecca Schmidt (Hiroshima Bunkyo Women's University), Gary Cook (Hiroshima Bunkyo Women's University), Lyndon Lusk Lehde (Hiroshima Bunkyo Women's University) and Azusa Kodate (Kokugakuin University)

1 Introduction

This sub-chapter describes and analyses the process of two curriculum renewal cycles undertaken by the Bunkyo English Communication Center (BECC) at Hiroshima Bunkyo Women's University (HBWU) from an action research perspective. A decision was made by management in early 2012 to reform the existing General English (GE) curriculum using the CEFR-J as a framework to increase the cohesion, transparency and focus of the curriculum (Council of Europe 2001). Given the CEFR-J self-assessment grid included newly released 'Can Do' descriptors specifically aimed at Japanese learners of English, it was chosen to provide better proficiency goals and accountability for the students of HBWU, who were required to successfully complete a 2-year GE curriculum prior to graduation, as is the case at most Japanese universities (Hosoki 2011). The first curriculum renewal cycle involved teacher training, creating new course and lesson goals based on 'Can Do' descriptors, and evaluating the existing curriculum by mapping lesson 'Can Do' descriptors against the CEFR-J's 'Can Do' descriptors and proficiency levels in order to assess the degree of alignment. This mapping process revealed various gaps in content and ability within the curriculum. Based on the lessons learned from the first curriculum renewal cycle, a second curriculum renewal cycle was initiated in early 2014 and is scheduled to be completed by January 2017. In this second cycle the entire GE curriculum is being remade based on target CEFR levels. The reasons for changing our curriculum renewal framework

Using the CEFR-J and the CEFR as frameworks for renewal

to the CEFR, and our recommended process for creating a CEFR-based curriculum are explained in the second half of this sub-chapter.

2 Literature review

One of the primary purposes of the CEFR is as a resource for the development of language curricula (Council of Europe 2001, Little 2006). There are several case studies published on using the CEFR as a framework for curriculum development (Faez, Majhanovich, Taylor, Smith and Crowley 2011, Faez, Taylor, Majhanovich, Brown and Smith 2011, Little and Lazenby Simpson 2004, Lockwood 2012, Manasseh 2004, Üstünlüoğlu, Zazaoğlu, Keskin, Sarayköylü and Akdoğan 2012, Wall 2004, Zárate and Alvarez 2005). However, it is difficult to find case studies on aligning an existing curriculum to the CEFR despite the availability of some 'how-to' type guides, such as in Hogan (2012), or North (2014, chapter 4). The only example we could find of an alignment attempt is Keddle's (2004) description of some of the difficulties encountered in integrating the CEFR into an existing secondary school language syllabus in Italy, in order to modify their existing grammar-driven curriculum.

Since the completion in March 2012 of the localised version of the CEFR for Japan, known as the CEFR-J, to the best of our knowledge there appear to be no published accounts of the alignment of an existing English language curriculum to the CEFR-J. Section 5 of this chapter aims to address this gap in the research by presenting a report of the process, the benefits, and the lessons learned from a CEFR-J curriculum alignment project. Section 6 of this chapter aims to make a useful contribution to the literature on designing CEFR-based curricula by describing in detail a curriculum-creation process that we found to be effective. We hope that this can serve as a useful model for other practitioners.

3 Context

3.1 The Bunkyo English Communication Center (BECC)

The BECC was established at Hiroshima Bunkyo Women's University in 2008 with the mission of providing a communicative English language curriculum for all first and second year students at the university (the GE curriculum). A Self-Access Center, called the BECC Self-Access Learning Center (hereafter referred to as the SALC), was also founded within the BECC to foster the development of student autonomous learning, and to support students' English language studies throughout and beyond their 2-year government-mandated language programme (see Thompson and Atkinson (2010) for an early description on how the SALC was integrated with curriculum content).

The GE curriculum caters to non-English-language majors from four of the university's departments: Early Childhood Education, Welfare, Nutrition and Psychology. The BECC also manages parts of the English language curriculum for English language majors, and continues working towards improving the learning materials and learner support available in the SALC.

3.2 The General English curriculum and the need for renewal

The original GE curriculum was designed to be a communicative and functional foreign language curriculum. It was based on a thematic and communicative curriculum originally intended for English language majors at Kanda University of International Studies, one of about 10 foreign studies universities in Japan. It emphasised integrated lessons involving all the four skills of speaking, listening, reading and writing, and also had a major focus on project-based and task-based learning (TBL). The GE curriculum aimed to be not only level appropriate, but also targeted towards students' interests (Thompson and Foale 2008). The GE curriculum is taught over two academic years of study, each of which consists of two semesters. The first year of this programme is referred to as Freshman English (FE), while the second year is referred to as Sophomore English (SE). Each of the three semesters of the 4-semester programme consisted of two major thematic units, with the final semester comprised of only a single unit, for a total of seven thematic units of study.

The original GE curriculum however, was found to be pitched a little too high for the target students, and was not well matched to their interests and needs, which were quite different from those of English majors at an international studies university. Significant revisions were therefore made from 2009 to 2011 with the intention of targeting the learners at the BECC more effectively. For example, a unit on Food and Health was created to match the interests of Nutrition majors, incorporating language functions such as giving instructions for cooking and describing health problems. Although these lessons appeared to be more appropriately targeted to the interests and abilities of the students, at the end of 2011 following the three years of revisions to the GE curriculum it was felt that the GE curriculum was fragmented and lacked cohesion. BECC management therefore made the decision that further curriculum renewal was required, and selected the CEFR-J as the overarching organising framework for a renewal project beginning in 2012. This process is described in section 5 and is analysed from an action research perspective, described in section 3.3.

3.3 Examining GE curriculum renewal from an action research perspective

The following descriptions and analyses of curriculum renewal in this chapter are organised using an action research framework. Action research is an approach to research which involves investigating a real-world problem, attempting to implement a solution, and then reflecting on the process and results of the implementation to better craft future approaches to the problem. Educational action research is distinct from formal educational research in several ways (State of New South Wales, Department of Education and Training 2010). On one hand, formal educational research generally involves testing abstract theories through extensive reviews of the literature, rigorous experimental design, and the use of statistics. Formal research also aims at objectivity. Action research, on the other hand, examines immediate social or educational problems, which are often small scale and local. The literature review in this case is more concerned with examples of similar interventions for similar problems in other contexts, and evidence can consist of only qualitative, or a mix of quantitative and qualitative data. As action researchers are often directly involved in their subject of study, a degree of subjectivity is seen as necessary and useful.

There are several approaches to action research in the literature, however a common core to all of the approaches is that action research is cyclical, with the results of one programme being used to inform the planning of the following cycle. More specifically, it requires the identification of an existing problem, data collection through qualitative and/or quantitative research methods, interpretation of the gathered evidence and an evaluation of the completed cycle, followed by the implementation of a new plan to address the identified issues. This implementation may lead to further research in the form of additional programmes; for as educators continue to gain a deeper understanding of their problem, they can redesign their research until a more desirable outcome is achieved (Creswell 2008, Stringer 2008).

For this chapter a traditional programme consisting of four stages is used: 1. Study and Plan, 2. Take Action, 3. Collect and Analyse Evidence, 4. Reflect (Creswell 2008, McNiff and Whitehead 2010, Stringer 2008).

4 Two programmes

This chapter is structured around two programmes divided into the four stages. The first programme is described and analysed in section 5, and took place from 2012 to 2013. The first cycle aimed to align the existing GE curriculum to the CEFR-J. The second programme began in 2014 and will be completed in January 2017. The second cycle is described and evaluated in section 6.

5 Curriculum renewal Programme 1 (2012–13): CEFR-J alignment

The following section 5.1 first explains the Study and Plan stage of the programme. This stage includes an explanation of why the CEFR-J was selected as the framework for curriculum renewal. Second, sections 5.2 and 5.3 detail how each of the stages of Take Action, Collect and Analyse Evidence in the programme were carried out throughout the alignment process. Finally, section 5.4 presents the 'Reflection' stage, and discusses the benefits and problems with the entire process and the recommendations for other institutions that may attempt a similar CEFR or CEFR-J alignment project.

5.1 Programme 1 Stage 1: Study and Plan

5.1.1 Reasons behind the alignment of the GE curriculum with the CEFR-J

The BECC opted to use the CEFR-J as its framework for curriculum renewal for two main reasons. The first is related to the success the CEFR has enjoyed in Europe and other locations. Specifically, using the CEFR as a framework for the development of language programmes has been argued to improve communication between relevant stakeholders in language education while fostering reflective practices in both learners and teachers and increasing cohesiveness and transparency of curricula (Council of Europe 2001). In addition, using the CEFR as a basis for the development or revision of language curricula has also been argued to increase student motivation by providing clear learning goals, a functional communicative focus for the content of pedagogy and allowing for the establishment of equivalencies with other institutions, while fostering reflective practices in both learners and teachers (Council of Europe 2001, Little 2006, North 2007, Tono and Negishi 2012). BECC management thought that by drawing from the philosophies of the CEFR and employing the CEFR-J's levels and descriptors, similar outcomes to those achieved in Europe could also be achieved within the GE curriculum at the BECC. The CEFR-J was conceptualised simply as an extension to the CEFR, and through its operationalisation it was thought that the lack of cohesion the BECC curriculum was judged to possess (described in section 3.2) could be addressed.

The second reason that the CEFR, and by extension, the CEFR-J was selected as the framework for GE curriculum alignment was that it was seen to provide a means to increase the university's competitiveness in attempting to maintain or increase the size of its student population. In recent years, this has become a significant issue for Japanese tertiary institutions as a declining birth rate in Japan has led to significant decreases in the annual total number of applicants to Japanese universities (Matsutani 2012). Indeed, such a trend has been observed outside of Japan, as reference to the CEFR has been noted as a means of securing a 'market advantage' (Elder 2007 as cited in Valax 2011), since an institution that is 'CEFR-aligned ... [is] probably going to survive' (Papageorgiou 2006 as cited in Valax 2011). BECC management agreed with these quotations, believing that employing the CEFR-J (as a counterpart to the CEFR) could provide a means by which our institution could stay competitive, while also mobilising our institution to present solid evidence of the efficacy of our language programme.

Completely recreating the curriculum to match the CEFR-J was initially considered, but it was undeniable that this would involve a large time commitment from an already busy teaching staff, so such a plan was rejected. In addition, although the existing curriculum lacked cohesion and an overarching structure, many of the lessons were felt by teachers to be engaging and useful for students. Rather than entirely scrapping the existing curriculum and starting anew, it was thus decided to align the existing curriculum by drawing on the CEFR-J's self-assessment grid descriptors. Such an approach is also recommended by one of the co-authors of the framework in his book *The CEFR in Practice*: 'in relating a curriculum to the CEFR, the most important point is to not throw away what already exists [since] what exists may well have been developed to suit the needs of the learners in context' (North 2014:111). A methodology was therefore sought which could assess which elements of the existing curriculum could be kept or modified into a new CEFR-J-aligned curriculum, and what new materials would need to be made, if any.

The process of the first attempt at aligning the GE curriculum to the CEFR-J involved six main components, as follows:

1. The rewriting of course proficiency goals in the form of CEFR descriptors in order to increase clarity and transparency (see section 5.2.12).
2. Familiarising teachers with the CEFR and the CEFR-J, training teachers in 'Can Do' descriptor writing and norming the process of matching 'Can Do' descriptors with CEFR-J self-assessment grid bands (see sections 5.2.1, 5.2.3, 5.2.7, 5.2.9, 5.2.11).
3. Designing standardised tests of listening, reading and speaking (see sections 5.2.13, 5.3.5).
4. The writing and inclusion of learner 'Can Do' descriptors on all lesson handouts so that learners can self-assess their ability to achieve lesson target tasks at the start and end of every lesson (see section 5.2.7), and getting expert feedback on these lesson 'Can Do' descriptors (see section 5.2.4).
5. The revising of activities in the SALC so that they aligned with the CEFR-J and more closely supported the curriculum's classroom activities (see the second part of this chapter).
6. The creation of a CEFR-aligned map of the curriculum which classified all lesson tasks according to descriptors on the CEFR-J self-assessment grid, meaning that lesson content was organisable by level of difficulty, language skill and topic (see section 5.2.6).

5.1.2 Timeline for Programme 1

After identifying several problems with the GE curriculum and choosing the CEFR-J as the framework for renewal to fix these problems (see section 3.2), a renewal plan began to emerge. Several steps were taken towards the goal of aligning the GE curriculum to the CEFR-J between 2012 and 2014 and these steps are summarised in Table 1.

Table 1 Curriculum renewal timeline (April 2012–February 2014)

Date	Important actions
April 2012	Made decision to base renewal of the GE curriculum and SALC activities on the CEFR-J.
May 2012	Teachers familiarised themselves with the CEFR, CEFR-J and related documents.
June 2012	Workshop on the history of use of the CEFR in Japan.
July 2012	Students and teachers completed CEFR-J survey to determine self-perceptions of level of the students through 'Can Do' descriptors.
October 2012	'Can Do' writing workshop #1 on why and how the BECC is using the CEFR-J framework; workshop on how to write 'Can Do' descriptors. Teachers divided into teams to write initial 'Can Do' descriptors for FE and SE lessons.
November 2012	Initial 'Can Do' descriptors completed and sent for expert feedback.
December 2012	Teacher 'Can Do' perception survey completed (SE curriculum).
January 2013	FE and SE semester 1 lesson revisions completed with initial 'Can Do' descriptors included on lesson handouts.
January 2013	Feedback on initial 'Can Do' descriptors received from the expert.
February 2013	Initial 'Can Do' descriptors mapped to the CEFR-J.
April 2013	New FE and SE contextualised CEFR-J statements for overall curriculum goals created. FE students started using new CEFR-J based SALC activities. (Continual revisions continued throughout the 2013/14 school year.)
May 2013	'Can Do' writing workshop #2: Review of accomplishments, discussion of feedback, review and practice of how to rewrite the lesson 'Can Do' descriptors, discussion and practice of writing student-friendly 'Can Do' descriptors.
July 2013	FE and SE semester 1 lesson revisions completed with revised 'Can Do' descriptors added.
July 2013	Second version of 'Can Do' descriptors completed for semester 1 lessons. Student-friendly 'Can Do' descriptors written for semester 1 lessons. Lesson summary documents, which briefly summarise the content of each lesson, completed.
November 2013	Task based language teaching workshop.
January 2014	'Can Do' writing workshop #3: Reviewed inconsistencies in 'Can Do' wording and 'Can Do' descriptors which could not be mapped. Familiarisation and mapping workshop: CEFR-J descriptor sorting exercises, attempt to map revised GE lessons to the CEFR-J.
February 2014	Final lesson revisions for semester 2 2014, new 'Can Do' descriptors and lesson summaries completed.
February 2014	Teachers gave feedback on their perceptions of GE curriculum renewal process through individual meetings and anonymous surveys.

5.1.3 An evolving curriculum renewal plan

The first cycle of curriculum renewal did not begin with a comprehensive overall plan, but instead evolved gradually as BECC management and staff became more familiar with the CEFR and the CEFR-J. As can be seen in Table 1, the entire renewal project began with the decision to use the CEFR-J as the framework to underpin the BECC's GE curriculum renewal (see section 3.2). How teachers were familiarised with the CEFR and the CEFR-J, and trained teachers in 'Can Do' descriptor writing, is explained in sections 5.2.3 and 5.2.7.

Section 5.3 describes the component of the overall alignment project referred to hereafter as the GE Curriculum–CEFR-J mapping, or simply 'mapping'. The goal of this component of the first curriculum renewal project was to provide information about five aspects of the GE curriculum's lesson materials:

1. The balance of individual language skills (section 5.3.2.1).
2. The level of difficulty of language tasks (section 5.3.2.2).
3. Whether a progression in difficulty was evident throughout the GE curriculum (section 5.3.2.3).
4. Whether the lesson content met the institution's stated target CEFR-J levels at exit of the two years of study (section 5.3.2.4).
5. Whether all of the language tasks and language functions implicit in the target CEFR-J level descriptors were covered by the existing GE curriculum (section 5.3.2.5).

If the resulting 'map' suggested any problems in any of these five areas, evidence-based feedback could then be used to direct specific modifications of future versions of the curriculum to ensure that the content of the curriculum was in fact mobilising students to achieve its objectives. However, as is explained in the reflection stage in Programme 1 (see section 5.4), this process did not achieve its intended aims due to oversights in the methodology employed. Reflecting on the process highlighted some of the confounding issues, which prevented us from making the observations about the curriculum we had hoped for. Nonetheless, we regard the mapping to be an endeavour worth engaging in, and in section 5.4.5.3, recommendations to address the issues are made for others to follow so that evidence-based feedback about numerous facets of a language curriculum can be obtained. The Take Action section (section 5.2) describes the rewriting of the course proficiency goals using CEFR-J descriptors (section 5.2.12), the development of CEFR-informed tests of listening, reading and speaking (section 5.2.13), and the process of creating learner-friendly 'Can Do' descriptors for all lesson handouts so that learners could self-assess their ability on lesson targets at the start and end of every lesson (section 5.2.7).

5.2 Programme 1 Stage 2: Take Action

The Take Action stage of Programme 1 began with staff completing some readings on the CEFR and the CEFR-J before attending a workshop formally introducing them to the history of CEFR usage in Japan (section 5.2.1). A survey on student and teacher perceptions of the CEFR-J level of language proficiency was then conducted, the results of which were used to inform subsequent stages of the programmes (section 5.2.2). The first formal training workshop in October 2012 led to staff being able to write localised, consistent 'Can Do' descriptors representative of the activities within the GE curriculum's lessons (section 5.2.3). External, expert feedback on the content of the 'Can Do' descriptors was obtained (section 5.2.4), which guided the modification of any 'Can Do' descriptors flagged by the expert as being potentially problematic. The updated 'Can Do' descriptors were then mapped to the CEFR-J self-assessment grid (section 5.2.5) and an overall curriculum map was produced. These processes were then analysed within the Collect and Analyse Evidence stage (section 5.3).

5.2.1 CEFR introduction workshop

In June 2012, in the first year of the alignment project, Fergus O'Dwyer (Osaka University) was invited to conduct a workshop at the BECC on the CEFR and its implementations in Japan. In it, he presented the history of the CEFR's use in curricula development at various universities in Japan and issues relevant to its implementation in the classroom. The workshop also outlined methods for teachers to execute a CEFR-J-based curriculum in the classroom by explaining how 'Can Do' descriptors were incorporated into a 4-stage learning cycle involving self-assessment, goal setting, task performance, and reflection (O'Dwyer 2010, O'Dwyer and Runnels 2014). In terms of curriculum renewal, the importance of having a bottom-up approach driven by teachers as well as a top-down mandate by the centre administration was stressed as a key aspect for success.

5.2.2 Teacher and student perceptions of CEFR-J levels survey

The results of a research project undertaken by a staff member were used to support the decision of making A1.3 the target for the first year English curriculum, and A2.2 for the second year. Although this decision had been obtained via a staff consensus within a meeting, a survey was conducted with all teachers and students. A summary of the results of this survey is given in section 5.3.1.

5.2.3 Training workshop: 'Can Do' descriptor creation

Given that an important component of the CEFR and CEFR-J is describing learner performance through 'Can Do' descriptors (Little 2006) it was decided that teachers would write 'Can Do' descriptors for all lessons in the

GE curriculum. In the first teacher training workshop held in October 2012, a BECC staff member, working in tight conjunction with BECC management, presented the reasons for the curriculum renewal and clarified why the CEFR-J was chosen as the framework to guide renewal. The vertical and horizontal axes of the CEFR grid, where the vertical axis defines the language skill and the horizontal axis defines the level of difficulty (North 2000) were explained. Then, North's (2000:343–246) five principles for writing 'Can Do' descriptors (positiveness, definitiveness, clarity, brevity, independence) were described, as it was these that would underpin the production of the BECC's 'Can Dos'. This was followed by 'Can Do' writing practice, with the goal of mobilising staff to produce locally standardised 'Can Do' descriptors. Essentially, a lesson task was presented to all attendees of the workshop. Participants worked in teams of three or four to produce a sample 'Can Do' descriptor for that task. All samples were then compared, and discussions occurred about where they were similar and different, and also about the advantages and disadvantages of each. This allowed for a gradual refinement of the language that was considered suitable to describe the GE curriculum lesson tasks. Further practice on different tasks occurred again until each group was producing nearly identical 'Can Do' descriptors for the presented task (see Semmelroth (2013) for a detailed description of this workshop). Based on this training, five pairs of teachers then worked on developing 'Can Do' descriptors which reflected the content and tasks performed by learners throughout all of the lessons of the 2-year GE curriculum lessons. All 'Can Do' descriptors were then amalgamated within a document and external feedback was sought.

5.2.4 Expert feedback

Feedback regarding the 'Can Do' descriptors written for all BECC GE lessons was obtained from a member of the Framework and Language Portfolio Special Interest Group (FLP SIG) of the Japan Association for Language Teaching, Dr. Naoyuki Naganuma (Tokai University). The FLP SIG was established to discuss the CEFR and European Language Portfolio (ELP) tools, undertake projects, and communicate results within contexts spanning elementary schools to universities in Japan (Framework and Language Portfolio Special Interest Group 2009). The following sections present the key points from Dr Naganuma's feedback.

5.2.4.1 Differentiation of activity and task

The lesson 'Can Do' descriptors often referred to language activities (e.g. grammar or vocabulary activities) rather than linguistic competences or functions. In this sense, they did not represent a communicative competency nor stand-alone criteria as defined by the CEFR (Council of Europe 2001). It was therefore recommended to rigorously separate language activities from linguistic competences when writing 'Can Do' descriptors. A focus on the core communicative goal of each lesson would then be necessary rather than listing every activity of the lesson. This action would eventually see the total number of 'Can Do' descriptors per lesson drop considerably from an average of six 'Can Do' descriptors reflecting various activities to a single 'Can Do' descriptor describing the lesson's one central task.

5.2.4.2 Consistency of the 'Can Do' descriptor wording

The wording of 'Can Do' descriptors varied somewhat in consistency. It was recommended that teachers agree on the wording of statements and how much detail each should provide (Green (2012) discusses the components of a 'Can Do' descriptor). For example, nuances of expressions that were used could vary (simple language versus simple prepared language), and some statements were very specific whereas others were vague. For example:

> I can write short one sentence opinions about the funniest comedian, prettiest actress or most handsome actor in Japan provided I can follow written examples.
>
> I can write short sentences about my hometown.

Furthermore, when statements gave examples to clarify meaning, there was a lack of consistency with the number of items included and their position, either within the statements or in brackets at the end.

> I can write one-word descriptions for a list of known places (e.g. New York), things of personal interest (e.g. my bike) and known people (e.g. my mother) using given examples.
>
> I can name and give the uses of various survival items (e.g. flashlight, knife, compass) when shown pictures provided I can use a dictionary.
>
> I can write answers to simple questions to show comprehension of a short clip from a television programme (e.g. character's name, occupation, location).

5.2.4.3 The necessity for a spiralling system

After observing the complete list of 'Can Do' descriptors Dr Naganuma noted that they all seemed to be largely unrelated to each other. This led to the question of whether there was any overlap in the contents of lessons, and a recommendation to ensure spiralling in the curriculum to facilitate language acquisition for students. A spiral curriculum is one in which concepts are initially introduced in simple form, and then the same concepts are revisited later in the curriculum, but are each time presented in more depth and complexity. Thus, an ascending spiral is formed in which the same concepts are presented repeatedly, each time in more detail (Bruner 2009).

5.2.5 'Can Do' descriptor mapping to the CEFR-J self-assessment grid

Once 'Can Do' descriptors were finalised following the feedback, teachers worked in pairs to map these statements to the CEFR-J grid. An example of a lesson 'Can Do' descriptor and its closest CEFR-J equivalent is given below:

> Lesson 'Can Do' descriptor
> I can listen for/answer written questions about the key points of a short speech describing a person's personality if spoken slowly, clearly and with chances for repetition.
> Closest CEFR-J 'Can Do' descriptor (Level A1.1)
> I can catch concrete information (e.g. places and times) on familiar topics encountered in everyday life, provided it is delivered in slow and clear speech.

Therefore, the lesson 'Can Do' descriptor above was allotted a CEFR-J difficulty level of A1.1. The same process was undertaken for each 'Can Do' descriptor by the same pair of teachers who created it. This process was completed in February 2013 (see Table 1).

5.2.6 The curriculum map

Following the matching of all of the lesson 'Can Do' descriptors with their closest equivalent CEFR-J descriptor, the lesson 'Can Do's were entered into an Excel spreadsheet which could be organised (using the sort feature) according to any of the following criteria, which acted as the headings of each column: unit of study, classroom handout, CEFR-J 'Can Do' descriptor, CEFR-J level, or language skill. This spreadsheet acted as the 'map' of the content of all lesson materials, providing an overview of two full years of the GE language programme. A snapshot of the document itself is provided in Figure 1. In the skill column, lower and upper refer to which of the two statements in the CEFR-J self-assessment grid for each level and skill the lesson 'Can Do' is associated with.

5.2.7 Training workshop for student-friendly 'Can Do' descriptors on lesson handouts

A major discovery following the initial round of 'Can Do' writing was that the lesson 'Can Do' descriptors were not appropriate to be included on lesson handouts. A second version of 'Can Do' descriptors more easily comprehensible for students needed to be created. The existing 'Can Do' descriptors were therefore referred to as teacher 'Can Do's and were used for identifying and summarising lesson language proficiency goals for teachers, as well as for the mapping process to determine where the current curriculum stood in terms of alignment with the CEFR-J. Conversely, the student 'Can Do' descriptors would be simplified versions of the teacher 'Can Do' descriptors, and would be added to the lessons for students to self-assess their

Figure 1 The GE curriculum map as shown in Excel*

Year	Unit	Lesson#	Lesson Can Do	CEFR-J level	Skill
FE	IU	1	I can introduce myself and ask other people for their name with prepared simple language.	A1.1	SI lower
FE	IU	1	I can ask/answer questions about when one's birthday is in simple language.	A1.1	SI lower
FE	IU	2	I can ask/answer questions about what hobbies another person or I do in our free time in simple prepared language.	A1.1	SI lower
FE	IU	3	I can unscramble and arrange the words of written sentences (of . .)	A1.1	R upper
FE	IU	3	I can match simple written classroom instructions with their video representations of the . . .	A1.1	R upper
FE	IU	5	I can write simple one sentence answers to written questions about my high school English classes.	A1.1	W lower

Note: SI = Spoken interaction; R = Reading; W = Writing

learning. Student self-assessment of proficiency both before and after each lesson is intended to help learners to engage in the learning cycle described by O'Dwyer (2010), Nagai and O'Dwyer (2011) and O'Dwyer and Runnels (2014). A second 'Can Do' writing workshop in May 2013 was therefore held to train teachers on the creation of student-friendly 'Can Do' descriptors. This workshop also familiarised new teachers and learning advisors with the curriculum renewal and refreshed and updated veteran teachers and learning advisors on the purpose of the curriculum renewal, while explaining progress, shortcomings and accomplishments of what had occurred so far. Following this workshop, issues pointed out by Dr Naganuma in the teacher 'Can Do' descriptors were also addressed, such as clarifying inconsistencies in wording so that statements were neither too vague nor too specific, and ensuring that 'Can Do' descriptors reflected communicative goals.

5.2.8 Student-friendly 'Can Do' descriptors

A useful way to break down the components of a 'Can Do' descriptor is into *performance*, *criteria* and *condition* (Tono and Negishi 2012). The performance component describes the language task to be performed, the criteria describes quality of language of input or output, and the condition describes under what circumstances (e.g. topic familiarity, or opportunity for

Using the CEFR-J and the CEFR as frameworks for renewal

repetition). Student-friendly 'Can Do' descriptors were created by removing the criteria and context components of the teacher 'Can Do' descriptors for lessons and simplifying the language of the remaining 'Can Do' descriptor as much as possible. An example is shown below with the criteria and context section of the lesson 'Can Do' descriptor for teachers underlined.

> Lesson 'Can Do' descriptor for teachers
> Students can ask and answer questions about song preferences <u>using simple words and phrases, provided they can use prepared example language.</u>

> Lesson 'Can Do' descriptor for students
> I can ask and answer questions about favourite songs.

Self-assessment checklists, which include Japanese translations, appear twice (at the start and end) on each lesson handout. The self-assessment wording, i.e. 'I can't do it', 'I can do it, but I need more practice', 'I can do it', 'I can do it easily' was modelled after the self-assessment checklists created in the SALC activities (see sections 3.2.3 and 5.5.2 of the second part of this chapter). An example lesson 'Can Do' checklist is shown in Figure 2.

Figure 2 An example of a self-assessment checklist at the start of a lesson handout

Check the boxes.				
	I can do it easily.	I can do it.	I can do it, but I need more practice.	I can't do it.
I can understand a travel blog. 私は旅行ブログを理解することができる。				
I can talk about travel experiences. 私は旅行経験について話すことができる。				
I can write a travel blog about a trip. 私は旅行についての旅行ブログを書くことができる。				

Before beginning each lesson, students read the 'Can Do' descriptors and consider how they relate to the content of the upcoming lesson. Students also self-assess their language proficiency by identifying which one of four proficiency descriptors they best fall into and checking the boxes. After completing the lesson, students must once again read the 'Can Do' descriptors and reflect on their language proficiency level by choosing one of the four

Assessment of CEFR-informed Language Teaching in Japan and Beyond

categories shown in Figure 2. A survey to determine the student perceptions of the inclusion of these self-assessment checklists was conducted, the results of which are described in section 5.3.2.6.

5.2.9 Further training to support curriculum renewal

Upon completion of the actions described in the previous sections, it had become apparent that few of the GE lessons actually followed their intended TBL approach. As tasks are recommended in the CEFR (see Council of Europe 2001, chapter 7), it was felt that increasing faculty knowledge of TBL would assist in the subsequent lesson revision and creation process. Thus, a workshop was held by Paul Leeming of Kinki University in November 2013. This workshop informed BECC teachers and learning advisors about the history and theories of TBL, examined a task-based lesson and then compared it to a current GE curriculum lesson to point out weaknesses and recognise specific areas that needed to be revised.

5.2.10 Lesson materials modifications

Since the commencement of the curriculum renewal project, the lesson materials had undergone some significant changes. In addition to the inclusion of self-assessment checklists on lesson handouts (as described in sections 5.2.3 and 5.2.8), throughout 2013, all FE lessons and half of the SE lessons had been revised with the stated intention of bringing them closer to the target CEFR-J bands of A1.3 for FE and A2.2 for SE. However, most lessons were revised based on teacher feedback to make them more teachable and engaging, rather than with a focus on bringing lessons closer to the CEFR-J. A new map was therefore needed to reflect these changes. At end of the 2013 academic year, in February 2014, a second mapping process was initiated with the intent of creating an updated map of the GE curriculum against the CEFR-J.

5.2.11 Training workshop for an updated curriculum map

To work towards the creation of a new map to quantify the modified GE curriculum, BECC teachers and learning advisors participated in a final training workshop in January 2014, nearly two years after the commencement of the CEFR-J GE curriculum renewal project. This workshop was held with the intentions of increasing teachers' familiarity with the target CEFR-J descriptors for the GE curriculum, and of reaching a consensus amongst teachers on the matching of some representative lesson 'Can Dos' with their nearest CEFR-J equivalent.

The process of matching lesson 'Can Do' descriptors to their closest CEFR-J descriptor for the purpose of gaining information for curriculum alignment to the CEFR-J is in many ways similar to the process of aligning tests to the CEFR by reaching agreement about what CEFR levels test questions assess. The procedures recommended in the manual for relating examinations to the CEFR (Council of Europe 2009) were thus consulted.

Using the CEFR-J and the CEFR as frameworks for renewal

The workshop was divided into two parts. In the first part of the workshop BECC teachers and learning advisors did a descriptor sorting exercise. Descriptor sorting exercises are recommended by the manual for familiarising expert panels with the CEFR before aligning tests to the CEFR. Descriptor sorting exercises were used in the Swiss project which developed the original CEFR descriptors (North 2000), and were also used in the process of validating the CEFR-J descriptors (Negishi, Takada and Tono 2013).

For the descriptor sorting exercise, pairs of teachers sorted either the upper or the lower of the two statements within each CEFR-J level for the five skills (listening, reading, spoken interaction, spoken production and writing) for levels Pre A1 to B1.1. This meant that each pair had a total of 35 descriptors to sort (the manual recommends that the total number of descriptors should not exceed 40). Secondly, pairs of participants combined into groups of four in which one pair had sorted descriptors for the upper band for each skill, and the other pair had sorted descriptors for the lower band for each skill. The groups then had to reach an agreement on the difficulty ordering of the 70 CEFR-J descriptors from Levels Pre A1 to B1.1. After all groups had finished, they were then allowed to compare their sorted descriptors with the actual CEFR-J grid and could discuss discrepancies.

In the second section of the workshop, six representative lesson 'Can Do' descriptors from the lessons revised in 2013 were chosen for norming purposes. These 'Can Do' descriptors were selected as they represented all of the five language skills represented in the CEFR-J (spoken production, spoken interaction, listening, reading and writing) and included aspects that might make them problematic or difficult to map. For each 'Can Do' descriptor in turn workshop participants assigned what they deemed to be the CEFR-J 'Can Do' descriptor from the self-assessment grid which matched most closely with the content of the lesson 'Can Do' descriptor. In an effort to reach a consensus on the best match, the whole group justified and discussed their selections. The six representative lesson 'Can Do' descriptors chosen for the workshop are listed below:

1. Students can catch key information from a simple clothes shopping dialogue, such as prices and colours, provided it is delivered slowly and clearly.
2. Students can ask and answer simple questions about weekend activities and everyday life if people speak clearly and formulaic language is provided.
3. Students can write a series of sentences about songs using simple words and basic expressions, provided they can refer to model text.
4. Students can give a brief presentation outlining a party they helped arrange with a group of classmates provided they can use prepared speech.

Assessment of CEFR-informed Language Teaching in Japan and Beyond

5. Students can understand a short text about a musician provided they can work with a partner and use a dictionary.
6. Students can shop online provided they are given a website link.

The outcomes of this process are described in section 5.4.5.2.

5.2.12 Adapting CEFR-J descriptors as new course proficiency goals

Another important action taken towards CEFR-J alignment of the GE curriculum was the creation of new course proficiency goals. Through discussion in committee meetings in 2012, and in accordance with the survey results described in section 5.3.1, a consensus amongst BECC teachers was reached to set English language proficiency targets at CEFR-J A1.3 for FE and CEFR-J A2.2 for SE. Accordingly, for 2013 new course proficiency goals were created by taking the CEFR-J descriptors at the two target levels, and adapting the 'performance' sections of the statements to match existing curriculum themes and content. Reformulation of 'Can Do' descriptors to adapt them to local contexts is encouraged within the CEFR (Council of Europe 2001, North no date). An example of how localised course proficiency goals were adapted from the CEFR-J is provided in Table 2.

Table 2 An example of localisation of a CEFR-J 'Can Do' descriptor for a course proficiency goal

CEFR-J A1.3 descriptor		
Performance	**Criteria**	**Condition**
I can ask and answer ... questions about familiar topics such as hobbies, club activities	Simple	Provided people speak clearly
FE course proficiency goal		
Performance	**Criteria**	**Condition**
Be able to ask and answer ... questions about familiar topics such as hobbies, university life, and weekend activities	Simple	Provided people speak clearly

CEFR-J A1.3 descriptor
I can ask and answer simple questions about familiar topics such as hobbies, club activities, provided people speak clearly.

New FE curriculum proficiency goal
By the end of a year of study Freshman English students will:
Be able to ask and answer simple questions about familiar topics such as hobbies, university life, and weekend activities provided people speak clearly.

As can be seen in the previous example, only the performance part of the CEFR-J descriptors was modified for new GE curriculum language proficiency goals. This maintained the difficulty level of the descriptors while adapting them to the local context. The new course goals covered all five language skills in the CEFR-J self-assessment grid. These are spoken interaction, spoken production, listening, reading and writing.

5.2.13 Redesigning institutional tests – the Bunkyo English Tests (BETs)

The final major action taken to align the GE curriculum with the CEFR-J from 2012 to 2014 was the creation of institutional standardised tests of reading and listening aligned to Level A2 of the CEFR, dubbed the Bunkyo English Tests (BETs). The BETs, which are standardised tests of English listening and reading ability, have several important functions within the GE curriculum. Firstly, as standardised tests, the BETs aim to give an objective measure of GE students' English reading and listening proficiency across their two years of study in the GE curriculum. This information is important for a variety of stakeholders including students, teachers, administrators, and parents of students. If BET results show that students' average reading and listening ability does not improve significantly from year to year, changes may need to be made to the GE curriculum or teaching approach. Secondly, BET results are used to stream students into classes divided by English language proficiency. Thirdly, the BETs are intended to provide positive washback on the GE curriculum through specifying what language tasks and text types are characteristic of the CEFR A2 level for reading and listening.

Finally, a standard-setting project was underway in 2016 to set cut points for BET scores. Cut points are the scores above which test takers are classified one way, and below which they are classified another way (Brown 2005). The first step in this standard-setting project was to set cut points for the reading section of the BET in August 2016. A panel made up of BECC teachers set cut points for the BET reading section at CEFR Levels A1, A2 and B1 using the bookmark method. (For more information about standard setting and the bookmark method, see the manual for relating language examinations to the CEFR (Council of Europe 2009)). We also plan to set BET cut points for listening, and once the cut points are complete, they will form part of the basis for issuing English language proficiency certificates at the A2 and B1 CEFR levels to GE graduates from 2017.

Due to a lack of illustrative examples of test questions benchmarked to the CEFR-J, the BET test tasks were modelled on tasks from *Cambridge English: Key (KET)* (University of Cambridge ESOL Examinations 2012a), which is targeted at the A2 level. Detailed specifications for the BETs were written, and around half of the tasks in the existing GE curriculum institutional reading and listening tests were remade to match the new test specifications. In 2014 further modifications were made to the BET specifications, and for their 2015 administrations, the BETs fully matched the new test specifications. There are three BETs: one for entering GE students, one for GE students at the end of their first year of study, and one for students graduating from the GE programme after two years of study. (For more information about the history of standardised reading and listening tests in the GE curriculum see Bower, Rutson-Griffiths and Sugg 2014).

5.3 Programme 1 Stage 3: Collect and Analyse Evidence

The third phase of the programme involved collecting and analysing evidence. In this section the results of each of the actions detailed in section 5.2 are analysed.

5.3.1 Teacher and student perceived CEFR-J level survey results

Using a 5-point scale, students responded to all CEFR-J 'Can Do' descriptors from A1.1 to A2.2. Teachers also rated what they perceived the abilities of 80% of students in their classes to be, according to the convention set by the prototype Swiss Portfolio (and also adopted by the Association of Language Testers in Europe) that mastery of a set of 'Can Do' descriptors for a level should be judged at a threshold of 80% (Council of Europe 2001:248). The results provided support for the target levels previously selected by staff, as it was found that the first year students' mean self-assessment rating across all skills was at an A1.3 level, while second year students' mean was between an A2.1 and A2.2. The teachers' ratings for the students were similar. Teachers' mean scores for the first year students were between an A1.2 and A1.3, although the teacher ratings were obtained for the skills of listening and reading alone and ratings on the remaining skills of spoken production, spoken interaction, and writing may have differed (the second year teachers did not participate in this study). The results of these surveys are described in further detail in Runnels (2013a, 2013b, 2013c).

5.3.2 The initial curriculum map

Following the completion of the curriculum map, the findings regarding the five aspects of the curriculum's content – the balance of language skills, level of difficulty, progression in difficulty, targeting with goal CEFR-J levels, and coverage of CEFR-J level descriptors – were analysed. To do this, each of the eight CEFR-J levels was assigned a number from 0 to 7 (where 0 and 7 represented 'Can Do' descriptors from Levels Pre A1 and B1.2 respectively), and each lesson 'Can Do' descriptor was represented with a corresponding single digit according to its CEFR-J level. The 8-point scale was then used for any calculations regarding the mean difficulty level or progression of difficulty through each lesson, unit, semester, or year and for determining how the curriculum compared to the target CEFR-J level for each academic year.

5.3.2.1 The balance of individual language skills

Figure 3 shows the balance of individual language skills for the lesson content of the GE curriculum. It can be seen that there was an overall imbalance of skills, with spoken interaction making up nearly half of the lesson content, while listening represents only a tenth of the total.

Figure 3 The balance of language skills across lesson content for the GE curriculum

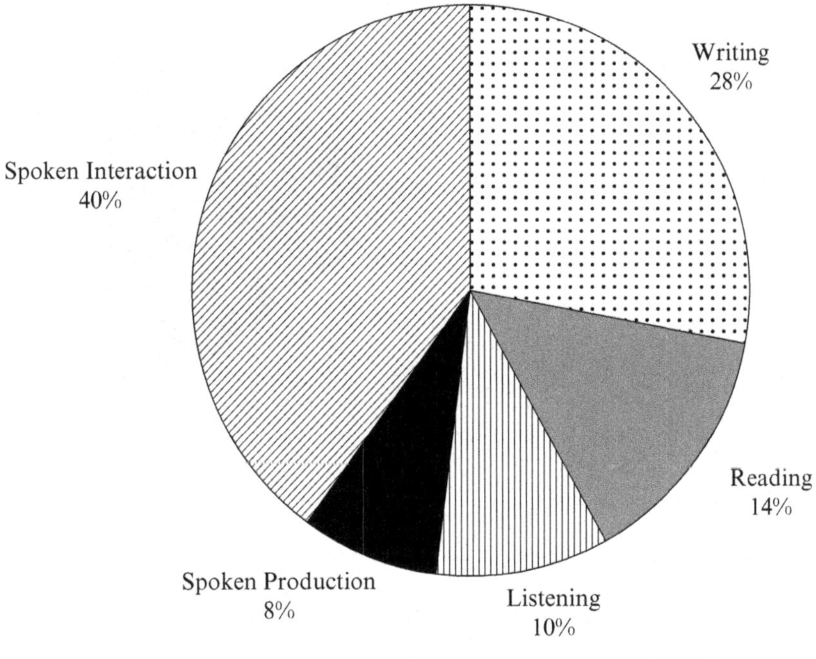

- Writing 28%
- Spoken Interaction 40%
- Reading 14%
- Spoken Production 8%
- Listening 10%

5.3.2.2 Difficulty of the GE curriculum

In terms of the level of difficulty of language tasks, Figure 4 shows that the GE curriculum spans difficulty levels Pre A1 through to B1.2, although very few tasks were deemed to be at either of those two levels. Nearly two thirds of all of the GE curriculum's tasks were between an A1.3 and an A2.2 level of difficulty.

5.3.2.3 Progression of difficulty of the GE curriculum

Regarding whether a progression of difficulty was evident throughout the 2-year GE curriculum, the map could be organised according to academic year, semester, week of study, unit or lesson. To determine the progression of difficulty, the mean for each thematic unit was calculated, using the same 8-point scale where the zero point on the scale corresponds to the CEFR-J

Figure 4 The level of difficulty of the lesson content for the GE curriculum

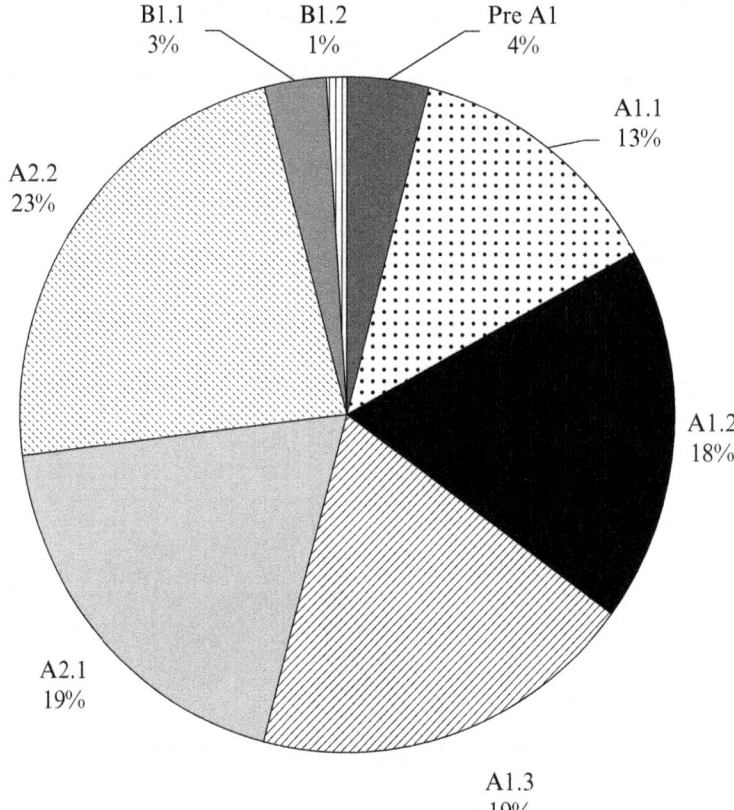

level Pre A1, and 7 represents a B1.2 level. Figure 5 shows the mean difficulty level for each of these units. The units are organised chronologically, and it is evident that the difficulty of the lesson content starts at approximately an A1.3 level (represented by 3 on the scale) in the first unit and finishes at an A2.1 level (represented by a 4 on the scale). With the exception of the third chronological unit, which drops towards an A1.2 level of difficulty, the mean difficulty of all material falls within the range of A1.3 and A2.1.

5.3.2.4 Targeting of GE curriculum

In relation to the fourth aspect of the curriculum's content, whether the lesson content met the institution's stated target CEFR-J levels of A1.3 at the exit of the first year, and A2.2 at the exit of the second year, it can be gleaned from Figure 5 that the mean difficulty level of the final unit from the first year (Unit 4) was at A1.2, although the mean difficulty level of the FE curriculum

Figure 5 The mean level of difficulty for each thematic unit of study

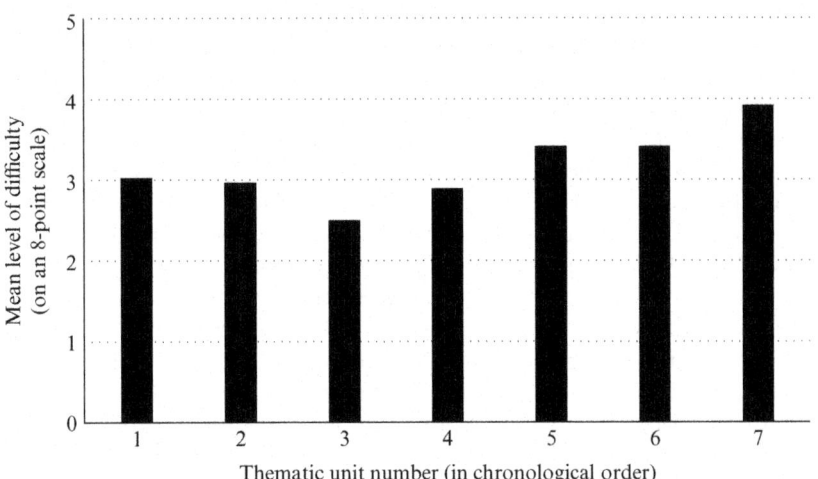

was at an A1.3 level, meeting the FE curriculum's stated target. The mean difficulty level of the seventh and final unit (which spanned an entire semester) was approximately at an A2.1 level, and approximately one level lower than the stated target. However, within this final unit, despite the mean being at an A2.1 level rather than at A2.2, 33.8%, or a third of the unit, was in fact at the A2.2 level of difficulty, with an additional 6.5% above that. This means that a significant number of easy tasks at Levels A1.3 or lower brought the mean down to A2.1, even though about 40% of the final unit was levelled at the exit target of the programme of A2.2. In terms of the mean difficulty for each year, the FE curriculum mean difficulty was about mid-way between A1.2 and A1.3 whereas for the SE curriculum it was about mid-way between A1.3 and A2.1, lower than the exit goal of A2.2.

5.3.2.5 Coverage of CEFR-J descriptors by the GE curriculum

The final component of the curriculum map analysis was to determine whether all language tasks and functions in the target CEFR-J level descriptors were covered by the existing curriculum. The material of the curriculum spans eight levels (Pre A1, A1.1, A1.2, A1.3, A2.1, A2.2, B1.1, B1.2) which are associated with a total of 80 different 'Can Do' descriptors (each CEFR-J level consists of a total of 10 statements, two for each of the five language skills). However, only a single statement from B1.2 appeared from the curriculum. It was thus removed from the following analysis, which focused only on the content of Levels Pre A1 to B1.1. Of the 70 statements within these levels, 14 of them (or 20%) are not represented in the curriculum whatsoever. Among the remaining 56 descriptors, six of them made up a total of

1.8% of the curriculum (or 0.3% each), appearing only once in the 2-year programme. Conversely, the most frequently occurring statement appeared 28 times across the curriculum, making up a total of 8.2% of the total lesson content.

When considering the distribution of represented statements for the programme's target exit levels of A1.3 and A2.2, for the former, the 10 statements from Level A1.3 appeared in the curriculum a total of 71 times. Each statement appeared at least twice, while the most frequently appearing statement appeared 20 times. Other statements appeared 4, 6, 11 or 18 times. All of the 10 CEFR-J A2.2 statements were also represented in the lessons. Of the 10, one of them only appeared once, whereas another appeared 28 times, or 35% of all statements. The remaining eight statements appeared 2, 4, 6, 9 or 16 times. Similar spans existed within every one of the CEFR-J levels meaning that some CEFR-J descriptors were not represented in the lesson content whatsoever, while others were represented numerous times throughout the curriculum. If the BECC management insists that all CEFR-J descriptors be represented in the curriculum equally, these findings suggest that some serious imbalances exist, and that significant modifications are required. On the other hand, the imbalance and focus on some statements or others might be seen as an advantage since they would ensure that learners become accustomed to performing tasks from those statements.

Ultimately, the curriculum map provided some useful feedback on the content of the curriculum. However, all of these findings were limited due to issues with the process, which are described in section 5.4.5.

5.3.2.6 Student feedback on self-assessment on lesson handout 'Can Do' descriptors

Lesson 'Can Do' descriptors were first included in SE lessons in 2011 as part of a previous curriculum renewal project. The main purpose of this project was to write new lessons for the second year portion of the curriculum. These lessons were based on *Waystage* (van Ek and Trim 1991b), which is associated with CEFR Level A2, and as part of the lesson-creation process 'Can Do' descriptors were written to include at the start and end of each lesson for students to self-evaluate their proficiency on the lesson content. A survey of 274 SE students in 2012 indicated positive student attitudes to these lesson 'Can Do' descriptors. Results from two of the survey's Likert scale items are shown in Figures 6 and 7. 83% of students either agreed or strongly agreed that 'Can Do' descriptors in the lesson handouts helped them to understand their weaknesses in English (Figure 6), and 84% of students also agreed that 'Can Do' descriptors in the lessons helped them to understand the goals of the lessons (Figure 7).

Figure 6 Student attitudes to lesson self-assessment checklists

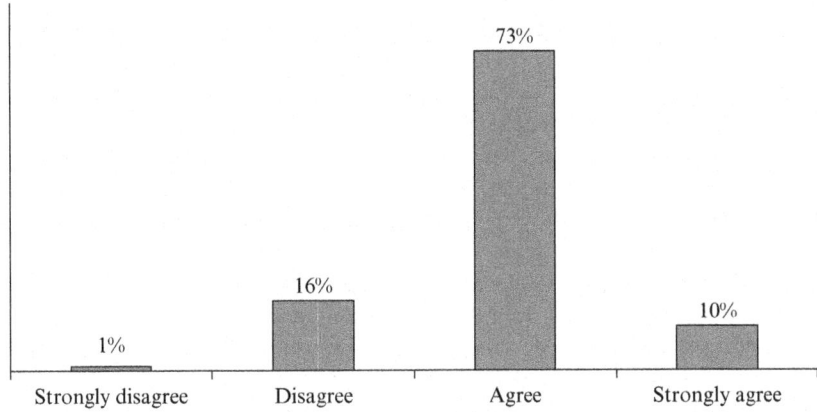

'Can Do' descriptors helped me to understand my weaknesses in English (n = 274)

Figure 7 Student attitudes to lesson self-assessment checklists

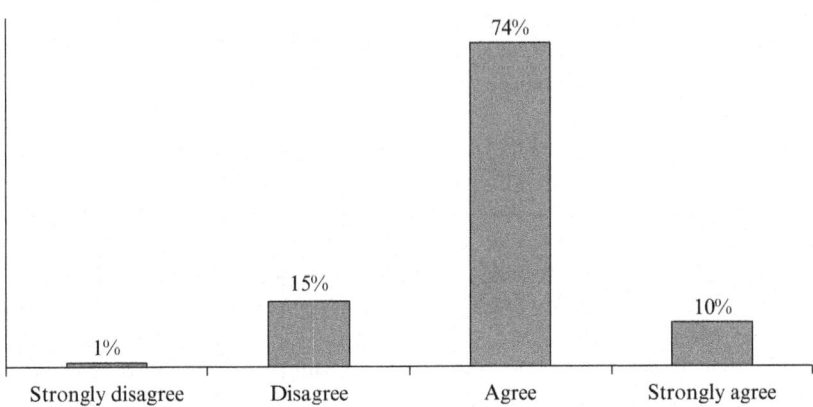

'Can Do' descriptors helped me to understand the goals of lessons (n = 274)

5.3.3 Observations on lesson material modifications

A major problem with the modifications made to lessons in the first cycle of curriculum renewal was a lack of top-down direction. Individual teachers were assigned lessons to revise, with an instruction to revise each lesson based on lesson feedback from other teachers, and with a view to aligning each lesson to the CEFR-J. However, a lack of clear directions on specific modifications to be made to lessons to bring them into alignment with the CEFR-J (due to problems with the mapping process) meant that most lessons were only revised in terms of making them more interesting and effective, not to bring their target task in line with a CEFR-J descriptor.

5.3.4 Updated curriculum map training workshop feedback

Several issues arose during the training session for the second mapping, both from the descriptor sorting exercise and from the norming workshop, which ultimately put a halt to the attempt to create an updated curriculum map. Specifically, it was found that some of the CEFR-J 'Can Do' descriptors contained ambiguous wording, which could not be clearly interpreted without the use of illustrative examples, or more detailed description. For example, the workshop participants were not able to reach a consensus on the meaning of and the difference between 'using familiar formulaic expressions' in the CEFR-J spoken interaction Level A1.1 descriptor and 'using a limited repertoire of expressions' in the A1.2 descriptor. In addition, for the reading descriptors participants commented that it was difficult to distinguish between the textual complexity of the different reading text types at different levels without illustrative examples.

Furthermore, there was much debate about whether the use of a dictionary should be permitted in the CEFR-J writing descriptors. Dictionary use is only mentioned in two CEFR-J writing descriptors at Levels A1.1 and A1.3, but most workshop participants felt the learners should be allowed to use dictionaries for writing tasks at the B levels. Finally, it was unclear how to map the lesson material statements that included classroom scaffolding, or task preparation, such as in the case of being able to refer to a model text for writing, or speaking tasks.

Many workshop participants had different interpretations about these issues based on their teaching experience and their readings from second language acquisition literature. These same issues had not arisen during the first mapping attempt, which had occurred just over a year prior, because no group norming session had taken place. Instead, for the first mapping, lesson 'Can Dos' had been divided to be classified by pairs of teachers, who each made their own pair interpretations of CEFR-J 'Can Do' descriptors for mapping. Ultimately, the differences of opinion in the second workshop could not be resolved with available CEFR-J resources, so the second mapping attempt was abandoned.

5.3.5 Redesigning institutional proficiency tests – The Bunkyo English Tests (BETs)

2015 BET results were analysed using the Rasch model. The Rasch model is a mathematical model commonly used in the social sciences for analysing test and survey data. Results from Rasch analysis of the 2015 iterations of the BETs confirmed that BET1 and BET2 were able to split test takers into two or three distinct groups for FE and SE course and class streaming purposes. However, the separate reading and listening sections of the BETs were unable to split test takers into three distinct groups for the purpose of placing test takers into A1, A2 and B1 groups for CEFR levelling and certification purposes. Table 3 shows the Rasch person separation, person reliability and strata statistics.

Table 3 Rasch person separation, person reliability and strata statistics for the 2015 BETs

Test	Person separation	Person reliability	Strata
BET1 Reading section	1.79	0.76	2.72
BET1 Listening section	1.16	0.57	1.49
BET1 Overall	2.11	0.82	3.14
BET2 Reading section	1.72	0.75	2.62
BET2 Listening section	0.91	0.45	1.55
BET2 Overall	1.91	0.79	2.88
BET3 Reading section	1.72	0.75	2.26
BET3 Listening section	1.33	0.64	2.10
BET3 Overall	2.11	0.82	3.14

The strata statistic in the right column shows how many groups of person ability the test items distinguished (separated by at least three standard errors of measurement) (Osborne 2008). As can be seen in Table 3, BET1 overall is able to split test takers into three groups (strata = 3.14), and BET 2 is able to split test takers into at least two groups (strata = 2.88), meaning that these tests were able to fulfil their purpose of streaming students into at least two course streams. However, the strata values for the individual reading and listening sections of the BETs were all below three, meaning that the 2015 BETs could not separate the test takers into three groups in order to place them at the A1, A2 and B1 levels. This means that changes need to be made to the BET design and questions in order to raise the strata values to at least three for the reading and listening sections. To improve the person separation, person reliability and strata statistics for the BET reading and listening sections for the 2016 BETs, more questions will be added to the 2016 iterations of the BETs and the test designers will attempt to revise the test questions so the difficulty range of the test questions better matches the ability of the test takers.

5.4 Programme 1 Stage 4: Reflect

As described in section 3.3, the Reflect stage of the programme entails a reflection on the completed cycle, analysed with a view to finding insights and lessons learned to aid in planning the next programme. This section presents the reflections on each of the major actions undertaken to align the GE curriculum to the CEFR-J described in both of the Programme 1's stages of Take Action and Collect and Analyse Evidence. The efficacy of the actions undertaken in teacher training workshops (section 5.4.1), internal survey research (section 5.3.1), lesson 'Can Do' descriptor self-assessment checklists (section 5.4.3), the new course proficiency goals using CEFR-J descriptors (section 5.4.4), and the curriculum maps (section 5.4.5) are all analysed. The benefits of the GE curriculum renewal are reflected on, and finally the lessons learned from the CEFR-J alignment attempt are given. A final overall reflection section is included (section 5.4.6) which describes the difficulties encountered in being early adopters of the CEFR-J self-assessment grid as a basis for curriculum renewal. The results of the entire section of 5.3 and reflections from 5.4 were drawn from to inform various aspects of Programme 2.

5.4.1 Reflections on teacher training workshops

One of the most important actions undertaken in the Take Action phase of the first programme was teacher training. In total, a series of five workshops were held throughout Programme 1, which spanned the 2-year period from 2012 to 2013, and were led both by external experts and also BECC teachers. These were the CEFR Introduction workshop (section 5.2.1), the initial 'Can Do' descriptor training workshop (section 5.2.3), the student-friendly 'Can Do' descriptor workshop (section 5.2.7), the TBL workshop (section 5.2.9) and the updated curriculum map workshop (section 5.2.11). Many of the benefits of the GE curriculum CEFR-J alignment project stemmed from teacher training.

When the decision was first made to align the GE curriculum to the CEFR-J in April 2012, knowledge and understanding of the CEFR and the CEFR-J was generally quite low amongst both teachers and management. As such, education about the CEFR and its principles and goals was identified as a priority to facilitate the renewal process. The first workshop on the introduction to the CEFR allowed for the establishment of a common understanding of the CEFR, and it laid the foundations for all of the actions subsequently undertaken. The first teacher training workshop on the creation of 'Can Do' descriptors was equally as important, as the results of this workshop were 'Can Do' descriptors for all lessons, and the initial curriculum map.

One major benefit realised through the remaining teacher training sessions was that teachers became aware of the overall proficiency goals and expectations of the CEFR-informed GE curriculum. Involving teachers in the process from the beginning also granted a sense of ownership of the new curriculum and revised lessons, which hopefully contributed to higher awareness of the goal-setting procedures when planning classes, and how the various classroom activities when teaching contributed to the achievement of these goals. 'Can Do' writing workshops not only provided guidance for writing 'Can Dos', but also provided a forum to clarify areas which teachers were unsure of and to share ideas. This further allowed the process to be more inclusive and brought it away from a top-down mandate. Finally, teacher training raised the overall level of knowledge about the CEFR, the CEFR-J and TBL in the BECC and led to active discussion amongst teachers about the best way to design materials, structure lessons, and the meaning of individual CEFR-J descriptors.

5.4.2 Reflections on expert feedback

The BECC curriculum renewal project benefited from the outside expert's feedback on 'Can Do' descriptors in three ways. Firstly, teacher awareness of what constitutes a language task was enhanced. Consequently, a definition of a language task for the second Programme 2014–16 curriculum renewal project was included in the BECC GE Curriculum Overview document (Bower, Rutson-Griffiths, Kodate, Foale, Lusk Lehde and Semmelroth 2014) written for the second phase of curriculum renewal (see section 6.1.1).

Secondly, feedback highlighted the necessity for additional 'Can Do' writing workshops to address the issues outlined in section 5.2.4. As a result, teachers gained increased knowledge of what constitutes a locally acceptable 'Can Do' descriptor, as well as being aware of the need for more uniformity in our writing approach.

Finally, the expert feedback alerted us to the lack of recycling of lesson contents and of clear progression between the two years of study, likely a result of lessons being previously created by teachers on two separate committees (FE and SE). This feedback, in addition to the results of an internal survey conducted amongst teachers and learning advisors regarding the curriculum renewal project, highlighted the need for connection between lessons, and more systematic review of previously learned language (vocabulary, grammar and language functions). As a consequence the FE and SE curriculum renewal committees were combined into a single committee from 2014.

5.4.3 Reflections on lesson 'Can Do' descriptor checklists

The provision of lesson 'Can Do' descriptors for students was an integral part of CEFR-J curriculum alignment, because setting clearly defined learning targets in the form of 'Can Do' descriptors is an important aim of the CEFR (Goullier 2007:6). Self-assessment using 'Can Dos' is also advocated by the CEFR and the accompanying ELP (Little 2006).

There were several benefits of adding 'Can Do' descriptor checklists to the GE lessons. It gave students an opportunity to evaluate and reflect on their progress, as well as creating clear language learning goals (Negishi et al 2013, Shimo and Nitta 2011). Furthermore, by having students become involved in the assessment process, they are more likely to increase their motivation to learn and monitor their own progress (Luoma 2013). Finally, this form of self-assessment is unlikely to become a discouraging process for students, as the wording of the descriptors emphasises what *can be* accomplished, rather than what cannot (Faez, Majhanovich et al 2011, Faez, Taylor et al 2011, Jacobsen 2011). This positive focus on accomplishment may provide students with the additional motivation they need to succeed in their second language learning (Jacobsen 2011).

5.4.4 Reflections on new course proficiency goals

The adoption and adaptation of CEFR-J 'Can Do' descriptors covering the five language skills of spoken interaction, spoken production, listening, reading and writing provided clearer language proficiency goals for the GE curriculum (see the Appendix for an example of the prior FE curriculum goals). The new course goals show to all stakeholders what tasks GE graduates are expected to be able to perform in English. Students understand more clearly what they are expected to learn, and also what they will be tested on. In addition, these goals allow curriculum developers to construct assessments that directly test the curriculum goals, which in turn provides information on whether or not the aims of the curriculum are being achieved. Finally, the new course goals also help university administrators understand what skills graduates are expected to have, which may help with promoting the language programme to prospective students and their parents. In other words, one of the major goals of the GE curriculum renewal project was achieved in that the CEFR-J increased the transparency of the curriculum itself, and also clarified the purpose of the entire renewal effort.

5.4.5 Reflections on the curriculum map

The creation of the curriculum map was the main focus of the first year of the curriculum renewal project. It entailed a labour-intensive process involving staff familiarisation with the CEFR, the process of learning to write 'Can Do' descriptors, and then align them with CEFR-J difficulty bands. Ultimately, the curriculum map provided some useful feedback on the content of the curriculum. However, the findings were limited due to some issues with the process. Flaws in the mapping process reduced the validity and utility of the map. Firstly, the map did not account for the amount of classroom time spent on practising the skills needed for each 'Can Do' descriptor. Secondly, no process was implemented to ensure a common understanding amongst teachers of the meaning of the CEFR-J descriptors before the mapping.

A second mapping attempt was therefore made at the end of 2013, beginning with the workshop described in section 5.2.11. The workshop aimed to facilitate a better common understanding between teachers and learning advisors by reaching a consensus on the nearest CEFR-J equivalents of some representative lesson 'Can Do' descriptors written for the updated lessons, with the end goal of producing an updated curriculum map. The second mapping attempt was, however, halted due to flaws which became evident in the mapping methodology, and difficulties encountered in reaching a consensus interpretation of the meaning of some CEFR-J descriptors (see section 5.4.5.2). Specific reflections, including benefits and shortcomings of the mapping attempts, are described in the following sections.

5.4.5.1 Benefits of the mapping attempts

A major benefit of the mapping process was an increased awareness amongst staff of the nature of the CEFR-J, in addition to fostering active and critical discussions of the structure and purpose of lessons, the role of the learner and teacher in the classroom and the importance of some degree of consistency in interpretations across teachers. It also led to an increase in overall general communication and collaboration among staff and provided a means for all team members to work towards a common goal.

Furthermore, the first CEFR-J GE curriculum map gave some useful information about the balance of each of the five CEFR-J language skills in the curriculum. At a glance, it was easy to see the approximate difficulty levels of lessons. It allowed for straightforward calculations of the mean difficulty of units, semesters and years of study. The map also provided evidence for the progression in difficulty over the two years of the GE programme, or in some cases, the lack thereof (Figure 4). It showed that the curriculum did indeed largely mobilise learners to be working towards the institution's target exit goals of A1.3 at the end of the first year and A2.2 at the end of the second. A need for more difficult tasks at the A2.2 level was indicated for the second year, as it had a mean difficulty closer to an A2.1 level than A2.2. Finally, the map showed that contents implicated by some of the CEFR-J descriptors were barely covered by the curriculum while others were emphasised significantly.

5.4.5.2 Problems with the mapping attempts

Unfortunately, due to flaws in the mapping process which became apparent after the map was created, the map was not entirely able to meet the specific objectives for which it was intended. For the first mapping process, one problem was that the number of 'Can Do' descriptors associated with each lesson differed, which meant that a varying amount of class time was spent on content supporting each 'Can Do' descriptor. Without controlling for the time it takes to complete the content implicated by each descriptor, the previously described findings regarding a balance of language skills, the difficulty and the progression of difficulty are inconclusive. For instance, although an imbalance of language skills was found across the curriculum (Figure 3), it is possible that the class time associated with the listening 'Can Do' descriptors (which were purported to make up 10% of the curriculum) equalled the class time spent on reading (which made up 14% of the curriculum's 'Can Do' descriptors), even though their percentage of the total number of 'Can Do' descriptors differed. This is also the case for the difficulty.

Although the curriculum was found to be made up of 23% of tasks at an A2.2 level (Figure 4), the time corresponding to the completion of those tasks may not also equal 23% of the year's class time. In fact, this is extremely likely since tasks at a Pre A1 level of difficulty are by definition easier to complete and therefore will take less time. Thus, two of the objectives of the mapping process – to determine the balance between language skills and the difficulty of each lesson – were not precisely achieved.

The findings on the progression of difficulty are slightly more conclusive, since in this case, the difference in difficulty does increase as learners proceed through the seven thematic units (Figure 5). A similar argument can be made for determining whether the target exit goals were met, since it is likely that more time was spent on tasks at A2.2 than tasks at the lower levels. In any case, the lack of control of timing meant that the findings described in section 5.3 had to be taken as broad estimates only, as the map was not able to provide adequate information for guiding future curriculum revisions.

Another problem with the mapping was that many of the competencies contained within the CEFR-J statements did not explicitly appear as lesson 'Can Do' descriptors since they do not correspond with actual classroom tasks on the materials, but are nonetheless part of everyday classroom interaction. For example, the CEFR-J listening A2.1 'Can Do' descriptor 'I can understand the main points of straightforward factual messages (e.g. a school assignment, a travel itinerary), provided speech is clearly articulated in a familiar accent' is actually practised in every class as students listen to and carry out the teacher's oral instructions. This descriptor is undoubtedly underrepresented in the curriculum map, because it does not appear as a 'Can Do' descriptor for each lesson.

Regarding the targeting of the curriculum's materials, a further issue was noted: although it was found that approximately a third of pedagogic content of the curriculum matched precisely with the institutional target levels (Figure 5, described in section 5.3.2.5), with some tasks levelled both above and below, it is perhaps no surprise that the target levels were attained since the creators of the statements also aligned their own descriptors. First year teachers created and mapped their own first year statements and second year teachers also did so for their own materials. This meant that teachers were involved in the creation of materials, the writing of 'Can Do' descriptors for their own materials and then the mapping of those 'Can Do' descriptors. If teachers had been blind to the lesson's materials from which the statement was derived, or even blind to the ultimate level target of the programme, the mapping may not have matched the goals so closely.

A further issue which was frequently raised by teachers was that many of the lesson 'Can Do' descriptors were difficult to map to the CEFR-J because the scaffolding on lesson handouts was so great for some of the classroom

Using the CEFR-J and the CEFR as frameworks for renewal

tasks. Teachers believed this meant that students did not actually move towards communicating the target language function independently throughout the lesson. Instead, when learners were supposed to be performing the communicative task which was the ultimate goal of the lesson, students read directly from the example language provided on their handout to complete the task. In contrast, the criteria of the CEFR-J 'Can Do' descriptors is that learners are able to use language without referring directly to an example. In this sense, the task that learners performed in the classroom did not match the tasks implicated by the CEFR-J descriptors, rendering the match teachers made between the lesson 'Can Do' descriptor and the CEFR-J 'Can Do' descriptor inaccurate. An example of this is from the following lesson 'Can Do' descriptor in 1), which was mapped as being closest to the CEFR-J A2.2 spoken interaction statement in 2):

1. I can ask/answer questions about what musical instruments my classmate or I can play in simple prepared language.
2. I can respond simply in basic everyday interactions such as talking about what I can/cannot do or describing colour using a limited repertoire of expressions.

This example shows that while the condition of the GE lesson 'Can Do' descriptor allows the learners to prepare language before speaking to their classmates, the closest CEFR-J 'Can Do' descriptor does not include such a provision. This apparent gap between many of the lesson tasks and tasks as described by the CEFR-J 'Can Do' descriptors led to active discussion amongst teachers as to whether the structure of lessons should be revised to remove perhaps excessive scaffolding from some final lesson tasks. However, this was a debated point, as some teachers thought that students should be able to perform the lesson 'Can Do' descriptor without written support by the end of a lesson, whilst others argued that students should be able to do this by the end of the semester, or by the end of a year of study, and that achieving this within a single lesson was neither important nor necessary. In any case, due to these issues and flaws in the mapping process, it was not possible to definitively claim that the BECC's GE curriculum was aligned to the CEFR-J.

5.4.5.3 Suggestions for an improved mapping methodology

For other institutions that may attempt to gather information to inform a CEFR or CEFR-J curriculum alignment process in future, we recommend a process which follows a similar procedure to the one that the BECC undertook, but with four main changes that we believe are required in order to result in a successful mapping process.

Firstly, a familiarisation session on the CEFR and/or the CEFR-J should be performed. Associated readings may also be assigned to help teachers deepen their understanding of the framework and its objectives. This was found to be a crucial step for the staff at the BECC. Following this, a session which outlines the entire mapping process before it begins would allow stakeholders to see the timeline that the project is expected to follow, their role in the whole process, and to resolve any queries they may have. Having a global understanding of the project is thought to benefit anyone involved and will likely increase the impact of some of the advantages the BECC experienced.

A second crucial step that the BECC missed in our first attempt, which the second mapping attempted to rectify, involved the descriptor sorting exercise and a standardising procedure of matching six representative lesson 'Can Do' descriptors to the CEFR-J (section 5.2.11). This is similar to the process of rater training for speaking and writing tests (see Harsch and Martin (2012) for a description of CEFR-informed rater training). However, teachers were not able to come to a consensus regarding which level of performance was implied by some lesson 'Can Do' descriptors. We suggest that illustrative examples of learner production for speaking and writing tasks at the different levels should be prepared and distributed to participants before or during the workshop. Having prepared examples for each level would allow participants to resolve any vagueness or discrepancies in performance at each level. This could also occur for receptive tasks, by providing staff with reading or listening texts targeted at different CEFR-J levels. Such texts may already exist in the institution's language curriculum. In any case, we would argue that performing the sorting task and standardising procedure will greatly help teachers when they break up to create the localised descriptors and then match them with the CEFR-J 'Can Do' descriptors. A further change to the process undertaken by the BECC which we believe is crucial to ensuring a successful mapping process is that different teachers than those responsible for writing the 'Can Dos' should be tasked with mapping the 'Can Dos' to reduce the chance of bias. Finally, and perhaps most importantly, each 'Can Do' descriptor should be tagged for an estimated amount of classroom time spent working towards its achievement such that the balance of language skills and difficulty levels can be calculated based on the time that is actually spent working in those areas. Taking all present discussions into account, the overall recommended process is outlined below:

- introduce the CEFR and the CEFR-J to staff and check their understanding of the framework
- assign readings if necessary, and have teachers perform a descriptor sorting task
- introduce the overall goals, rationale and procedure of the alignment project to staff including the stakeholders' roles (ensure that all staff understand the purpose of the curriculum and how it can be addressed via undertaking this project)
- using samples of materials to be aligned, norm teachers on the creation

of locally appropriate/useable 'Can Do' descriptors and the classroom materials associated with each CEFR-J level (ideally taken directly from the curriculum)
- assign lessons to teams/pairs for 'Can Do' descriptor development (meanwhile, ensure that teachers are logging approximate time spent on lesson tasks so that time associated with each 'Can Do' descriptor can be calculated)
- compile all 'Can Do' descriptors, check for consistency, get external feedback on statements, modify or eliminate as appropriate (ensure that classroom time spent on each is included)
- assign 'Can Do' descriptors to teams/pairs for matching with a CEFR-J/CEFR level, check for consistency, get external feedback, modify level assignment as appropriate
- compile the following information in one re-arrangeable spreadsheet: handout number, unit, CEFR-J level, language skill, semester, academic year of study, local 'Can Do' descriptor
- using all information in the compiled document, calculate time spent working within each language skill, CEFR-J level, within each CEFR-J 'Can Do' descriptor
- perform similar calculations for each lesson/week/handout/unit or whatever breakdown is necessary according to the local context.

Decisions to be made prior to commencing the mapping process' analysis:

- the ideal balance of language skills for the course (e.g. an emphasis on spoken interaction with little listening is acceptable)
- the expected difficulty levels of the course (at both the micro lesson level and macro levels including semester and year, e.g. most materials in the first year at around an A1.3 level, most materials in the second year at an A2.2 level)
- the intended progression of difficulty throughout the course (i.e. nothing in first year should proceed above an A1 level, whereas nothing in second year should drop below an A2; or, should the first unit be targeted at an A1.1 with the difficulty increasing over time? Or is a span of difficulties within a single lesson acceptable?)
- the extent of coverage of the CEFR/CEFR-J grid that should be addressed within the course's curriculum.

Following the decisions and calculations, the next steps are:

- identify any imbalances in language skill that require rectifying (i.e. a programme which emphasises verbal communication may not take issue with a curriculum which reflects a 70% focus on spoken interaction)

- identify the percentage of time spent working within each CEFR-J difficulty level (identify any required modifications according to local preferences, i.e. if the target is for students to be working at an A2.2 level, and much of the curriculum fell at a B2.2, these tasks likely require simplification)
- explore the progression in difficulty within each lesson, week, unit, semester, academic year and through the entire programme (identify required modifications or reshuffling of lessons depending on local requirements),
- identify CEFR-J statements which are not being covered by the curriculum or those which are overrepresented (again, this may or may not present an issue and depends on local circumstances relevant to the course/institution/department etc.).
- (Recognise/remember/account for the fact that some statements are not explicitly included, but that learners are encountering tasks implicated by those statements on a regular basis.)

Completing the above process will not only produce evidence of a number of features of a course's curriculum, but it will also provide evidence-based rationale for future modifications of the curriculum in order to ensure its alignment with the CEFR-J. Furthermore, the 'Can Do' descriptors created by teachers may be modified to create student-friendly 'Can Dos' which can be used at the start and end of each lesson's materials for the purposes of self-assessment (see section 5.2.8).

5.4.5.4 Closing comments on the mapping

The mapping process described herein intended to provide a clear picture of the content of lessons with a view to determining how well the existing curriculum matched the CEFR-J. The planned outcome of this process was to, 1) identify areas of the curriculum that required adjusting in order to bring it into better alignment with the CEFR-J target levels of A1.3 for the first year course and A2.2 for the second year course, 2) ensure that the curriculum gradually increased in difficulty, and 3) provide a balanced curricular focus across all language skills. However, due to problems which became apparent with the mapping methodology, the final map was neither able to provide a definitive answer as to whether the content of lessons matched the CEFR-J, nor specific directions as to what kind of modifications would be necessary for increased alignment. Furthermore, the second attempt at mapping, which intended to address the shortcomings of the first process, was unsuccessful due to lack of consensus among teachers about how to interpret the meaning of some CEFR-J descriptors.

The most important initial decision that will be faced by other institutions that may seek to adopt the CEFR-J as the framework for in-house curricula and materials is whether to align existing materials to the CEFR-J or to redesign the curriculum from scratch based on target CEFR-J proficiency levels. The two major factors influencing the BECC's decision to map the GE curriculum to the CEFR-J were the perception that modifying the existing curriculum would be less time consuming than developing an entirely new one, and a reluctance to abandon existing lesson materials targeted to the specific population of learners. However, based on the experience of this project, we would caution that attempting to align an existing curriculum to the CEFR-J could be just as time consuming as making an entirely new curriculum.

Finally, a major assumption of the mapping approach described in this chapter was that CEFR alignment is largely equated with the use of 'Can Do' descriptors. Indeed, such assertions have been made before and Alderson (2007 cited in Valax 2011) has noted the claims by many textbook publishers that their products are 'linked' to the CEFR are 'worrisome', since these linkages have occurred without any explanation of what they entail or what they mean. Tsagari (2006) has demonstrated the pervasiveness of these claims by providing lists of learning materials (textbooks) with stated equivalences to CEFR levels in their new editions, despite very few changes in content from previous editions (beyond the inclusion of 'Can Do' descriptors). Ultimately, for the BECC, the CEFR-J provided the basis for a process of quantifying a curriculum, which resulted in some general information to guide subsequent curriculum modifications. However, after reflecting on the project we realise that CEFR adopters must go beyond the use of only 'Can Do' descriptor scales in order to claim effective CEFR alignment. In addition to the descriptor scales, other aspects including the vocabulary, grammar, functions and notions covered by the curriculum, fostering of learner autonomy, and pedagogical approach should be considered as part of alignment.

Although some valuable lessons were learned from the curriculum mapping attempts described here, numerous issues with the process that was undertaken, including a narrow focus on 'Can Do' descriptors, led BECC management to make a decision in 2014 to create an entirely new curriculum based on target CEFR levels. This involved making all new lessons, rather than continuing to attempt to readjust the existing curriculum to match the CEFR-J. For other institutions considering engaging in similar CEFR or CEFR-J alignment projects we would recommend that rather than attempting a CEFR curriculum alignment utilising solely 'Can Do' descriptors from the CEFR-J self-assessment grid, administrators also consider utilising additional CEFR-related resources to ensure that curriculum alignment consists not just of language functions as represented by 'Can Do' descriptors, but also alignment of themes, topics, vocabulary, grammar, text types, text and task complexity, along with adoption of the educational philosophies of the CEFR.

5.4.6 Overall reflection

The following sections summarise our overall reflections on our 2-year attempt to align the existing GE curriculum to the CEFR-J.

5.4.6.1 Challenges of being a CEFR-J early adopter

In hindsight many of the problems we encountered in the curriculum alignment attempt from 2012 to 2013 stemmed from attempting to implement an untested localised version of the CEFR, the CEFR-J. The following sections describe and reflect on these problems.

5.4.6.1.1 Lack of curriculum alignment models

Being an early CEFR-J adopter presented some serious challenges for planning a curriculum renewal based on the CEFR-J. Having no previous examples of aligning a curriculum to the CEFR-J meant that we, as curriculum developers, were unable to reference our progress and were often left to improvise implementation procedures. Additionally, both management and teachers were still becoming more familiar with the CEFR and CEFR-J documents throughout the 2012–13 curriculum renewal cycle.

5.4.6.1.2 Shortage of CEFR-J supporting resources

Unlike the CEFR, there are no illustrative examples of student output at each CEFR-J level, which made it difficult for teachers to interpret the exact meaning of several CEFR-J 'Can Do' descriptors due to occasional vague and ambiguous wording. As discussed by Negishi et al (2013), there can be different ways to interpret the CEFR-J descriptors. For example, in the below CEFR-J 'Can Do' descriptor for reading at the A2.1 level it is not clear exactly what is meant by the adjectives 'short' and 'simple'.

> I can understand short narratives and biographies written in simple words.

It would greatly benefit users of the CEFR-J in the future if illustrative examples were to be made showing typical student output at the different levels for the productive skills, and examples of suitable texts at each level for the receptive skills.

5.4.6.2 Summary of benefits

Various benefits for stakeholders of the BECC are attributed to the first programme of the GE curriculum renewal project:

- increased teacher awareness of the differences between language tasks and language activities (section 5.2.4.1)
- increased teacher knowledge of how to write sound 'Can Do' descriptors (sections 2.1.1 and 2.1.2)

Using the CEFR-J and the CEFR as frameworks for renewal

- clearer course proficiency goals via the adoption and adaptation of CEFR-J 'Can Do' descriptors (sections 5.2.12 and 5.4.4)
- standardised, CEFR-aligned tests to give objective measures of GE students' English reading and listening proficiencies (section 5.2.13)
- future direction for improvement in the next stage of curriculum renewal with more connection between lessons and systematic revision to facilitate students' language acquisition.

5.4.6.3 Summary of shortcomings and lessons learned

The attempt to align the existing curriculum to the CEFR-J also had a number of shortcomings. A significant limitation was that the attempted mapping of the curriculum to the CEFR-J did not give sufficient information on the extent to which the curriculum matched the CEFR-J. Although it was possible to quantify the number of 'Can Do' descriptors that matched each CEFR-J skill and band, it was not possible to quantify how much class time was spent working on tasks associated with each 'Can Do' descriptor. Thus, it was difficult to determine how balanced the curriculum was in its coverage of various language skills.

The mapping process also did not reveal whether the spiralling process recommended by the external expert (described in section 5.2.4.3) was being successfully implemented in lessons, units or across the whole course. It also became clear during a workshop in early 2014 that some of the activities included in the classroom materials were not easily represented by 'Can Do' descriptors made according to the process described in section 5.2.3. As some of the lesson 'Can Do' descriptors were deemed to be 'unmappable' due to the fact that they referred to classroom activities and were not language focused, this caused further problems with the mapping attempt.

Other shortcomings were identified as being related to the curriculum itself. An apparent imbalance in the skills and level of difficulty covered in the curriculum was revealed by the mapping process. Although the mapping was flawed, the large imbalance in 'Can Do' descriptors for each skill revealed is unlikely to be solely due to problems with representing time on task for each statement. In addition, lesson revisions that subsequently took place in an effort to align the curriculum more closely with the CEFR-J improved each individual lesson, but did not address the more fundamental problems with the curriculum as a whole, such as whether lessons were progressing in difficulty in relation to each other and the overall skill balance.

Given the difficulties in mapping the existing curriculum to the CEFR-J, and the realisation that a more systematic revision of the curriculum was necessary to ensure full and balanced coverage of CEFR-based course goals, a decision was made to remake the curriculum rather than continue to try to revise what currently existed. This was not just the decision of the BECC management, but was a perception shared by most teachers. In an end-of-semester survey to identify the most urgent curriculum needs for the following year, teachers rated the statement 'Linking lessons, and building in more systematic recycling of language' to be most urgent out of eight options. The sections 6.1.4.1 to 6.1.4.5 explain how this redesign is being undertaken.

6 Curriculum renewal Programme 2 (2014–16): Making a CEFR-based curriculum

Section 6 outlines the plan and the early stages of a second cycle of curriculum renewal beginning in 2014 and scheduled to finish in mid–2016. This second curriculum renewal cycle aims to create a new GE curriculum based on the CEFR. The major reason for this decision is that at present the CEFR offers a much richer array of available supporting resources than the CEFR-J. As with the CEFR-J alignment project described in section 5, this section is also structured around the stages of a programme; however, as the current cycle is in its early stages, only the Study and Plan stage is presented in detail. The Take Action stage, and Collect and Analyse Evidence stage are only briefly presented based on some preliminary evidence from a July 2015 teacher survey and student course evaluation results.

6.1 Programme 2: Study and Plan

6.1.1 Making a GE curriculum overview

The first step in planning the second curriculum renewal cycle was creating a GE curriculum overview. At the end of the 2013/14 academic year an anonymous survey was administered to all BECC teachers to ascertain their views on the GE curriculum renewal process in 2013. In addition, short individual discussions were held by one of the project leaders with each BECC teacher with the same aim. One issue that arose in the interviews and the survey was the lack of any document which stated the aims and educational philosophy of the GE curriculum, along with specific guidelines on how to write a GE lesson handout. As one respondent stated in the survey: 'After 6 years we still don't know what a "BECC lesson" is, never mind a BECC curriculum. To address this concern, a General English Curriculum Overview (Bower, Rutson-Griffiths, Kodate et al 2014) was written in semester 1 2014. The overview clearly states the aims of the GE curriculum, along with its overarching framework (the CEFR), and the GE syllabus structure. In addition, the overview gives detailed specifications for designing a typical GE lesson handout, along with a lesson handout example.

6.1.2 Utilising a wider range of CEFR-related resources

As mentioned above, one major benefit of utilising the CEFR rather than the CEFR-J is the vast number of resources available. At the time of curriculum renewal, the CEFR-J consisted only of a single self-assessment grid, and some vocabulary lists (this situation has improved somewhat since, with the publication of a CEFR-J guidebook including a descriptor database (Tono 2013)), whereas the CEFR had a plethora of available supporting materials. Many of these CEFR-related resources are being utilised in the creation of various aspects of the new curriculum to ensure it is aligned with its intended CEFR levels. Reading and listening texts and tasks for new lessons are being based on the specifications for the BETs, which themselves are based on the Cambridge English A2 level *Cambridge English: Key* and B1 level *Cambridge English: Preliminary* (see section 5.2.13). Vocabulary used in the new curriculum is based on *Cambridge English: Key* (University of Cambridge ESOL Examinations 2012c) and *Cambridge English: Preliminary* (University of Cambridge ESOL Examinations 2012d) vocabulary lists, and the English Vocabulary Profile (University of Cambridge 2012). Grammar points included in lessons are taken from the *Waystage 1990* (van Ek and Trim 1991b) and *Threshold 1990* (van Ek and Trim 1991a) documents and supplemented by the *British Council/EAQUALS Core Inventory* (North, Ortega and Sheehan 2010). The vast array of textbooks available at the A2 and B1 levels is also being referred to, to ensure that lesson activities are generally level appropriate. By utilising CEFR-based resources in designing all aspects of the curriculum's content and assessment, it is hoped that the resulting lessons and assessments will be tightly aligned to the CEFR in all aspects, and thus provide level-appropriate language instruction for BECC students.

6.1.3 Getting an objective measure of student proficiency: The Oxford Online Placement Test

To gain an objective measure of BECC incoming first year students' English levels, the Oxford Online Placement Test (OOPT) was administered to a representative sample (n = 71) of the 2014 FE cohort (n = 292) in May 2014. This placement test from Oxford University Press covers reading, grammar, vocabulary and listening skills (Pollit 2009, Purpura 2010). Reasons for choosing this test included the ease of administration (online) and the provision of student CEFR levels with OOPT results.

The outcome indicated that the majority of entering GE students were either at CEFR A1 (44%) or CEFR A2 (42%). Outliers were at Pre A1 (9%), B1 (4%) and B2 (1%) levels. The result that almost half of entering GE students were shown to be at A2 level or higher necessitated a rethinking of the BECC GE curriculum goals. As nearly half of GE students entered at A2 level, the current goal of CEFR-J Level A2.2 after two years of study did not make sense for these students.

6.1.4 2014–16 plan for remaking the curriculum

6.1.4.1 Justification for creating two course streams

The Association of Language Testers in Europe (ALTE) guide (Table 4) suggests the number of hours of guided learning required to obtain each CEFR proficiency level.

Table 4 Required study time (guided learning) for each CEFR proficiency level

Target level	Average number of hours of study needed for someone who is one level below	Average number of hours of study needed for someone who is a beginner (from 0 = cumulative)
A1	90–100	90–100
A2	90–100	180–200
B1	170–200	350–400
B2	150–200	500–600
C1	200–300	700–800
C2	300–400	1,000–1,200

Source: Association of Language Testers in Europe (ALTE) (as cited in European Organization for Nuclear Research 2013).

In the BECC GE curriculum, students receive approximately 180 hours of guided language learning over a 2-year period. Given this amount of tuition, and considering the results outlined in section 6.1.3, it would seem reasonable for students entering at A1 or Pre A1 level to achieve an A2 level. However, students already entering at A2 level need the opportunity to reach a higher level, thus it was decided to create two course streams. One stream aims to bring students from Pre A1 or A1 to A2 level, and the other stream aims to bring students from A2 level to B1 level.

6.1.4.2 3-year timeline

The 3-year timeline for creating the new curriculum and its assessments is presented in Table 5. The curriculum creation plan includes making new lesson handouts and materials, making in-class assessments including vocabulary tests, and making speaking tests and revised BETs. As well as lessons required for the new curriculum, in-class assessments, vocabulary tests, speaking tests and updated BETs will be created concurrently. Due to the volume of work required, this process is anticipated to take a total of three years.

Using the CEFR-J and the CEFR as frameworks for renewal

Table 5 3-year timeline for second curriculum renewal phase

Academic year	Curriculum duties	Assessment duties
2014 semester 1	Create curriculum overview and curriculum renewal plan	None
2014 semester 2	Create first year semester 1 materials	Create first year semester 1 vocabulary and speaking tests
2015 semester 1	Create first year semester 2 materials	Create first year semester 2 vocabulary and speaking tests
2015 semester 2	Create second year semester 1 materials	Create second year semester 1 vocabulary and speaking tests. Update BETs 1 and 2 to reflect new curriculum
2016 semester 1	Create second year semester 2 materials	Create second year semester 2 vocabulary and speaking tests
2016 semester 2	Make any necessary lesson revisions	Update BET 3 to reflect new curriculum

6.1.4.3 Syllabus design methodology

Creating the new syllabus consisted of two stages: initial design, and feedback and development. Early in the initial design stage, the syllabus was conceived as one course delivered over two years, with each year consisting of two semesters, and each semester consisting of 30 90-minute classes. BECC management carried out the initial design stages. To ensure full coverage of the CEFR, it was decided to cover the 13 themes suggested in Waystage (van Ek and Trim 1991b). As some of the suggested topics appeared to be unequal in classroom time required, some themes were merged to create 12 curriculum units and two reviews, with each unit intended to take approximately eight to nine classes to complete. Table 6 shows the distribution of these topics across the two years.

Table 6 New GE curriculum units and topics

Academic year	Curriculum units	Waystage topics
Year 1, semester 1	Introduction unit	Personal identification
	Everyday life	Daily life
	My home	House and home, environment
Year 1, semester 2	Travel	Travel, weather
	Relationships	Relations with other people
	Leisure time	Free time, entertainment
Year 2, semester 1	Orientation	(Review of first year topics)
	Health	Health and body care
	Services	Services
Year 2, semester 2	Food and drink	Food and drink
	Shopping	Shopping
	Places	Places, language
	Review	(Review of all topics)

After the distribution of topics had been decided, lesson ideas for each unit were drafted, based on the specific notions listed under each topic in Waystage and Vantage (van Ek and Trim 2001). These lesson ideas were collected in online collaborative documents (Google Docs), and the feedback and development stage was commenced. The documents were opened to teachers who were asked to input their feedback on the lesson ideas drafted in the initial design stage, and to develop them further by adding more ideas and suggestions. These ideas were then used as a basis for the lesson-writing process (see the next section).

6.1.4.4 Lesson design methodology

The lesson ideas just described were based on a set lesson design that was developed at the same time as the syllabus. As discussed in 6.1.1, teachers had expressed concern that there was no set design for GE lessons. To address these concerns, and improve the consistency of lessons written by different teachers, a lesson design was devised.

As described previously, CEFR 'Can Do' descriptors are to be used as end-of-course goals for the new curriculum. A curriculum in which goals are chosen, and then content and methodology are subsequently chosen to support the achievement of these goals may be referred to as backwards design (Richards 2013). As goals and content had already been decided, only methodology remained. The course goals for the new curriculum, being taken from the CEFR descriptors, describe goals in terms of what learners are able to do, or tasks. According to Ellis (2013:5), a task-based curriculum is 'a syllabus in which the content is specified entirely in terms of the tasks to be performed (i.e. it is not based on linguistic specifications)'. Therefore the decision was taken to create a lesson structure that utilises a TBL methodology that reflects the task-based nature of the curriculum. Although the CEFR does not seek to impose any particular methodology (see Council of Europe 2001, section 6.4), the CEFR does describe language ability in terms of tasks that learners are able to perform (Council of Europe 2001, chapter 7), and it was felt that a TBL lesson design would ensure the strongest possible anchoring of each lesson to the CEFR.

As TBL is 'usually characterised as an approach, rather than a method' (Richards and Rodgers 2014:174), it was felt to be an appropriately flexible framework to design a lesson structure. Drawing on a number of resources (Ellis 2003, Nunan 2006, Willis and Willis 2007), a lesson design structure was created, with each lesson to include a warm-up, a vocabulary review, facilitating tasks and main task, and a focus on form. The creation of a lesson structure allows each lesson to be clearly anchored to the CEFR: vocabulary used in lessons is CEFR based (see section 5.1.2), the main task of each lesson is directly based on a task from the CEFR, the Eaquals (2015) bank of descriptors, or the Association of Language Testers in Europe (2002) 'Can

Using the CEFR-J and the CEFR as frameworks for renewal

Do' descriptors bank, and grammar points covered in the focus on form sections are selected from *Waystage 1990* (van Ek and Trim 1991b), *Vantage* (van Ek and Trim 2001) and the *British Council – EAQUALS Core Inventory for General English* (North et al 2010).

6.1.4.5 Lesson creation process

The lesson creation process was based on the lesson structure and on the curriculum structure described in the previous sections. Teachers are assigned a lesson at the start of each semester. They look at the collaborative ideas documents to find suggestions for lesson tasks and pre-tasks and 'Can Do' descriptors for the lesson. They may also refer to other resources, such as commercial textbooks. Teachers then submit their ideas, based on the lesson structure, to the assistant director and co-ordinators. After receiving feedback, teachers then create two lessons, one at the A1–A2 level and one at the A2–B1 level, utilising the resources described in 6.1.2 to select appropriate vocabulary and grammar and to write level-appropriate listening and reading texts and tasks. The completed lessons are then submitted to the assistant director and co-ordinators for a final check before being added to the curriculum.

6.2 Programme 2 Stage 2: Take Action

The whole curriculum creation process will be completed in January 2017. The creation of lesson materials for the 2-year curriculum using the process outlined in 6.1.4.5 was completed in August 2016.

6.3 Programme 2 Stage 3: Collect and Analyse Evidence

6.3.1 Teacher and learning advisor curriculum renewal survey

A survey was administered to BECC teachers and learning advisors at the end of semester 1 2015 to elicit their opinions of the second curriculum cycle thus far. The main points from the survey responses are summarised in point form below. Overall, respondents were very positive about the curriculum renewal process:

- the lesson creation and feedback timeline and process was perceived to be busy but efficient
- respondents thought that the new lessons matched the ability level of the students better than the old lessons
- respondents agreed that course goals and lesson goals in the form of 'Can Do' descriptors tied to the CEFR clarified the aims of the curriculum for all stakeholders

- there was unanimous agreement from survey respondents on the CEFR being the most suitable framework for GE curriculum renewal.

Some concerns were raised however:

- there was too much lesson material for FE semester 1 to cover in class
- respondents commented that simpler lessons are needed for the lowest proficiency students (Pre A1)
- some assessments did not match lesson content well
- there were not enough lesson tasks similar to the speaking test tasks
- there was insufficient focus on classroom process language in the handouts.

6.3.2 FE semester 1 course evaluation results

A comparison of the results of an FE course evaluation survey administered at the end of semester 1 in 2014 with one administered at the end of semester 1 in 2015 provides some evidence for improvements in learning outcomes as a result of the second renewal cycle. The mean Likert scale scores on a scale from one to five, for five FE course evaluation questions, are shown in the table below. The scale was 5 = strongly agree, 4 = agree, 3 = neutral, 2 = disagree, 1 = strongly disagree.

Table 7 A comparison between 2014 and 2015 semester 1 FE student course evaluation results

Statement	Mean 2014 (N = 286)	Mean 2015 (N = 271)	Difference
このコースでスピーキング能力が上がった **The course has improved my speaking skills**	3.73	3.87	0.14
英語の語彙が増えた **My English vocabulary has increased**	3.72	3.91	0.19
授業のおかげで他の国や文化により理解を深めることができた **The course has improved my understanding of other countries and other cultures**	4.10	3.92	−0.18
授業のおかげで英語のコミュニケーション能力が上がった **The course has improved my English communication skills**	3.89	4.02	0.13
授業のおかげで授業で使用する英語言語能力が上がった **The course has improved my English classroom language skills**	3.82	3.96	0.14

It can be seen from Table 7 that mean scores improved for all of the questions except for students' perception that the course improved their understanding of other countries and cultures, which decreased. To see if these Likert scale score increases were statistically significant a non-parametric test of equivalence, the Mann-Whitney U test, was run in SPSS. The results of this test are shown in Table 8.

Table 8 Results of a Mann-Whitney U test comparing 2014 and 2015 semester 1 FE student course evaluation results

Statement	Asymptotic Significance (2-tailed) Mann-Whitney U Test
このコースでスピーキング能力が上がった **The course has improved my speaking skills**	0.020
英語の語彙が増えた **My English vocabulary has increased**	0.002
授業のおかげで他の国や文化により理解を深めることができた **The course has improved my understanding of other countries and other cultures**	0.017
授業のおかげで英語のコミュニケーション能力が上がった **The course has improved my English communication skills**	0.023
授業のおかげで授業で使用する英語言語能力が上がった **The course has improved my English classroom language skills**	0.019

The results of the Mann-Whitney U test show that the differences between the 2014 and 2015 surveys are statistically significant at $p<.05$ for all of the questions. However, a Bonferroni correction to the significance level needs to be made because five separate hypothesis tests were run at the same time. The Bonferroni correction reduces the significance level to $p<.01$, meaning that only the second statement 'My English vocabulary has increased' is statistically significant. Nevertheless, these results indicate that students who completed the semester 1 FE courses in 2015 after the second CEFR-based curriculum renewal cycle believed that they had better overall learning outcomes than students who completed the semester 1 FE course in 2014 after the first CEFR-J-based renewal cycle. One notable exception is that 2015 FE students overall did not feel that the course had improved their understanding of other countries and other cultures as much as the 2014 cohort. However, this is not a major concern as increasing understanding of other countries and cultures was not one of the stated goals of the revised 2015 FE curriculum.

6.4 Programme 2 Stage 4: Reflect

Based on teacher and Learning Advisor (LA) feedback on the first half of the 2014–16 curriculum renewal process from the survey results summarised in section 6.3, it can be seen that teachers and LAs at the BECC generally felt engaged and positive about both the process and products of the new CEFR-based curriculum creation. They also saw the CEFR as the best available framework to guide this renewal.

To address the concerns raised by the survey respondents, lesson assessments will be made by the General English Assessment Committee, a specialised group of teachers, rather than by individual teachers from semester 2 2015 (which starts in October). In addition, an effort will be made to reduce the amount of lesson material each semester to make sure that it is more easily covered.

7 Concluding comments

The first programme of curriculum renewal from 2012–13 did not achieve its stated goal of aligning the GE curriculum to the CEFR-J. In hindsight, basing GE curriculum renewal only on the CEFR-J, which at that time consisted simply of a single self-assessment grid and vocabulary lists, was not an ideal choice. Problems arose in interpreting the CEFR-J 'Can Do' descriptors, and in attempting to systematically assess the extent of alignment of the current curriculum to the CEFR-J. On the other hand, many benefits arose from the first cycle of GE curriculum renewal. These benefits were increased knowledge amongst BECC management and teachers of the CEFR, 'Can Do' descriptors, and TBL. In addition, the renewal process instigated clarification of the educational approach and goals of the GE curriculum. The CEFR also helped in designing standardised reading, speaking and listening assessments. Finally, the lessons learned from the first curriculum renewal cycle formed the foundations for planning the current GE curriculum renewal cycle, in which lesson structure, vocabulary, grammar, language functions, overall syllabus content and assessment are all much more clearly defined and based systematically on the CEFR.

We came to the clear conclusion that rather than aligning our existing curriculum to the CEFR-J it was preferable to redesign the entire curriculum based on the target CEFR levels. This is consistent with Keddle's (2004) experience in which she eventually decided to create CEFR-based syllabuses from scratch, after attempting to integrate the CEFR into an existing secondary school syllabus in Italy.

Considering our experiences from three years of firstly attempting to align and secondly to develop a CEFR-based language curriculum, we recommend taking the steps outlined below to create a CEFR-based curriculum from scratch.

7.1 General steps for CEFR-based curriculum creation

- Have a representative sample of students take a CEFR placement test. Suitable tests may include the OOPT (Pollit 2009, Purpura 2010), the English First Standard English Test (English First 2014), or the Cambridge English Placement Test (see English UK (2011) for a brief description).
- Decide on an appropriate number of course streams to match the levels of your students.
- Choose or adapt CEFR 'Can Do' descriptors as overall curriculum goals for each course stream.
- Make a curriculum overview document to explain the aims, pedagogical philosophy and methodological approach of the curriculum.
- Drawing on appropriate CEFR-related documents make a syllabus outline which shows the breakdown of units and lessons. Key documents for developing our syllabus outlines were *Waystage 1990* (van Ek and Trim 1991b) and *Threshold 1990* (van Ek and Trim 1991a).
- Make a timeline for developing lesson materials and assessments.
- Make CEFR-related resources for curriculum development easily available for teachers. As mentioned above, resources we found to be useful include vocabulary lists from the Cambridge English suite of exams (University of Cambridge ESOL Examinations 2012a, 2012b), the English Vocabulary Profile (University of Cambridge 2012), *Threshold 1990* (van Ek and Trim 1991a) and *Waystage 1990* (van Ek and Trim 1991b), the *British Council – EAQUALS Core Inventory for General English* (North et al 2010), and examples of textbooks at the curriculum target CEFR levels.
- Give a workshop on the reasons for making the new curriculum, the rationale for using the CEFR as the framework of reference for curriculum development, and how to make a CEFR-informed lesson.
- Solicit teacher ideas for lesson content on a unit-by-unit basis to provide a starting point for teachers to create individual lessons and to create a sense of ownership. We found that Google Docs provide a convenient medium for this, as teachers can enter their ideas simultaneously from any internet-connected device.
- Teachers develop actual lessons and assessments.
- Give systematic feedback to ensure the consistency and quality of the formatting and structure of lessons. Feedback should also make sure that each lesson focuses on a specific CEFR-related 'Can Do' descriptor or statements.

- Allow time for lesson revisions and final checks.
- Organise the recording of lesson listening passages and videos.
- Organise the translation of lesson 'Can Do' descriptors for student self-assessment checklists.
- Begin using the new curriculum. For a longer curriculum such as our GE curriculum it may be necessary to continue developing later units while using the first few units (see section 6.1.4.3, Figure 7).
- Once lessons are complete, each lesson designer adds more specific lesson information to the syllabus document, such as the lesson target 'Can Do' descriptor, grammar, vocabulary and target language functions about each lesson.
- After the entire curriculum is completed, begin the process of feedback and reflection with a view to making revisions.

7.2 A CEFR-curriculum creation model

As was discussed in section 2, a lack of previous examples of CEFR-informed curriculum alignment and development models initially presented a significant hurdle for the curriculum renewal project at the BECC. Through the description and analysis of procedures in this chapter however, a model has emerged which mirrors the components of well-established curriculum development Analyse–Design–Develop–Implement–Evaluate (ADDIE) models (Branch 2009, Forest 2014), typically used in the field of instructional design. Many resources regarding the usage of ADDIE exist, one of which[1] poses general questions that should be asked throughout the development of curricula. However, these resources are not necessarily specific to language education, and certainly not specific to CEFR-informed curriculum creation. Incorporating the general steps for CEFR curriculum creation presented in section 7.1 with the five phases of the ADDIE model (Forest 2014) produces what we believe is the first CEFR-curriculum creation framework derived through an action research project. Figure 8 shows each of the CEFR-curriculum creation steps within the five stages of the ADDIE model.

The following sub-chapter 9B has a detailed account of aligning SAC activities to the CEFR-J and the CEFR. Sub-chapter 9C contains a summative reflection of the overall benefits and challenges of firstly using the CEFR-J, and then the CEFR as the framework for curriculum renewal.

---

1 See raleighway.com/addie/analyze.htm

Figure 8 The CEFR-curriculum creation model

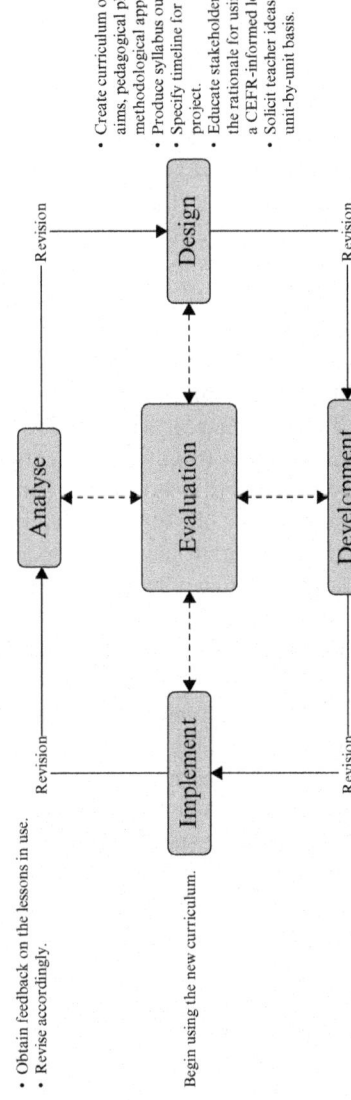

9B Developing ELP-informed self-access centre learning materials to support a curriculum aligned to the CEFR

Azusa Kodate (Kokugakuin University)

1 Introduction

Skills such as setting learning goals and monitoring and evaluating learning are said to be essential for successful language learning. In the CEFR, the development of such skills is emphasised as a fundamental learning objective, and not simply a by-product of a given course. In Japan, the CEFR has been adopted and adapted to play major roles in language curriculum revisions in many different contexts (Nagai and O'Dwyer 2011). Attempts also have been made, in classroom contexts, to incorporate activities which promote the development of skills necessary for autonomous language learning. Where self-access centres fit into this schema, however, has not been subject to a great deal of attention. This sub-chapter will describe how learning advisors at the Self-Access Learning Center (SALC) at Hiroshima Bunkyo Women's University's BECC have developed in-house materials based on the ELP, CEFR-J, and CEFR to support the GE English lessons (see sub-chapter 9A). It will also discuss how these materials have been operationalised to support students' learning outside the language classroom and how they help promote skills for learning as part of the overall curriculum.

As mentioned in sub-chapter 9A, 'the original curriculum aimed to be a task-based, communicative curriculum that encouraged learner autonomy' (Thompson and Foale 2008). In actuality, however, very little support for autonomous learning existed within the GE curriculum. Also, the degree of understanding and perception of learner autonomy varied greatly among the group of BECC teachers. In order to fill the gap between the curriculum and its goal, as well as to provide students with more coherent, thorough educational support both in and outside the classroom, the SALC and the curriculum have been taking a highly integrated model (Gardner and Miller 1999) and operationalised many aspects of educational activities together at the BECC since 2012.

As described in depth in the sub-chapter 9A, both the SALC and GE lessons started undergoing educational contents renewal based on CEFR-J alignment in April 2012. Since 2014, the project has shifted its direction by adopting the CEFR. Throughout the entire period of the project, the primary contribution of the SALC is to provide the GE lessons with learning materials

Using the CEFR-J and the CEFR as frameworks for renewal

that have a strong focus on learning how to learn and raising self-awareness along with language exercises. The purpose of the SALC activities in relation to the BECC GE curriculum as a whole, therefore, can be described as the following two points:

a. To achieve the learner autonomy objective of the GE curriculum.
b. To support, reinforce, and further develop students' understanding of the GE lesson contents.

Whereas the lesson renewal process has been carried out by classroom teachers, the SALC activities renewal has been delivered by the learning advisors who are based in the SALC. The SALC activities are an important component of the GE curriculum, and as such an extensive range of learning resources were designed based on the CEFR-J and CEFR to support the learner autonomy objective of the curriculum. The detailed process of the materials development and features of the activities are discussed in this sub-chapter.

The materials development project in the SALC has been carried out by three dedicated learning advisors, in close co-ordination with lesson developers. When the initial project was launched in 2012, there were 13 full-time lecturers in the BECC, amongst which three were learning advisors in the SALC and 10 of them were classroom teachers. The mission of the BECC SALC learning advisors is to promote learner autonomy amongst students in Hiroshima Bunkyo Women's University, and they are mainly responsible for giving personalised English language learning support to individual students and develop in-house learning materials to ensure that the SALC resources are accessible to users. Learning advisors' roles are considerably different from those of classroom teachers, in that their principal goal is to provide learner training and thus interact with students adapting their degree of direction depending on a student's level of self-directedness (Grow 1991). The details of the context at a much wider institutional level are described in sub-chapter 9A. In the next section, therefore, the background to the goal of learner autonomy in the curriculum and the self-access learning materials which were developed to support the lessons to create a more comprehensive curriculum are discussed in more detail.

2 Rationale for the emphasis on learner autonomy

2.1 The CEFR

The CEFR implies learner autonomy by the concept of 'ability to learn'. This is common across the documents which consist of the foundation of the framework, namely *Breakthrough* (Trim 2009), *Waystage* (van Ek and Trim 1991b), *Threshold* (van Ek and Trim 1991a) and *Vantage* (van Ek and Trim 2001). According to the 'Learning to Learn' section in each document:

'the skills involved in learning to learn are not simply a by-product of some courses, but an essential aspect of that objective, which all teaching towards that objective should promote. As such, they form an integral part of the objective, not an optional extra' and there is need for formulating 'the learning to learn component in terms of a learning objective, but a fairly high level of generality' in order to nurture autonomous learning skills and meet the individual learner's differences. This clearly indicates that the purpose of the CEFR is not simply to develop learners' language abilities, but also to enable them as autonomous individuals in various learning situations including and beyond language learning. As empirical research in social psychology argues that autonomy is a basic human need, it is essential for our intrinsic motivation and proactive interests in much wider contexts (Little 2004). Autonomous learners can connect what they have learned and tasks given to them, and apply their knowledge and skills even outside the language classroom (Trim 2009, van Ek and Trim 1991a, 1991b, 2001). This acquisition of autonomous learning skills and attitude as well as pragmatic communicative competence are important aims of the BECC GE curriculum. Given the clear links between the rationale behind the CEFR and GE lesson objectives, it seemed highly congruent for the SALC to model activities closely after the CEFR, particularly in supporting learner autonomy aspects. Learner autonomy is also addressed in sub-chapter 9A.

Although learner autonomy plays an important role within the CEFR, how CEFR elements could be integrated in our supplemental learning materials (i.e. the SALC activities) was a challenging question for the SALC. What became extremely useful were the principles of the European Language Portfolio (ELP).

2.2 The ELP

The ELP was developed by the Language Policy Division of the Council of Europe and launched in 2001. It reflects the Council of Europe's concern with developing mutual understanding among European citizens, protecting linguistic and cultural diversity, developing capacity for lifelong independent language learning, enhancing transparency and coherence in language learning programmes, and facilitating mobility by creating common reference. In achieving these objectives, the ELP should be designed in such a way to record all experience of language learning, and it has to be the property of individual learners with which learners can plan, monitor, and evaluate their own learning based on the learning record being kept. To this end, the ELP, when implemented successfully, can provide learners with guidance and direction, and fulfil its reporting function. Although there are socially and contextually inapplicable elements of the ELP to the BECC SALC context such as that the ELP should not support the learning of only one

Using the CEFR-J and the CEFR as frameworks for renewal

language, the following key features were adapted to the materials development project.

2.2.1 The ELP is the property of the learner

According to the Council of Europe (2004), the ELP should belong to individual learners to enhance sense of ownership and responsibility in learning. One of the fundamental approaches to this is regular self-assessment, and this should always be independent of teacher assessment. Although in formal learning contexts teachers are responsible for developing learners' skills for self-assessment, teacher assessment should not be used to correct the learners' self-assessment. To this end, any type of self-assessment or self-reflection is not assessed by teachers (see sections 3.2.3 and 5.5.2 of this sub-chapter).

2.2.2 The ELP is based on the common reference levels of the CEFR

Any ELP should be coherent and consistent in line with the common reference levels of the CEFR. It must also include appropriately formulated and detailed 'Can Do' checklists to help learners assess their language competencies within these levels. The Language Policy Division also suggests presenting the reference levels in the learners' target language at least partly in order to enhance its pedagogical function and accessibility of those who examine it. All the SALC activities are aligned to the CEFR. Both levels and 'Can Do' descriptors are presented in English and Japanese to ensure understanding of students and teachers.

2.2.3 The ELP is a tool to promote learner autonomy

This aspect of the ELP is interdependent on the function of the ELP (as described in section 2.2.1) and should be used to involve learners in planning, monitoring and evaluating processes. The ELP, therefore, is intended to be a learner's guide, not just a means to record their learning. In the following sections, how these principles of the CEFR and ELP were implemented in the actual materials development project is illustrated in detail.

3 Cycle 1: CEFR-J-based project

3.1 Rationale for adopting the CEFR-J

Tono (2013) describes the CEFR-J as a more localised, specified version of the CEFR to meet Japanese learners' needs. He refers to the CEFR as being rather 'UK-centred' and needing to be understood within the framework of the European social context. As Negishi et al (2013) also point out, given the reality of which over 80% of Japanese English learners fall into the A levels, adopting the CEFR-J, which offers more finely divided steps particularly in

Assessment of CEFR-informed Language Teaching in Japan and Beyond

A levels, seemed to make better sense. To the SALC, being able to provide students with learning options that were narrowed down to serve individual needs and differences was an attractive aspect. Last but not least, building the SALC activities based upon the framework which was adopted in the curriculum also seemed to be a sensible option to provide more direct support.

Activities were developed from the lowest level (Pre A1) to slightly higher levels than those set for the classroom curriculum. Receptive skills activities (listening and reading) were developed up to B2.2 and productive skills (writing, speaking) up to B1.2 and B2.1 respectively. The materials developers set levels to ensure that newly developed activities would cover a wide range of levels across skills, in order to meet the needs and levels of ability of all students (including outliers who might fall out of the range of the freshman and sophomore materials at the upper or lower ends). As of March 2016, the total of these activities numbers more than 90.

3.2 Materials development process

Due to relatively low levels of English language proficiency amongst the students at the university, Pre A1 level activity development was deemed necessary to support the weakest students. For the same reason, activities at the C levels were not developed at the initial stage of the project.

As a first step, the titles and contents of the existing SALC activities were compared against the CEFR-J 'Can Do' descriptors to find out what gaps existed, and what content needed to be created to match the Freshman and Sophomore lesson contents. Additional 'Can Do' descriptors were developed based on students' perceived interests and immediate concerns in order to increase intrinsic interest.

The contents of the activities were developed based on the CEFR-J 'Can Do' descriptors (Tono 2012) and other relevant resources such as *Waystage* (van Ek and Trim 1991b), *Threshold* (van Ek and Trim 1991a), *Cambridge English: Key* (University of Cambridge ESOL Examinations 2012a), *Cambridge English: Preliminary* (University of Cambridge ESOL Examinations 2012b), and English Vocabulary Profile (University of Cambridge). The topics of the activities at each level in each skill were also discussed among the material developers. At this stage, the contents of the curriculum were also investigated to create some overlaps between the activities and the lesson contents.

In line with the emphasis on learning to learn aspects of the CEFR, some of the important features of the activities from the SALC perspectives are 'Can Do' descriptors at the beginning of each activity (goal setting), the achievement checklist (monitoring), the commentary section to go with the checklists (self-evaluation), and lists of recommended learning resources for

Using the CEFR-J and the CEFR as frameworks for renewal

further learning to encourage students' active involvement in their learning. The details of those features are illustrated in the following sections.

3.2.1 Learner involvement

What teachers should do to promote learner autonomy can be summarised into three pedagogical principles, namely 'learner involvement', 'learner reflection' and 'appropriate target language use' (Little 2006). According to the Council of Europe (2004), learners should be involved in their own learning and given ownership of learning objectives and the learning process.

In the SALC activities, learner involvement was encouraged by getting students to become responsible for and aware of their learning processes. This includes understanding the objective in each activity, making decisions about which activities to work on, when to work on the activities, accessing a wide range of learning resources and facilities in achieving each activity objective, and self-assessing their own learning progress. Many activities were also designed in ways that require students' physical presence in the SALC (answer keys and supplemental resources that were required to do the activities were also stored in the SALC in order to create opportunities for students to visit the centre to be familiar with the educational services and facilities).

Another point being made to encourage learner involvement was to present a 'Can Do' descriptor at the beginning of the activity to show the learner the goal to achieve. In order to ensure students' understanding of the 'Can Do' descriptors, they are presented both in English and Japanese at all levels. Though the use of the target language is encouraged both in the instructions and actual activities and tasks, it was agreed that Japanese language support for somewhat complex concepts and contents would be up to the CEFR-J A2.2 level. The reason why this level was set as the threshold was because learners should be able to 'understand clearly written instructions' (Tono 2012) from above B1.1.

As mentioned in sub-chapter 9A, the process of writing 'Can Do' descriptors for the SALC activities was also based on features defined by the Council of Europe (2001:205–7) following North (2000:343–346), namely positiveness, definitiveness, clarity, brevity, independence, action-orientedness, and the nature of plurilingualism. Unlike the ones in the GE curriculum, the 'Can Do' descriptors in the SALC activities included further components of criteria and context. This is to help students accurately understand the aim of each activity and assess their own ability as precisely as they can. Having no immediate support or guidance from teachers, making the purpose clear was particularly important. The following are some examples of typical 'Can Do' descriptors:

Original 'Can Do' descriptor from the CEFR-J 'Can Do' descriptors [Reading A1]

'I can understand very short, simple, everyday text, such as simple posters and invitation cards.'

Contextualized 'Can Do' descriptor in the SALC activity [Reading A1]
ポスターに掲載された大学内の施設利用の広告について、短く基本的な文章で書かれた内容を読み、理解することができる。*('I can read and understand a poster advertising university services.')*

3.2.2 Appropriate target language use

One of the principles of the ELP raised in section 3.2.1, appropriate target language use, was also adopted in the material development process. As Little (2006) discusses, appropriate target language use is important for it becomes a source for learner involvement and reflection, and in this sense, these three elements interrelate with one another.

The instructions are written in English across all the levels. When making instructions for learning materials for use in self-access learning, wording and the degree of direction required have to be carefully adjusted to support learners' understanding depending on their language level and level of self-directedness. At lower levels, instructions have been made as simple as possible with greater support such as examples and visual aids. Instructions slowly increase in complexity over higher levels.

Another feature of the activity instructions is that they require a great amount of learner involvement. In many activities, students are asked to find designated resources from a variety of sections in the SALC to complete an activity (e.g. 'Go to the . . . section in the SALC and find a movie called . . .'). To do so, they may need to borrow materials and/or equipment or even seek assistance from a teacher or friend in the SALC (e.g. 'Go to the lounge area to find a teacher'). In some activities at higher levels, more discretion is left to students to choose resources they wish to use (for a discussion of 'choice of procedure' in developing learner autonomy, see Sheerin 1989:24).

Furthermore, by linking the activity contents to the learning resources available in the SALC, the majority of the activities are designed in ways to get students to complete them within the SALC. There are several points in doing so. First, the activities could provide students with opportunities to become familiar with the centre. Second, students will have to be in the English-only environment while they are working on their activities, which may contribute to students' language acquisition. Having student-users physically in the SALC is also positive, especially for any SACs where they are under pressure from their schools to show evidence of students' needs.

In comparison to traditional classroom instructions where supplementary directions and support from teachers are often provided, however, ones in self-access materials can easily generate frustration among learners if not carefully designed and delivered as it is easy for students to get lost and lose motivation. In the SALC activities, the following solutions were brought in in order to ease the accessibility of the materials. These are explicitly addressed and explained to students in orientations, which are an integral part of the delivery of these materials.

3.2.3 Learner reflection

Self-assessment by reflecting on learning processes and the target language play an important role (Little 2006). Many students are, however, not equipped with the necessary critical, constructive skills and they need directions.

Similarly to the classroom lesson handouts, a 'Can Do' descriptor is presented at the beginning of all the SALC activities, and is restated again at the end in both English and Japanese. At the end of an activity, there is a self-assessment checklist provided. Each student needs to choose the degree to which they think their achievement is best described from 'I can do it easily', 'I can do it', 'I can do it, but I need more practice' or 'I can't do it', and those criteria are standardised along with the ones that appear in lesson materials as shown in sub-chapter 9A. As specified in the principles of the ELP (Council of Europe 2004), this aspect of self-assessment is the foremost important element of the SALC activities in achieving the learner autonomy goal of the BECC GE curriculum (see sub-chapter 9A). After the final self-assessment checklist in each SALC activity the student was then asked to give reasons why they answered the way they did in a written form. This was revised to a more forward-looking reflection by asking what would be a next step if the student chose either of the first two options, and what would help them to be able to say that they 'Can Do' it if they chose a later one.

Encouraging learners to reflect on their learning processes and enabling them to see the positive and negative qualities of their learning efforts is an essential part of learner training of the SALC activities. This is then fed back into the students' decision-making process of what activity to work on next and whether they need to do any extra work to reinforce/supplement their understanding, which all relates back to the fundamental principles of learner autonomy, namely planning, monitoring, and evaluating one's learning.

The GE curriculum's assessment policy for the student reflection section follows what is being emphasised by the Council of Europe (2004:4) in that the reflection section is not assessed or corrected by teachers, and that it is purely for learners to reflect on their own learning processes and abilities. In order to select activities, students are provided with a detailed list of 'Can Do' descriptors developed specifically for the purpose of self-assessment in the activity orientation. Inclusion of the self-assessment grid is one of the requirements specified in the ELP (2004:4). Students are then instructed to select activities at the right level based on their initial self-perception. However, as discussed by Little (2009:159), there is always one general concern regarding self-assessment: 'How can learners assess themselves? They simply don't know enough'. According to Little (2010), this view misses the point that the self-assessment concerned in the CEFR and ELP is referenced in the first instance to behavioural criteria, and it is not requiring learners to refer to detailed linguistic aspects. Instead, it is asking learners to judge their communicative proficiency in more general terms. From the SALC perspective, too, what we expect from students is not accuracy in their assessment, but gradual adjustment in their behaviour in selecting activities and perceptions of their abilities based on their reflective practices encouraged by SALC activities.

3.2.4 Learner involvement

One of the crucial roles that the SALC should play is to give students a wide range of learning opportunities and resources to meet individual needs, and ensure that the support they need is sufficiently and promptly provided. Such support can also further encourage those learners who may not go on to the next step of their learning otherwise. In order to fulfil this role, the SALC activities include a list of recommended learning resources, provided after the reflective commentary section described in 3.2.3. These are selected to provide students with further learning opportunities based on the content of each activity. In order to ensure high accessibility for students (as well as for classroom teachers and learning advisors who wish to direct their students to some useful resources), the list provides detailed information as to where they can find those resources. The idea was that those students who stated a need to study more would look at the list to get a hints of what can be done next. By carefully designing the order of the contents, too, the SALC activities are trying to pursue more learner involvement.

3.2.5 Logistics

The SALC activities were worth 10% of each semester's grade for the GE lessons. Each activity was designed to take 40 to 60 minutes on average, although this varies depending on the individual learner's ability and familiarity with contents in each activity. Students were required to do at least five activities (i.e. one each for reading, writing, listening, spoken interaction, spoken production) per semester. Thus, approximately 3 to 5 hours are necessary to complete the minimum number of activities required in the curriculum. Activities are completed outside the classroom to encourage students' independent learning. Students are, therefore, responsible for planning when they work on the activities to meet submission deadlines set by their classroom teachers.

The activities are used by all the first and second year students as part of the compulsory language courses, regardless of their majors. A thorough orientation about how to select activities, and how, when, and where to complete the activities is provided by learning advisors and classroom teachers at the beginning of the first semester for all the first years.

4 Positives and negatives of the SALC activities (Cycle 1)

4.1 Survey results and reflection of the contents of the activities

A survey was conducted in an online format as part of the BECC Course Evaluation in Semester 2, 2013, which received responses from 310 first year students for the section which asked their impressions about the new SALC activities.

4.1.1 Positives

As many of the activities were designed requiring students' physical attendance in the SALC, it gave students opportunities to become familiar with the facilities, services, and even staff of the centre. Of the total survey respondents, 46% agreed that the activities helped them learn more about how to use the SALC. By developing the activities that tied the centre and GE lessons closely, better accessibility and approachability for students was facilitated, and, therefore, the SALC activities provided an effective introduction to a new learning environment.

4.1.2 Negatives

Of the respondents, 55% answered that they are not sure about the effectiveness of the activities in helping them reinforce their understanding of the BECC GE lessons, and another 12% of the respondents answered that the activities were not effective for the same purpose. One of the biggest issues we became aware of was the lack of language training elements in the activities. For example, if a 'Can Do' descriptor says 'I can talk about my family using simple language', its activity asked the student to talk about their family using some simple English without any preparation. The activity, thus, did not provide any preparatory or practice section, and it specifically told the student not to use a dictionary, notes, or other support. In other words, the SALC activities failed to scaffold students' language understanding, but instead became a set of small tests that do not offer students concrete solutions or help them to be better at each CEFR-J 'Can Do' descriptor. Originally being developed to supplement the lessons, the SALC activities were designed as rather evaluative learning resources that students could use to self-assess their progress, promoting a variety of learning resources and means as well as reflective skills. Linguistic scaffolding elements were, therefore, deliberately excluded from the activities. In order to support students' needs, however, more facilitating contents and stronger links with lessons became necessary in the next stage of the project.

4.2 Teachers' perception of the SALC activities

Though no formal analysis has been carried out at this stage, some feedback from the teachers (non-materials developers) was received on a more casual basis. The following descriptions are, therefore, anecdotal yet may interest some parties who are considering a similar project.

4.2.1 Positives

According to some teachers, having the dedicated 'Recommended learning resources' section at the end of every activity was helpful because it allowed them, some of whom may not have in-depth knowledge about the SALC learning resources, to direct their students to the resources listed when they thought that their students needed more language practice. One teacher gave extra credit for those students who used a recommended learning resource and did extra work voluntarily (and presented the evidence). Although this extra effort was supported by the incentive of a 'better grade', some may object that in an ideal world, 'autonomy' should come from within. Such encouragement was supported as a means to bridge the gap between 'autonomous learning' and 'classroom learning'.

4.2.2 Negatives

It seemed that for some classroom teachers, the SALC activities became a burden as extra things to mark. This was indicated by the grading system, which gave a full mark if all the sections were filled regardless of the actual quality, half the full mark if partially skipped, and none if not done or not submitted. This may also be due to the fact that the reflective commentary section, the most important section from the SALC's perspective, allowed students to use Japanese. Because the instructions and students' comments were both written in Japanese, it was not possible, or was at least extra time consuming, for the non-Japanese classroom teachers to understand what their students went through in this particular section. Lacking understanding of the learner autonomy aspect of the curriculum goal and its link to the purpose of the CEFR, sense of ownership (as the classroom teachers were not involved in the materials development process), and sufficient time and workforce (as there were only a very limited number of staff given the volume of all the other responsibilities being assigned) may also have influenced how the activities were perceived by the classroom teachers.

Using the CEFR-J and the CEFR as frameworks for renewal

5 Cycle 2: CEFR-based project

In order to improve the initial sets of the activities, the following aspects were given special focus in the second cycle, which began in 2014 in semester 2:

5.1 Providing more language training elements
5.2 Providing real-life contents
5.3 Providing balanced, valid activity contents
5.4 Strengthening the link with the GE lesson contents
5.5 Adding more supporting elements to foster learner autonomy
5.6 Improving the logistics

5.1 Providing more language training elements

As mentioned in section 4, to support the curriculum at the SALC and focus on training both cognitive and metacognitive aspects rather than the language dimension, scaffolding elements were purposefully eliminated from the initial set of activities. This was also because covering non-linguistic aspects such as goal-setting skills, learning how to use a variety of learning resources, and reflecting on learning processes was set as the priority at the SALC in support of achieving the learner autonomy goal of the GE lessons. The nature of the activities, however, generated dissatisfaction and questions among the students as described in section 4.1. After conducting the survey, the materials developers strongly felt that it was necessary to change the activity contents to be more vocabulary and grammar focused with more supporting features. In order to achieve this, the so-called PPP strategy (Presentation, Practice, Production) was adopted as the basic framework. Although the materials developers were aware of contradiction against the Lexical Approach and TBL teaching on which the GE lessons are based, the approach seemed to be useful in terms of complementing and supplementing the lessons. In other words, if the lessons are described as being 'bottom-up' and 'implicit', the SALC activities support students' development of their understanding at more micro levels by providing 'top-down', 'explicit' learning contents.

5.2 Providing real-life contents

As illustrated in the CEFR-J 'Can Do' descriptors, the framework was rather 'classroom-focused', and discrepancies in the contents of the CEFR and CEFR-J became a major concern among the materials developers. Adopting Breakthrough (Trim 2009), Waystage (van Ek and Trim 1991b), Threshold (van Ek and Trim 1991a), the self-assessment grid (Council of Europe 2001:26–27), and Descriptive Categories (Council of Europe 2001:48–49), which are directly borrowed from the CEFR, helped in solving the problem.

At the initial planning stage, the list of Descriptive Categories was particularly useful to brainstorm the context of each activity. The materials developers also modified some parts of the list to make it more suitable for current Japanese contexts (e.g. adding 'Sempai/Kohai (senior students/junior students)' in the Public/Persons column and 'Temples/Shrines' in the Public/Locations column).

5.3 Providing balanced, valid activity contents

In the first cycle of materials development, the types of activities (e.g. fill-in-the-blanks, having a conversation with a teacher, matching words, listening to native speakers, writing/reading postcards) selected for the activities were not co-ordinated among the materials developers. They largely followed their observation of what the students may need to decide the types and contents of the activities. In terms of the contents, there were a lot of overlaps across all the skills as there was a lot of similar wording in the CEFR-J descriptors and these were followed closely.
Examples:

> CEFR-J Writing A1.2: I can write message cards (e.g. birthday cards) and short memos about events of personal relevance, using simple words and basic expressions.
> CEFR-J Reading A1.2: I can understand very short, simple, everyday texts, such as simple posters and invitation cards.
> Tono (2012)

This was not necessarily negative as those repetitions could reinforce students' understanding by providing opportunities for both input and output rehearsing. Also, developed purely in-house, the activities reflected what the students needed well, yet influence of potential bias and subjectivity could not be completely denied. For those reasons, a more systematic approach to the materials development project was desirable. Two ways to solve those issues have been adopted. One is to create a database of all the activities. This provides information about each activity's level, title, 'Can Do' descriptor, corresponding Descriptive Categories (Council of Europe 2001:48–49), corresponding BECC GE curriculum lesson(s), target grammar/vocabulary, and type of pre/while/post-task activities. The database is shared online among the materials developers and curriculum co-ordinators for referencing purposes. In this way, over-representing similar topics and types was avoided. For a better distribution and a variety of types of activities as well as for establishing a theoretical basis for each stage, the learning strategies presented by Paris, Wasik and Turner (1996) were adapted for all skills with necessary modifications.

Those strategies were embedded in the drop-down menu in the activity templates for the materials developers' reference when deciding a type of activity for the pre-, while-, and post-task sections. Having the theoretical framework as the basis of the activity structure has been valuable to avoid producing mundane, repetitive language exercises. Having those ready-made options as a reference also enhanced the efficiency and productivity of the creation process. Those elements were adapted in combination with the PPP model (see section 5.1 of this part) for all the skills. How the activities were then developed based on those elements is explained in the following sections.

5.3.1 Pre-task

To ease the introductory process to each activity, one more step was added as a warm-up exercise. In this section, a preparatory activity which is closely linked to the key language task is presented, often eliciting students' prior knowledge. For example, an email sample is given in a warm-up section in a reading activity. Students are asked some questions about the basic information in the contents such as 'Who wrote this email?' and 'How often do you write an email to your friend?'.

5.3.2 Presentation and practice

As described earlier, direct, explicit grammar/vocabulary focus is provided in the second cycle. This means that target grammar and vocabulary are presented before the main task in each activity. Often this part is followed by an exercise, which tests students' basic understanding of the key language feature presented in an activity. These instructions usually come with Japanese language support.

5.3.3 Main task

The main task was also created based on the list suggested by Paris et al (1996). To give some examples, these are 'comprehension', 'skimming', and 'scanning' activities. It should be noted that for many of the productive skill activities (i.e. speaking and writing), this section also plays the role of the 'production' part of the PPP model, whereas with receptive skills (i.e. listening and reading), such 'production' parts are usually given in the post-task section as an activity to reinforce students' grammar and vocabulary understanding.

5.3.4 Post-task

In order to raise students' awareness in different approaches to language learning, they revisit the main task, but using a different approach from the one(s) they employed in the previous section(s) this time. As described previously, Paris' list was adapted to create this section.

5.3.5 Review

In order to further consolidate students' understanding of the target language, a reviewing activity was included after post-task activities. In most of the activities, this section caters for language rehearsals. It should also be noted that for many of the receptive skill activities (i.e. reading and listening), this section also plays the role of the 'production' part of the PPP model, because the main task for reading and listening activities does not entail production activities in itself.

5.4 Strengthening the link with the GE lesson contents

Although in the first cycle the link between SALC activities and GE lessons was taken into account, the degree was not strictly controlled. In order to provide students with more support for understanding lesson contents as well as to attain classroom teachers' 'buy-in', more collaboration and information sharing became an important element in the second cycle. To reinforce the links between the SALC activities and the GE lesson contents, communication between the SALC co-ordinator and the GE curriculum co-ordinators has been strengthened through regular meetings, email exchanges, and informal conversation.

5.5 Adding more supporting elements to foster learner autonomy

5.5.1 Learner involvement

One of the concerns from the SALC perspective was to what extent the newly modified activities should maintain their learner training aspects. Especially given a number of negative comments on the purpose of the activities not being clear in the results of the student survey, clarification of this aspect needed to be made.

A detailed introductory section of the purpose of the activities was made based on this principle. In the new section, each activity is introduced in terms of its purpose and target grammar and/or vocabulary in which students are expected to learn. As Little (2006) argues, principles such as learner involvement and learner reflection implicate each other. For example, we cannot engage learners in reflection unless we also involve them in their own learning. Consequently, in the new model, greater emphasis was placed on the first stage of the activity presenting more detailed aims and target language. To ensure students' better understanding of this part, all the information is provided in Japanese at all levels. Other features such as getting learners to find necessary information and their own learning resources to complete the activity are inherited from the older version.

Using the CEFR-J and the CEFR as frameworks for renewal

5.5.2 Learner reflection

It became clear to the materials developers that even when the reflection section required only a minimum amount of work in the activities of the first cycle, many students were unsure about how to cope with this section. The modified version, therefore, takes a more guided approach. First, students are asked to do the 'Can Do' self-checklist, which is the same as the one that was made in the CEFR-J cycle. In this section, students are instructed to evaluate their own achievement against the four 'Can Do' descriptors ('I can do it easily', 'I can do it', 'I can do it, but still need more practice', and 'I can't do it'). Next, students are asked their reasons for the result of the checklist. This was initially eliminated from the first cycle, but in order to get them to think more carefully about their response to the checklist it was brought back in. Finally, as we realised that many students struggled to answer the open-ended question of 'What should you do next?' in the first cycle, a more ready-made section was developed in the second cycle. By showing some possible options for the next steps (i.e. 'I'm going to work on a lower level activity', 'I'm going to work on a higher level activity', 'I'm not sure so will ask for advice from a teacher', 'I'm going to work on the recommended learning resources listed below', 'I'm not going to do anything as I'm satisfied') this may support learners who are not yet ready to clarify their own direction.

5.5.3 Appropriate amount of target language use

In the initial model, the materials developers followed a strict rule of 'English only' when writing activity instructions. After conducting the survey, however, we thought that this generated ambiguity and confusion among students in understanding the contents of the activities. This may be partly because those instructions needed to be written in detail, giving all the necessary information for students to complete the activities in a self-access environment. Unlike lesson materials, which teachers can adapt by adding support and information as necessary, the SALC activities which students are required to complete outside the classroom inevitably entail some challenges like this. For this reason, the opportunity for appropriate target language use is now limited to the content of the actual main task, and Japanese translations are provided for the English instructions where necessary.

5.6 Improving the logistics

After the second renewal cycle, the SALC activities continued to be worth 10% of each semester's grade for the GE courses. Whereas it was kept to a maximum of two pages originally in the first cycle due to the time restraint between the activities and the GE lessons (see section 3.2.5 of this part), each activity is 12 pages long on average in the current version. With the revised SALC activities, both GE first and second year students are required to complete at least four activities (reading, writing, listening and speaking) per semester. Another major change is that the activities are now downloadable from an online platform, and students have their own online folder to save the completed activities in. These online folders are shared with their classroom teachers, which means that the feedback can be given spontaneously, and it is effortless for both the students and teachers to keep track of what activities they did, when they did them, how much they improved, and what would be the next action to be taken for further development of their language ability. This trait is also one of the key functions of the ELP, which highlights the importance of learner accountability (Council of Europe 2004). Another improvement is that an online platform has been set for teachers to give feedback to the materials developers. This enhanced the speed of content improvement and problem-solving processes.

6 Positives and negatives of the SALC activities (Cycle 2)

A survey was conducted online as part of the BECC Course Evaluation in semester 1 2015. For the General English classes, 73 first year students answered the section which asked their perception about the CEFR-based SALC activities. Note that the contents of the survey were modified this time due to changes in activity contents and delivery system, and the sample size for the survey was much smaller than the last time (see section 4.1 of this part). It is therefore necessary to re-conduct the survey to get more statistically valid data (Fowler 2009). As part of a preliminary study, however, student responses to some of the key questions are going to be examined in the following section.

6.1 Survey results and reflection of the contents of the activities

Of the respondents, 53% agreed that the activities helped them learn more about how to use the SALC. In comparison to the result from the last survey (see section 4.1 of this part), it improved by 7%. Also, approximately 50% of the entire respondents answered that they feel more comfortable going to the SALC as a result of doing the SALC activities.

The results of the survey this time also showed that 50% of the respondents felt that the activities helped them understand the BECC GE classes, which improved by more than 10% from the last survey result. Nonetheless, the improvement described above is still marginal regardless of the major changes in the second materials development cycle. Particularly, with much greater emphasis on the language aspect, those results were rather unexpected among the materials developers. There may be a number of factors to explain this, and some of the assumptions are raised below.

6.1.1 Mismatch in levels

It is possible that students are not choosing the right activities for their actual language levels. As students have the discretion of what activities they work on, if they choose ones that are considerably lower or higher than their actual language levels, they may not gain as much as they could otherwise (research into this mismatch has been carried out). From the SALC perspective, where learner training is the foremost essential point, such mismatch in the learner's actual level, self-perception, and ability to judge the right content is not an issue at the beginning. Rather, the important point would be the step after this, which is whether students can take the right action based on the reflection of their own learning processes. This point, however, needs to be clearly communicated with students beforehand and reminders from teachers over the semester would be crucial. An appropriate amount of teacher intervention to guide students to the right activities could work effectively, too. It is also possible, especially with first year students, among whom 7% fall into the level below A1 and 43% fall into A1 according to results of the OOPT administered for GE students (see sub-chapter 9A, section 6.1.3) in 2015, that having activities which are below A1 (e.g. Pre A1 in the CEFR-J) to support their basic understanding of A1 and above may be necessary.

6.1.2 Non-overlap with GE course contents

The materials developers aimed at 60% overlap with the lesson contents in the second cycle. This means that the remaining 40% of activities were not directly linked with what students learn in GE lessons. Although the activity contents were developed carefully based on relevant references, it is possible that those students who chose activities which were not related to the topics being covered in the GE lessons did not see the immediate benefit of doing SALC activities. This point was not emphasised in the student orientation; nor are activities designed so students can identify which are directly linked to the GE lessons and which are not. These points need to be taken into account during the next step of the project.

6.1.3 Teacher perception and roles

As also highlighted in section 2.1.4 of this sub-chapter, teacher perception of the SALC activities improved a lot in the second cycle due to close collaboration and communication amongst the staff. The next step would be to improve the feedback and grading system to achieve the learner autonomy objective as a whole. In the second cycle as in the first cycle, the teacher feedback is only given as a numeral grade, and this is only assessed based on the completion level, rather than the actual contents.

7 Implications for other institutions

In this final section, implications for future projects by other institutions will be addressed by reflecting on our own projects.

7.1 Communication and collaboration between the SALC and lessons

One of the most effective practices would be the collaboration between the SALC learning advisors and classroom teachers. As mentioned earlier in this chapter, often the roles of the language classroom and self-access centres are considered to be separate, but the close link between those two made it possible to produce higher quality activities and more thorough educational support. Particularly, referencing the vocabulary lists from the same sources, following similar materials design, exchanging ideas, and sharing information helped the entire curriculum grow into a more coherent, supportive, and reinforcing programme to meet our students' needs at both group and personal levels. As both sides had their own agendas to prioritise, maintaining a close link was not always straightforward. Thus, strong leadership to connect the two sides is essential. In addition to the points mentioned above, getting teachers' direct involvement to develop activity contents would be an ideal approach to a project of this type. However, this can only be done when an institution has a relatively large capacity in terms of its human resources, and educational goals and values are shared among staff.

7.2 Shared purposes

Though we did receive some positive feedback from the students through the survey, the general impression of the students was that doing the activities was only a part of many other assignments that they have to do in order to get a better grade. To this end, the attempt to develop a sense of ownership in students is still questionable at this stage. The least attempt that could be made would be to clarify the meaning and purpose of the activities. This could be done by an orientation session, and by adding an extra section to each activity explicitly showing the goal of the activity, for example. Another crucial point would be to provide opportunities in which teachers can get to know the activities and rationales behind their creation before implementing anything with students, because classroom teachers are powerful influencers. As it has been emphasised throughout this sub-chapter, one of the keys to a successful project would be shared purposes among SALC learning advisors and classroom teachers.

7.3 Introduction of a more systematic and thorough portfolio

The point has been raised among the materials developers that having a proper 'portfolio' such as the ELP may improve the students' perception of the activities. A series of visible learning products presented together with a record of students' progress, of which the students have ownership, may help them see the purposes of the activities and get motivated in language learning. This, however, requires not only an agreement at an institutional level, but also more collaboration and co-operation between the language classroom and the SALC. Currently, in the second cycle, we are using an online platform to save students' activities, and it seems like we are following the ELP requirement on the surface. To achieve this, however, such a portfolio needs to contain all of the students' learning record, not just the SALC activities, but also what is learned in language lessons and what students did in their independent learning outside the classroom. This will without doubt require radical changes to how and to what extent the concept of learner autonomy is perceived and understood among the staff. Furthermore, principles and concept will need to be the core drive of the language education being provided.

7.4 Providing a wider range of support

When creating courses and materials based on the CEFR, materials developers tend to focus just on the existing levels (i.e. A1 to C2). After comparing the results of the OOPT, students' reflective comments in the activities, and the results of the survey, we realised that the volume of supporting materials for the lowest level, A1, was insufficient. As one of the goals of the SALC activities is to 'support, reinforce, and further develop students' understanding of the GE lesson contents', it appears necessary to scaffold lower students' understanding from more basic areas.

7.5 Support from administrative staff

This type of institutional project requires great commitment and work from all the related parties, including administrative staff members. Managing the activity section on a daily basis (if it physically exists in a centre), providing assistance to the materials developers in designing activities, supporting students with technical problems doing the activities, and reporting issues with the design and contents of the activities in a timely manner (because SALC counter staff are constantly monitoring students' activities taking place in the SALC) played a crucial role in the successful implementation.

7.6 Capacity for ongoing revision

Due to the scale of the project and limited human resources, our project is yet to be completed (as of academic year 2015). It will also be subject to ongoing revision to maintain the quality, as well as to keep up to date with the direction of the curriculum. Utilising ICT devices (i.e. iPads in this case) and directing students to SALC or online resources as part of the activities implies that continuous research and improvement are necessary to keep track of the resources available in the centre and of fast-changing technology available for education.

7.7 Emphasis on learner training

The SALC at Hiroshima Bunkyo Women's University has been granted a well-designed learning space, full-time teaching and administrative staff, and learning resources selected by language professionals. These factors definitely gave the materials developers much wider choices in terms of the variety of activity contents to develop, but at the same time, we are aware of the reality that many institutions are not granted such support or resources. As illustrated in sections 3.2.1, 3.2.2, and 3.2.3 in this part, emphasis should be on learner training rather than how much language educational service your programme can offer, if your primary goal is to promote learner autonomy. To this end, designing materials in ways to scaffold learners' planning, monitoring, and reflective skills, as well as establishing systems for provision of necessary feedback and support, whether it is verbal or written, targeted to individuals or to much wider learner groups, would be crucial in creating the kind of activities described throughout this part.

8 Conclusion

In this sub-chapter, promotion of learner autonomy through language learning materials within the CEFR-J/CEFR-aligned language curriculum was introduced based around the principle of the ELP. To date, at our institution, the ELP has been adopted only as a framework, and the actual implementation of the physical portfolio has not been carried out. In order to achieve this, it requires more coherent, radical changes at a wider institutional level. There has to be thorough discussion and understanding of how the portfolio should be used, how learner autonomy can be promoted through actual lessons, and how students' work and portfolios can be looked at as sources for teacher assessment who should give feedback on student reflection. This also has implications on how the SALC and classroom work together, which may ultimately mean hiring more staff and more collaboration between the two for an optimal educational effect. As discussed in the next sub-chapter, there is no doubt that the educational services we provide as a whole have made a lot of progress (thus far). As highlighted in section 5, improvements have been made to enhance students' learning with special attention to maintaining the balance of the dimensions of linguistic and learner autonomy. In order to achieve the GE curriculum goals, both the SALC and classroom teachers must make such efforts when introducing the ELP as a tool to promote more integrated, effective language education.

9C The key questions in Bunkyo

Jack Bower (Hiroshima Bunkyo Women's University), Arthur Rutson-Griffiths (Hiroshima Bunkyo Women's University), Gary Cook (Hiroshima Bunkyo Women's University), Rebecca Schmidt (Hiroshima Bunkyo Women's University), Lyndon Lusk Lehde (Hiroshima Bunkyo Women's University), Azusa Kodate (Kokugakuin University), Judith Runnels (University of Bedfordshire)

1 Introduction

Sub-chapters 9A and 9B described and analysed the processes undertaken, firstly in an attempt to align the General English (GE) curriculum at the Bunkyo English Communication Center (BECC) at Hiroshima Bunkyo Women's University (HBWU) to the CEFR-J from 2012 to 2013, and secondly to create a new GE curriculum from scratch based on the CEFR from 2014 to 2016. This sub-chapter represents the fourth stage, *reflection*, of the programmes presented in sub-chapter 9A. We reflect on the overall benefits of, and problems encountered in, adopting the CEFR-J and the CEFR as frameworks for curriculum renewal.

Salient points from this reflection highlight the importance of training teachers and learning advisors on the CEFR with particular regard to 'Can Do' descriptors; having clear course goals categorised by skill (Listening, Reading, Writing, Spoken Production and Interaction) which are assessable through both self-evaluation such as in Self-Access Learning Center (SALC) activities, and other forms of assessment such as standardised tests with CEFR-based rubrics; and providing the basis for a collaborative environment by asking for and collating lesson ideas from all teachers which are then implemented into a curriculum with consistent lesson design. The following reflections are structured around the key questions of this volume. These reflections also draw on data from a survey answered by BECC teachers and learning advisors in July 2015 regarding the curriculum renewal process.

2 Questions in regard to curricula

2.1 What practices have been seen to be effective?

The CEFR-informed curriculum renewal activities that we have found to be effective are teacher training workshops, writing and implementing lesson 'Can Do' descriptors, adapting new course goals, creating new SALC activities and introducing standardised assessments. One practice that was seen to be largely ineffective was an attempt in the 2012–13 curriculum renewal to map and then align lesson content to the CEFR-J, although recommendations were made which we believe would ensure an effective mapping process.

2.1.1 Teacher training workshops

Teacher training workshops were seen to be effective in raising teacher knowledge of the CEFR and the CEFR-J (section 5.4.1 of sub-chapter 9A). Through the series of training workshops conducted for teachers on how to write consistent 'Can Do' descriptors, the quality of lesson 'Can Do' descriptors rose steadily. Expert feedback was also effective in showing us problems with the way 'Can Do' descriptors had been written, a lack of connection between lessons, and a lack of systematic recycling of language functions and vocabulary.

2.1.2 Lesson 'Can Do' descriptors

The inclusion of self-assessment checklists using simplified 'Can Do' descriptors in lesson handouts is beneficial to students for several reasons. In addition to clarifying the lesson aims, it helps students to evaluate and reflect on their progress. Through this process of self-evaluation, students may become more motivated to set and achieve language learning goals, helping them to develop a more autonomous learning style (Luoma 2013). Furthermore, these statements focus on what can be accomplished, which could help boost students' self-confidence as language learners regardless of their current proficiency level (Faez, Majhanovich et al 2011, Faez, Taylor et al 2011). For teachers, the addition of 'Can Do' descriptors to lessons creates a sense of accountability to ensure they adequately prepare their students for assessment purposes. Teachers also commented in the July 2015 survey that they found the new 'Can Do' descriptors to be clear and simple for both teachers and students and helped clarify the goals of lessons.

2.1.3 CEFR-based course goals

From April 2013, new course goals were created for both the GE freshmen and sophomore curricula and then again revised for the 2015/16 academic year. As explained in sub-chapter 9A (see section 5.4.4), these goals in the form of 'Can Do' descriptors create transparency in what is expected of students among all stakeholders – current students, prospective students, parents of students, teachers, learning advisors and administrators. Breaking down objectives by skill (Listening, Reading, Writing, and Spoken Production and Interaction) gives clear outcome-based focuses for lessons, examinations, SALC activities and homework. Students are also given the opportunity at the end of the year to assess their progress through self-assessment of the overall course goals as part of a course evaluation survey. This added reflection process may help learners to reflect on their progress through the year. Furthermore, the information gained from the student self-assessment surveys helps teachers in their roles as material and test developers. As one survey respondent in the July 2015 teacher survey noted, 'I think having CEFR-based course goals was the strength of the renewal process, for our students will be able to monitor their progress at the BECC for two years'.

2.1.4 SALC activities

Another effective practice was increased collaboration between the classroom and the SALC. Often the roles of classrooms and SACs are considered to be separate, but in our context, these two practices are integrated as much as possible to implement the CEFR(-J)-based curriculum. Practically, this is seen in the 2014–16 curriculum renewal cycle in the use of the CEFR and its resources as a basis for creating both the new curriculum and SALC activities. One example of this is the use of the same vocabulary list for creating all curriculum and SALC materials. For teachers, having SALC activities based on the CEFR allowed them to provide better guidance for students' self-study and to better understand the purpose of the SALC activities. Several teachers in the 2015 survey noted the improved link between the curriculum and SALC activities, and were satisfied with the increased overlap between the lessons and activities.

As the SALC activities are directly linked to class grades, any major changes and decisions to be made are communicated to all the classroom teachers. Particularly with the curriculum co-ordinators, plans are always shared to ensure that what the classroom and the SALC are going to do is aligned to the institutional goals. An online feedback form is also available to the teachers so they can comment on any points of the activities. Teachers are also requested to join and run a 90-minute SALC activity orientation for first year students.

2.1.5 Standardised assessments

As described in sub-chapter 9A section 5.2.13, standardised reading and listening tests have been created for the GE curriculum to stream students into classes and to track their progress across their two years of study. These assessments are based on *Cambridge English: Key* (University of Cambridge ESOL Examinations 2012a) and *Cambridge English: Preliminary* (University of Cambridge ESOL Examinations 2012b) which are aligned to CEFR Levels A2 and B1 respectively. From semester 1 2015, standardised CEFR-aligned tests of speaking were also used. The creation of in-house tests has had a number of benefits for the curriculum. Firstly, the presence of these tests provides an incentive for teachers to cover the materials in the shared curriculum instead of teaching whatever they wish, thus helping to standardise the CEFR-based education that students receive in the BECC, regardless of their teacher. Secondly, the tests will be able provide teachers and students with a measurement of their progress throughout the course and in relation to the course goals. Section 2.5 in this sub-chapter gives further details on the effectiveness of these tests in measuring student ability.

As well as the tests themselves, test specifications were created. The test specifications include information such as the 'Can Do' descriptors targeted by each test task type, word counts, grammatical complexity and vocabulary range for reading and listening texts. Test specifications allow for the standardisation of test tasks and test administrations (Carr 2011). These test specifications are also used as a reference for writing, reading and listening texts in lesson handouts. This ensures that reading and listening passages used in the classroom are CEFR based and are at an appropriate level for students. This also exposes students to tasks that they are likely to encounter on the tests. According to Messick:

> Ideally, the move from learning exercise to test exercise should be seamless. As a consequence, for optimal positive washback there should be little if any difference between activities involved in learning the language and activities involved in preparing for the test (1996:1).

As well as benefitting students, having curriculum and assessment based on the same specifications increases the likelihood that students are being assessed on material that they have covered in class, increasing content validity and giving teachers an accurate measure of the effectiveness of the curriculum in improving students' skills. The introduction of CEFR-based rubrics for in-class assessment of presentations and writing has also had a positive impact. One teacher noted in the 2015 survey that with the new rubrics 'we can all come to some kind of standard with [grading] presentations and writing'. The presence of CEFR-based assessment has undoubtedly been effective in promoting CEFR-based classroom materials.

2.1.6 General English (GE) curriculum mapping to the CEFR-J

As explained in sub-chapter 9A, in 2012–13 two attempts were made to 'map' the existing GE curriculum to the CEFR-J by matching lesson 'Can Do' descriptors to their nearest CEFR-J equivalent to form a map of GE curriculum coverage of the CEFR-J. Benefits of the mapping process were increased knowledge of faculty about the CEFR, and reflection on the strengths and weaknesses of the 2012–13 GE curriculum. Mapping also fostered faculty discussion of what the aims of the GE curriculum should be, what is the most effective GE lesson structure, and our preferred pedagogical approach. These conversations led to the creation of a GE curriculum overview document in early 2014 which clearly explains these areas in regard to the GE curriculum.

The mapping process also made it evident to all stakeholders why a rewrite of the curriculum from scratch was necessary for it to be properly aligned to the CEFR-J. The lessons learned from the mapping attempt created the foundation of the subsequent curriculum renewal plan to design a curriculum aligned to the CEFR, explained in section 6 of sub-chapter 9A.

Unfortunately, flaws in the mapping methodology led to the final map not being entirely usable for its intended purposes. No account was taken of the classroom time spent on each 'Can Do' descriptor in the mapping, and several lesson tasks did not readily match CEFR-J 'Can Do' descriptors, making them problematic to map. Furthermore, no norming process was undertaken to ensure a mutual understanding of how to map lesson 'Can Do' descriptors in the first mapping attempt. The second mapping attempt was eventually called to a halt due to an inability to reach such a consensus. For other institutions attempting a mapping process, we would recommend a norming session to try and reach agreement on how various terms included in the CEFR and CEFR-J match the curriculum being mapped. We would also suggest including a rough estimate of how long the tasks or lesson associated with a 'Can Do' descriptor take to complete in the classroom to give a more accurate representation of how long students spend on each skill at each level. The problems with the mapping attempt are explained in more detail in sub-chapter 9A, section 5.4.5.2, and our recommended mapping procedure is described in section 5.4.5.3.

2.2 How are all stakeholders involved? Can the people engaging in CEFR-based teaching and learning develop a sense of ownership?

We believe that all stakeholders in our institution are involved in using the CEFR, and classroom teachers and learning advisors in particular have developed a strong sense of ownership as evidenced by the results of the July 2015 teacher and learning advisor survey.

2.2.1 Classroom teachers and learning advisors

All teachers are heavily involved in the process of GE curriculum renewal through writing and revising classroom lessons. Learning advisors are similarly involved in writing SALC activities. Teachers and learning advisors are also given the opportunity to comment on the overall CEFR-based curriculum renewal in anonymous surveys, one-on-one meetings with management, and in regular committee meetings. These feedback opportunities are held in principle at least once per semester, and in the case of committee meetings more frequently. We have found these opportunities to give feedback and share concerns to be a valuable part of the process and would encourage others to use these practices even when there are no specific problems or points to discuss. Participation in these projects gives both teachers and learning advisors an increased sense of ownership.

2.2.2 Students

Students are involved in engaging with the CEFR in a number of ways. A SALC orientation is held in April of GE students' first year in order for them to understand what the SALC activities are for, how they can make use of them, and to raise students' awareness of the importance of learner responsibility.

'Can Do' checklists were used in 2013 and 2014 to help students select appropriate SALC activities to complete for their area(s) of need. Students first completed the 'Can Do' checklist which ranged in order from Pre A1 to B2 levels, then used the results to choose SALC activities to target their priority areas of language at a suitable level. The checklist was designed so students had to keep their own copy during their first two years of GE to be able to see the progress of their learning and find their own learning goals. More information about the SALC activities is given in sub-chapter 9B.

Regarding the SALC activities, the general impression we receive from students is that doing the activities is only a part of many other assignments that they have to do in order to get better grades. To this end, the attempt to develop a sense of ownership in students is still questionable at this stage. It has been discussed among the materials development team that having a proper 'portfolio' may improve the situation. This, however, requires agreement at an institutional level and is a substantial challenge. This will be considered again after the current curriculum renewal process is completed (see section 6.1.4.2 in sub-chapter 9A).

2.2.3 Management

From a management perspective, the experience of three years of curriculum renewal has highlighted the need for clear communication with all stakeholders about the purpose and goals of CEFR adoption, the need for a feedback system to get honest opinions and ideas from teachers and learning advisors involved in curriculum renewal, the importance of having a clear step-by-step plan, and a willingness to change plans when necessary. Furthermore, it became clear that providing a clear structural template for lesson handouts and an accompanying pedagogical framework to ensure a consistency of lesson design by different teachers was needed. In our case we chose a task-based approach, in which each lesson builds towards a single main communicative task.

Communication among the staff and a collaborative environment are crucial for a quality and sustainable project. Also, strong leadership and tactful feedback from leaders will help create more cohesion between individual lessons, in order to prevent lessons from differing drastically from one to the other depending on the style of the teacher who created it. The feedback system introduced for the 2014–16 renewal cycle, described in 9A section 6.1.4.3, has so far proven successful in ensuring that all lessons in the curriculum are consistent in methodology and are directly linked to curricular goals. In short, this system involves three stages of feedback upon initial lesson ideas, the first draft of a lesson and its materials, and the final lesson. This system was praised by a number of teachers in the 2015 feedback survey, with some requests for even more detailed comments and feedback. Teachers also commented that lessons in the new curriculum are more uniform in style and more integrated with each other and with the SALC activities, which we believe is in large part thanks to the feedback system. We would recommend a similar process for other institutions thinking of writing in-house materials made by a number of teachers.

2.3 Has the CEFR promoted a system for in-house evaluation of curricula and learning targets?

The CEFR has definitely served as a valuable framework for reflecting on the GE curriculum as a whole. It has provided the basis for overhauling the entire curriculum. This includes learning targets, lesson content, assessment, vocabulary, and the SALC activities. Our initial project to align the GE curriculum to the CEFR-J brought to light the need for a much more fundamental change to the curriculum to bring it in line with the CEFR. These fundamental changes included the need for a more uniform lesson structure, more spiralling of vocabulary and grammar, clearer main tasks and lesson goals, more receptive activities and more level-appropriate lessons for our students. We also recognised the need for more assessment of the four skills, as our old curriculum was more heavily weighted to assessing spoken production.

2.4 Do curricula and courses include transparent and concrete learning objectives, with accepted 'Can Do' descriptors at the centre?

In the 2012–13 curriculum renewal cycle, adopting CEFR-J 'Can Do' descriptors and modifying them slightly to fit the context of the GE curriculum in the BECC was seen to be a significant improvement on the old course goals. As described in sub-chapter 9A, section 5.2.12, specific course goals for the five skills covered by the CEFR-J (spoken interaction, spoken production, listening, reading and writing) were adapted for each of the GE first and second year courses. In addition, learning targets for lessons were made transparent through creating 'Can Do' descriptors for each lesson. To make these learning objectives clear to students, translations of the course goals were provided to students at the start of each academic year. Lesson 'Can Do' descriptors, appearing in self-assessment checklists at the start and end of each lesson, were also deliberately simplified and translated to make them easily comprehensible for students.

In the 2014–16 curriculum renewal cycle, new course goals are being adopted directly from CEFR 'Can Do' descriptors at the target levels for each of the two course streams. Lesson 'Can Do' descriptors for the newly created lessons are being adopted and modified from the CEFR scales, from the Eaquals (2015) bank of descriptors and from the ALTE (Association of Language Testers in Europe 2002) 'Can Do' descriptors. In the 2012–13 curriculum, it was common to have three to five 'Can Do' descriptors for a lesson. However, in the 2014–16 cycle each lesson has a single 'Can Do' descriptor which describes the main communicative task of the lesson. This has a number of benefits. With a number of 'Can Do' descriptors, it was not clear what the main goal of the lesson was. This often led to a collection of somewhat unrelated activities in a lesson, which covered all of the 'Can Do' descriptors, but with no obvious candidate for the main outcome of the lesson. One statement, clearly related to the main task, allows material writers to build the activities in a lesson upon one another to focus on helping students to be able to perform the main task. It helps teachers in class understand the purpose of each activity, and which are suitable to modify or skip in the case of not having enough time. It may also help students when reflecting upon their performance before and after a lesson; it is probably easier to consider one's performance on a single 'Can Do' descriptor than five at once, particularly when some of those statements are not clearly linked to a lesson activity. For these reasons, we would recommend one 'Can Do' descriptor per lesson over multiple statements.

2.5 Is it possible to compare the results of instruction in different classes?

Results of instruction between classes can be compared through standardised reading and listening tests (as described in section 2.1.5 of this sub-chapter). These tests, known as the Bunkyo English Tests (BETs), allow for comparison of the results of instruction in different GE classes after one year, and again after two years of study in the GE programme. For example, statistical tests (ANOVA) applied to results of the 2014 BET2 and BET3, administered to finishing first year and second year students respectively, showed no significant difference in mean overall BET scores between classes in the same ability stream. This provides some evidence that the quality of teaching (at least for the skills of reading and listening) is consistent across GE classes taught by different teachers. (Due to considerations of space, the detailed statistical analyses are not included here, but these can be provided upon request.)

Furthermore, since 2011 teachers have undergone GE speaking test norming sessions in order to establish uniformity in their grading practices. Since 2013, teachers have swapped classes to rate speaking tests and reduce the possibility of teacher bias. From semester 1 2015, CEFR-aligned speaking tests based on *Cambridge English: Key* and *Cambridge English: Preliminary* speaking task types were used. This has also provided an incentive for teachers to prepare students adequately for the tests. From 2015, speaking tests are double graded to allow for more consistent comparison of results between different classes.

3 Questions in regard to classroom instruction

3.1 Do 'Can Do' checklists serve as the key reference point for processes of reflective teaching/learning in which self-assessment plays a central role? How?

'Can Do' descriptors certainly serve as the key reference point for reflective teaching and learning in the GE curriculum. 'Can Do' self-assessment checklists, which are placed at the beginning and end of lesson handouts, foster the implementation of a learning cycle, and these statements are written in simple English for students and are also translated into Japanese. Students check the 'Can Do' descriptors before a lesson, which both clarifies the lesson aims for students, and fosters reflection on their ability to perform the communicative language goal of the lesson. After the lesson, students check the checklist again, which helps them to evaluate how much they have progressed in their ability to perform the communicative functions of the lesson, and hopefully to take further action by utilising the reflective section in the SALC activities, as well as the learning resources recommended (see sub-chapter 9B for more details) if they feel that they need more practice. Furthermore, data from a survey conducted in 2012 indicated that students feel that 'Can Do' descriptors help them to understand their weaknesses in English and lesson goals (see sub-chapter 9A, section 5.3.2.6). More specifically and technically written 'Can Do' descriptors were also written for each lesson. These more detailed descriptors provide teachers with clear descriptions of the communicative language target of each lesson and also form part of the GE syllabus document, which catalogues all of the language performance aims of the GE curriculum.

3.2 What are the interpretations of teachers, students and other stakeholders of the philosophy and ideas of the CEFR?

Interpretations of the philosophy and ideas of the CEFR have been broadly positive among teachers. One reason for this may be the background of staff in the centre, where the vast majority of teaching and advising staff's postgraduate study has been in teaching methodology such as TESOL or TEFL. This background may well predispose staff to interpret the CEFR's philosophy favourably, as communicative, learner-centred approaches are commonly taught in master's courses in English language teaching.

Results of a teacher and learning advisor survey administered at the end of the 2013/14 academic year showed that although overall teachers agreed that an external standard framework was necessary for the BECC GE curriculum to benefit all stakeholders, there were some reservations about the CEFR-J being the best option. This can be seen in the comments below in response to the following question asked of teachers in an anonymous curriculum renewal survey: 'Do you think the CEFR-J is a suitable framework for GE curriculum renewal?'

> Teacher A: I don't think there's any viable alternative (apart from the CEFR). The problem is that it's (the CEFR-J) not enough by itself (you also need to decide on topics, methodology, assessment etc.).
>
> Teacher B: We need to add to this framework so as to cater our curriculum to our students' needs and future goals. By itself, the CEFR-J does not provide curriculum designers with the information they need to achieve such a task.

These survey results are part of the reason that the CEFR was chosen as the framework for the second curriculum renewal cycle currently underway, rather than continuing to use the CEFR-J. Another contributing factor was a statement sorting exercise carried out in January 2014, in which teachers paired up and attempted to sort the CEFR-J self-assessment into levels. We had a lot of problems in identifying the differences between some of the lower levels, particularly in reading and spoken interaction. Until illustrative samples of level-appropriate input and learner output at each of the CEFR-J levels are made available, this will remain a problem. We also found that CEFR-J statements are often very specific and are not easy to base multiple lessons on. For example, the Reading A1.1 statement 'I can understand a fast-food restaurant menu that has pictures or photos, and choose the food and drink in [sic] the menu' is not, we feel, well suited as a base for designing lessons. A redesign of SALC activities also revealed problems, where old activities written based on CEFR-J statements were not easily aligned to CEFR descriptors at the same level, suggesting that at lower levels the CEFR-J and CEFR are not as well matched as we desire for our needs.

The extent to which students embrace the CEFR's philosophy and ideas has not yet been fully investigated in our institution. However, data from surveys on students' use of 'Can Do' descriptors (see sub-chapter 9A, section 5.3.2.6) and general attitudes towards English suggest that students are receptive to concepts that are part of CEFR, such as planning their own learning and using language as a communicative tool. For many students at our institution, the traditional grammar-translation methods of language instruction that they encountered before entering university have not served them well. As discussed in a study conducted by Miura (2010), many Japanese high school students experience a sharp drop in their motivation to learn English after taking their university entrance examinations. This suggests the lack of long-term learning goals beyond high-stake tests. Considering this background, students may be willing to engage with new approaches of the CEFR when they begin tertiary education.

3.3 Are the CEFR-based materials (textbooks, teaching content, etc.) action-oriented and easily applicable by both teachers and students?

The lesson materials in the GE curriculum are action-oriented in that they attempt to teach students how to communicate effectively in various real-world language tasks, as is advocated in the CEFR (Council of Europe 2001) and the *Waystage 1990* (van Ek and Trim 1991b) and *Threshold 1990* (van Ek and Trim 1991a) documents. The extent to which these materials are applicable to situations outside the classroom is not clear; although a number of students participate in study abroad programmes or have part-time jobs that may allow them to make use of their English skills, a thorough needs analysis of our student population has not yet been undertaken.

In general, based on feedback from regular curriculum committee meetings and an online lesson feedback system, lessons are seen as easily applicable by teachers. However, one notable drawback has been the time pressure on teachers to create and teach new CEFR-based materials within a busy semester. This system has teachers critiquing, sharing ideas and suggesting improvements for each lesson in the GE curriculum. One key issue regarding applicability of material has been a debate created over the greater needs of our student population, for example, whether students would benefit more from using English as a tourist in a foreign country, or Japanese shop staff serving English-speaking tourists. This issue, which not only has consequences for lessons but for assessment purposes, could be best solved by an extensive needs analysis as mentioned previously.

3.4 Can all readily see the benefits of the CEFR-based approach for their own teaching/learning?

We have some evidence through survey results that students see the value of self-assessment checklists at the beginning and end of lessons. A significant majority of students indicated that they see the value of such checklists for clarifying the goals of lessons, and for helping them to reflect on their strengths and weaknesses in English.

The teacher survey carried out in July 2015 asked teachers and learning advisors directly whether they thought the CEFR was a suitable framework for curriculum renewal. All respondents answered that it was, which suggests that acceptance of the CEFR is widespread in our institution. As teachers, we feel that basing the new curriculum renewal on the CEFR has clarified the goals for each lesson and highlighted the importance of focusing on clear communicative functions over form. 'Can Do' descriptors not only provide goals and learning reflection for students, but also allow us as teachers to reflect on how well we taught the language function for each individual lesson. Having the CEFR as an overall framework also gives us confidence that we are covering a broad and appropriate range of topics with our classes. Having evidence from assessments gives us further confidence that the materials are generally at the right level for the students we teach.

3.5 Is autonomous learning beyond the specified materials (e.g. textbooks) supported and encouraged? If so, how?

Autonomous learning is supported through the SALC and SALC activities, which students are required to complete as part of their GE course. As 'Can Do' descriptors that students encounter in their lessons are based on the same CEFR descriptors as SALC activities, students are able to clearly identify activities that can help them build upon lesson materials that they wish to work on further. Moreover, SALC activities all contain suggested resources available in the SALC, encouraging students to further explore learning processes and ensuring that they have a whole network of resources available to them for autonomous learning. Students are also supported through various means such as orientations and learning advising sessions provided by the SALC.

4 Conclusion

Through our three-and-a-half years of curriculum renewal, we have discovered a number of practices that we feel are effective and would be applicable in other institutions. These include workshops about the CEFR and 'Can Do' descriptors to help teachers understand some of the principles behind the approach of the CEFR, writing course goals based on CEFR 'Can Do' descriptors, and using CEFR 'Can Do' descriptors to write 'Can Do' descriptors for individual lessons. We have found that having a standard lesson format and a feedback process have helped to ensure lessons are well integrated with course goals and build upon one another. Basing other aspects of the curriculum, such as SALC activities, vocabulary lists, and the choice of lesson grammar on CEFR-related resources has also contributed to the close integration and appropriate levelling of the curriculum. We have also found that these practices have helped to foster a good understanding and acceptance of the CEFR among the faculty, and may be helping to foster reflective learning among our students.

In addition, basing GE curriculum assessments on the target CEFR levels has enabled us to create standardised tests of reading, speaking and listening, and standardised rubrics for writing tasks and presentations. One benefit of this standardisation is increased consistency of assessment across GE classes. Another important benefit is positive washback on the content of GE lessons. During the 2014–15 lesson-writing process, several lesson tasks have been deliberately included which prepare students for the types of reading, listening and speaking tasks targeted at the CEFR A2 and B1 levels, which are found in the GE standardised tests.

At the time of writing, after three-and-a-half years of curriculum renewal based firstly on the CEFR-J and then on the CEFR, we are able to present our recommended process of CEFR-based curriculum creation. As described in sub-chapter 9A section 7.2, the steps involved can be clearly presented using the ADDIE model (Forest 2014). This model, whose name stands for Analyse, Design, Develop, Implement, Evaluate, provides educators with a series of steps for planning, implementing, and appraising a curriculum. The steps taken at the BECC, which we also recommend to other practitioners, are summarised below.

ANALYSE (pre-planning, thinking about your course)

- Identify audience: students' CEFR level.
- Identify objectives: choose CEFR 'Can Do' descriptors as overall curriculum goals.

- Choose number of course streams to match the levels of your students.
- Create a curriculum overview which describes the aims, pedagogical philosophy and methodological approach of the curriculum.

DESIGN (design your course on paper)

- Create a syllabus outline.
- Educate stakeholders on the new curriculum, the rationale for using the CEFR as the framework of reference for curriculum development, and how to make a CEFR-informed lesson.
- Select a 'Can Do' descriptor for each lesson.
- Solicit teacher ideas for lesson content on a unit-by-unit basis to provide a starting point for teachers to create individual lessons and to create a sense of ownership.

DEVELOP (develop course materials and assemble)

- Teachers develop actual lessons and assessments (including listening passages and videos, and translated self-assessment checklists).
- Give systematic feedback to ensure the consistency and quality of the formatting and structure of lessons. Feedback should also make sure that each lesson focuses on a specific CEFR-related 'Can Do' descriptor or statements.
- Allow time for lesson revisions and final checks.
- Once lessons are complete, each lesson designer adds more specific lesson information, such as the lesson target 'Can Do' descriptor, grammar, vocabulary and target language functions about each lesson, to the syllabus document.

IMPLEMENT (begin teaching)

- Begin using the new curriculum.

EVALUATE (look at course outcomes with a critical eye)

- After the entire curriculum is completed, begin the process of feedback and reflection with a view to making revisions.
- Use appropriate assessment tools to evaluate whether course goals are being met.

References

Association of Language Testers in Europe (2002) *The ALTE Can Do project: Articles and Can Do statements produced by the members of ALTE 1992–2002*, available online: www.cambridgeenglish.org/images/28906-alte-can-do-document.pdf

Bower, J, Rutson-Griffiths, A and Sugg, R (2014) Setting and raising standards: A rationale for, and the structure of the Bunkyo English Tests, *Hiroshima Bunkyo Women's University Bulletin* 49, 65–78, available online: harp.lib.hiroshima-u.ac.jp/h-bunkyo/detail/1216920150204165253;jsessionid=BF59C15C5D3D975 C501417C4C891F2F5

Bower, J, Rutson-Griffiths, A, Kodate, A, Foale, C, Lusk Lehde, L and Semmelroth, A (2014) *BECC General English curriculum overview 2014/15*, unpublished internal document, Bunkyo English Communication Center.

Branch, R M (2009) *Instructional Design: The ADDIE Approach*, New York: Springer.

Brown, J D (2005) *Testing in Language Programs*, New York: McGraw-Hill.

Bruner, J (2009) *The Process of Education*, London: Harvard University Press.

Carr, N (2011) *Designing and Analysing Language Tests*, Oxford: Oxford University Press.

Council of Europe (2001) *Common European Framework of Reference for Languages: Learning, Teaching, Assessment*, Cambridge: Cambridge University Press.

Council of Europe (2004) *European Language Portfolio (ELP): Principles and Guidelines. With Added Explanatory Notes*, Strasbourg: Council of Europe.

Council of Europe (2009) *Relating Language Examinations to the Common European Framework of Reference for Languages: Learning, Teaching, Assessment (CEFR)*, Strasbourg: Council of Europe.

Creswell, J W (2008) *Educational Research: Planning, Conducting, and Evaluating Quantitative and Qualitative Research*, Upper Saddle River: Prentice Hall.

Eaquals (2015) *Revision and refinement of CEFR descriptors*, available online: www.eaquals.org/resources/revision-and-refinement-of-cefr-descriptors

Ellis, R (2003) *Task-based Language Learning and Teaching*, Oxford: Oxford University Press.

Ellis, R (2013) Task-based language teaching: Responding to the critics, *University of Sydney Papers in TESOL* 8, 1–27.

English First (2014) *EF Standard English Test: Technical Background Report*, available online: www.efset.org/about/science-and-research/?lang=en

English UK (2011) *Guide to the Cambridge English Placement Test for English UK Members*, available online: www.englishuk.com/uploads/assets/training/Guide_to_the_CEPT_for_English_UK_Members.pdf

European Organization for Nuclear Research (2013) *Language Guidelines Within the CERN Learning and Development Policy*, Geneva: European Organization for Nuclear Research.

Faez, F, Majhanovich, S, Taylor, S, Smith, M and Crowley, K (2011) The power of CEFR-informed instruction in French as a second language classrooms in Ontario, *The Canadian Journal of Applied Linguistics* 14 (2), 1–19.

Faez, F, Taylor, S, Majhanovich, S, Brown, P and Smith, M (2011) Teacher reactions to CEFR's task-based approach for FSL classrooms, *Synergies Europe* 6, 109–120.

Forest, E (2014) *The ADDIE Model: Instructional Design*, available online: educationaltechnology.net/the-addie-model-instructional-design

Fowler, F (2009) *Survey Research Methods*, California: Sage Publications.
Framework and Language Portfolio Special Interest Group (2009) *Framework & Language Portfolio Newsletter #1*, available online: sites.google.com/site/flpsig/home/FLPSIG
Gardner, D and Miller, L (1999) *Establishing Self-access*, Cambridge: Cambridge University Press.
Goullier, F (2007) *Council of Europe tools for language teaching: Common European framework and portfolios*, available online: www.coe.int/t/dg4/linguistic/Source/Goullier_Outils_EN.pdf
Green, A (2012) *Language Functions Revisited: Theoretical and Empirical Bases for Language Construct Definition Across the Ability Range*, English Profile Studies volume 2, Cambridge: UCLES/Cambridge University Press.
Grow, G (1991) Teaching learners to be self-directed, *Adult Education Quarterly* 41 (3), 125–149.
Harsch, C and Martin, G (2012) Adapting CEF-descriptors for rating purposes: Validation by a combined rater training and scale revision approach, *Assessing Writing* 17 (4), 228–250.
Hogan, M J (2012) *The CEFR and ELT in Australia: Getting Them Together*, available online: www.neas.org.au/conference/presentations/conf12Hogan.pdf
Hosoki, Y (2011) English education in Japan: Transitions and challenges, *Kyushu kokusai daigaku kokusai kankeigaku ronshu [Kyushu International University International Relations Journal]* 6 (1–2), 199–215, available online: www.kiu.ac.jp/organization/library/memoir/img/pdf/kokusai6-1_2–006hosoki.pdf
Jacobsen, N (2011) Giving kids a can do attitude, *Learning Languages: The Professional Journal of the National Network for Early Language Learning* 16 (2), 22–25.
Keddle, J (2004) The CEF and the secondary school syllabus, in Morrow, K (Ed) *Insights from the Common European Framework*, Oxford: Oxford University Press, 43–54.
Little, D (2004) Democracy, discourse and learner autonomy in the foreign language classroom, *Utbildning & Demokrati* 13 (3), 105–126.
Little, D (2006) The Common European Framework of Reference for Languages: Content, purpose, origin, reception and impact, *Language Teaching* 39, 167–190.
Little, D (2009) Learner autonomy, the European Language Portfolio and teacher development, in Pemberton, R, Toogood, S and Barfield, A (Eds) *Maintaining Control: Autonomy and Language Learning*, Hong Kong: Hong Kong University Press, 147–172.
Little, D (2010) *The Linguistic and Educational Integration of Children and Adolescents from Migrant Backgrounds*, Strasbourg: Council of Europe.
Little, D and Lazenby Simpson, B (2004) Using the CEF to develop an ESL curriculum for newcomer pupils in Irish primary schools, in Morrow, K (Ed) *Insights from the Common European Framework*, Oxford: Oxford University Press, 91–108.
Lockwood, J (2012) Developing an English for specific purpose curriculum for Asian call centers: How theory can inform practice, *English for Specific Purposes* 31 (1), 14–24.
Luoma, S (2013) *Self-assessment: The Encyclopedia of Applied Linguistics*, Oxford: Blackwell Publishing Ltd.
Manasseh, A (2004) Using the CEF to develop English courses for teenagers at the British Council Milan, in Morrow, K (Ed) *Insights from the Common European Framework*, Oxford: Oxford University Press, 109–120.

Matsutani, M (2012) Student count, knowledge sliding, *Japan Times*, available online: www.japantimes.co.jp/news/2012/01/10/reference/student-count-knowledge-sliding

McNiff, J and Whitehead, J (2010) *You and Your Action Research Project* (3rd edition), Abingdon: Routledge.

Messick, S (1996) Validity and washback in language testing, *Language Testing* 13 (3), 241–256.

Miura, T (2010) A retrospective survey of L2 learning motivational changes, *JALT Journal* 32 (1), 29–53.

Nagai, N and O'Dwyer, F (2011) The actual and potential impacts of the CEFR on language education in Japan, *Synergies Europe* 6, 141–152.

Negishi, M, Takada, T and Tono, Y (2013) A progress report on the development of the CEFR-J, in Galaczi, E D and Weir, C J (Eds) *Exploring Language Frameworks: Proceedings of the ALTE Kraków Conference, July 2011*, Studies in Language Testing volume 36, Cambridge: Cambridge University Press, 135–163.

North, B (no date) Introduction, in *The European Association for Quality Language Services, CEFR curriculum case studies: Examples from different contexts of implementing 'Can do' descriptors from the Common European Framework of Reference*, available online: clients.squareeye.net/uploads/eaquals/EAQUALS%20CEFR%20Case%20Studies%20Final.pdf

North, B (2000) *The Development of a Common Framework scale of Language Proficiency*, New York: Peter Lang.

North, B (2007) The CEFR common reference levels: Validated reference points and local strategies, *Language Policy Forum Report*, 19–29.

North, B (2014) *The CEFR in Practice*, English Profile Studies volume 4, Cambridge: UCLES/Cambridge University Press.

North, B, Ortega, A and Sheehan, S (2010) *British Council – EAQUALS Core Inventory for General English*, available online: www.teachingenglish.org.uk/sites/teacheng/files/Z243%20E&E%20EQUALS%20BROCHURErevised6.pdf

Nunan, D (2006) *Task-based Language Teaching*, Cambridge: Cambridge University Press.

O'Dwyer, F (2010) Can Do statements at the center of involving learners in the self-assessment, goal-setting and reflection learning cycle, in Schmidt, M G, Naganuma, N, O'Dwyer, F, Imig, A and Sakai, K (Eds) *Can Do Statements in Language Education in Japan and Beyond – Applications of the CEFR* (2nd edition), Tokyo: Asahi Press, 218–234.

O'Dwyer, F and Runnels, J (2014) Bringing learner self-regulation practices forward, *Studies in Self-Access Learning Journal* 5 (4), 404–422.

Osborne, J W (2008) *Best Practices in Quantitative Methods*, London: Sage.

Paris, S G, Wasik, B A and Turner, J C (1996) The development of strategic readers, in Barr, R, Kamil, M, Mosenthal, P and Pearson, P D (Eds) *Handbook of Reading Research* (2nd edition), New York: Psychology Press 609–640.

Pollit, A (2009) *The Oxford Online Placement Test: The Meaning of OOPT Scores*, available online: www.oxfordenglishtesting.com

Purpura, J E (2010) *The Oxford Online Placement Test: What Does it Measure and How?* available online: www.oxfordenglishtesting.com/uploadedfiles/6_New_Look_and_Feel/Content/oopt_measure.pdf

Richards, J C (2013) Curriculum approaches in language teaching: Forward, central, and backward design, *RELC Journal* 44 (1), 5–33.

Richards, J C and Rodgers, T S (2014) *Approaches and Methods in Language Teaching*, Cambridge: Cambridge University Press.

Runnels, J (2013a) A preliminary exploration of the relationship between student ability, self-assessment and teacher assessment on the CEFR-J's 'Can Do' statements, *Framework and Language Portfolio SIG Newsletter* 9, 6–18.

Runnels, J (2013b) Examining the difficulty pathways of can-do statements from a localized version of the CEFR, *Applied Research on the English Language* 2 (1), 25–32.

Runnels, J (2013c) Preliminary validation of the A1 and A2 sub-levels of the CEFR-J, *Shiken Research Bulletin* 17 (1), 3–10, available online: teval.jalt.org/sites/teval.jalt.org/files/SRB-17-1-Runnels_0.pdf

Semmelroth, A (2013) The early stages of aligning a curriculum to the CEFR-J: Writing can-do statements, *Framework and Language Portfolio SIG Newsletter* 10, 6–19.

Sheerin, S (1989) *Self-access*, Oxford: Oxford University Press.

Shimo, E and Nitta, K (2011) Developing can-do checklists as a self-evaluation tool for university-level English classes, *Kinki University Center for Liberal Arts and Foreign Language Education Journal* 2 (1), 225–245, available online: kurepo.clib.kindai.ac.jp/modules/xoonips/detail.php?id=AA12508620–20111130–0225

State of New South Wales, Department of Education and Training (2010) *Action Research in Education*, available online: www.det.nsw.edu.au/proflearn/docs/pdf/actreguide.pdf

Stringer, E (2008) *Action Research in Education*, Upper Saddle River: Pearson.

Thompson, G and Atkinson, L (2010) Integrating self-access into the curriculum: Our experience, *Studies in Self-Access Learning Journal* 1 (1), 47–58.

Thompson, G and Foale, C (2008) Adapting the BEPP model: The BECC curriculum project, *Studies in Linguistics & Language Teaching* 19, 253–289.

Tono, Y (2012) *CEFR-J*, available online: www.cefr-j.org/download.html

Tono, Y (2013) *CAN-DO risuto seisaku katsuyo eigo totatsudo shihyo CEFR-J gaidobukku [CEFR-J Guidebook: Making and Using Can-do Lists: An Index of English Level of Achievement]*, Tokyo: Taishukan Shoten.

Tono, Y and Negishi, M (2012) The CEFR-J: Adapting the CEFR for English teaching in Japan, *Framework and Language Portfolio SIG Newsletter* 8, 5–12, available online: dl.dropboxusercontent.com/u/33808898/FLP%20SIG%20NL%208%20Sep2012%20CEFR-J.pdf

Trim, J L M (2009) *Breakthrough*, Cambridge: Cambridge University Press.

Tsagari, D (2006) *Linking EFL textbook materials to exam specifications*, paper presented at the Third Annual Conference of EALTA, Kraków, Poland.

University of Cambridge (2012) *About the English Vocabulary Profile*, available online: www.englishprofile.org/wordlists

University of Cambridge ESOL Examinations (2012a) *Cambridge English Key: Key English Test (KET) CEFR Level A2 Handbook for Teachers*, Cambridge: UCLES.

University of Cambridge ESOL Examinations (2012b) *Cambridge English Preliminary: Preliminary English test (PET) CEFR Level B1 Handbook for Teachers*, Cambridge: UCLES.

University of Cambridge ESOL Examinations (2012c) *Vocabulary List: Key English Test (KET), Key English Test for Schools (KETfS)*, Cambridge: UCLES.

University of Cambridge ESOL Examinations (2012d) *Vocabulary List: Preliminary English Test (PET), Preliminary English Test for Schools (PETfS)*, Cambridge: UCLES.

Üstünlüoğlu, E, Zazaoğlu, K F A, Keskin, M N, Sarayköylü, B and Akdoğan, G (2012) Developing a CEF-based curriculum: A case study, *International Journal of Instruction* 5 (1), 115–128.

Valax, P (2011) *The Common European Framework of Reference for Languages: A Critical Analysis of its Impact on a Sample of Teachers and Curricula within and beyond Europe*, available online: researchcommons.waikato.ac.nz/bitstream/handle/10289/5546/thesis.pdf?sequence=3

van Ek, J A and Trim, J L M (1991a) *Threshold 1990*, Cambridge: Cambridge University Press.

van Ek, J A and Trim, J L M (1991b) *Waystage 1990*, Cambridge: Cambridge University Press.

van Ek, J A and Trim, J L M (2001) *Vantage*, Cambridge: Cambridge University Press.

Wall, P (2004) Using the CEF to develop English courses for teenagers at the British Council Milan, in Morrow, K (Ed) *Insights from the Common European Framework*, Oxford: Oxford University Press, 121–130.

Willis, D and Willis, J (2007) *Doing Task-based Teaching*, Oxford: Oxford University Press.

Zárate, J A and Álvarez, J A (2005) A perspective of the implications of the common European framework implementation in the Colombian sociocultural context, *Colombian Applied Linguistics Journal* 7, 7–26.

Appendix

2012 Freshman English proficiency goals

At the end of this course, you will have:

- used English in a lot of different situations, and improved your ability to speak and listen to English in conversation and discussions (e.g. interviews, conversations, discussions, problem-solving)
- learned about how to understand and write in English to make communicative texts (e.g. emails, postcards, and letters)
- developed your basic English vocabulary – particularly useful phrases for communication
- used a range of grammar and vocabulary to communicate ideas with your teacher and classmates
- learned some presentation skills and practised giving short presentations in English (e.g. eye contact, gestures, voice)
- developed your understanding of other cultures and about communicating in English
- been able to practise autonomous learning and developed strategies and knowledge about how to better control and organise your learning (e.g. planning projects, carrying out SALC independent learning activities, and working collaboratively)
- developed teamwork and leadership skills (e.g. co-operating with others, project planning)
- learned some ways for sustaining your language learning in the future (e.g. independent learning).

Section 4
Portfolio approaches

10 A CEFR-informed e-portfolio in blended learning at a German university

Astrid Buschmann-Göbels
Bärbel Kühn
University of Bremen

1 Introduction

This chapter introduces one form of the European Language Portfolio (ELP); the e-portfolio Elektronisches Europäisches Portfolio der Sprachen (EPOS, translated as Electronic European Portfolio of Languages). In the Language Centre of the University of Bremen, the EPOS is used in conjunction with a tutorial programme. We aim to outline how portfolios informed by the Common European Framework of Reference for Languages (CEFR, Council of Europe 2001) work well when they are put online as part of a blended learning package supported by tutoring. The chapter suggests that others who wish to implement a 'Can Do' language learning approach should seriously consider this type of implementation of the ELP, in combination with associated technology.

2 The European Language Portfolio approach and e-portfolios

As the first chapter of this volume noted, the ELP approach developed initially in Europe very much informs the portfolio approaches adopted in Japan (see Chapters 11–13). As users of the ELP must understand the principles of the CEFR, we first briefly outline the underlying principles of the ELP approach, before describing e-portfolios. For other ELP-related discussions in this volume, see section 2.1.2 of Chapter 1, section 1 of Chapter 7, section 2.2 of sub-chapter 9B, section 1 of Chapter 11 and section 3 of Chapter 12.

Little (2012) states that the ELP has two functions: a pedagogic function – to support the development of learner autonomy, plurilingualism and intercultural awareness and competence – and a reporting function: to allow users to record their language learning achievements and their experience of learning and using languages. Many tend to emphasise the ELP's reporting function (Little 2012:9). In our opinion there are at least two reasons for this. Firstly, the ELP provides practical evidence of second/foreign language communicative proficiency and intercultural experience. This helps the reporting of language learning achievement in an internationally transparent manner. Secondly: the CEFR and ELP were conceived to promote European mobility. The Europass (europass.cedefop.europa.eu/en/about) document is promoted by the European Commission to make language skills and qualifications clearly and easily understood in Europe, and is used to foster European mobility. The most important recording tool of the ELP, the passport, was the starting point of the Europass. It is unfortunate that the Europass is not integrated with the pedagogical use of the ELP. As stated in the Council of Europe's ELP guidelines (2011) this pedagogical function 'values the full range of the learners' language and intercultural competences and experiences regardless of whether acquired within or outside formal education' (Council of Europe 2011:5). It is a tool to promote learner autonomy. (For more about approaches to learner autonomy see section 2 of Chapter 1, section 4 of Chapter 6, section 3 of Chapter 8, section 1 of sub-chapter 9B, and section 2.2 of Chapter 12.) Seen from a political view there are good reasons for the passport, but seen from a pedagogical view the use of the passport alone, with a focus on the reporting function, is not sufficient for the effective learning of a language. The pedagogical practices outlined in this chapter suggest how use of an ELP-informed approach can also emphasise learning in terms of the pedagogical function.

The ELP guidelines state that the 'basic division' of the ELP into three parts has to be respected: the language passport, the language biography and the dossier (Council of Europe 2011:7). The passport should provide the results of self-assessment (sometimes combined with teacher assessment), the dossier should provide certificates and examples of best practice, while the language biography should be used to reflect on one's own learning process. In principle, each part should serve two functions: to strengthen reflection about the process of learning, and to keep a record of learning results as a showcase for employers and other institutions mentioned previously. In general, the dossier and passport are more suitable for the reporting function, while the biography is more suitable for the pedagogical function. It is not always easy to seamlessly integrate the two functions within one learning programme. In our experience, both functions can be realised via the implementation of blended learning and use of modern technology to create an e-portfolio. One such example is the EPOS, developed by the language centre in Bremen.

2.1 EPOS – The Bremen e-portfolio

At one level, an e-portfolio is nothing more than a digital collection of artefacts that belong to or represent a person. In an academic context, these artefacts might include a student's essays, posters, photographs, videos, artwork, and other course-related assignments. Additionally, the artefacts might also pertain to other aspects of a student's life, such as volunteer experiences, employment history, extracurricular activities, and so on. However, while these digital artefacts are important, they are static products. They are simply things that the student has produced or done or experienced, and a good e-portfolio ought to be more than just a collection of products. It should also be a process – specifically, the process of generating new or deeper learning by reflecting on one's existing learning. It's important, then, to think of an e-portfolio as both a product (a digital collection of artefacts) and as a process (of reflecting on those artefacts and what they represent). Before the EPOS was conceived there had only been an accredited Eaquals/ALTE e-portfolio.

The implementation of EPOS, in our opinion, effectively implements a pedagogic function. This is exemplified by the various elements and functions of the EPOS: self-evaluation, setting learning objectives, a journal to reflect and document the learning process, a dossier to document proof of progress, a biography to reflect on language learning experiences. The most important part is the 'pages' function, where users can present learning examples (e.g. self-evaluation, journal, dossier) to others, and the 'groups' function, where it is possible to collaborate, give feedback upon, and share projects.

The use of EPOS encourages a collaborative approach, similar in a way to online social networking. Just as learners are used to posting comments in language learning blogs or on other social media websites, learners are quite motivated to post and share their learning outcomes in EPOS. Web 2.0 tools are part of our students' living environment, and it is important to differentiate between the conscious use of Web 2.0 technologies like E-Tandem or Distance Tandem (when learners learn by email, phone (e.g. Skype) or other media, in contrast to face-to-face Tandem, where learners meet in person), language learning blogs, wikis etc., and the non-reflective use of non-didactic materials like blogs or chats in the target language, or playing computer games. This is exactly where our tutorial programme (through a combination of project work, peer learning, portfolio work and learning counselling under the umbrella of the e-portfolio EPOS) comes into play. Learners construct their own learning process and create their own learning spaces.

Having summarised in brief the e-portfolio, we now turn to the main point of the chapter: how the use of the EPOS is a good example of how CEFR-based portfolios work well when they are put online as part of a blended learning package supported by tutoring.

3 The tutorial programme of the Bremen Language Centre

In the last decade, the needs of possible clients at university language centres have changed significantly. As a result, the demands placed on the centres have also expanded. Students enter university with a heterogeneous background. Heterogeneity, in this context, refers to multiple factors: language competences; age; gender; cultural and social background; professional competences; diverse mother tongues and learning biographies; different learning styles and motivations; different degree courses; and prior knowledge. Advisors and course instructors have to teach these mixed-ability groups. Language centres also have to react and adapt to the new learning behaviour and learning culture (e.g. learning 'on the go' in a variety of learning spaces, via modern technology). At the Fremdsprachenzentrum der Hochschulen im Land Bremen (FZHB, the Language Centre for Higher Education institutions in the federal state of Bremen), we have developed several course formats to meet the needs of our learners:

- language courses (during and between semesters)
- intensive courses
- blended learning courses
- informal/semi-informal learning scenarios (out-of-classroom learning).

The 'Autonomous language learning with tutorial advisory service' tutorial programme, which is central to meeting learner needs in the FZHB, has been running since 2007. Student tutors are specially trained to support language learners in planning, performing and evaluating their own learning process. The tutorial programme is one example of how the University of Bremen serves heterogeneous learner groups and tries to bridge the learners' interests and the university's needs. The following summarises the programmes. For a thorough description of the tutorial programmes as well as an empirical study of its motivating effects and its sustainability, see Buschmann-Göbels, Bornickel and Nijnikova (2015).

The tutorial programme is open for learners of any language. Participants of the programme can use all materials available at our independent learning centre for free. Once a week they have individual meetings with their tutors for language counselling. These sessions also take place at our independent learning-centre and last for about 20 minutes each. Currently, the FZHB has a team of 18 student tutors. These tutors are trained in two full-day workshops as language advisors. Their job is to accompany autonomous language learners and their learning processes. More precisely, the training workshop focuses on the following aspects:

A CEFR-informed e-portfolio in blended learning at a German university

- strategies of autonomous language learning
- setting learning objectives
- select adequate language learning materials
- ways of assessing learning processes
- time management
- how to conduct learning advisory meetings
- project work
- ways to reflect and assess one's own learning process and the process of other learners
- introduction to the e-portfolio EPOS.

Furthermore, the new tutors sit in on diverse language advisory meetings of tutors already working in the programme as well as shadowing their work. Additionally, the whole team, including the project-coordinator, Astrid Buschmann-Göbels, as well as a colleague of German as a Foreign Language, Christine Rodewald, meet every week for supervision and further on-the-job training. Depending on the workload, the participants can get up to 3 ECTS (European Credit Transfer System) points for active participation (ECTS credits are a numeric value which represent the workload students must complete to pass each course unit); 1 ECTS corresponds to 30 hours of learning. Thus, to achieve 3 ECTS points, students have to attest to a workload of 90 hours in their portfolio. The participants can decide themselves how much time they will invest in their language learning. The weekly learning advisory hours with their tutors are obligatory, as is documentation and reflection of their learning in an e-portfolio, work on a project of their choice and presentation of this project at the end of the programme.

The overall aim of the tutorial programme is to accompany autonomous learners, to encourage them and finally to enable them to plan, conduct and evaluate their own learning process. In concrete terms, the aims of the tutorial programme are:

- to improve the students' ability to study through individual, personal learning counselling
- to achieve sustainability in language learning by supporting learner autonomy and focusing on action and competence orientation
- to individualise our offer of language courses to meet heterogeneous groups of students and their different profiles, curricula and timetables.

The tutor's role primarily is capacity building. This means that the tutors:

- help set reasonable learning goals for their tutees
- work out a corresponding learning plan
- support them with strategies for autonomous learning

- recommend suitable materials, if necessary
- help learners with their time management
- introduce them to our e-portfolio EPOS and give them regular feedback on their learning diaries and dossiers
- support them in their project work.

This project work is closely connected to the set learning goals. These goals are directly related to the CEFR descriptors, as the next sub-section shows.

3.1 The use of EPOS in the tutorial programme – planning and reflecting on the learning process

We will now describe how learners can plan and reflect upon their learning with the help of the EPOS and the tutorial programme. The first learning advisory meeting between a tutor and his/her tutee is devoted to a needs analysis of the tutee. Therefore, we have developed a questionnaire to record the learners' language learning biography. Then, the motivation for learning a certain language is detected. In the next step, the learners are introduced to our e-portfolio and its main functions (see Figure 1):

- self-evaluation: integration of several descriptor lists; comparison of levels
- learning objectives: set according to the ticked descriptors in the self-evaluation section; learners can phrase these as they wish
- journal: reflecting and documenting the learning process
- dossier: documentation proof of progress; possibility to download any data file or data format
- biography: language learning experiences
- pages: presenting learning examples (e.g. self-evaluation, journal, dossier) to other learners and their teachers and tutors
- groups: all members of a group share their work and can work on it collaboratively and give feedback, etc.

After a thorough explanation of all the functions of EPOS, the learner is asked to conduct a first self-assessment of their current language competences using the self-assessment grid (Figure 2). Self-assessment is carried out by using electronic checklists of 'I can-descriptors', offered by EPOS. These checklists are based on the CEFR 'Can Do' descriptors and learners can choose from two different sets of descriptor lists: one by the European Confederation of Language Centres in Higher Education (CercleS, www.cercles.org/en), the other by the European Language Council/Conseil Européen pour les Langues (ELC/CEL, www.celelc.org). The descriptor

A CEFR-informed e-portfolio in blended learning at a German university

Figure 1 EPOS at a glance

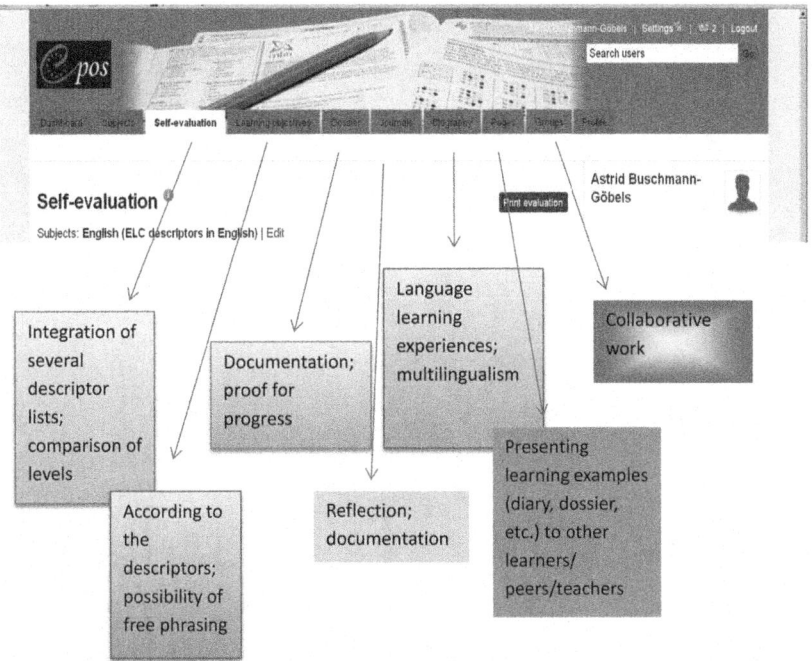

sets are available in English, French and German. Apart from the competence level for the skills 'listening', 'speaking', 'reading' and 'writing', further competences can be added. Each time, the learner clicks a competence menu, e.g. speaking, a drop-down menu opens showing all relevant descriptors for this competence (see the Figure 2 example 'spoken interaction A1'). These descriptors are of course based on the CEFR.

When working with the descriptors, learners can tick whether they have already mastered different competences. They can also specify a certain descriptor as a learning objective. This is then automatically transferred to the list of learning objectives in the EPOS menu. This example clearly shows one of the benefits of EPOS – the interconnectedness of its several functions.

In the end, the learners get a graphic representation of their self-assessment. The more a box is filled, the more the learner has achieved at that level (see Figure 3). Thus, they immediately see their abilities at a glance.

Learners can share their self-evaluation, as well as any other part of their EPOS, with their tutors or with peers by using the 'page' function. This function is a kind of electronic poster that can be filled with anything from the portfolio the learner would like to share with their tutor or peer learners. Tutors and peer learners then have the option to comment on the shared items. Hence, EPOS is an interactive, dynamic tool to reflect, progress, monitor and

Figure 2 Example of self-assessment grid

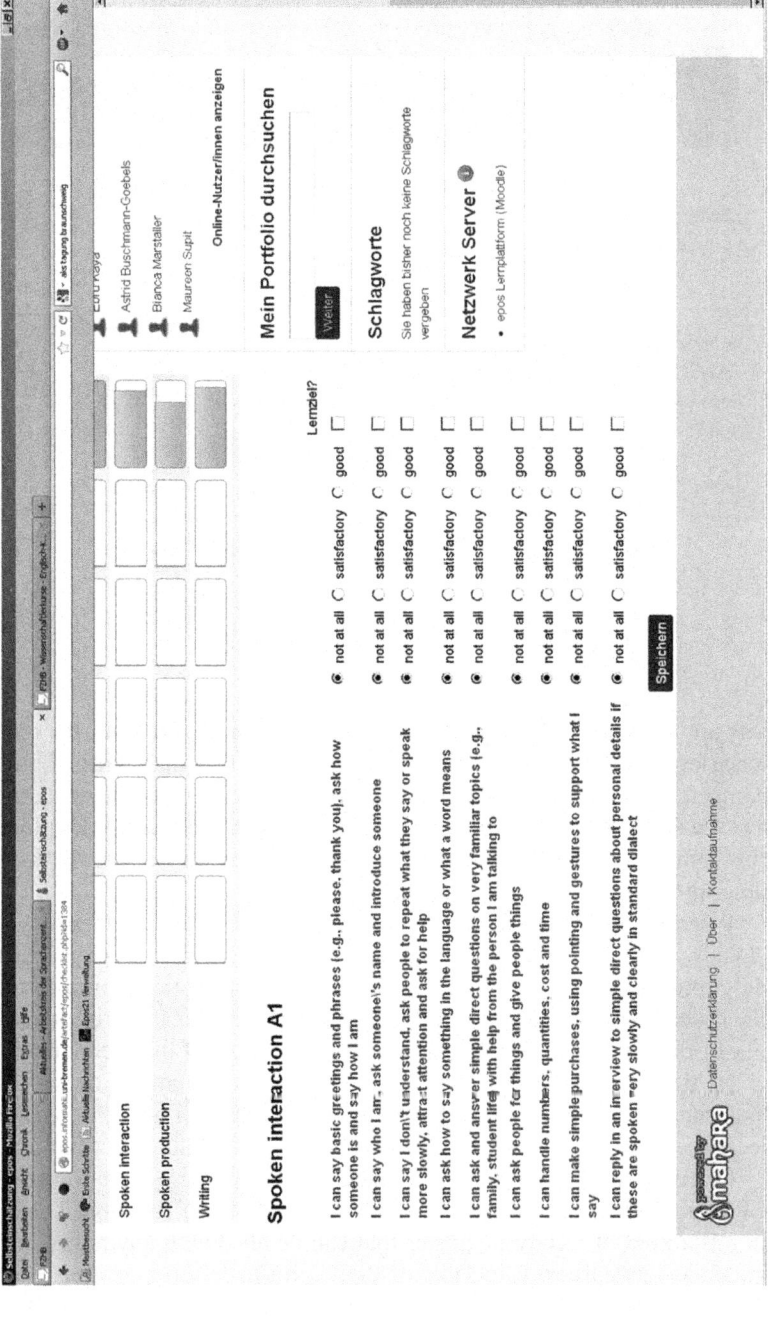

Figure 3 Self-evaluation in EPOS

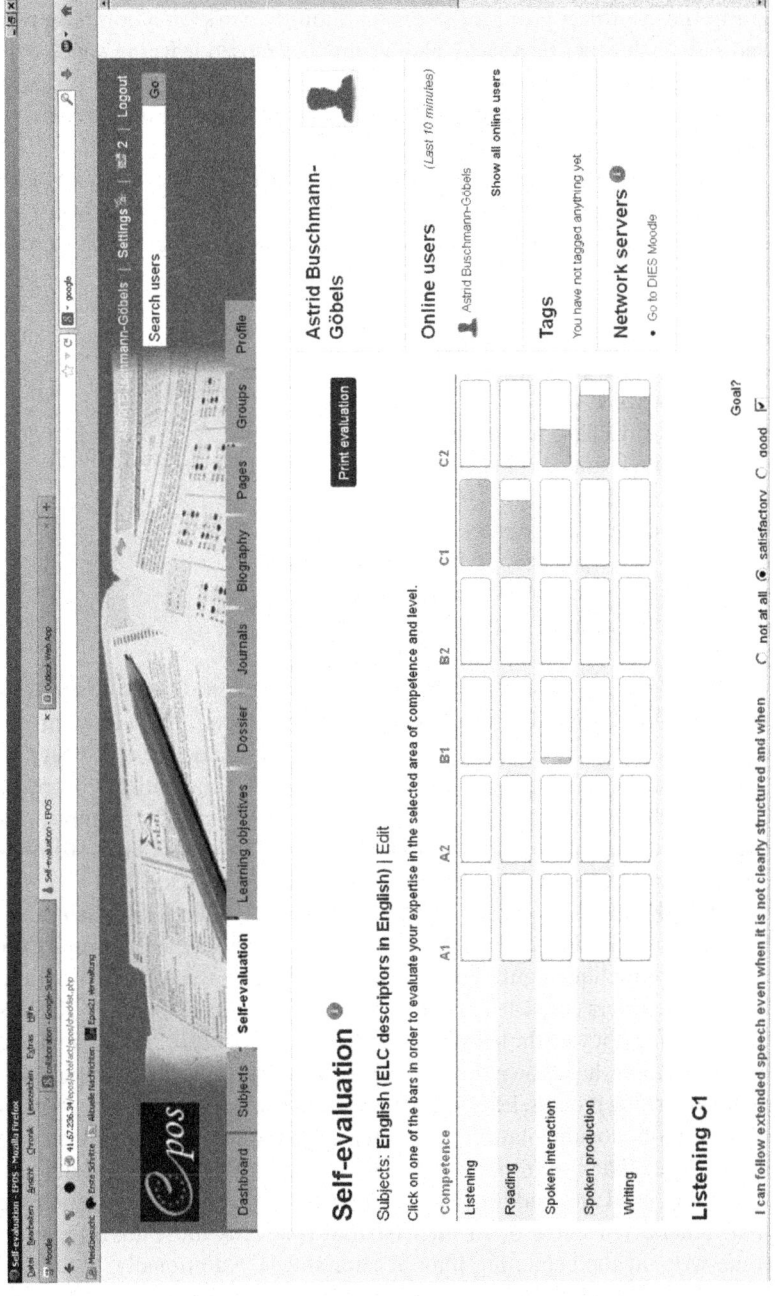

evaluate learning. By using the 'group' function of EPOS, members of a set group (i.e. a project group of peers) can jointly work on a common project and give each other feedback. The 'group' is a closed learning space with all group members being responsible for the group. Anything that is posted by a group member is automatically shared with the other group members, who are then able to give feedback etc.

A thorough reflection of each individual learning process is done by using the 'journal' function. By the optional use of some guiding questions, learners reflect on their learning. Examples for these guiding questions are the following:

- What learning objective did I work on?
- Which materials did I use?
- What worked well?
- Where did I have problems?
- How much time did I spend on my language learning?
- Where did I learn?
- How did I make progress (give examples)?
- Which strategies and methods did I apply?
- Do I stick to my timetable?
- What do I want to discuss with my tutor?

The e-portfolio allows them to add any type of file (audio, video, music, pictures, etc.) to their diary and design their 'products'. Thus, they can create digital posters in EPOS, using a variety of graphic devices to design their 'pages' described above. Learners, for example, have the option to copy parts of their self-assessment, their learning goals, diary entries, pictures, audio/ video files to their poster and finally upload it to share it with their tutor, with peer learners and with the teacher in order to get feedback.

While the tutors meet their tutees every week, the length of their counselling session varies. Depending on the degree of autonomy, learners make use of learning counselling regularly or on demand. Within the tutorial programme, language learners can learn according to their own pace. Being the agents of their learning, they set the learning objectives. Experience, especially in the tutorial programme, has shown that learners seek a kind of flexible companionship in their learning process. EPOS is an important tool for this, as it allows individual reflection, documentation and evaluation as well as getting and giving and receiving feedback to/from other learners. 'Flexible' here means that learners sometimes need more advisory support at some stages of the learning process than others. Thus, it is often the case that they seek more advisory support (time-wise) at the beginning than at later stages. Additionally, 'flexible' also refers to the format of an e-portfolio. Feedback and other forms of exchanges on the learning process take place whenever and wherever is required. Learners get face-to-face feedback during the advisory meetings, taking place in our self-access centre, as well as online via EPOS. Besides, the 'Can Do'-descriptors in EPOS are a great way for learners to clearly assess where they are and where they want to go. Hence, the 'Can Do' descriptor lists actually show them their abilities. When doing another self-assessment at the end of the tutorial programme, the learners immediately see their progress in every competence, as EPOS directly compares the assessment grids from the beginning and end of the programme. To sum up, at the FZHB we use EPOS as a tool:

- to assess, reflect and document individual learning
- to set learning objectives
- to collect materials in a variety of formats
- for communication among learners and among learners and tutors
- for collaborative work
- for task-based learning.

A closer look at the counselling concept described reveals that the tutorial programme follows a non-directive model. The tutors show the learners' possible options, strategies and materials and reflect the learners' progress. In the end, the learners have to decide how to proceed and which decisions to make. In other words, the tutors try to motivate learners to construct their own way of learning. This is exactly what Reinders (2009) demonstrates when talking about learner autonomy. The learner is responsible, but they do not necessarily learn alone so much as construct their learning via contact and comparisons with others:

> Autonomy, then, is an intimately personal affair. It is about your life, about what you want to achieve, and what you enjoy. In this way, it is the only way to learn successfully in the long term. Because no-one knows you better than you do, and no-one can make your choices for you, autonomy requires you to get to know yourself better. Becoming autonomous is a process of discovery. Because autonomy is about you and starts from within you, it cannot be forced upon you. You, and you alone, can make the decision to start this journey. But just as good travellers listen to others and learn from their experiences, good learners are not islands. They rely on others to offer insights, and occasionally, show them the way (Reinders 2009).

Autonomous language learning cannot be forced upon someone from outside and cannot be made obligatory: it must develop from the learners themselves. The learners regularly work on their subject-specific project, which is a free-choice project. Above all, it should be fun to do. Here again we have the action-oriented approach. The learner is responsible for taking charge of their own learning and to be the agent of their learning process.

This ensures a high degree of authenticity and, as the following quotation by Lindgren and McDaniel shows, is the most sustainable way of learning:

> The notion of agency as contributing to cognitive processes involved in learning comes primarily from the Piagetian notion of constructivism where knowledge is seen as "constructed" through a process of taking actions in one's environment and making adjustments to existing knowledge structures based on the outcome of those actions. The implication is that the most transformative learning experiences will be those that are directed by the learner's own endeavours and curiosities (Lindgren and McDaniel 2012:346).

In pursuing the goals pursued in the tutorial programme, learners receive training in language as well as subject-specific and intercultural competences. Our independent learning centre serves to meet at least two needs. It offers 1) a physical space for learning/for decisions on learning goals, projects, materials and 2) an inner (psychological) space to become aware of one's own learning process and discover strategies, presuppositions on learning and other affective aspects of learning.

4 Discussion

In this section we first address the key questions found in section 2.1.1 of Chapter 1, which concern specific implementations of the CEFR:

- What type of implementation has been adopted for curricula? What specific practices have been implemented? What practices have been seen to be effective?
- How are all stakeholders involved? Can the people engaging in CEFR-based teaching and learning develop a sense of ownership? How?

In our opinion the most effective practical teaching is the one which is developed by teachers themselves and the most effective concepts are those which are learner oriented. When we had to implement curricula top-down only by instruction there have often been gaps between the written curriculum and the curriculum as actually taught. In these courses the washback effect of textbooks and of tests and certificates was in reality accidental. It rather strengthened the position of the teachers when they were able to discuss and develop descriptors, tests and methods across languages, at events like teacher conferences. Our new experience confirms this: in the tutorial programme, the tutors develop a sense of ownership. The tutors are the ones responsible for guiding and advising the learning process. This encompasses the responsibility for planning, performing and evaluating the learning process. In doing so, the learners set their learning objectives, monitor their learning process,

A CEFR-informed e-portfolio in blended learning at a German university

Figure 4 Components of tutorial programme and their grade of importance

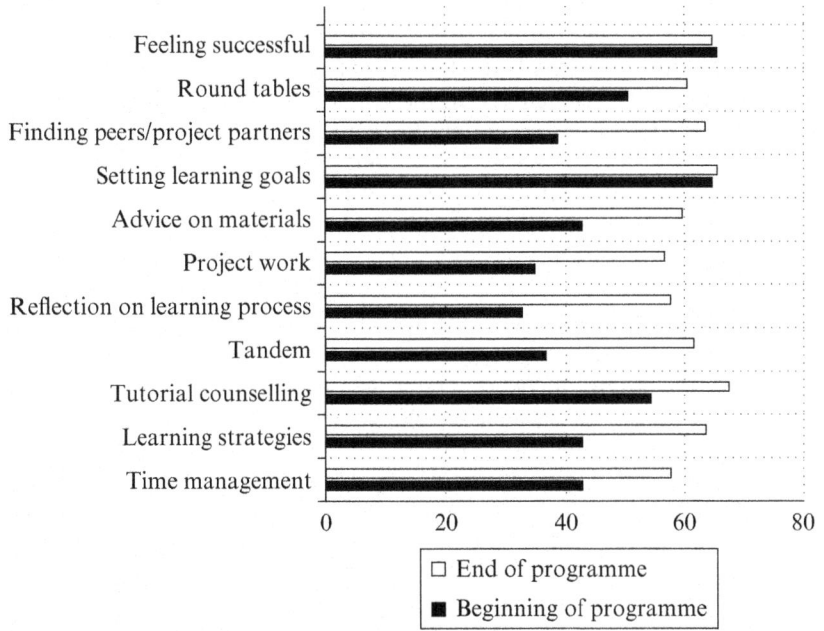

and adapt the strategies and materials to their needs. In collaboration with peers and a tutor as a student counsellor, the learners continuously reflect upon their own learning, using the online portfolio EPOS as well as peer and tutorial feedback. Figure 4 shows all the relevant components of the tutorial programme. An exemplary survey with a questionnaire as well as oral interviews were conducted among 68 learners of German, based on the principles of qualitative contents analysis (QCA). This survey was taken twice: at the beginning as well as at the end of the tutorial programme. Figure 4 shows the results. The x axis represents the number of the participants who answered and the y axis represents the items of the questionnaire. For more information see Buschmann-Göbels et al (2015).

It is noticeable that in almost every case learners assign a higher relevance to the components of the programme at the end of the programme as compared to their evaluation at the beginning. This seems to indicate that the tutorial programme has led them to autonomous learning. We can say that learners can readily see the benefits of an ELP-based approach for their own learning.

Furthermore, the tutorial programme is now one prominent service facility of the University of Bremen. Due to the steadily increasing number of participants, which we feel demonstrates that autonomous learning is possible with the tutorial advisory service, other European language centres are interested in implementing elements of the practices outlined above. The EPOS association of 10 German and other European universities – in Germany, Bremen, Bochum, Coburg, Paderborn, Potsdam, Stuttgart (with four universities) and Saarbrücken; in the UK, the London School of Economics (LSE) and King's College, London; in Italy, Bolzano – does a lot to develop courses, teacher training programmes and (last but not least) co-operation by regular meetings and newsletters to foster this. In the near future, we envisage further collaboration with the departments of the University of Bremen to establish a pool of subject-related project topics. The use of EPOS is an important tool in that respect.

The use of EPOS strengthens the offering of the CEFR 'Can Do' descriptors for several pedagogical functions: goal setting, project planning, biography and diary writing, and working together with peers via interactive tools. These processes are closely linked to the sets of descriptors. To illustrate, the self-assessment function (based on the CEFR descriptors) is directly linked to the option of setting learning goals. The project planning then is linked with the goal setting and as such, is based on the descriptors. In the diary, learners reflect on their learning process and refer to the set learning goals. It is important not to confuse testing for teachers and testing for students themselves. It is one of the principles of the ELP that the portfolio is the property of the learner: they do not have to show their daily reflections to the teachers via these tools. Students can ask for help and have to pass the examinations at the end of courses or modules. They can also share their learning projects to receive feedback. This helps the reflective competencies of autonomous learners.

It is important to remember, in terms of the goals of this volume (outlining effective implementation of CEFR-informed learning), that the learning objectives of each course at FZHB are based on the CEFR descriptors, adapting them to match the actual needs of the language students. Lesson plans and the co-operation of the students ensure transparency via the use of the online platform Moodle. Formative assessment, working as peers or in groups and performance learning tasks through projects are supported by EPOS. In addition, students use the e-portfolio EPOS to provide their learning results including certificates to teachers, employers, other universities etc. to make their progress visible. This is possible due to the European Language Passport, which is part of EPOS and illustrates the learners' language competences. Teachers use the CEFR descriptors in discussion and workshops for making chosen descriptor lists and classroom results comparable and transparent. This underlying foundation of commitment to the use of the CEFR makes the implementation of the EPOS and tutorial programmes very possible and effective. In general, as outlined in this section, we also try to implement a learner-centred and action-oriented approach. Language learning should be authentic. Authentic learning must not only use naturalistic, non-edited materials, but, moreover, be relevant to the students. In this way, learning can occur like it does in informal learning in daily life. If it matters to learners, they will gain the most out of it. We conclude the chapter by offering advice to others who may consider implementing such practices.

4.1 General steps for using a tutorial programme in conjunction with a CEFR-informed e-portfolio

- Set the overall aim of a tutorial programme (e.g. to foster autonomous language learning and to offer individual language advisory service)
- choose the languages the student can learn in the programme
- establish criteria for the selection of tutors
- develop a training programme for the tutors (e.g. strategies and methods of autonomous language learning, the CEFR as a tool for self-assessment, pedagogy of e-portfolio EPOS, project-based learning, working as a language advisor)
- choose relevant sets of descriptors for the portfolio
- show the options of an e-portfolio for autonomous language learning: formative self- and peer-assessment, setting concrete learning objectives, working collaboratively on a project with peers
- set up individual weekly meetings of tutor and tutee for reflection the learning process
- have both tutees and tutors keep their notes (work drafts, projects as well as advisory comments in the e-portfolio)
- offer regular short workshops on topics of autonomous language learning (e.g. time management, task-based learning, how to set sensible learning objectives)
- ensure a final evaluation of the whole programme as well as of the individual learning process
- use the final evaluation to plan the future learning steps.

The main focus in the tutorial programme is to enable the participants to assess their own learning process within a CEFR-informed learning environment. In programmes of higher education and development the ELP can be used to promote awareness of the common levels of the CEFR and to encourage reflective, learner-centred approaches to language learning and teaching. The Bremen tutorial programme demonstrates that successful language learning can be facilitated with the help of an e-portfolio. Will it be the same in language education outside of Europe? Will, for example, Japanese culture and Japanese language learning traditions be open enough to accept the principles and goals of the CEFR and ELP? How will classes used to – as we assume – more instructive teaching react to the type of learning promoted by task-based or project-based learning? These are questions we cannot answer ourselves. We are ending the chapter by putting them to you, the reader, in the hope that you can find some answers in the following chapters.

References

Buschmann-Göbels, A, Bornickel, M and Nijnikova, M (2015) Lernberatung und tutorielle Lernbegleitung heterogener Lerngruppen zwischen individuellen Bedürfnissen und fachlichen Anforderungen [Meet the needs – Language counselling and tutorial advisory service of heterogeneous learner groups between individual needs and professional demands], *Zeitschrift für interkulturellen Fremdsprachenunterricht [Journal for Intercultural Foreign Language Teaching]* 20 (1), available online: tujournals.ulb.tu-darmstadt.de/index.php/zif/article/view/197/190

Council of Europe (2001) *Common European Framework of Reference for Languages: Learning, Teaching, Assessment*, Cambridge: Cambridge University Press.

Council of Europe (2011) *European Language Portfolio (ELP): Principles and Guidelines,* Strasbourg: Council of Europe, available online: www.coe.int/t/dg4/education/elp/elp-reg/Source/Templates/ELP_Annotated_PrinciplesGuidelines_EN.pdf

Lindgren, R and McDaniel, R (2012) Transforming online learning through narrative and student agency, *Educational Technology and Society* 15 (4), 344–355.

Little, D (2012) The European Language Portfolio: History, key concerns, future prospects, in Kühn, B and Pérez Cavana, M L (Eds) *Perspectives from the European Language Portfolio: Learner Autonomy and Self-Assessment*, London: Routledge, 7–21.

Reinders, H (2009) *Innovation in Teaching*, available online: innovationinteaching.org/autonomy/practical-tips

11 Using the CEFR-based European Language Portfolio in a non-CEFR English course

Paul Wicking
Meijo University

1 Introduction

Many educators in Japan work in situations where they are not able to design their own syllabus or choose their own textbooks. In such situations, it is possible to weave the CEFR-based European Language Portfolio (ELP) into the fabric of a standardised English course that is not based on the Common European Framework of Reference for Languages (CEFR, Council of Europe 2001) descriptors. By doing so teachers are able to move the curriculum in a more action-oriented direction. The following outlines one way in which this was done at a Japanese university. Student opinions about the portfolio will be discussed, highlighting the language portfolio's successes as well as challenges for the future.

The ELP has been used for over a decade throughout Europe as a way of taking the CEFR descriptors and applying them to the classroom in a practical way. The two main functions of this document are evaluative and pedagogical. It aims to formally record learning and intercultural experiences of diverse kinds, and also to provide direction and purpose in future language study. Both teachers and learners alike have reported the positive results of using the ELP, in such areas as motivational orientations (Glover, Miric and Aksu 2005, Sisamakis 2006), promoting learner autonomy (Gonzalez 2009, Little 2009), and enabling students to function actively and independently (Yilmaz and Akcan 2012). O'Dwyer introduced the ELP to a Japanese university class and also reported a positive effect on learner autonomy and motivation (O'Dwyer 2011).

2 Development and implementation

Following the principles outlined in Schneider and Lenz (2001), a version of the ELP was developed for use in a Japanese university. The Japanese

Language Portfolio (JLP) contained three sections: the language passport, the language bibliography and the dossier. Instructions were provided in English and Japanese. The main point of departure with the ELP was the self-assessment framework. Instead of the CEFR 'Can Do' descriptors, the CEFR-J descriptors were used. The CEFR-J aims to more accurately describe the achievement levels of Japanese students by breaking down the levels into detailed sub-sections (Tono (Ed) 2013).

2.1 Procedure for implementation

The portfolio was introduced into six classes in the General English programme of the university. Altogether, 125 students were involved in the study. Students were introduced to the JLP at the beginning of the fall semester. Classes ranged from A1 to B1 levels on the CEFR, with between 16 and 25 students in each class. The syllabus followed the units in a standard 4-skills textbook, *American Headway* (Soars and Soars 2009), which is not based on the CEFR. The focus of the course was speaking and writing.

2.1.1 Stage 1: Pre-course planning

As the JLP was based on the CEFR-J, care was taken to go through the content of each lesson in the textbook and link it to a CEFR-J 'Can Do' descriptor. For example, the theme of Unit 9 was 'Food you like!' with the target grammar being count and non-count nouns. This was linked in with the CEFR-J Level A2.2 'Can Do' descriptor: 'I can interact in predictable everyday situations (e.g., a shop) using a wide range of words and expressions.' During the lesson, students did role plays set in a grocery store, asking for 'a banana' and 'some milk'. In this way, Unit 9 was linked to an appropriate 'Can Do' descriptor taken from the CEFR-J. In a similar fashion, all the units from the textbook were tied to an appropriate 'Can Do' descriptor. The focus of the course was speaking and writing, so all of these 'Can Do' descriptors were taken from the 'Writing', 'Spoken Production' and 'Spoken Interaction' sections. The elementary level classes focused on A1.3 and A2.1, while the intermediate level classes focused on A2.2 and B1.1.

2.1.2 Stage 2: Commencement of the course and subsequent lessons

In the first class, students were given an opportunity to complete the language passport section and the first part of the language biography. At the beginning of every subsequent class, students were shown the 'Can Do' descriptor which corresponded to the goals of that lesson. For example, Unit 5 in the textbook focused on the question, 'Where do you live?' Before the lesson began, students were directed to the descriptor: 'I can give simple directions from place to place, using basic expressions such as "turn right" and "go straight", along with sequencers such as "first", "then", "next".' (CEFR-J A2.1) After reading the descriptor, the lesson got underway. Beginning with a 'Can Do' descriptor provided a clarity and focus to the lesson which enabled students to aim towards a concrete goal.

During the final few minutes of class, students opened their JLPs and engaged in reflection and self-assessment. This was a simple process which involved checking a box. There were three boxes, simply labelled with either O ('can do it'); Δ ('unsure'); and X ('can't do it'). In this way, the descriptors in the JLP framed the beginning and ending of each lesson. A simplified 90-minute lesson plan is given as an example (Table 1).

Table 1 Simplified 90-minute lesson plan using the JLP

Time	Activity
2 mins	Students open their JLP and read the descriptor for that lesson. For example: 'A2.1: I can give simple directions from place to place, using basic expressions such as "turn right" and "go straight", along with sequencers such as "first", "then" and "next".'
85 mins	Lesson proceeds from the textbook, with a focus on giving directions.
3 mins	Students engage in self-assessment.

Each 'Can Do' descriptor that was used provided the focus of a lesson twice during the semester. This allowed students to revisit the target ability and try again if they weren't able to achieve it the first time.

As well as regularly checking these boxes to record their progress, students also completed writing tasks which were collected and added to the dossier section at the back of the JLP. The writing competences described in the CEFR-J are sufficiently broad enough to enable textbook activities to be used as practice. For example, a descriptor from A2.1 reads: 'I can write texts of some length in simple English, using basic, concrete vocabulary and simple phrases and sentences, linking sentences with simple connectives like "and", "but" and "because".' Such a broad description fit with almost all the writing tasks from the textbook.

2.1.3 Stage 3: Post-course reflection

Upon completion of the course, students' JLPs were collected and the results of their self-reflections were analysed. The 'Can Do' descriptors with which students struggled most then provided the focus for the next year's class, so more attention is given to those areas in which students felt they were weak.

3 Student opinions of the JLP

Students were given a questionnaire survey to evaluate their perceptions and attitudes towards the JLP. The most positive feedback concerned students being able to see progress in learning and being able to assess their competence (36 comments). 'I can understand at a glance my own English ability', wrote one student, while some other comments were 'My language ability is able to be looked at objectively', 'I can get a general feeling for my practical ability', and 'it was very useful for getting a handle on my actual level of English'. As the CEFR-J uses a quite detailed breakdown of descriptors, students said they appreciated being able to know their strong and weak areas of competence.

The second thing students liked best about their portfolio was that they could show their language learning history (11 comments). One student liked that 'the results from past exams can be seen', and another wrote, 'I'm able to bring together everything I've experienced in English up until now', and '[the language portfolio] makes it easy for me to look back and reflect on my English study'. Many students had a sense of satisfaction in looking back over their past learning experiences, both within and without the formal education system. They could better understand where they had come from and how they had progressed as language learners.

On the other hand, students wrote that the JLP did not encourage them to take a more proactive role in pursuing English learning outside of the classroom. The most common recurring comment as to what students liked least about the JLP was that they didn't understand it (16 comments). For example, 'there were a lot of difficult questions that I couldn't understand', 'the basis for making a judgment [about the 'Can Do' descriptors] was too vague' and 'it was difficult to evaluate my own level using the CEFR-J'. One learner wrote, 'The basis for judging X, Δ, and O was unclear'.

Many of the negative comments were made by students who commented they didn't see the relevance of the JLP to their study. 'I don't think this is necessary for English study', wrote one learner, and another, 'Because this is self-evaluation, it doesn't have any meaning'.

4 Discussion

Generally, it seems that students were unsure of the reasons behind the use of the JLP and did not clearly understand its role in promoting language learning. Some students indicated that the 'Can Do' descriptors were difficult to understand, while others lacked faith in their ability to evaluate their own achievement. However, there was also a not insignificant number of students who said they did understand the purposes of the JLP and could see its value in guiding their language study. As they were clearly able to document their progress, the JLP helped foster a sense of achievement which is something sorely missing from much of Japanese education (Clark 2010). If these small successes of the JLP in enabling students to evaluate their own learning could be built upon, then the JLP could prove to be a positive force for self-directed language learning.

One criticism that cannot be ignored was that only 46% of respondents said that time spent keeping their language portfolio was 'well spent', indicating that many students felt they could have used their time better in other activities. Perhaps this may have been a problem with the implementation rather than the JLP itself. It's likely that many students would not have engaged in much self-reflection and assessment before, so may have been a little perplexed. As has been noted:

> ... the teacher also needs to justify the benefits of reflection to the students and explain why she is asking them to reflect on their learning and assess their communicative knowledge, skills and attitudes. Once the students realize the purpose of reflection and self-assessment they have crossed the basic *motivational threshold* for reflective activities in class (Kohonen 2002:88, author's emphases).

Training and guidance in doing self-evaluation would go a long way towards supporting students and making clear the benefits of self-regulated learning (Sato 2010).

4.1 General steps for using a version of the ELP in a non-CEFR-informed course

- Create the ELP document, based on the principles found in Schneider and Lenz (2001).
- Examine the syllabus of the non-CEFR-informed course, and link each language goal with a related 'Can Do' descriptor from the CEFR (or CEFR-J).
- Give each lesson a specific goal oriented around those 'Can Do' descriptors.
- At the beginning of the course, introduce students to the ELP, explaining how it can be used to improve the language learning process and outcomes.
- Guide students in the principles and processes of self-evaluation, without assuming that they can do this unaided.
- Inform students of the lesson goal at the start of every class, and have them do self-assessment at the end of the class, by recording their achievement in the ELP.
- Have students keep their drafts and final products of their work in the dossier section.
- At the end of the course, students look back through their ELP to see where their strengths and weaknesses lie, and use this information to plan the next step of their language learning.

5 Future directions

Judging by student responses, this method of employing a CEFR-based language portfolio with a non-CEFR-informed syllabus is promising, but still has a long way to go in terms of making itself more relevant and appealing. Two suggestions are offered as a way forward.

Firstly, in order to make the most of the framework, the CEFR (or CEFR-J) should be taken as the main pillar of the syllabus, and then the textbook could be wrapped around that. In other words, rather than following the textbook unit by unit and matching it up with an appropriate 'Can Do' descriptor, the CEFR descriptors could provide the focus of each lesson and then suitable activities found in the book. Which would mean, of course, that the book would not be followed in a linear fashion.

Secondly, there is great potential for using a JLP as a resource for student conferences. As part of their final assessment, students could spend time talking with their teacher about their learning progress and future goals, making use of the 'Can Do' descriptors and the dossier to demonstrate language attainment. Such formative assessment processes would help learners to continue studying long after the course has ended.

While the JLP itself might be a useful pedagogical tool, it seems clear that there needs to be careful thought put in to the way it is implemented. Much care and deliberation needs to be taken in explaining the goals of the JLP, and in making evident the value of its pedagogical and reporting functions. Students will also need to be trained in the process of self-evaluation. This was a foreign concept for many of the respondents, and they struggled with it. To help with that, it is recommended that students write in their JLP every lesson. One student liked this process because 'I can understand the goal of every lesson, and keep it in mind as I'm studying'. Of course, if the curriculum is not based on CEFR-J descriptors, the portfolio developer could use the learning goals of his or her particular language programme.

All in all, the most important factor in the successful introduction of a language portfolio is this: it must be woven tightly through the fabric of the course of study, and not just tacked on the outside as an added extra. As a standalone tool that is largely extraneous to the course syllabus, the ELP has little chance of success, as the case in Europe has shown (Little 2014). When the ELP is tightly integrated at all stages of the course, making the learning goals explicit and giving shape and direction to language study, there are great potential benefits for the students. It is hoped that this short chapter is helpful to educators in attaining that end.

References

Clark, G (2010) Saving Japan's universities, *The Japan Times*, available online: www.japantimes.co.jp/opinion/2010/08/17/commentary/saving-japans-universities

Council of Europe (2001) *Common European Framework of Reference for Languages: Learning, Teaching, Assessment*, Cambridge: Cambridge University Press.

Glover, P, Miric, I and Aksu, M (2005) Preparing for the European Language Portfolio: Internet connections, *Turkish Online Journal of Distance Education* 6 (1), 84–98.

Gonzalez, J (2009) Promoting student autonomy through the use of the European Language Portfolio, *ETJ Journal* 63 (4), 373–382.

Kohonen, V (2002) The European language portfolio: From portfolio assessment to portfolio-oriented language learning, *Quo vadis foreign language education?* 27, 77–95, available online: www.script.men.lu/activinno/portfolio/kohonen_european_language_portfolio.pdf

Little, D (2009) *The European Language Portfolio: Where pedagogy and assessment meet*, paper prepared for the 8th International Seminar on the European Language Portfolio, Graz, 2009.

Little, D (2014) *The CEFR from the perspective of the European Language Portfolio*, keynote presentation given at the CEFR Web Conference, March 2014.

O'Dwyer, F (2011) Using a European Language Portfolio for self-assessment, goal-setting and reflection, *OnCUE Journal* 5 (2/3), 49–61.

Sato, Y (2010) Using can do statements to promote reflective learning, in Schmidt, M G, Naganuma, N, O'Dwyer, F, Imig, A and Sakai, K (Eds) *Can Do Statements in Language Education in Japan and Beyond – Applications of the CEFR* (2nd edition), Tokyo: Asahi Press, 184–199.

Schneider, G and Lenz, P (2001) *European Language Portfolio: Guide for Developers*, Strasbourg: Council of Europe.

Sisamakis, E (2006) *The European Language Portfolio in Irish post-primary education: A longitudinal empirical evaluation*, unpublished PhD thesis, Trinity College Dublin.

Soars, L and Soars, J (2009) *American Headway* (2nd edition), Oxford: Oxford University Press.

Tono, Y (Ed) (2013) *The CEFR-J Handbook: A Resource Book for Using Can-do Descriptors for English Language Teaching*, Tokyo: Taishukanshoten.

Yilmaz, S and Akcan, S (2012) Implementing the European Language Portfolio in a Turkish context, *ELT Journal* 66 (2), 166–174.

12 Developing a portfolio for English as a tool for global communication

Yukie Saito
Waseda University

1 Introduction

This chapter describes how the 'Can Do' descriptors of the Common European Framework of Reference for Languages (CEFR, Council of Europe 2001) and the European Language Portfolio (ELP) can be used to create a portfolio specific to the needs and expectations of a particular situation for students to learn English as a tool for global communication. I exemplify how 'Can Do' checklists serve as the key reference point for processes of self-assessment and reflective learning. The portfolio to learn English as a tool for global communication I introduce in this chapter includes a dossier and a language biography, which are designed to reflect the cyclical phases of self-regulated learning: a forethought phase, a performance phase, and a self-reflection phase (Zimmerman 1990).

2 Teaching context

The portfolio was designed for a course to teach freshmen English as general communication. I am in charge of four classes and in each class there are about 30 students whose levels range from A2 level to B1 level of the CEFR (Council of Europe 2001). The course covers one semester with 15 lessons of 90 minutes each. The main objectives of the courses set by the faculty are to be able to listen to English at B1 level, participate in spoken English discussion in a small group, report in English to the class on group discussion, and give a presentation in English to the whole class. Although the objectives are set, there is no designated textbook and the contents covered in this course are left to each teacher's discretion. During the first year of teaching the course, I adopted an English Language Teaching (ELT) textbook but I felt that the contents were not enough to achieve the objective for A2 to B1+ students. In addition, I felt the strong need to reflect the needs of globalisation while teaching English. Thus, I decided to make a portfolio which could be used as a textbook and promote their English learning as a tool for global communication.

Developing a portfolio for English as a tool for global communication

2.1 English as a tool for global communication

Universities in Japan are expected to reflect the rapid pace of globalisation in their English education, and offer courses in which students can acquire English as a tool for global communication. Such communication requires plurilingual and pluricultural competence. These competences are defined as 'the ability to use languages for the purposes of communication and to take part in intercultural interaction, where a person, viewed as a social agent has proficiency, of varying degrees, in several languages and experience of several cultures' (Council of Europe 2001:168). I referenced and adapted this definition in the development of my own portfolio.

I also included a reference to concrete descriptors from the 'Can Do' descriptors for spoken production in the CEFR for B2. The descriptors of the B2 level were chosen because most of the students' levels ranged from A2 to B1, with the majority of the students placed at the B1 level; thus, setting the achievement level of B2 for this particular semester course was considered appropriate. The following are examples of the descriptors for the B2 level on the CEFR.

> Addressing Audiences:
> Can give a clear, systematically developed presentation, with highlighting of significant points, and relevant supporting detail.
>
> Informal Discussion:
> Can account for and sustain his/her opinions in discussion by providing relevant explanations, arguments and opinions.
>
> Formal Discussion and Meetings:
> Can express his/her ideas and opinions with precision, and present and respond to complex lines of argument convincingly.
> (Council of Europe 2001:60, 77, 78)

With the reference to the descriptors of spoken production for B2 from the CEFR as well as the framework's concept of plurilingual and pluricultural competence, I developed a definition of English as a tool for global communication as follows:

> The ability in English to think critically and objectively, and to convey thoughts and ideas in an organized manner through pair work, discussion, and presentation as well as the ability in English to understand and convey other cultures as well as our own cultures.

2.2 Self-regulated learning

The definition of English as a tool for global communication described in section 2.1 is also used for additional objectives of the course. In order for students to acquire English as a tool for global communication, it will be essential for them to be self-regulated learners. Self-regulation is the self-directive process by which learners transform their mental abilities into academic skills. These are important because a major academic function of education is the development of lifelong learning (Zimmerman 2002). Self-regulated students are meta-cognitively, motivationally, and behaviourally active participants in their own learning (Zimmerman 1986). Figure 1 shows phases of self-regulated learning (Zimmerman 2002).

Figure 1 Cyclical phases of self-regulated learning (adapted from Zimmerman 2002:67)

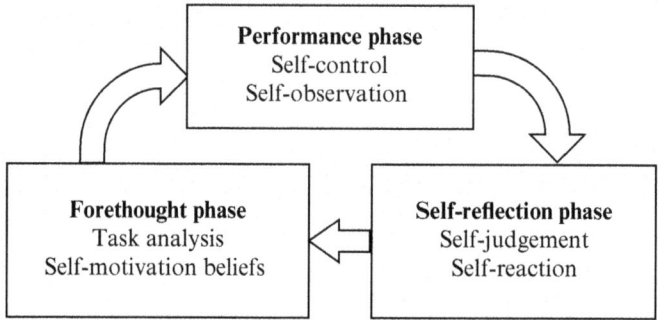

In this cyclical process, there are three stages for self-regulation: the forethought phase, the performance phase, and the self-reflection phase. At the forethought phase, learners analyse tasks and set motivational beliefs such as belief that they can accomplish certain tasks. Based on the analysis of tasks, they can set goals and adopt strategies. At the performance phase, they observe their learning behaviour to see if they are learning effectively and make attempts to control their behaviour. At the self-reflection phase, they can judge themselves and react to the previous performance. The feedback from the self-judgement stage can then be used in another forethought phase.

3 The language portfolio for English as a tool for global communication

The European Language Portfolio (ELP) is defined as a document in which those who are learning or have learned a language can record and reflect on their language learning and cultural experiences (Council of Europe 2001).

The ELP is composed of three sections: a language passport, a language biography and a dossier. The language passport summarises learners' linguistic ability by recording their history of learning foreign languages, formal language qualifications and proficiency in different languages. A language biography is used to set language learning goals, and to monitor and assess learning processes and progress. A dossier offers the learner the opportunity to store work in progress and present the work (Little, Goullier and Hughes 2011). The language portfolio that I drafted for students to acquire English as a tool for global communication (hereafter ETGC) includes a language biography with 'Can Do' descriptors for goal setting, self-evaluation and self-reflection, and a dossier to keep a record of the process of ongoing learning. 'Can Do' descriptors for goal setting also reflect the forethought phase and 'Can Do' descriptors in self-motivation, and self-reflection echoes the third phase in the cyclical phases of self-regulated learning (Zimmerman 2002).

3.1 Contents of the portfolio for ETGC

On page 1 of the portfolio, the definition of ETGC described in section 2.1 is included as the objectives of the course, in addition to how student performance is to be graded. On page 2, there is a space where they can write what they would like to achieve in the four main language skills (listening, reading, speaking, and writing), and how they intend to work to achieve the goals. The inclusion of goal setting by students is to reflect the forethought phase in the cyclical phases of self-regulated learning. On page 3, the contents that will be covered in each class and space in which they can write their self-evaluation after each lesson are included, which is shown in Table 1. The contents covered in the portfolio were for students to achieve the objectives set for them to learn English as a tool for global communication through helping them to become self-regulated learners. Taking into consideration that this course was the first for the freshmen, the contents were drafted from easy tasks such as asking questions to a classmate, and talking about the classmate to a new partner, to more challenging tasks such as making a problem-solving presentation as a group.

In the previous portfolio that I drafted (Saito 2015), 'Can Do' descriptors for each lesson were not included. However, in this revised portfolio, to help students understand the main goal and sub-goals for each lesson and to evaluate their own learning more objectively, 'Can Do' descriptors for each lesson were included in the language biography. The biography section for each lesson with 1) Contents, 2) Goal and Sub-Goals, 3) Self-Evaluation, 4) Self-Evaluation: 'Can Do' descriptors, and 5) Self-Reflection was added to the portfolio for ETGC, which is shown in Table 2. In section 1, Contents, students can understand the main content of the lesson and tasks that they

Assessment of CEFR-informed Language Teaching in Japan and Beyond

Table 1 The contents and self-evaluation sheet

Lesson	Contents	Looking back on today's lesson, write comments
1	Orientation, Self-introduction, Introduction to Presentations	
2	Family and Friends	
3	Family and Friends	
4	Individual Presentation (What I have been most concerned about)	
5	Individual Presentation (What I have been most concerned about)	
6	News in Japan	
7	Social Issues in Japan	
8	Cultures in Japan	
9	A Group Presentation about News, Social Issues, and Cultures in Japan	
10	Cultures in the World	
11	News in the World	
12	Various Issues the World is Facing	
13	Review and Preparation of Group Presentation	
14	Review and Preparation of Group Presentation	
15	Group Presentation	

Table 2 A sample language biography for ETGC, Lesson 10

1) Contents	2) Goal and Sub-Goals	3) Self-Evaluation
Cultures in the World	Main Goal: I can understand and convey other cultures.	
Task 1: Ask and answer questions about travelling.	Sub-goal 1: I can ask and answer questions about travelling.	
Task 2: Brainstorm about unique cultures in the world.	Sub-goal 2: I can brainstorm unique cultures in the world.	
Task 3: Investigate one culture of one country.	Sub-goal 3: I can investigate one culture of one country.	
Task 4: Convey the findings in an organised manner through a presentation.	Sub-goal 4: I can convey the findings in an organised manner through a presentation.	
Task 5: Tell my opinion about how to be a global-minded person.	Sub-goal 5: I can say my opinion about how to be a global-minded person.	

4) Self-Evaluation: Can Do descriptors
If you think you can do it well, draw three stars. ☆☆☆
If you think you can do it a little, draw two stars. ☆☆
If you think you cannot do it at all now, draw nothing.

5) Self-Reflection
Write down what you have been able to do.
Write down what you will have to improve.
Write down how you will improve the area in detail.

are going to work on. In section 2, Goal and Sub-Goals, students can understand the main goal and sub-goals they are expected to achieve. Table 2 shows one example of a language biography for ETGC from Lesson 10. In Lesson 10, the main goal is to be able to understand and convey other cultures, which is a part of the objectives of the course and based on CEFR definitions of pluricultural competence. Sub-goals are also set for each task. In Table 2, sub-goal 4 ('I can convey the findings in an organised manner through a presentation') and sub-goal 5 ('I can say my opinion about how to be a global-minded person') reflect 'Can Do' descriptors for the spoken production for Level B2 quoted in section 2.1. In section 3, 'Self-Evaluation', students can evaluate their learning after the class using 'Can Do' descriptors from section 4, 'Self-Evaluation: 'Can Do' descriptors'. In section 5, 'Self-Reflection', students can reflect on their learning and think about what they have been able to achieve, what they will have to improve, and what they will try to do to improve the weak areas.

Table 3 shows an excerpt of a dossier for Lesson 10 in which students record their learning process. In Lesson 10, they work on Tasks 1 to 5 (see Table 2). The first task is to conceive questions related to travelling with a partner and then they ask the questions they created to a new partner. This task is to be introduced as a warm-up activity to move to the following main tasks. In Task 2, they are to investigate unique cultures from around the world on the internet and they are encouraged to investigate as many unique cultures as possible. In the following Task 3, they will choose and investigate one cultural aspect of one country on the internet and take notes to inform other students of the summary of their findings. Based on the summary, in Task 4 they will make a mini-presentation about the findings to other students. They are expected to convey the findings in an organised manner. This is introduced as a group activity. While listening to others, they take notes. After studying a variety of cultures in Task 5, they will discuss how and what should be done towards different and unique cultures in order to become a global-minded person. They will share the results of the discussions in the class. For example, in the previous semester in Task 5, first they brainstormed in a group through drawing a mind map and then they shared the opinions from each group in the whole class. In the dossier part of Task 5 in Table 3, some students wrote opinions such as understanding the importance of accepting and being tolerant of different cultures, not valuing everything from one's own culture's norms, and learning other languages.

Assessment of CEFR-informed Language Teaching in Japan and Beyond

Table 3 A sample dossier for ETGC

Task 2: Unique cultures in many countries. Write about many unique cultures in the world with your group members.

Task 3: Choose one country and look into the unique culture of the country with partners. Take notes during your discussion and using the memo, report it to other students.

Name of a country you chose
Unique culture in the country

Task 4: Make a presentation of the findings in Task 3. While listening to others, take notes.

Presenters' names	Names of countries	Unique cultures of the countries

Task 5: Every country and every region has different and unique cultures. To be a global-minded person, how and what should we do towards different and unique cultures in the world?

3.2 Classroom practice with the portfolio for ETGC

In the first class, the paper-based portfolio, including the dossier and the language biography, was distributed to each student. With the portfolio, the objectives, the contents of the course, and the method of evaluation were explained. This process is important for students to understand what they will study and what they should aim at. Students also wrote their own goals for the four skills. This process is introduced to reflect the forethought phase in the cyclical phases of self-regulated learning. After the explanation of the course, they introduced themselves and learned how to make effective presentations. For about 10 minutes before the end of the class, they reflected on their learning and wrote self-evaluations about the lesson in the portfolio.

In every class, students bring their own portfolios and write about the ongoing process of learning. For instance, in the second class, students are to create questions with a partner, ask the questions to a new partner, draw a mind map based on the answers from the partner, and write a paragraph about the second partner who has just answered the questions. All of the process can be written and kept in the dossier in the portfolio; therefore they can observe their own learning process. This is also the self-reflection phase of the cyclical phases of self-regulated learning.

The final task of this course is to make a problem-solving presentation. This task is included to help them achieve the course objective of 'having the ability in English to think critically and objectively, and to convey thoughts and ideas in an organised manner through pair work, discussion, and presentation'. Before the final presentation, they brainstorm social issues in the world in a group, share them with the class, and finally choose and investigate one problem as a group. In the group, they discuss possible causes behind the problem, negative effects resulting from the problem, and possible solutions. They can take notes about all of the brainstorming ideas and the results of the discussion in the dossier on the portfolio. Using the notes effectively, they make a problem-solving presentation about one social issue in the world including possible causes, negative effects, and possible solutions. This part of the dossier is used not only to observe their ongoing learning but also to move forward to the next step and to the final step, the final group presentation.

Ten minutes before the end of each class are allocated to reflect on their own learning and write on the self-evaluation sheet (as shown by Table 1) and the language biography for ETGC shown by Table 2. Taking self-evaluation time in every lesson mirrors the self-reflection phase in the cyclical phases of self-regulated learning, and to help learners make self-evaluation a habit of learning.

4 Student reflections about the use of the portfolio

After four classes in the spring semester, I asked the students if the portfolio helps them set goals, and observe and evaluate their learning. Regarding goals, one student wrote that the portfolio helps the student understand the goal for each class because they are clearly stated, and another student wrote that they can be easily ready for each class because what they should learn is presented. Many students wrote that the use of the portfolio helps them reflect on their own learning, with one student writing that 'I understand that I have come to enjoy speaking English by reading previous comments'. Another student wrote that just writing self-evaluation such as writing what did not go well is useful for self-evaluation, while another commented that: 'I can read the comments I wrote every time, so I can see the process of my growth'. The learners feel that the portfolio also helps them move on to the next study unit by reflecting on the class and confirming what they learned in the class.

As for the part of the dossier in which they can record their learning process, one student wrote that the portfolio is very easy to use because it is composed of a textbook and a notebook. However, a couple of students wrote that more space is needed to take notes such as new words or sentences. Another suggestion from one student is that extra handouts might be needed when assignments in the portfolio will have to be submitted because when the portfolio is collected, students cannot review and prepare for studying for the next class.

Overall, the comments from the students show that the portfolio enables them to set goals, observe, and evaluate their learning; however, as the students suggested, more revisions to the portfolio are needed.

5 Thoughts on using a language portfolio

General steps for making and using a language portfolio are provided below:

- Make a definition of ETGC with a reference to the CEFR and 'Can Do' descriptors of the CEFR.
- Create a language portfolio reflecting the cyclical phase of self-regulated learning theory, which enables students to understand objectives of the course and create goals and sub-goals for each lesson, to set their own learning goals, and to observe and reflect on their learning.
- The language portfolio for ETGC includes the following contents:
  o the objective of the course, which was the definition of English as a tool for global communication
  o a syllabus on which contents are to be covered in each lesson
  o a dossier for each lesson in which they can record their learning process
  o a language biography for each lesson in which the goals and sub-goals are listed, and a space for self-evaluation after each lesson is provided
  o a dossier section for each lesson is presented first so that students can write during the lesson and a language biography section is included after the dossier section so that they can reflect on their learning.
- Distribute the language portfolio to each student in the first class. Explain the course objective and the contents covered in each class and the purpose of using the portfolio to promote self-regulated learning.
- At the beginning of each class, inform students of the main goal and sub-goals for the class. During the class, let them take notes in the portfolio

Developing a portfolio for English as a tool for global communication

while they are working on tasks. Before the end of the class, let them reflect on their learning using the portfolio.
- Before the end of the course, let students reflect on what they studied in the course and write what they have come to be able to do and what they will have to improve.

5.1 Suggestions for future applications of the portfolio

The portfolio was designed to help students to use English as a tool for global communication, and also to help them become more self-regulated learners. Overall, the students' responses show that the use of the portfolio was helpful for them to set goals, observe, and evaluate their learning, and facilitate their discussions and presentations during the semester. They were also able to achieve, to some degree, the course objective of learning English as a tool for global communication. Thus, employing the concept of pluriculturalism and 'Can Do' descriptors of the CEFR is considered to be a strong basis for the instruction of teaching and learning English as a tool for global communication. For future application of the portfolio, I would like to propose two suggestions.

The first suggestion is to include more space in the portfolio following the suggestions of the students. In fact, sometimes there was not enough space to take notes while they were working on the tasks. In the end, the students had to use other paper to take notes and keep the paper in the portfolio. Therefore, enough space for every task should be included in the portfolio.

The second suggestion is to make the last pages of each section in the portfolio homework pages to be turned in when they have to submit an assignment. As the students' comments imply, they were not able to review what they studied and to prepare for the next lesson when the assignments in the portfolio needed to be collected. Thus, to improve the situation the last pages of the portfolio can be allocated to the pages for the homework which is to be collected. Then, students can complete their assignment, cut off the page, and submit it.

Finally, sometimes it was difficult to take 10 minutes before the end of each lesson since many tasks are to be covered in every lesson. Thus, in case the self-reflection time cannot be allocated, they can be encouraged to write self-reflection at home, which may possibly lead to promoting autonomy.

5.2 Conclusion: Language portfolio for ETGC reflecting self-regulated learning

The rapid pace of globalisation has placed the expectation on students to acquire English as a tool for global communication. Based on the definition I proposed with reference to the concept of pluriculturalism and 'Can Do' descriptors of the CEFR, a portfolio for students to learn English as a tool for global communication (ETGC) was drafted. For students to be able to acquire ETGC effectively, helping them to become self-regulated learners was thought to be important. Thus, the cyclical phases of self-regulated learning, the forethought phase, the performance phase, and the self-reflection phase (Zimmerman 2002), are reflected in the language biography and the dossier in the language portfolio for ETGC.

Overall, this portfolio for ETGC shows that pluriculturalism and 'Can Do' descriptors of the CEFR can be adapted to learn ETGC, reflecting globalisation and that the language biography and the dossier can be adapted to facilitate students' self-regulated learning of ETGC.

References

Council of Europe (2001) *Common European Framework of Reference for Languages: Learning, Teaching, Assessment*, Cambridge: Cambridge University Press.

Little, D, Goullier, F and Hughes, G (2011) *The European Language Portfolio: The Story so Far (1991–2011)*, Strasbourg: Council of Europe.

Saito, Y (2015) Suggestions to university English education towards globalization: English as a tool for global communication, *The Japan Association for Global Competency Education* 2 (1), 43–59.

Zimmerman, B J (1986) Development of self-regulated learning: Which are the key sub-processes? *Contemporary Educational Psychology* 16, 307–313.

Zimmerman, B J (1990) Self-regulated learning and academic achievement: An overview, *Educational Psychologies* 25 (1), 3–17.

Zimmerman, B J (2002) Becoming a self-regulated learner: An overview, *Theory into Practice* 41 (2), 63–70.

13 Using the 'Can Do' descriptor list as a checklist for short-term Chinese study in China

Qu Ming
Muroran Institute of Technology

1 Introduction

This chapter outlines how 'Can Do' checklists serve as a key reference point for processes of self-assessment and reflective learning based around study trips abroad arranged by the Muroran Institute of Technology (Muroran IT). Muroran IT is located in Hokkaido, Japan. The university consists of only one department – the Faculty of Technology. Every year there are over 600 freshmen, 90% of whom are male. A second foreign language is compulsory for the 1st year students: they can choose from Chinese, German or Russian. The courses cover one semester, with 15 weekly lessons of 90 minutes each. There are around 25 students in each class, with 12 sections each for Chinese and German, and two sections for Russian. All foreign languages must be taught according to the A1 level of the Common European Framework of Reference for Languages (CEFR, Council of Europe 2001). Based on the regulations of Muroran IT, the education goal of the foreign language course is: through foreign language learning, enhance the understanding of different cultures, and cultivate the capacity for communication in a foreign language[1].

Muroran IT currently conducts two short-term study abroad programmes: a 10-day Chinese study programme in China, and a 2-week English study programme in Europe. Because the programmes are of such a short duration, most students cannot recognise what they have learned in China or Europe after their return to Japan. To date, teachers have evaluated a student's Chinese ability by grading their grammar and vocabulary on a paper test; however, while the score gives an indication of a student's knowledge of Chinese, it does not adequately describe whether they can actually use the language. In order to show the learning/educational goals more explicitly, we

---

1 「外国語学習を通じて、異文化理解を深める、外国語による受信・発信能力を涵養する。」(translated by Qu Ming).

used a 'Can Do' descriptor list as a checklist for the self-assessment of actual Chinese ability for the short-term study programme in China.

This article aims to provide detailed information on two points: first, how we created the 'Can Do' descriptor list and second, how we utilise it as a checklist.

2 The process of creating the 'Can Do' descriptor list

A 'Can Do' descriptor list describes what a language learner can do in a foreign language. For example: give a self-introduction, introduce their family members, buy a train ticket, order food in a restaurant, introduce Japanese culture and Japanese food, and so on. In order to create the 'Can Do' descriptor list for the Chinese class at Muroran IT, we carried out two surveys, an interview with the teachers and a questionnaire survey of the students. There were four distinct stages in the creation of the 'Can Do' descriptor list:

1. Create a draft questionnaire based on Chinese teaching guidelines and other resources.
2. Perform interviews with teachers.
3. Conduct a survey of the students.
4. Decide the final list by analysing the level of difficulty of each item.

In Stage 1, we created a draft questionnaire based on the accreditation criteria of HSK (*Hànyǔ Shuǐpíng Kǎoshì*, a Chinese test administered by Hanban, a non-government organisation affiliated with the Ministry of Education of the People's Republic of China; for more information, see www.hskj.jp), CHUKEN (a Chinese test administrated by the Society for Testing Chinese Proficiency, Japan; for more information, see www.chuken.gr.jp), the CEFR, and the content of the Chinese textbook used at Muroran IT. The syllabus guidelines for Chinese teaching in Muroran IT require most of the students to achieve CEFR Level A1 in their first year, so we generally chose descriptors in the A1 range from the above references. At this point, the 'Can Do' descriptor list included 22 items, 19 communication activity items, two communication language competence items, and 1 communication strategy item. Among the 19 communication activity items, the majority were categorised into three domains (Council of Europe 2001:45): four items in the personal domain, five items in the educational domain, and six items in the public domain. Most of the activities in the personal and educational domains were monologue activities whereas all the activities in the public domain were interactive activities.

In Stage 2, we interviewed four experienced Chinese language teachers employed at Muroran IT, asking them to describe the abilities they felt were absolutely necessary for the students to gain, especially for the students of our university (whose major is science). The Chinese language teachers provided a good deal of advice during this process. For example, the draft questionnaire included the following two items: 'I can describe one's appearance', and 'I can describe the house I live in', but as all teachers argued that Japanese people seldom describe one's appearance or one's house they recommended these two items be deleted. Further, they suggested that 'email address' be added to the item 'Can give brief information regarding address, telephone number, nationality, age, and so on', arguing that email address information is now frequently used. At this point, the revised 'Can Do' descriptor list included 20 'Can Do' descriptors, including the teachers' suggestions.

In Stage 3, using these 20 items, we surveyed all of the students who studied Chinese in their first year and asked them two questions: which ability they wanted to develop, and how they could do it. They were given three choices for the first question:
- It is very important to learn this item?
- It is necessary to learn this item?
- It is not necessary to learn this item?

They were given four choices for the second question:
- I can do it well
- I can almost do it
- I can do it a little
- I cannot do it.

At this stage, we deleted another item, 'I can do basic greetings', as most of the students said they could do it well.

Finally, in Stage 4 we chose the items which most students wanted to develop and said they could perform only a little or not at all for a tentative 'Can Do' descriptor list. There were 19 'Can Do' descriptor items in this version of the 'Can Do' descriptor list.

At first, the 'Can Do' descriptor list (shown in Table 1) was created as a list of explicit learning/educational goals. In the second term, we found it to be an effective tool for encouraging the students' autonomous learning. We therefore decided to use it as a checklist to evaluate students' ability to actually use Chinese when they go to China. The score achieved on a paper test can give an indication of a student's knowledge, but it cannot evaluate whether they can actually use the language or not. In Japan, in particular, it is said that most students know a great deal of vocabulary and grammar, but they cannot actually apply it in real-life communication. To rectify this, we asked the students to use the 'Can Do' descriptor list to self-assess their Chinese speaking ability.

Table 1 The 'Can Do' statement list used in this study

Learning/ educational goals	Items (19)	Domain
Communicative activities	• Can do a brief self-introduction. • Can simply introduce one's family members, friends and the people around her/him. • Can handle numbers, quantities, cost and time. • Can say what he/she likes and dislikes about sports or hobbies. • Can give brief information on address, telephone number, email address, nationality, age, and so on.	Personal domain
	• Can explain what he/she likes or dislikes about school subjects. • Can ask Chinese teachers questions and ask for help when he/she has problems. • Can talk about schedules, plans, and goals of their school life. • Can give a brief introduction to their club activities. • Can give a brief introduction on one's own educational background.	Educational domain
	• Can cope with routine situations in post offices, such as buying stamps, sending letters, and mailing boxes, bags, etc. • Can cope with routine situations in banks, such as withdrawing money, exchanging money, etc. • Can get simple information about travel or using public transport: buses, trains, taxis, purchasing tickets. • Can ask somebody the way and give directions. • Can make simple transactions in hotels, giving numbers and dates, one's own name, nationality, address, age, date of birth, etc. • Can make simple transactions in restaurants, asking about things, ordering food, etc.	Public domain
Communicative language competence	• Can give a simple description of an ordinary event continuously for 1 minute. • Can express beliefs, opinions, agreement and disagreement politely.	
Communicative strategies	• Can start again using a different tactic when communication breaks down.	

3 Using the 'Can Do' list as a checklist for a short-term study programme in China

The students were asked to check the 'Can Do' items before and after they went to China. After using the language in actual communicative situations in China, the students were asked to report which 'Can Do' items they performed (a) successfully (indicated by ○), (b) partially (indicated by △), or

(c) 'failed to perform' here and below (indicated by x). For the items they reported as 'partially' and 'failure', they were asked to analyse the reasons for this and report on what they could do to solve their communicative problems. Table 2 is the checklist for one of the students.

Our analysis of the students' reports revealed several interesting findings that have notable pedagogical implications for teaching Chinese as a second language in Japan. The first point is that after 10 days of study and language practice in China, most students said that they found monologue activities were easier than interactive activities. This is because the students found that the Chinese generally speak very quickly and the students were, therefore, unable to understand what people were saying on first hearing. Under such conditions and due to the students' lack of knowledge of communication strategies, most of the communication simply broke down. For example, one student described his experience in China as follows:

> In Japan, we were taught that when you go shopping, you should say 我想要×× ("*Wǒ xiǎng yào*" "I want ××") first, and then ask 多少钱 ("*Duōshao qián?*" "How much does it cost?"). The staff will then give the price (for example 50 yuan), and I should give them money, and say 给你50元 ("*Gěi nǐ 50 yuán.*" "Here is 50 yuan"). But when I said "I want ××", the staff just said "ha??" It seemed that they could not understand what I said. I tried to say it again, but they still could not understand me, I have no way to solve this, and the communication broke down ... I think it is important to master some tactics in order to solve communication problems; for example, rewording the message for the purpose of clarification, or using gestures to solve the problems.

This shows that, as the student said, mastering communication strategies (for instance, asking for clarification, coining new words, using non-verbal strategies, etc.) is necessary, even for 1st year students, when they undertake actual communication. At present, there are few Chinese textbooks that deal with communication strategies. Therefore, I think this should be one area in which we improve our Chinese curriculum in the future.

Another finding is that for most students their experience of real communication was markedly different from what they had learned in the classroom prior to going to China. For example, when you buy something in the market the sellers don't say the words that the students had learned in their textbook; they never say 你好 ('*Nǐ hǎo*' 'Hello') or 谢谢 ('*Xièxie*' 'Thank you'). Instead of such greetings, the students were asked if they wanted a plastic bag, or if they had the exact amount of money, neither of which they had learned from the textbook used in Muroran IT. The students therefore suggested that in order to understand authentic Chinese, they should learn not only from the textbook but also from other media such as television programmes or

Table 2 A student's checklist before and after he went to China

Learning/ educational goals	Items (19)	Pre-visit	Post-visit	Domain
Communicative activities	• Can do a brief self-introduction.	(o)	(o)	Personal domain
	• Can simply introduce one's family members, friends and the people around her/him.	(o)	(o)	
	• Can handle numbers, quantities, cost and time.	(△)	(o)	
	• Can say what he/she likes and dislikes about sports or hobbies.	(o)	(o)	
	• Can give brief information on address, telephone number, email address, nationality, age, and so on.	(o)	(o)	
	• Can explain what he/she likes or dislikes about school subjects.	(x)	(△)	Educational domain
	• Can ask Chinese teachers questions and ask for help when he/she has problems.	(x)	(△)	
	• Can talk about schedules, plans, and goals of their school life.	(x)	(△)	
	• Can give a brief introduction to their club activities.	(△)	(o)	
	• Can give a brief introduction on one's own educational background.	(△)	(o)	
	• Can cope with routine situations in post offices, such as buying stamps, sending letters, and mailing boxes, bags, etc.	(x)	(△)	Public domain
	• Can cope with routine situations in banks, such as withdrawing money, exchanging money, etc.	(x)	(△)	
	• Can get simple information about travel or using public transport: buses, trains, taxis, purchasing tickets.	(x)	(△)	
	• Can ask somebody the way and give directions.	(x)	(△)	
	• Can make simple transactions in hotels, giving numbers and dates, one's own name, nationality, address, age, date of birth, etc.	(x)	(△)	
	• Can make simple transactions in restaurants, asking about things, ordering food, etc.	(△)	(△)	
Communicative language competence	• Can give a simple description of an ordinary event continuously for 1 minute.	(x)	(△)	
	• Can express beliefs, opinions, agreement and disagreement politely.	(x)	(x)	
Communicative strategies	• Can start again using a different tactic when communication breaks down.	(x)	(x)	

Using the 'Can Do' descriptor list as a checklist for short-term Chinese study

YouTube, and the students even suggested that having a Chinese friend might be the best way to learn the living language. One of the students described his experience in China as follows:

> Once, in China, my hotel room key didn't work. I told the staff and asked if they could help me. I thought they would say 好 ("*Hǎo*" "Yes, OK") or 不好 ("*Bù hǎo*" "No, I can't"), but they answered in some other Chinese that I could not understand or even guess at. Also, when I went shopping in China, they never used the sentences I learned as conventional phrases in Japan. Sometimes they asked me if I needed a plastic bag, or if I had the exact amount of money. If I only learn Chinese from the textbook, I will never conduct actual communication smoothly, I think I need to learn more widely from the other media, and should also learn more autonomously and independently.

It is a very good result that the student realised that language should be learned from more media and should also be learned more autonomously and independently. At the same time, it is also a good opportunity for language teachers to consider how to use authentic content in future classes. Using authentic materials can provide exposure to real language, relate more closely to learners' needs and maybe have a positive effect on learner motivation. Authentic materials on the other hand often contain difficult language, obscure or unnecessary vocabulary items and complex language structures, which causes a burden for the teacher in lower-level classes. Therefore, appropriate use of authentic materials remains an issue for the teachers.

The students made progress in most of the items of the checklist: they mostly marked the checklist items with x or △ before they went to China whereas they marked them with △ or ○ after they came back to Japan. On the other hand, a lot of students said that there was no change in social language competence items ('can express beliefs, opinions, agreement and disagreement politely'). Similarly, the ability to change communication strategy ('can start again using a different tactic when communication breaks down') was also discovered to be a weak point in our teaching of Chinese in Japan. For example, one student said to her middle-aged male Chinese teacher: 老师，你很可爱 ('*Lǎoshī, nǐ hěn kěài*' 'Sensei, you are very cute'). In China, it is very bad manners to say such things directly to one's teacher, especially one of such an age and sex. As we all know, knowing a language goes beyond the knowledge of grammatical rules, vocabulary items and the pronunciation of these items. Successful language learning requires language users to understand the culture underlying the language in order to get the meaning across. In order to teach students social language knowledge, we need to introduce culture in the foreign language classroom and develop our teaching and learning programme of basic social language knowledge in the future.

4 Conclusions

Learner-centred teaching is proposed in Muroran IT. Using the 'Can Do' descriptor list as a checklist gave the students a chance to assess their ability to actually use Chinese and think about the problems they face in using the language. The 'Can Do' descriptor list works like a guidebook: it can tell the students how and what Chinese they should learn both in China and in Japan. By filling out the 'Can Do' descriptor list, the students found and analysed their communication problems by themselves and arrived at conclusions by which they could try to solve their problems, also by themselves. In this way, the 'Can Do' descriptor list enables the students to recognise what they can and cannot do when using Chinese, and is an effective tool for motivating the students' autonomous learning.

4.1 General steps for creating a 'Can Do' descriptor list to evaluate students' communicative ability

- *Create a draft questionnaire.* This should be created to match the level of the target students, and it should be created based on both internal (for example, the education goals of the university or other school or some special guidelines of that institution) and external (for example, the guidelines for reputable external tests) guidelines.
- *Interview the teachers.* Show the draft to some experienced teachers and ask them if it is appropriate for the students in your university. You should create a 'Can Do' descriptor list which is appropriate to the particular needs and features of the students. Add the teachers' advice and revise the draft list accordingly.
- *Distribute a questionnaire survey to students.* Show the draft to the students and ask them what they think is necessary to learn and to what level they think they can accomplish those communication goals at present. Accommodate the students' wishes to increase their incentive to learn.
- *Decide the final list by analysing the level of difficulty of each item.*

As educational/learning goals, we should choose items which the students think are important or necessary to learn and that they can only do a little or not at all.

4.2 Suggestions looking forward

First, when we create the 'Can Do' list we should involve both the teachers and the students and create it together, perhaps along with other interested parties. In this way, they can all have a very good understanding of the 'Can Do' descriptor list itself.

Secondly, after using the 'Can Do' descriptor list, reflective activities are very important. It is therefore vital to ask the students to undertake a self-assessment using the 'Can Do' descriptor list and report what they can and cannot do. Analysing the reasons for their failures and reporting on what they could do to solve their communicative problems is also very important. This allows them to solve the problems by themselves. Once they can find and solve the problem by themselves, they can start their autonomous learning.

References

Council of Europe (2001) *Common European Framework of Reference for Languages: Learning, Teaching, Assessment*, Cambridge: Cambridge University Press.

Section 5
Conclusion

14 Bringing critical and constructive assessments of CEFR-informed language teaching forward

Fergus O'Dwyer, Morten Hunke, Alexander Imig, Noriko Nagai, Naoyuki Naganuma and Maria Gabriela Schmidt

1 Introduction

The final results of this volume are presented in this chapter as a synthesised assessment of all the learning practices discussed within. By outlining the positive points of all the pedagogical practices described, an exemplar for future initiatives is provided. An action research perspective (see sub-section 2.1 of Chapter 1, section 3 of Chapter 6, and sub-section 3.3 of sub-chapter 9A for more about this type of research) suggests ways in which the Common European Framework of Reference for Languages (CEFR, Council of Europe 2001) can be effectively contextualised. However, the more the CEFR is adapted to a specific context, the greater the possibility that the original language proficiency scales of the CEFR will be altered in an unhelpful way. The localisation of the CEFR proficiency levels means a departure from the CEFR global standards and raises issues such as how closely the localised scales are related to the CEFR scales. The localisation must be done to fit each language course but should be done in principled ways so that the original levels are kept intact. We first address the issue of CEFR-informed textbooks, before addressing the principal issue of implementation of the CEFR in curricula, and finally in the language learning classroom.

2 Action research and textbooks

Chapter 4 highlights how a learner-centred approach to adopting the principles of the CEFR can be used to reinvigorate a particular language education sector. Some prominent practices in language learning and teaching (e.g. an emphasis on learning strategies, foregrounding the process of going back and forth between output and input to promote inner learning) are combined with use of the Japan Foundation Standard (JFS), a CEFR-based framework. Transparent and concrete learning objectives are at the centre of the curricula and learning targets, and 'Can Do' checklists serve as the key reference point for processes of reflective learning in which self-assessment plays a central role. The approach also manages to incorporate other elements of the CEFR, for example intercultural understanding. The best 'Can Do' descriptors should be selected to form both the objectives of the lessons of the textbook and an index for assessment. This is a valuable exemplar for further textbook creation along CEFR-informed lines.

The same can be said for the English for Academic Purposes (EAP) textbook discussed in Chapter 5. At tertiary level in Japan, where in many cases individual teachers work alone, there is little co-ordination between classes. There is also the related issue of the lack of links between what is learned at high school and university. Scaffolded, CEFR-informed curricula could be one solution, and this textbook provides a logical step from high school to university, and more critical thinking at tertiary level. The focus is to use the CEFR for action-oriented learning, with the purpose of creating level-appropriate learning materials informed by the CEFR levels and scales. The textbook encourages learners to engage with the scales of the CEFR, for example by asking learners to judge, and provide reasons, if the main points of an argument 'are explained in detail, with precision' (Council of Europe 2001:77). Once aware of what is expected, the learners can take action, step by step. By creating, planning, and working towards the goals of presenting arguments 'with precision', learners have to work out for themselves how the action of precisely presenting main arguments is performed, and then work towards efficiently using language in this way, step by step. Focusing on language features is one part of this action, but focus on language alone will not be sufficient. The learning outcome of writing with precision will only be successfully achieved by carefully focusing on the development of ideas through language. One important goal of the CEFR is suggested to learners: learner autonomy and lifelong learning. The learners see the logical steps to aim for next, and work towards achieving these steps. The editors of the textbook (Naganuma, Nagai and O'Dwyer (Eds) 2015) aimed to help learners navigating the lofty goals the CEFR has set for language learners and educators. These scaffolded steps can be implemented in a coherent manner by other textbooks. We now turn to using the CEFR in institutions and curricula, the main focus of the volume.

3 Language curricula

The following section summarises each case study in Chapters 6 to 9 of the volume, noting the positive points of the practices, with some possible improvements. We suggest that readers, while considering the various needs, aims, rationale and outcomes, think about which aspects they can replicate in order to improve upon the particular situation at the institution where they are teaching. As noted in sub-section 2.2 of Chapter 1, the key questions of the volume can make up a grid (Table 1) which can be used to assess and design elements of learning programmes (through curricula alignment, 'Can Do' contextualisation, incorporating principles of the CEFR like learner involvement and autonomy, etc.). We present this grid here, with a reference system (Keys 1–8) for the purpose of organising the following text.

Table 1 Assessment grid for learning programmes

Language learner can receive tuition informed by the following * = reasonably well, ** = well, *** = very well	*	**	***
Key 1: Teachers, students and other stakeholders accept the philosophy and ideas of the CEFR (e.g. learner-centred, forward-looking assessment)			
Key 2: In-house evaluation of curricula and learning targets, informed by the CEFR			
Key 3: It is possible to compare the results of instruction in different classes			
Key 4: People engaging in CEFR-informed teaching and learning develop a sense of ownership			
Key 5: All stakeholders are involved			
Key 6: All can readily apply, and see the benefits of the CEFR-informed approach for their own teaching/learning			
Key 7: 'Can Do' checklists serve as the key reference point for processes of reflective teaching/learning in which self-assessment plays a central role			
Key 8: Autonomous learning beyond the specified materials (e.g. textbooks) is supported and encouraged			

The reflections in Chapter 6 are useful for future practices of contextualising the CEFR within institutions where familiarity with the CEFR is low, and viewed with a certain amount of suspicion. Implementation is very much a top-down approach in Vietnam, focusing on using the CEFR as a testing and assessment tool for gatekeeping and validation purposes. As a result, there is a sense of distrust in the top-down policy among staff and students, with an over-focus on levels, with an under-appreciation of the underlying principles and practices. The teacher training and development practices developed in Hue are necessary to learn how to accommodate heterogeneous levels, and find agreement on which learning materials should be used to help learners feel they 'Can Do' things with the language. This chapter provides a template for institutions elsewhere in Vietnam and beyond to develop effective practices from the bottom-up, progressing the gradual process of going from little to greater acceptance of the CEFR in terms of four of the keys (1: acceptance of the ideas of the CEFR; 4: developing a sense of ownership; 5: involvement of stakeholders; 6: readily seeing benefits of a CEFR-informed approach).

Chapter 7 acknowledges the challenge facing large language programmes: maintaining pedagogically consistent methods across the many teachers, classes and students. The writers tackle this by prioritising helping students understand how to learn a language while promoting autonomous learning practices. While the full-time staff have 'bought-in' to this concept, it is difficult to force teachers to explicitly introduce these concepts into classroom activities, as they have not had sufficient exposure to the descriptors and their levels. They find it challenging to link activities and learning outcomes. The approach is to hope familiarisation will occur through socialisation and intermittent faculty development sessions. Stakeholders do not need to be aware of the framework within which they work to implement it. What is important is that teachers come on board, so that the learning enterprise links the top (e.g. progress through the levels of the CEFR via the scaled 'Can Do' descriptors, and career goals of learners) and bottom (e.g. activities of the next class).

The 'Can Do' descriptors in this context are suitably adapted and contextualised (e.g. the inclusion of additional qualifying words or explanation such as 'for half a minute', 'if preparation time is given' and 'while making use of dictionaries'). This provides a guide for teachers designing class activities, and also helps learners clarify the gap between current and desired performance in tangible ways. In these ways the practices are both action-oriented, and easily applicable. There are some concerns that statements about grammatical accuracy are used (North 2014:125). The writers recognise that an action research cycle-type activity to work on validation of the learning goals would be very helpful. Overall though, the learner-centred approach takes the local context into consideration (numbering levels according to Japanese tradition with the lowest level at 4 and the highest at 1), but also providing implicit motivation by naming B2+ as 'global', highlighting that while it may be a real challenge for the students it would be very rewarding to reach there or somewhere close. The processes are made more familiar to the user by informing them not only by briefing but by a handbook which can be accessed at any time. Similar to the two previous chapters, Chapter 7 presents ideas for those in similarly large-scale institutions who need to bring about a greater involvement and acceptance of the ideals of the CEFR (Key 1 and 5) in order to renew and bring transparency to curricula (Key 2), with 'Can Do' descriptors at the centre of the learning enterprise (Key 7). The writers introduce structured practices that encourage autonomous learning (Key 8).

Chapter 8 outlines how the CEFR can be used to bolster national priorities that filter down to universities through policy documents to develop 'global human resources': communication, cultural knowledge and understanding, and working skills. This is a good example of how using the underlying principles of the framework (multi-purpose, flexible, open, dynamic, user-friendly, and non-dogmatic), rather than the 'Can Do' descriptors of the CEFR, can be the starting point for action-oriented curriculum renewal (Key 1). The integration of an information and communications technology (ICT) platform and a content and language integrated learning (CLIL) aspect alongside the implementation of a CEFR-informed curriculum renewal also contributes to effective pedagogy. The 'Can Do' and CEFR approach are implicit: the teachers and students are unaware of the CEFR as a benchmark. Such a familiarisation process may not be feasible in this case. As long as the sound pedagogic goals are being implemented, this is perfectly fine. What is important is the need for engagement and widespread buy-in, which may not be maintained if the active individuals are not a constant presence. It would also be useful for self-reflection to understand the 'Can Do' descriptors behind the concept though, as this would be very useful for future learning activities outside of the traditional learning setting. The most prominent point for us in this case study is the support of autonomous learning beyond the classroom (Key 8), and the presentation of one way to implicitly cause acceptance of the ideas of the CEFR.

The motivation for the use of the CEFR in curriculum renewal in Chapter 9, to develop a sustainable teaching and learning environment to increase competitiveness in the face of a shrinking student population, is relevant for a lot of institutions. The real strong point of this outstanding contribution, which is at the core of this publication, is the extent to which the stakeholders are involved in using the CEFR (Key 5): a bottom-up approach is also combined with top-down support from administration. The classroom teachers and learning advisors in particular have developed a strong sense of ownership of the CEFR (Key 4). We suggest this stems from the familiarisation process of training workshops and the formation of teams to work on 'Can Do' lists for lessons. An important consideration was in relating the curriculum to the CEFR, not throwing away what already exists, once it is found to suit the needs of the learners in context. The process has not always gone smoothly, but there is the flexibility to change track and work on new action research cycles. Lessons are to start with a comprehensive overall plan (as the group did not), but also be ready to evolve gradually (as they are doing). This flexibility is easy to manage with a group of 10 full-time teachers. This staffing situation itself is an important contextual choice. To successfully redo and improve institution-wise curricula twice in such a short time (three years) is extremely rare.

The results, and future results, of Chapter 9 work towards meeting three main criteria of successful projects (North 2014:145): while future needs analysis is required there has been an efficient selection of 'Can Do' descriptors (see sub-section 6.1.4.4 of sub-chapter 9A), an informed contextualisation (with twin lists for staff and simpler versions for learners), and focused validation steps. The introduction of tests recognises the close interdependence between curriculum, pedagogy, and assessment that the CEFR implies (Little 2010:160). It can be argued that there is more room for reflective learning, with the current self-assessment focusing on checking 'Can Do' lists before and after classes. This is recognised in the second part of Chapter 9, and it remains to be seen if the ELP-type activities are implemented: specifically how learner autonomy can be promoted through actual lessons, how students' work is a source for teacher assessment, and how to give feedback on student reflections. Reflective learning has yet to be internalised into students' learning repertoire, both in self-access learning centre and classroom activities. Further challenges are recognised: CEFR adopters must go beyond the use of only 'Can Do' descriptor scales in order to claim true CEFR alignment. There is not enough reflection on how well learners are progressing according to the CEFR illustrative scales in this case. This should also be combined with the 'spiralled curriculum' formed when the same concepts are presented repeatedly, each time in more detail (Bruner 2009). It is very important to explain to the students why it is important to not only fill in forms, but use this way of self-reflection to improve their learning. To introduce the principles of the ELP is a very important and powerful aspect of guided learning. Overall though, this case is an exemplar for others who wish to harness the power of the first six keys (Key 4 and 5 are mentioned above; Key 1: acceptance of ideas of the CEFR within the institution; 2 and 3: evaluation of transparent curricula informed by the CEFR). As a result all can readily see the benefits of the CEFR-informed approach (Key 6).

Readers may refer to elements of Chapter 6 for Key 7 ('Can Do' checklists serving as the key reference point for reflective learning and self-assessment plays a central role) and Key 8 (the support of autonomous learning). Chapters 7 and 9 also show promise in the latter key. As noted in Chapter 6 though, one major challenge is applying the principles of the pedagogical function of the CEFR and ELP (i.e. learner involvement and reflection). For this reason classroom ideas found in the final section of the volume highlight how this has been foregrounded by enthusiastic practitioners in their classrooms.

4 Portfolio-based teaching

As noted in section 3 of Chapter 1, Chapter 10, 'A CEFR-informed e-portfolio in blended learning at a German university' by Astrid Buschmann-Göbels and Bärbel Kühn of the University of Bremen, discusses both the use of the CEFR in curricula and how CEFR-informed e-portfolios are implemented in blended learning supported by tutoring. The contextual choices taken in Bremen are based on a high level of familiarity with the CEFR. This allows the tutorial learning programme at the Language Centre there to set an example of how to work and learn with the principles of the CEFR and the European Language Portfolio (ELP). This is bolstered by the fact that Europe embraces a culture that encourages competence standards by focusing on the use of the 'Can Do' descriptors of the CEFR and the European

Qualifications Framework (EQF). While the reporting (of language learner experience and competency) function is generally foregrounded in Europe and worldwide, the writers suggest that in Bremen there is a strong belief that the ELP should be at the centre of learning, with a focus on a pedagogic function (foregrounding learner involvement and promoting learner autonomy). In the future, the institution plans further collaboration with the departments of the university to establish a pool of subject-related project topics, with the use of EPOS being an important tool in that respect. This is very important in terms of the impact of portfolios beyond the scope of university language centres. We suggest the exemplar elements of these practices include how the 'Can Do' checklists serve as the key reference point for reflective learning (Key 7), with autonomous learning clearly encouraged (Key 8). The level of familiarity encourages the 'buy-in' and involvement of stakeholders (Key 4 and 5) in the ideas of the CEFR (Key 1), which results in all seeing the learning benefits (Key 6). Chapter 10 features in this volume as it is an exemplar of how to use e-portfolios in conjunction with a tutoring system. We hope this is something that will play an important role in the future implementation of the CEFR in Japan and elsewhere. The classroom ideas that are discussed in the following chapters can be improved by integrating some elements of the e-portfolio and tutoring approaches. Nevertheless, there are several noteworthy practices contained in Chapters 11 to 13.

Chapter 11 illustrates how to make non-CEFR-informed materials (textbooks) action-oriented and easily applicable by both teachers and students. This demonstrates how CEFR and ELP adaptation can be used and implemented as a reflection and achievement tool for any teaching (material) that is not originally CEFR informed. It also presents the challenges, and the steps enthusiastic teachers must go through to effectively contextualise their classes and make classes more principled. These include making the ELP itself more relevant and appealing. Learners require more explanation of why the ELP is important and effective. This is similar in ways to what was experienced at Bunkyo (Chapter 9), as the marking of the sheets alone is not effective self-assessment or self-reflection. Reflective practices need to be integrated into learner behaviour in a more sustained manner. Chapter 12 exemplifies this, by outlining how 'Can Do' checklists serve as the key reference point for processes of reflective learning in which self-assessment plays a central role. This comes in a strong form of self-regulated learning (cyclical phases of self-regulated learning, forethought phase, performance phase, and self-reflection phase). The ELP is the property of the learner, but also part of the classroom teaching as well. Integrating the practices clearly into classroom practices separates this example from surface-only implementation of the CEFR (e.g. textbooks which merely present 'Can Do' descriptors at the top of pages). There is also a connection with how the writers of Chapter 5 have tried to configure textbook practices to clearly integrate the illustrative scales of the CEFR.

Assessment of CEFR-informed Language Teaching in Japan and Beyond

The remaining classroom example (Chapter 13) highlights the need and importance of a 'Can Do' list for Chinese, or indeed for any language learning enterprise. 'Can Do' lists are created with all instructors teaching the same content for each language at the faculty, and used to help students realise the need of communication abilities which are not included in a basic, regular textbook. They can therefore control their own learning. The 'Can Do' descriptor list is just like a guidebook: it informs the students how and what Chinese they should learn both in China and in Japan. The learners reflecting before and after their study trip abroad draws their attention to the strengths and gaps in their learning (e.g. being able to interact with shop assistants in an informal and non-standardised manner). This process illuminates a relevant learning map for students. These practices are timely and forward looking, supporting current and future student learning. Other related practices include the exchange of information to improve learning (e.g. teacher and peer dialogue around learning, like defining a good task performance), and promoting reflective gap-closing practices (O'Dwyer and de Boer 2015) that involve developing assessment, self-assessment and reflection abilities in order to progress learning. The latter provide opportunities to close the gap between current and desired performance.

5 Bringing critical and constructive assessments of the CEFR-informed language teaching forward

The case studies featured here represent some successfully implemented CEFR-informed practices. As mentioned, readers can highlight both the aspects they can replicate and find suggestions to improve their pedagogic practices. We sum up the key strands of this volume in the following keywords: action research, contextual choices, engagement, familiarisation, and (applying) principles. When using the CEFR in language learning enterprises it is very important to consider the contextual choices, one of which is the level of familiarity of stakeholders with the principles and practices of the CEFR. We suggest the most important of these principles, at least in Japan, are the promotion of transparency (in learning goals), and learner autonomy: helping learners identify and work towards bridging the gap between current and desired performance. An action research perspective can be applied by educators, and groups of educators and other stakeholders, to engage together to incrementally improve practices towards these and other relevant goals. We humbly suggest that this volume is one resource to access when working towards harnessing the simple power of the CEFR.

References

Bruner, J (2009) *The Process of Education*, London: Harvard University Press.

Council of Europe (2001) *Common European Framework of Reference for Languages: Learning, Teaching, Assessment*, Cambridge: Cambridge University Press.

Little, D (2010) The European Language Portfolio and self-assessment: Using 'I can' checklists to plan, monitor and evaluate language learning, in Schmidt, M G, Naganuma, N, O'Dwyer, F, Imig, A and Sakai, K (Eds) *Can Do Statements in Language Education in Japan and Beyond – Applications of the CEFR* (2nd edition), Tokyo: Asahi Press, 157–166.

Naganuma, N, Nagai, N and O'Dwyer, F (Eds) (2015) *Connections to Thinking in English: The CEFR-informed Textbook Series A2+/B1 to B1+*, Tokyo: Asahi Press.

North, B (2014) *The CEFR in Practice*, English Profile Studies volume 4, Cambridge: UCLES/Cambridge University Press.

O'Dwyer, F and de Boer, M (2015) Approaches to assessment in CLIL classrooms: Two case studies, *Language Learning in Higher Education* 5 (2), 397–421.

Author index

A
Akdoğan, G 177
Aksu, M 285
Alderson, J C 42, 211
Alvarez, J A 177
ALTE *see* Association of Language Testers in Europe (ALTE)
Association of Language Testers in Europe (ALTE) 194, 216, 218, 254, 271
Atkinson, L 177
Atobe, S 24, 28

B
Bachman, L F 125
Barboni, S 4
Bornickel, M 272, 281
Bower, J, 194, 203, 214
Branch, R M 224
Broek, S 6
Brown, H D 71
Brown, J D 193
Brown, P 177, 204, 208
Bruner, J 186, 320
Burns, A 104
Buschmann-Göbels, A 272, 281
Butler, Y G 168
Byram, M 4, 6, 21, 29

C
Cambridge English 42, 193, 215, 223, 230, 250, 255,
Carr, N 250
Chamot, A U 71
Chauncey Group International 121
Clare, A 103
Clark, G 288
Clement, R 6
Collett, P 24, 139
Cosgrove, A 103
Coste, D 3, 5
Council of Europe 3, 5, 9, 13, 18, 25, 33, 37, 38, 49, 57, 67, 77, 79, 80, 87, 92, 97, 98, 118, 119, 121, 123, 128, 129, 136, 142, 155, 157, 158, 160, 165, 170, 171, 175, 176, 177, 180, 185, 190, 192, 193, 194, 218, 228, 229, 231, 231, 233, 237, 238, 242, 257, 269, 270, 285, 292, 293, 294, 303, 304, 315, 316
Coxhead, A 126, 153
Creswell, J W 179
Crowley, K 177, 204, 248

D
Davies, P A 103
Deaux, G 29
de Boer, M 155, 168, 170, 322
DIALANG 42
Dougiamas, M 158
Dummett, P 106

E
Eaquals 215, 218, 219, 223, 254, 271
Eiken Foundation of Japan 20, 49, 51, 54, 55, 56, 61
Ellis, R 68, 69, 218
English First 223
English UK 223
European Centre for Modern Languages 25, 41
European Organization for Nuclear Research 216

F
Faez, F 177, 204, 248
Falla, T 103
Figueras, N 6, 18, 29
Filipović, L 81–84, 100
Foale, A 178, 203, 214, 226
Forest, E 224, 259
Fowler, F 242
Fulcher, G 138

G
Gardner, D 226
Germain-Rutherford, A 6
Glover, P, 285
Goullier, F 203, 295
Gonzalez, J 285
Green, A 186
Grow, G 227

Author index

H
Habakari, S 57
Hamana, E 29
Hamid, M O 97, 101, 107
Harada, Y 24, 28
Harsch, C 208
Hawkins, J A 81, 83, 84, 100
Hodel, H 57
Hogan, M J 177
Holzman, L 163
Horiguchi, S 24, 28
Hosoki, Y 176
Hu, G 97
Hughes, J 106, 295
Huhta, A 42
Hymes, D 125

I
Imig, A 9, 20, 23, 24
Imoto, Y 24, 28, 29
Iwasa, Y 29

J
Jacobsen, N 204
Japan Association of Language Teaching Framework and Language Portfolio Special Interest Group 4, 6, 20,
Japan Broadcasting Corporation 20
Japan Foundation 12, 20, 22,
Jones, D 54

K
Kaisetsu kyoiku roppo henshu iinkai 53
Keddle, J 177, 222
Kemmis, S 104
Keskin, M N 177
Kimura, K 57
Kindai University Faculty of Applied Sociology, Department of General Education, English Language Learning Program Management Team 125
Kitagawa, T 29
Kodate, A 203, 214
Kohonen, V 57, 289
Koike, I 19, 26, 51
Kono, T 29
Krause-Ono, M 24
Kuroiwa, Y 29

L
Lazenby Simpson, B 177
Le, V C 98
Lindgren, R 280
Little, D 5, 8, 57, 62, 100, 119, 125, 139, 177, 180, 184, 203, 228, 231, 232, 233, 234, 240, 269, 270, 285, 290, 295, 319
Lockwood, J 177

Luoma, S 203, 248
Luske Lehde, L 203, 214

M
Macaro, E 119
Majhanovich, S 177, 204, 248
Majima, J 12, 19, 20, 23
Manasseh, A 177
Martin, G 208
Martyniuk, W 6, 7, 33, 37, 38
Matsubara, K, 29
Matsutani, M 180
McConnell, D 162
McDaniel, R 280
McKay, S L 97
McNiff, J 9, 104, 175, 179
McTaggart, R 104
Meijer, D 57
Messick, S 250
Miller, L 226
Ministry of Education and Training 97, 98, 99
Ministry of Education, Culture, Sports, Science and Technology 12, 20, 49, 50, 51, 52, 53, 54, 56, 78 79, 81, 122
Miric, I 285
Miura, T 257
Mochizuki, N, 29
Morrow, K 6

N
Nagai, N 4, 9, 22, 23, 24, 77, 79, 139, 188, 226, 316
Naganuma, N 20, 23, 24, 77, 79, 122, 316
Nagasue, A 122
Negishi, M 6, 12, 19, 20, 22, 23, 45, 51, 79, 175, 180, 188, 191, 203, 212, 229
Newman, F 163
Nguyen, T M H 98
Nguyen, V H 97, 101, 107
Nitta, K 120, 203
Nijnikova, M 272, 281
Noijons, J 6, 7, 33, 37, 38
North, B 5, 6, 10, 11, 13, 20, 42, 81, 100, 102, 132, 138, 142, 177, 180, 181, 185, 191, 192, 215, 219, 223, 231, 318, 319
Nunan, D 218

O
Ohashi, R 19
O'Dwyer, F 4, 9, 20, 22, 23, 24, 77, 79, 139, 168, 184, 188, 226, 285, 316, 322
O'Malley, J M 71
Onaka, N 155
Ortega, A 81, 215, 219, 223
Osborne, J W 201
Oyabu, K 31

Assessment of CEFR-informed Language Teaching in Japan and Beyond

P
Paris, S G 238, 239
Palmer, D 125
Parmenter, L 3, 4, 6, 21, 29
Paydon, S 138
Perclova, R 57
Pham, T H N 13, 98, 101, 114
Piccardo, E 6
Pollit, A 42, 215, 223
Porto, M 4
Purpura, J E 42, 215, 223

R
Ramirez, C 128
Reinders, H 279
Research and Validation Group, University of Cambridge 125
Richards, J C 218
Ridley, J 119
Robertson, C 138
Rodgers, T S 218
Rogers, E M 35, 39
Roth, A 103
Runnels, J 44, 184, 188, 194
Rutson-Griffiths, A 194, 203, 214

S
Sakai, S 20, 23, 24, 25
Sarayköylü, B 177
Saito, Y 295
Sato, M 119, 131, 139
Sato, Y 24, 119, 289
Schärer, R 62
Schmid-Burleson,B 103
Schmidt, M G 20, 23, 24
Schneider, G 119, 125, 285, 289
Semmelroth, A 185, 203, 214
Sheehan, S 81, 215, 219, 223
Sheerin, S 232
Shimo, E 120, 137, 203
Shimozaki, M 29
Shufflebeam, D L 11
Sisamakis, E 285
Slater, A 29
Smith, A 139
Smith, M 177, 204, 248
Soars, J 286
Soars, L 286
Society for Testing English Proficiency 121
State of New South Wales, Department of Education and Training 179
Steiner-Khamsi,G 98
Stephenson, H 106
Sugg, R 194,
Sugitani, M 4, 19, 20, 21, 22, 23, 24, 30, 31
Sullivan, K 24, 139

Swan, M 168
Swain, M 71

T
Takada, T 51, 57, 191, 203, 212, 229
Takala, S 6
Taylor, S 177, 204, 248
Test of English for Academic Purposes 20
The Japan Foundation 12, 20, 22, 67, 68, 73, 74, 75, 315
The Japan Foundation Japanese Language Institute 74, 75
Thompson, G 177, 178, 226
Tomita, Y 4, 19, 20, 21, 22, 23, 24, 30, 31
Tomura, R, 57
Tono, Y 6, 11, 12, 19, 20, 23, 44, 45, 51, 79, 81, 175, 180, 188, 191, 203, 212, 215, 229, 230, 231, 238, 286
Trim, J L M 81, 100, 198, 215, 217, 218, 219, 223, 227, 228, 230, 237, 257
Tsagari, D 211
Tsutimoto, C 29
Turner, J C 238, 239

U
University of Cambridge 125, 215, 223, 230
University of Cambridge ESOL Examinations 193, 215, 223, 230, 250
Üstünluoğlü, E 177

V
Valax, P 38, 39, 180, 211
Van den Ende, I 6
van Ek, J A 81, 198, 215, 217, 218, 219, 223, 227, 228, 230, 237, 257

W
Wada, M 49, 54, 56, 61
Wall, P 177
Ware, J L 138
Wasik, B A 238, 239
Watanabe, Y, 29
Whitehead, J 9, 104, 175, 179
Williams, S H 58
Willis, D 168, 218
Willis, J 168, 218
Wilson, J J 103
Wright, S 98

Y
Yoshijima, S 19
Yui, R 29

Z
Zarate, J A 177
Zazaoğlu, K F A 177
Zimmerman, B J 292, 294, 295, 302

Subject index

A
Alignment
 individual achievement to global standards 4
Action-oriented approach 9–10, 13, 23, 52–53, 59–61, 67, 74, 78, 82–93, 112–113, 119–120, 140–141, 155–174, 231, 257–258, 279–283, 285, 316, 318, 321
Academic Word List 126, 146, 153
Action research approach 175, 179
 Collect and Analyse Evidence 179, 194–200, 219
 Reflect 179, 200–211, 222
 Study and Plan 179, 180–183, 214–219
 Take Action 179, 184–194, 219–222
ADDIE *see* Analyse-Design-Develop-Implement-Evaluate model (ADDIE)
AJE *see* Japan Association for Language Teaching (AJE)
ALTE *see* Association of Language Testers in Europe (ALTE)
Analyse-Design-Develop-Implement-Evaluate model (ADDIE) 224–225, 259–261
Assessment
 Bunkyo English Test (BET) redesign 193, 200
 Bunkyo English Test (BET) specifications 255, 261
 criteria 59–60
 dynamic assessment xii, 168, 171, 173
 formative assessment 282, 290
 Cambridge English: Key (KET) modelling 193
 method 52, 56, 62
 Oxford Online Placement Test (OOPT) 42, 47, 215, 223, 243, 245, 263
 rubrics 128, 138, 145, 162–164, 166, 247, 250, 259
 standardised tests 22, 61, 113, 181, 193, 247, 259
 streaming 30, 200–201

Association of Language Testers of Europe (ALTE) 63, 194, 216, 218, 254, 261, 263, 271
Authentic communication 53, 133, 145, 307
Authentic materials 309
Autonomous learning *see* Learner autonomy

B
BECC *see* Bunkyo English Communication Center (BECC)
Behavioural objective 52
BET *see* Bunkyo English Test (BET)
Blended learning viii, 14, 15, 103, 115, 269–284, 320
Bunkyo English Communication Center (BECC) xii, xv, 176–178, 180, 182–185, 190–193, 198, 202, 203, 207–208, 211–217, 219, 222, 224, 226–228, 233, 235, 238, 242, 247–250, 254, 256, 259, 261, 264

C
Cambridge English exams 45
'Can Do' descriptors 3, 4, 5, 6, 8, 10, 12, 14, 15, 22, 23, 24, 25, 31, 32, 36, 43, 44, 52, 53, 55, 58, 59, 64, 67, 68, 69, 70, 73, 74, 75, 78, 82, 87, 88, 90, 91, 92, 101, 105, 106, 108, 109, 110, 111, 120, 122, 127, 128, 132, 136, 137, 138, 139, 141, 145, 146, 149, 155, 165, 166, 167, 168, 169, 170, 176, 181, 182, 183, 184, 185, 186, 187, 188, 189, 190, 191, 192, 194, 197, 198, 199, 200, 202, 203, 204, 205, 206, 207, 208, 209, 210, 211, 212, 213, 218, 219, 222, 223, 224, 225, 229, 230, 231, 233, 237, 241, 247, 248, 249, 250, 251, 254, 255, 256, 257, 258, 259, 263, 274, 282, 286, 287, 288, 289, 290, 292, 293, 295, 297, 300, 301, 302, 305, 316, 318, 319, 320, 321
'Can Do' lists xiv, 12, 17, 30, 43, 44, 47, 49, 50, 51, 52, 53, 54, 55, 56, 59, 61, 62, 63, 64, 78, 79, 121, 122, 157, 158, 160, 163, 166, 167, 169, 170, 319, 322

CEFR *see* Common European Framework of Reference for Languages (CEFR)
Common European Framework of Reference for Languages (CEFR) 3, 16, 18, 20, 45, 46, 47, 48, 49, 62, 63, 67, 76, 77, 81, 93, 97, 116, 117, 118, 146, 155, 173, 175, 261, 262, 265, 269, 284, 285, 291, 292, 302, 303, 311, 315, 323
  aims 3, 6, 9, 10, 11, 19, 25, 30, 31, 51, 141, 162, 177, 203, 211, 219, 283, 286, 320
  application of the 5, 16, 19, 20, 22, 23, 28, 30, 34, 40, 41, 44, 45, 46, 47, 62, 64, 97, 101, 114, 115, 138, 146, 147, 263, 291, 323
  as a common language 4, 5, 51, 61
  assessment grid for learning programmes 10, 317, 320
  CEFR-informed textbooks 20, 74, 78, 80, 315
  contextualisation of 5, 10, 41, 79, 317, 319
  critical assessment of the 4
  criticism of 5, 24, 25, 114, 205
  familiarisation 13, 14, 118, 132, 138, 142, 171, 182, 204, 207, 318–319, 322
  implementation 44, 45, 62, 115, 138, 145, 148, 160, 161, 169, 171, 184, 280, 282, 315, 319, 321
  influence/impact 5, 19, 20, 21, 22, 29, 32, 37, 47, 49
  informed curriculum 23, 224, 248, 319
  informed practices 11, 12, 14, 40, 322
  international use of 4, 47
  Japanese version *see* CEFR-J
  lack of understanding 35, 36, 40
  levels 5, 12, 30, 31, 92, 101, 146, 147, 157, 176, 190, 193, 211, 215, 222, 223, 250, 259, 316
  local standards 23, 36, 44, 98
  policy issues of the 3, 6, 21
  principles and practices of 4, 5, 7, 8, 9, 10, 11, 12, 14, 25, 40, 53, 67, 74, 77, 78, 79, 81, 91, 129, 138, 139, 142, 143, 144, 146, 202, 229, 269, 315, 317, 320, 322
  proficiency levels 6, 23, 31, 32, 51, 54, 60, 61, 100, 102, 121, 176, 211, 315
  proficiency scale (6-level) 3, 315
  pre-A1 6, 23, 51, 191, 194, 195, 196, 197, 206, 215, 216, 220, 230, 243, 252
  requirements when used by teachers 19, 36–37, 41–45, 50, 98–115, 133, 144–146, 207–211, 216
  self-assessment grid 8, 176, 181, 184, 187, 191, 193, 202, 211, 215
  supplementary resources 20, 35–45, 77–93, 211, 214–215, 223, 249, 259

  skills 51, 77, 169, 191, 193, 204, 205, 226, 228
  use 3, 4, 5, 6, 7, 8, 10, 11, 12, 13, 14, 15, 16, 17, 18, 19, 21, 22, 23, 24, 25, 26, 28, 30, 31, 32, 33, 34, 35, 36, 37, 38, 40, 41, 42, 43, 44, 46, 50, 51, 54, 61, 78, 81, 88, 92, 98, 99, 100, 101, 102, 106, 107, 108, 109, 111, 113, 114, 115, 121, 136, 155, 159, 160, 167, 168, 170, 180, 182, 183, 184, 191, 194, 200, 203, 204, 205, 206, 209, 210, 211, 212, 218, 222, 249, 250, 253, 256, 270, 274, 282, 283, 286, 288, 290, 304, 315, 316, 318, 319, 320, 321
Common European Framework of Reference (CEFR) in Japan 70, 72, 74, 76, 77, 78, 79, 80, 81, 82, 84, 86, 88, 90, 92, 94, 98, 100, 102, 104, 106, 108, 110, 112, 114, 116, 120, 122, 124, 126, 128, 130, 132, 134, 136, 138, 140, 142, 144, 146, 148, 150, 152, 154, 156, 158, 160, 162, 166, 168, 170, 172, 174, 175, 176, 177, 178, 180, 182, 184, 186, 188, 190, 192, 194, 196, 198, 200, 202, 204, 206, 208, 210, 212, 214, 216, 218, 220, 222, 224, 226, 228, 229, 230, 232, 234, 236, 238, 240, 242, 244, 246, 248, 250, 252, 254, 256, 258, 260, 262, 263, 264, 266, 270, 272, 274, 278, 280, 282, 284, 286, 288, 290, 294, 296, 298, 300, 302, 304, 306, 308, 310, 316, 318, 320, 321, 322
  history 18, 19, 20, 21, 23, 44, 184
  Japanese translation 19, 20, 21, 26, 189
  present role 11, 18, 226
  usage 18, 19, 24, 27, 28, 35, 44, 184
CEFR-J 8, 15, 6, 11, 13, 14, 17, 18, 19, 20, 21, 23, 26, 30, 38, 39, 42, 43, 44, 45, 47, 48, 50, 51, 56, 62, 63, 64, 79, 81, 93, 94, 175, 176, 177, 178, 179, 180, 181, 182, 183, 184, 185, 187, 190, 191, 192, 193, 194, 195, 196, 197, 198, 199, 200, 201, 202, 203, 204, 205, 206, 207, 208, 209, 210, 211, 212, 213, 214, 215, 221, 222, 224, 226, 227, 229, 230, 231, 235, 237, 238, 241, 242, 243, 246, 247, 248, 251, 253, 254, 256, 257, 259, 263, 264, 286, 287, 288, 289, 290, 291
  proficiency levels 176, 211
  resources 17, 38, 47, 64, 94, 200, 212, 214, 291
  self-assessment grid 176, 181, 184, 187, 191, 193, 202, 211, 215
  pre-A1 6, 23, 51, 191, 194, 197, 206, 243
  use 13, 44, 94, 175, 176, 177, 179, 181, 182, 183, 185, 187, 189, 191, 193, 194,

Subject index

195, 197, 199, 200, 201, 202, 203, 205, 207, 209, 211, 213, 215, 217, 219, 221, 223, 224, 227, 229, 231, 233, 235, 237, 239, 241, 243, 245, 247, 249, 251, 253, 255, 257, 259, 261, 263, 264, 265, 288, 291
Classroom language education 5
Communicative ability 69, 310
Curriculum
  behavioural objective 293, 294
  development 23, 35–36, 38, 114, 136, 141–142, 144, 177, 223–225, 260
  foreign language 175, 178
  key questions for 7–8, 90
  university 171

D

Delivery and Organization scales 79–80
Descriptive and Argumentative scales 80, 87–88
DIALANG 42, 45

E

EAP *see* English for Academic Purposes (EAP)
ECML *see* European Centre of Modern Languages
EFL *see* English as a foreign language (EFL)
English as a foreign language (EFL) 14, 30, 33, 175, 264
English for Academic Purposes (EAP) 12, 20, 29, 47, 77, 81, 316
English language education 19, 28, 49, 64, 115, 116, 146, 175
English language programme 31, 32, 118, 123
ELP *see* European Language Portfolio (ELP)
e-portfolio 14, 15, 90, 269, 270, 271, 273, 274, 278, 282, 283, 320, 321
  Elektronisches Europaisches Portfolio der Sprachen (EPOS) 15, 269, 270, 271, 273, 274, 275, 278, 279, 281, 282, 283, 321
EPOS *see* e-portfolio, Elektronisches Europaisches Portfolio der Sprachen (EPOS)
European Centre of Modern Languages (ECML) 25
European Language Passport 282
Europass 270
European Language Portfolio (ELP) 5, 8, 9, 12, 14, 15–16, 26, 42, 45, 57, 62–64, 72, 77, 79, 81, 82, 87, 91, 106, 118, 119, 125, 147, 185, 203, 226, 228, 229, 232, 233, 234, 242, 245, 246, 247, 261–262, 269, 270, 281, 282, 283, 284, 285, 286, 289, 290–292, 294, 295, 302, 320, 321, 323
  in Japan 26–27, 57–59, 62, 72–73, 77, 79, 81–82, 91, 106, 118, 119, 125, 185, 203, 226–247, 285–286, 289–290, 292–302, 320, 321
  in a non-CEFR informed course 14, 285–291, 321
Evaluation 17, 63, 81, 93, 134, 225, 235, 242, 295, 296, 297
  expert feedback 14, 181, 182, 184, 203
explicit learning 12, 68, 69, 71, 237, 305
Extensive reading 127

F

Faculty Development (FD) 13, 131–132, 135–138, 318
FD *see* Faculty Development (FD)
Foreign language education (in Japan) 18–19, 22, 24, 25, 28, 29, 38, 44
Foreign languages (other than English)
  Chinese and Ming 33, 46, 99, 124, 303–307, 310, 322
  French 19, 28, 29, 30, 31, 33, 99, 124, 261, 275
  German 19, 28, 29, 30, 31, 273, 275, 281, 303
  Japanese 12, 19, 22, 23, 33, 44, 67, 68, 69, 74
Foreign language programmes 23, 29, 30, 99
Forethought phase 292, 294–295, 298, 302, 321
Fremdsprachenzentrum der Hochschulen im Land Bremen (FZHB) 272, 279, 282
FZHB *see* Fremdsprachenzentrum der Hochschulen im Land Bremen (FZHB)

G

Goethe-Institut Start Deutsch 31
General Service List 126, 148
General Test of English Language Proficiency (G-TELP) 30
Global Test of English Communication (GTEC) 30, 122, 147
Goal setting/learning goal 25, 79, 88, 92, 126, 133, 134, 135 136, 137, 139, 141, 144, 180, 202, 203, 226, 237, 248, 252, 257, 263, 273, 274, 278, 280, 281, 282, 290, 291, 295, 300, 310, 318, 322
G-TELP *see* General Test of English Language Proficiency (G-TELP)
GTEC *see* Global Test of English Communication (GTEC)

I
ICT *see* Learning management system (LMS), Information and Communications Technology (ICT)
Implicit learning 12, 68, 69, 70
Individual learning 6, 278, 279, 283
Inferencing 71, 75
Informal learning 272, 283
Input 71, 76, 159, 188, 218, 238, 257, 315
Institutional size 123
Intercultural understanding 67, 68, 72, 124, 316
International influence 47

J
JALT *see* Japanese Association of Language Teaching (JALT)
Japanese Association of Language Teaching (JALT) 4, 6, 20–21, 33, 47, 93, 147–148, 173, 263–264
 Framework and Language Portfolio Special Interest Group (FLP SIG) 4, 6, 17, 20–21, 33, 46, 48, 90, 93–94, 185
Japan Association for Language Teaching (AJE) 6, 19–21, 46, 93, 147–148, 173, 185
Japan Broadcasting Cooperation (NHK) 20, 21, 44, 46
Japan Foundation (JF) 12, 20–22, 46, 67–68, 73–76, 315
Japan Foundation Standard for Japanese Language Education (JFS) 22, 67–68, 74, 315
Japanese Eiken Foundation for English 20
Japanese Language Proficiency Test (JLPT) 20, 67
Japanese as a foreign language (JFL) 12, 19, 21, 28
JF *see* Japan Foundation (JF)
JFS *see* Japan Foundation Standard for Japanese Language Education (JFS)
JLPT *see* Japanese Language Proficiency Test (JLPT)
JSPS *see* Research projects, Grant in Aid Japan Society for the Promotion of Science (JSPS)

K
Katsudo (communicative language activities) 68–70, 74, 76
KCF *see* Kindai Common Framework (KCF) Curriculum
Kindai Common Framework (KCF) Curriculum
 'Can Do' descriptors and CEFR descriptors 122–123, 132–146

 goals 119–121, 124–126, 130–139, 142
 levels 121
 methods and measures 125–131
 ownership (of) 134–135
 purpose 120–121
 revision 124

L
Language biography 57, 125, 270, 286, 292, 295, 296, 297, 298, 299, 300, 302
Language Center(s)
 University of Bremen 269, 272, 281, 282, 320
Language functions 178, 183, 203, 211, 222, 224–225, 248, 260, 262
Language learning biography 274
Language learning counselling
 counselling 279, 281, 284
 learning counselling 271, 273, 278
 language counselling 272, 284
Language learning strategies 76, 110, 111, 114, 238, 281, 315
Language passport 57, 125, 270, 282, 286, 295
Language portfolio 4–6, 12, 14, 16, 17, 20, 26, 42, 45, 48, 57, 62–64, 72, 77, 81, 87–88, 90, 93–94, 106, 118, 147, 185, 228, 261–262, 264, 269, 284–292, 292–295, 300–302, 320, 323
Language portfolio for Japanese University 90
Learner
 learner as a language user 53–54, 60, 99, 102, 110, 120, 309
 learner as stakeholder 13, 26, 76
 learner-centred pedagogy 3, 7, 10, 74, 119, 173, 256, 282, 283, 310, 315, 317, 318
 learner involvement in pedagogical decisions 15, 57, 231, 232, 234, 236, 240, 317, 320, 321
Learner autonomy 5, 8, 10, 16, 24, 25, 52, 56, 57, 59, 61, 64, 79, 82, 92, 106, 110, 111, 115, 119, 122, 137, 142, 143, 146, 147, 148, 211, 226, 227, 228, 229, 231, 232, 233, 236, 237, 240, 241, 243, 245, 246, 247, 262, 269, 270, 273, 279, 284, 285, 316, 320, 321, 322
 ability to learn 227
 autonomous learning 4, 9, 10, 12, 22, 26, 75, 110, 115, 120, 122, 142, 143, 144, 145, 146, 170, 175, 177, 226, 228, 248, 258, 259, 266, 273, 281, 305, 310, 311, 317, 318, 319, 320, 321
 autonomy, 5, 10, 43, 62, 77, 113, 119, 120, 127, 137, 142, 147, 228, 233, 236, 240, 262, 270, 273, 278, 279, 284, 301, 316, 317

330

Subject index

behavioural objective 234, 294
ELP 5, 8, 9, 12, 15, 26, 57, 62, 72, 77, 79, 81, 91, 106, 118–119, 125, 185, 203, 226, 228–229, 232–233, 242, 245–247, 261, 269–270, 281–286, 289–290, 292, 294, 320, 321
  evaluation 60, 73, 88, 110–111, 120–123, 126, 129, 131–134, 137, 140–146, 198, 203, 228–233, 244, 247–248, 255, 271–281, 287–290, 295–301
  goal-setting 126, 135, 137, 144
  learner involvement 15, 57, 231, 232, 234, 240, 317, 320, 321
  learning how to learn 227
  monitoring 11, 160, 226, 229, 230, 233, 245, 246
  planning 25, 41, 43, 55, 88, 92, 137, 171, 172, 179, 201, 202, 214, 229, 233, 234, 239, 246, 257, 259, 266, 272, 274, 280, 282, 286, 316
  reflection 8, 9, 12, 14, 57, 58, 59, 64, 74, 80, 82, 87, 88, 97, 104, 107, 109, 111, 114, 126, 129, 134, 135, 137, 139, 143, 183, 184, 201, 212, 224, 229, 231, 232, 233, 235, 241, 242, 246, 247, 249, 251, 255, 258, 260, 263, 270, 273, 278, 283, 287, 289, 291, 292, 294, 295, 299, 301, 302, 319, 320, 321, 322
  self-directedness 8, 227, 232, 262, 288, 294
Learner novice 43
Learner reflection 14, 57–58, 231, 233, 240–242
  activities 233–234
  implementation 14
Learning attainment target 12, 43, 50–54, 56–57, 59–64
Learning cycle 88, 89, 91, 93, 184, 188, 255, 263
Learning goals 25, 79, 88, 92, 133–134, 136, 139, 141, 180, 203, 226, 244, 248, 252, 257, 273–274, 278, 280–282, 290, 295, 300, 303–306, 308, 310, 318, 322
Learning management system (LMS) 158
  Moodle 158, 160, 162–163, 173, 282
  Information and Communications Technology (ICT) 155, 158–161, 165–173, 246, 318
  Information and Communications Technology (ICT) contents platform 155, 159–161, 167–169
Learning outcome 9–11, 31–32, 43, 59, 92, 98, 101–102, 105–110, 112–117, 138, 141–142, 220–221, 271, 316, 318
Learning spaces 271, 272
Lesson material 59, 60, 183, 187, 190, 199, 200, 211, 219, 220, 222, 223, 233, 241, 257, 258

alignment with CEFR-J 183, 187, 190, 199–200, 211
difficulty 7, 31, 36, 44, 55, 56, 74, 86, 120, 122, 123, 128, 143, 150, 151, 163, 181, 183, 185, 187, 191, 193, 194, 195, 196, 197, 201, 204, 205, 206, 208, 209, 210, 213, 264, 304, 310
Level of proficiency 103, 107–108, 112
Lifelong learning 5, 52–53, 61, 63, 294, 316
Linguistic pluralism 14, 124
LMS *see* Learning management system (LMS)

M

Marugoto 12, 67, 68, 69, 70, 71, 72, 73, 74, 76
METI *see* Ministry of Economy, Trade, and Industry
MEXT *see* Ministry of Education, Culture, Sports and Science and Technology, Japan
Minna no 'Can-do' Website 68, 70, 73
Ministry of Economy, Trade, and Industry (METI) 155, 156, 157, 161, 165, 170, 171, 172, 173
Ministry of Education, Culture, Sports and Science and Technology, Japan (MEXT) 12, 20, 29, 32, 38, 39, 43, 49, 50, 51, 52, 53, 54, 57, 60, 61, 62, 78, 122
Moodle 158, 160, 162, 163, 173, 282
Motivation 50, 100, 119, 169, 180, 203, 228, 232, 257, 263, 272, 274, 285, 289, 294–295, 309, 318–319
My next language learning target 88

N

NHK *see* Japan Broadcasting Cooperation (NHK)

O

OOPT *see* Assessment, Oxford Online Placement Test (OOPT)
Oral testing 128, 147
Out-of-classroom learning 272
Output 36, 42, 71, 76, 188, 212, 238, 257, 315
Output hypothesis 71
Oxford Online Placement Test (OOPT) 215

P

Partner Exchange Teacher (PET) System 128, 130, 133, 134, 135, 136, 140, 145, 264

Performance 23, 36, 37, 52, 56, 60, 68, 70, 73, 74, 78, 81, 102, 127, 129, 133, 136, 140, 147, 168, 184, 188, 192, 193, 208, 254, 256, 282, 292, 294, 295, 302, 318, 321, 322
Performance phase 292, 294, 302, 321
PET *see* Partner Exchange Teacher (PET) System
Pluricultural competence 293, 297
Plurilingual competence 293
Plurilingualism 3, 231, 269
Portfolio approach 14, 15, 22, 72, 75, 267, 269
PPP *see* Presentation-Practice-Production (PPP) model
Presentation-Practice-Production (PPP) model 68, 74, 237, 240, 241
Proficiency standards 4, 22, 23
Project work 271, 273–274, 281

Q

Questionnaire 26, 33, 55, 121, 137, 274, 281, 287, 304–305, 310

R

Real-life communication 305
Reception 161, 172, 262
Reflection 8, 9, 12, 14, 49, 57, 58–59, 64, 72, 74, 80, 82, 87–88, 92, 97, 102, 104–105, 107, 109, 111, 114, 126, 129, 134–135, 137, 139, 142–144, 180, 183–184, 201–205, 212, 224, 231–233, 235, 240–243, 246–249, 251, 255, 258, 260, 263, 270, 273, 278, 282, 283, 287, 289, 291, 299, 320–322
Reflective learning 8–9, 15, 35, 47, 57, 59, 67, 82, 87, 90, 93, 139, 147, 169, 259, 291–292, 303, 316, 319–321
Research projects
  Grant in Aid Japan Society for the Promotion of Science (JSPS) 3, 18, 64, 93
  Kaken database 26–29, 93
  Japanese universities 20, 33, 37, 176, 180
Rikai (communicative language competences) 68–69, 71, 73, 76
Reference point 8–10, 15, 59, 90, 106, 137, 169, 255, 263, 292, 303, 317, 320–321

S

Scaled descriptors 23
Secondary school 12, 21, 38, 42–44, 49–63, 81, 82, 98, 108, 177, 222
Self-access centre (SAC) 175, 224, 226, 232, 244, 249, 279

learning advisors 15, 111, 188, 190–191, 203–204, 219, 226–227, 234–235, 244, 247–249, 251–253, 319
Self Access Learning Center (SALC)
  activities 182, 189, 227–237, 240–243, 245, 247–249, 252–253, 255, 257–259
  accessibility 229, 234, 235
  instructions 32, 36, 43, 127, 133, 137, 141, 143, 149, 178, 206, 231–232, 236, 239, 241, 286
  target language 57–58, 61, 71, 147, 207, 224–225, 229, 231–233, 240–241, 260, 271, 182, 189, 227, 228, 229, 230, 231, 232, 233, 234, 235, 236, 237, 241, 242, 243, 245, 249, 252, 253, 255, 257, 258, 259
Self-assessment
  self-assessment checklist 23, 73, 82, 85, 189, 190, 199, 202, 225, 233, 248, 254–255, 258, 260
  self-assessment grid 8, 23, 51, 176, 181, 184, 187, 191, 193, 202, 211, 215, 222, 233, 237, 274, 276
  self-assessment part of Elektronisches Europaisches Portfolio der Sprachen (EPOS) 14, 16, 60, 189, 203, 233, 262, 274
Self-efficacy 43, 88
Self-evaluation 12, 21, 38
Self-regulated learners (students) 294–295, 301–302
Self-regulated learning 15, 115, 289, 292–302, 321
Self-reflection 129, 137, 229, 287, 289, 292, 294–302, 319, 320, 321
Short-term study 303–306
Social agent 53, 160–161, 293
Social language knowledge 309
Stakeholders 5, 7, 8, 9, 10, 12, 13, 14, 18, 19, 22, 23, 24, 25, 28, 29, 30, 32, 33, 35, 36, 37, 38, 39, 40, 41, 42, 44, 57, 73, 118, 120, 132, 134, 138, 144, 145, 155, 166, 167, 169, 180, 193, 204, 208, 212, 219, 225, 249, 251, 256, 260, 280, 317, 319, 321, 322
  Hiroshima Bunkyo Womens' University 29, 176–177, 226–227, 246–247, 261
  Ibaraki University 18, 24, 32, 77
  Management 252
  Mie University 30, 31
  Muroran Institute of Technology 24, 303
  Osaka University 20, 23, 32, 46, 47, 184
  Kanazawa University 29, 30, 31, 32, 47
  Keio University 24, 28
  teachers' perception 19, 26, 33–34, 54–55, 236

Subject index

Tsukuba University 45
Yokohama National University 30, 31
Standard assignments 131–134
Syllabus 6, 30–34, 78, 125–129, 134–136, 139–146, 177, 214, 217–218, 222–225, 256, 260, 285, 286, 289, 290, 300, 304
Syllabus design
   activity structure 240
   benchmarks 37, 43, 160, 161, 163, 166, 167, 168, 170, 171
   face–to–face 136, 162, 163, 165, 173, 271, 279
   self–study courses 159
   skills development 50–53, 118–124, 127–134, 139, 142, 145, 155–161, 163, 167–172, 178, 187, 191–197, 204–210, 213–221, 247–257, 266, 295, 298
   stakeholders 7–10, 24–25, 29, 32–33, 36–42, 57–58, 118–120, 132, 138–142, 144–145, 166–170, 180, 204–208, 212–213, 225, 251–252, 256–258, 317–322
   tools–and–results activity 163

T

Target language use 57–58, 231–232, 241
Task, assessment and evaluation 85, 88, 92, 136–137
Task-based activities 69
Task-based approach 125, 253, 261
Teacher assessment 229, 246, 264, 270, 320
Teacher training 12, 35–36, 38, 42, 99–100, 116, 171, 176, 185, 202, 248, 282, 317
Teachers
   full-time teachers 13, 111, 118, 124, 125, 131, 132, 139, 145, 163, 167, 319
   part-time teachers 13, 15, 36, 124, 131, 136, 138, 167, 171
   requirements when using the Common European Framework of Reference (CEFR) 19, 36–37, 41–45, 50, 98–115, 133, 144–146, 207–211, 216
   teacher-centred 12, 24, 62, 133
   teacher in classroom 12, 35, 43, 61, 77, 78, 81, 105, 132, 138, 145, 147, 171, 184, 205, 227, 234, 236, 240, 242, 244, 247, 249, 251, 252, 261, 318, 319

teacher networks 2, 3, 6, 90, 321
teacher role(s) 158, 171, 243, 244, 249
teacher stakeholders 7, 9, 10, 13, 19, 20, 22, 23, 32, 35, 36, 51, 118, 132, 138, 169, 193, 256, 317
Teaching material 28–29, 39, 67, 81, 99, 110
TEAP *see* Test of English for Academic Purposes (TEAP)
Test design 22, 201
Test of English as a Foreign Language (TOEFL) 30, 32, 51
Test of English for Academic Purposes (TEAP) 20–21, 47
Test of English for International Communication (TOEIC) 30, 32, 120, 121, 122, 146, 149
Textbook(s) 3, 7, 9–10, 12, 20–21, 29, 44, 52, 55, 57, 60, 67 69, 73–75, 77–83, 85, 87–93, 103–106, 109–111, 113–115, 122, 125, 127, 138–140, 142, 145, 151–152, 166, 169–170, 211, 215, 219, 223, 257–258, 264, 280, 285–287, 290, 292, 300, 304, 307, 309, 315–317, 321–323
TOEFL *see* Test of English as a Foreign Language (TOEFL)
TOEIC *see* Test of English for International Communication (TOEIC)
Tolerance of ambiguity 71
Top-down approach 114–115, 317
Traditional teaching practice 51
Training for stakeholders and teachers 12, 14, 24, 35–38, 40–43, 67, 98–100, 108, 111, 113, 138, 146, 171, 176, 181, 184–185, 187, 190, 200, 202–203, 247–248, 282–283, 289, 317, 319
Tutorial programme 269, 271–274, 278–283

U

Unified evaluation system 126, 133–134
Universities 6, 7, 19, 20, 26, 27, 28, 29, 30, 31, 32, 33, 37, 44, 78, 81, 98, 102, 118, 184, 185, 282, 291, 318

W

Writing tasks 59, 77, 200, 208, 259, 287

333